Touring the Western North Carolina Backroads

Also by Carolyn Sakowski

Touring the East Tennessee Backroads, second edition
Travel North Carolina: Going Native in the Old North State, fourth edition (with Sue
  Clark, Angela Harwood, Steve Kirk, Artie Sparrow, and Anne Holcomb Waters)

Third Edition

Touring the Western North Carolina Backroads

Carolyn Sakowski

BLAIR

Durham, North Carolina
www.blairpub.com

BLAIR

Printed in the United States of America

COVER IMAGES

TOP: *View from Appalachian Trail near Yellow Mountain Gap*
BOTTOM: *Upper Creek Falls / Quilt square on Ashe County barn / View of Grandfather Mountain*
BACK COVER: *Hawksbill*

Library of Congress Cataloging-in-Publication Data

Sakowski, Carolyn, 1948-
 Touring the western North Carolina backroads / by Carolyn Sakowski. — 3rd ed.
  p.   cm. — (Touring the backroads series)
 Includes bibliographical references and index.
 ISBN 978-0-89587-559-4 (alk. paper) — ISBN 978-0-89587-560-0 (ebook) 1. North Carolina—Tours.
2. Automobile travel—North Carolina—Guidebooks. 3. Historic sites—North Carolina—Guidebooks. 4. North Carolina—History, Local. I. Title.
 F261.S24 2011
 917.5604'44—dc23
              2011024027

To Alton

Contents

Preface   xiii
Acknowledgments   xvii

Tour 1: The Tour of the Lakes   2
Bryson City–Fontana Lake–Tapoco–Joyce Kilmer Memorial Forest–Robbinsville

Tour 2: The Chief Junaluska Tour   18
Robbinsville–Topton–Andrews–Tatham Gap–Cherohala Skyway–Tellico Plains–
    Coker Creek–Murphy

Tour 3: The Cherokee County Tour   34
Andrews–Marble–Peachtree–Murphy–Lake Hiwassee–Fields of the
    Wood–Murphy

Tour 4: The Standing Indian Tour   46
Murphy–Brasstown–Hayesville–Chunky Gal Mountain–Standing Indian Moun-
    tain–Winding Stair Gap–Franklin

Tour 5: The Nantahala Tour   60
    Franklin–Cowee Valley–Nantahala Gorge–Wayah Bald–Franklin

Tour 6: The Highlands Tour   74
Franklin–Cullasaja Gorge–Highlands–Stumphouse Tunnel–Whiteside
    Cove–Highlands

Tour 7: The Cashiers Tour   90
Sapphire–Gorges State Park–Whitewater Falls–Cashiers–Whiteside Mountain–
    Glenville Lake–Judaculla Rock–Cullowhee–Sylva–Dillsboro

Tour 8: The Cradle of Forestry Tour   106
Pisgah Forest–Forest Heritage National Scenic Byway–Cradle of Forestry–Sunburst–Tanasee Bald–Lake Toxaway

Tour 9: The Historic Flat Rock Tour   120
Loop of Historic Flat Rock Community

Tour 10: The Hunting Country Tour   132
Saluda–Tryon–Old Hunting Country

Tour 11: The Hickory Nut Gorge Tour   144
Hickory Nut Gap–Bat Cave–Hickory Nut Gorge–Chimney Rock–Lake Lure–Columbus

Tour 12: The Haywood to Madison Tour   158
Cove Creek–Haywood County–Hot Springs–Paint Rock Corridor–Marshall–Woodfin

Tour 13: The Mars Hill to Burnsville Tour   174
Mars Hill–Sam's Gap–Ernestville–Spivey Gap–Cane River–Burnsville–Pensacola

Tour 14: The Overmountain Victory Trail Tour   188
Pleasant Gardens–Lake Tahoma–Mount Mitchell–Micaville–Penland–Spruce Pine–Plum Tree–Cranberry

Tour 15: The Roan Mountain Tour   204
Elk Park–Roan Mountain–Bakersville–Kona–Burnsville

Tour 16: The Valle Crucis Tour   214
Blowing Rock–Shulls Mill–Valle Crucis–Banner Elk–Elk Park

Tour 17: The Globe Tour   230
Blowing Rock–The Globe–Gragg–Yonahlossee Trail–Blowing Rock

Tour 18: The Brown Mountain Tour   240
Morganton–Brown Mountain–Wilson Creek–Mortimer–Edgemont–Harper Creek and Lost Cove–Jonas Ridge

Tour 19: The Table Rock Tour   252
Morganton–Sitting Bear–Hawksbill–Table Rock–Morganton

Tour 20: The Old Buffalo Trail Tour   262
Deep Gap–Todd–Meat Camp–Elk Knob State Park–Sutherland Valley–Trade–Zionville–Cove Creek–Boone

Tour 21: The New River Tour   274
Roaring Gap–Stone Mountain–Shatley Springs–Healing Springs–West Jefferson–New River State Park–Glendale Springs

Appendix   292
Bibliography   302
Index   306

TOURS

1   The Tour of the Lakes
2   The Chief Junaluska Tour
3   The Cherokee County Tour
4   The Standing Indian Tour
5   The Nantahala Tour
6   The Highlands Tour
7   The Cashiers Tour
8   The Cradle of Forestry Tour
9   The Historic Flat Rock Tour
10   The Hunting Country Tour
11   The Hickory Nut Gorge Tour

12   The Haywood to Madison Tour
13   The Mars Hill to Burnsville Tour
14   The Overmountain Victory Trail Tour
15   The Roan Mountain Tour
16   The Valle Crucis Tour
17   The Globe Tour
18   The Brown Mountain Tour
19   The Table Rock Tour
20   The Old Buffalo Trail Tour
21   The New River Tour

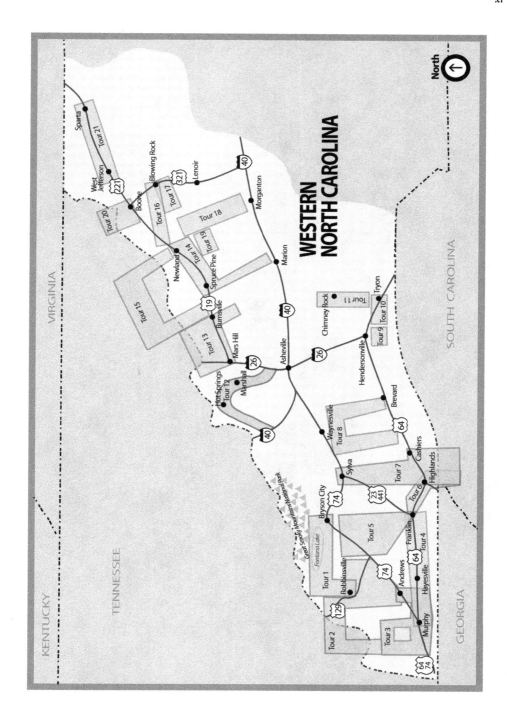

WESTERN
NORTH CAROLINA

Preface

To say that a lot has changed in western North Carolina since the second edition of this book was published in 1995 is quite the understatement. I do admit to apprehensions when I began redriving the nearly 4,000 miles covered in all 21 tours. However, my concerns about the disappearance of the region's rich history because of increased development were largely unfounded. In fact, some sites that would seem the most vulnerable are now more protected.

I did find that the two least-developed counties in the second edition—Ashe and Alleghany—are presently experiencing the same kinds of "progress" seen in other counties. That is especially true of the portions of Ashe and Alleghany along the New River.

However, many improvements have been made, especially in state and national parks and national forests. Some of those improvements—such as new shelters, trails, observation decks, railings, and even restroom facilities—were built when the federal and state governments had more funds available; some that were under construction as this volume was written were funded by the American Recovery and Investment Act. Two examples of improvements made in recent years are the new visitors' center at Stone Mountain State Park, which features exhibits about the locale and its inhabitants (human and otherwise), and the Wilson Creek Visitors' Center, which has a collection of historic photographs.

One exciting development is the creation of four new state parks in the region—Gorges, Elk Knob, Grandfather Mountain, and Chimney Rock—all of which protect natural areas that were under threat of development.

I was also relieved to see that the Eastern Band of the Cherokee Indians had used its newfound casino wealth to purchase several sites sacred to the Cherokees, such as Kituwah Indian Mound and the Ralph Preston Historic Cowee Mound. Under Cherokee control, these sites are now accessible to archaeologists who can learn more about the earlier civilizations that lived here. The locations will be protected for future generations.

And lastly, I have to gush about the Cherohala Skyway. Construction on this

34-mile roadway was about a year away from completion when the last edition was published. Just looking at where the projected highway was going to be located led me to think it would be magnificent. It has exceeded my expectations. The views atop the ridges are stunning, especially since almost all the eye can see is national-forest land, so evidence of man is limited.

Although those of us who knew the mountain area 40 to 50 years ago may lament what is lost, we can still celebrate what has been retained. We may experience a sense of loss for the slower pace that the old two-lane serpentine roads mandated, but we can't deny that we enjoy the convenience of the new four-lanes as well. This book seeks to recapture that feeling of slowing down and enjoying the passing scenery and the culture. Though it is growing difficult to trace a route that doesn't cross a well-traveled, commercialized segment of highway, it is still possible to travel backroads through areas reminiscent of bygone eras.

In order to avoid the most publicized of the tourist areas, I have tried to steer clear of interstates and four-lane highways, although some like the Great Smoky Mountain Expressway provide stunning scenic vistas. Since the Blue Ridge Parkway and Great Smoky Mountains National Park have been the subjects of numerous guidebooks, I have omitted them except for a few side trips.

Occasionally, I found it necessary to travel on dirt or gravel roads to stay on the "backroads," but I have tried to alert readers when they can anticipate rough roads. Travelers should also be forewarned that forest roads (designated F.R.) are usually old logging roads that are not as well maintained as the state highway system. State highways (designed N.C.) are usually paved and well maintained. State roads (designated S.R.) vary greatly in quality. Some are paved and some are gravel, but most can be negotiated even by recreational vehicles unless otherwise noted in the text.

Since the last edition of this book, the state has placed green road signs on most of its highways. But travelers can often find the state road number designations on the posts holding the signs as well.

This book is not meant to be a mere listing of directions for scenic routes. To gain a true feeling for the mountains as they once were, it is necessary to learn something about the history of the region. Because most areas of the North Carolina mountains were isolated and developed slowly, the history of the region has been neglected. Frequently, there are only one or two sources for a county's history, usually self-published books written by people in the community with enough foresight to realize the need to preserve a history that was quickly being forgotten. Sources are difficult to track down. I have tried to select highlights from as many sources as possible to turn this book into something that is as much a history of western North Carolina as a tourist guidebook.

In choosing the 21 tours, I tried to select routes that combine rich historical tradition, amusing stories about local characters, tidbits of folklore and legend, and exceptional scenery. I know I have not included all the routes that meet those criteria, but I hope I have at least made a good start.

Each tour has a map and photographs to give travelers some idea what they may see along the route. I have also compiled a bibliography for those who would like to read more about western North Carolina. The appendix lists agencies that can supply more detailed maps and information.

Thanks to the Internet, it is now possible to view historical photographs of some of the people and locations from earlier years that I describe in this book. Because I lacked the space to include all such materials in this guide, I have set up a special website for viewing these materials. The website will also allow me to provide updates after this edition is published and to share readers' observations. The URL is www.touringbackroads.com.

Many travelers have had occasion to say, "I wonder where that road goes." This guide is designed to supply the answer, as well as the impetus to follow that road. Whether you are traveling through the area for a few days, vacationing for a longer period, looking for new experiences off the main highways during your frequent visits, or merely satisfying your curiosity about the area where you live, I hope that your backroads journeys bring you a little closer to the history, people, and beauty of western North Carolina.

Acknowledgments

I would like to thank the following people for their help with this third edition: Susan Chappell and Steve Pagano at Gorges State Park; Kelly Safley at Elk Knob State Park; Randy Burgess with Pisgah National Forest; T. J. Holland at the Junaluska Memorial and Museum; Melinda Young with the Polk County Travel & Tourism office; Sandy Stevenson at the Madison County Visitors' Center; Emily Elders with the Jackson County Recreation and Parks Department; and Karen Nagle from Mountain Magnolia Inn in Hot Springs.

I especially thank my very good friends Susan Ervin of Franklin and Randy Russell and Janet Barnett of Asheville for their hospitality and friendship.

I also want to continue to acknowledge the people who helped me put together the first two editions, which remain the core of this book. In some cases, those people have retired or passed on. In other cases, the governmental offices don't even exist any longer because they have been merged into other districts.

The following offered helpful suggestions: George Ellison of Bryson City; Alice White of the Cherokee County Historical Museum; Cynthia and Wayne Modlin of Macon County; Gert McIntosh of Highlands; Georgia Paxton and John Wesley Jones of Flat Rock; Clarice Weaver of Ashe County; Shirley Wayland of Watauga County; and Mrs. Douglas Barnett of Morganton.

Several professionals from the United States Forest Service offered recommendations. They include Charles Miller of the Tusquitee Ranger District; Don Fisher of the Pisgah Ranger District; Michael Cook of the French Broad Ranger District; Gary Bennett of the Highlands Ranger District; and Bill Lee of the Wayah Ranger District.

Others to whom I am indebted for their time or assistance include Bob Greene of Brown Mountain Beach; Jennifer Wilson of Roan Mountain State Park; Linda Deyton and Grant Ward of Yancey County; Phyllis Burroughs of Avery County; Karen Doll of Lenoir; Rita Bond of Cashiers; Lucile Roberts of Madison County; Jo Greene of Ashe County; Beverly Means of Bryson City; the staff of the Toecane Ranger District; Michael Anderson of the Grandfather Ranger District; Frank Roth of the French Broad Ranger District; Judy Green of the Highlands Ranger District; and Joe Barnett of the Cheoah Ranger District.

The book would not have been possible without the help and support of the generous staff of John F. Blair, Publisher—Margaret Couch, Brooke Csuka, Jaci Gentile, Debbie Hampton, Angela Harwood, Steve Kirk, Heath Simpson, and Artie Sparrow.

Finally, I thank my mother, Alice Sakowski, and my in-laws, Charles and Mary Franklin, for their support through all three editions.

Touring the
Western
North Carolina
Backroads

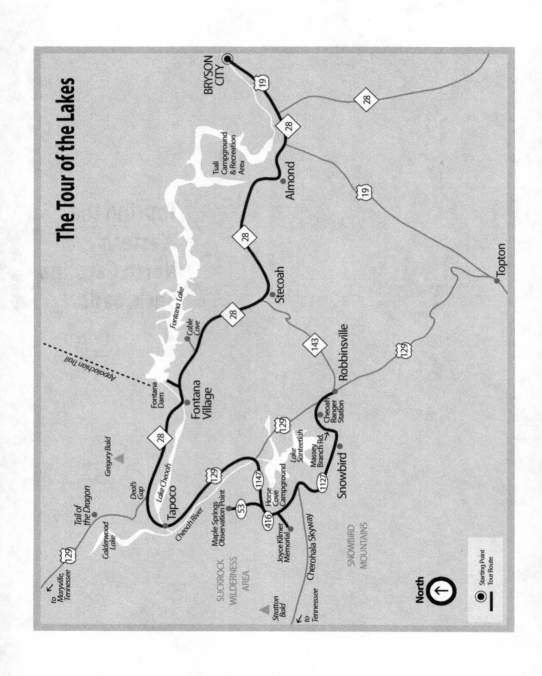

The Tour of the Lakes

TOUR 1
The Tour of the Lakes

This tour begins in Bryson City, the county seat of Swain County. It follows Fontana Lake to Lake Cheoah and the village of Tapoco. Next, it follows the Cheoah River to Lake Santeetlah, then heads toward Joyce Kilmer Memorial Forest and Slickrock Wilderness Area. It continues around Lake Santeetlah to the Snowbird Mountains before reaching Robbinsville, the county seat of Graham County.

Total mileage: approximately 90 miles

The tour begins at the easternmost exit for Bryson City, Exit 69 (Hyatt Creek/Elba) off U.S. 74 (Great Smoky Mountains Expressway). At the end of the ramp, turn right onto Hyatt Creek Road, then make an immediate left onto Walker Woody Road (S.R. 1168). Drive 1.4 miles alongside the Tuckasegee River to the junction with U.S. 19. Turn right onto Governors Island Road (U.S. 19) and drive 0.6 mile to a historical marker noting that Yonaguska lived in this area. Drive 0.1 mile farther to the sacred Cherokee site of Kituwah, an ancient mound that is considered one of the seven mother towns of early Cherokees in the Southeast. The Eastern Band of the Cherokee Indians purchased the site in 1996. An archaeological survey the following year found remains of an 18th-century village, but the density of artifacts indicated a longer period of settlement. There was also evidence of a hearth site in the center, which might indicate this location held the sacred fire.

The settlement was destroyed in 1776 by British forces, who ravaged all the Cherokee towns in the region. The area was later called Bear's Town or Big Bear Farm because it was the home of the Cherokee chief Big Bear. An important leader in the late 1800s and early 1900s, Big Bear was granted a reservation of 640 acres in the treaty of 1819 because he was "believed to be a person of industry and capable of managing his property with discretion," in the language of the treaty itself.

Later, another important Cherokee chief, Yonaguska, or Drowning Bear, lived in the same location. At the age of 60, Yonaguska suffered a severe illness that

Kituwah Indian Mound

caused him to go into a coma. Thinking he was dead, his people began mourning. Twenty-four hours later, Yonaguska regained consciousness and announced that he had visited the spirit world.

Yonaguska was known to use alcohol to excess. Upon his recovery from the coma, he called a council. "In an eloquent speech that moved some of his audience to tears, [Yonaguska] declared that God had permitted him to return to earth especially that he might warn his people and banish whisky from among them," according to James Mooney, an anthropologist who published extensive information collected during his stay with the Cherokees from 1887 to 1890. The chief asked his adopted son, Will Thomas—later an important leader of the Cherokees himself—to write an abstinence pledge. The rest of the council was convinced to sign it. From that moment until Yonaguska's death in 1839—less than a year after the Cherokee Removal—whiskey was "unknown among the East Cherokee," according to Mooney.

Though he counseled friendship with the white man, Yonaguska was always suspicious of missionaries. When the Bible was translated into Cherokee, he would not allow it to be read to his people until he heard it first. After listening to several chapters, Yonaguska remarked, "Well, it seems to be a good book—strange that the white people are not better, after having had it so long."

Following years of agricultural use, during which time the site was known as Ferguson's Field, the mound was considerably smaller than it was originally. Today, it is about 170 feet in diameter and only five feet tall.

Retrace your route on U.S. 19 to the Tuckasegee River. Follow U.S. 19 as it veers right after crossing the river. It is 2 miles to the center of Bryson City at the intersection of Main and Everett streets, where the former Swain County Courthouse stands.

Bryson City was built in a bowl-like depression formed by the Tuckasegee River in the Cowee Mountain range, which connects the Smokies to the north with the Balsams to the southeast.

On the grounds of the old courthouse is a historical marker noting that Cherokees who were supposedly part of Tsali's group were executed near here in 1838. The story of Tsali has come to symbolize the Cherokees' treatment during the Removal of 1838 along the Trail of Tears. Over the years, many sources have distorted the facts about Tsali, but he remains a hero. The myth that has evolved embodies Cherokee resistance to a brutal and inhumane policy. As detailed more fully in "The Chief Junaluska Tour" and "The Cherokee County Tour," the American government ordered the forcible removal of the Cherokees from their lands in the East to territory set aside for them in Oklahoma. When the Cherokees stubbornly refused to move, General Winfield Scott and a group of 7,000 men were dispatched to enforce the evacuation.

In late 1838, during one roundup of the reluctant Cherokees, an old man named Tsali (sometimes anglicized to Charley), his wife, his brother, his three sons, and their families were seized. According to Mooney, while the group was being taken to Fort Lindsay, a stockade near the junction of the Tuckasegee and Little Tennessee rivers, the members plotted an escape, with the women hiding weapons in their clothing. Other sources maintain that the escape was a spontaneous reaction when soldiers prodded Tsali's wife with their bayonets in an effort to get her to move faster. Tsali and his group attacked the soldiers, killing anywhere from one to four of them, again depending on the source. Official military reports say that two soldiers were killed and one was seriously wounded. Tsali's band fled to a cave in the Smokies on the Left Fork of Deep Creek.

At this point, the versions of the story split dramatically. The version that is usually told says that a group of rebel Cherokees led by Euchella (also written as Oochella or Utsala) was quartered at the head of the Oconaluftee River. When Tsali and his group escaped, General Scott seized upon the incident as an opportunity for compromise. He approached Will Thomas—Yonaguska's adopted son, "a trader who for more than twenty years had been closely identified with the Cherokee and possessed their full confidence," according to Mooney—and made his proposal. If Tsali and his followers would agree to turn themselves in, the other fugitives hiding in the Smokies would be "allowed to stay unmolested until an effort could be made to secure permission from the general government for them to remain," again according to Mooney.

Thomas approached Euchella with the proposal. Euchella realized it was futile for his small band of starving men to continue resisting Scott's several thousand, but he was also bitter because his own wife and son had starved to death while hiding out. He finally consented, rationalizing that it was better that a few should be sacrificed than that all should die.

Thomas then rejected General Scott's offer of an escort and rode off to find Tsali. Tsali listened to Thomas in silence before answering, "I will come in. I don't want to be hunted down by my own people." Tsali, his brother, and his two oldest sons surrendered. They were executed by a Cherokee firing squad near the mouth of the Tuckasegee. Wasituna, Tsali's 14-year-old son, was spared because Scott insisted, "We do not shoot children."

Several historians have rejected this version after examining the official military documents. Will Thomas did indeed play an important role, but one quite different from the romantic version above. The band of Cherokees living in Quallatown had received permission to stay in western North Carolina. Fearing that the Cherokees who evaded the roundup might jeopardize that permission, Thomas had been helping the soldiers from the start.

Euchella had successfully defended the rights to his land claim in the state supreme court years before, but he did not trust the soldiers to adhere to legalities (see "The Nantahala Tour" for more details about this court case). He fled into the mountains with a small group, and his wife and son died of starvation while in hiding. After the Tsali incident, Thomas did convince Euchella to assist in capturing Tsali's band in exchange for permission to stay in the area. Euchella's men did capture Tsali and his group, but there is no evidence that Will Thomas journeyed to Tsali's hideout and convinced him to surrender. There is also no evidence that Tsali came in voluntarily to sacrifice his life for his people.

Military documents also indicate that Tsali was not the primary target of the army's search. His two sons and a son-in-law were captured by Euchella's men. They were executed by Euchella's band on November 23. On the following day, Colonel William S. Foster and the Fourth Infantry left the area. It was not General Scott but Colonel Foster who issued a proclamation exempting Euchella and his band from removal, in consideration of their assistance in the search for the murderers. Foster announced to Euchella and his warriors that the Removal was officially ended and that they should notify any Indians still in hiding to join their brothers at Quallatown. Since he noted in his report that he considered his orders completed, Foster apparently did not think Tsali had played a major role in the murder of the soldiers. Euchella's band captured Tsali the day the soldiers left and executed him the following day near where the historical marker stands in Bryson City.

A highly dramatized version of Tsali's sad story is retold at the Mountainside Theatre in the community of Cherokee every night during summer. The outdoor drama *Unto These Hills* may be factually inaccurate, but sometimes tearjerkers can produce positive results.

Will Thomas continued to be instrumental in pleading the Cherokee cause to Congress. In 1842, the Cherokees still living in the Appalachian Mountains were granted permission to remain. In 1846, the Eastern Band of the Cherokees was officially recognized. Since North Carolina refused to grant Indians rights as landowners, Thomas became their authorized agent, purchasing land in what are now Swain, Jackson, and Graham counties for them. When the War Between the States broke out, Thomas organized 200 Cherokees into the Thomas Legion, which fought on the side of the Confederacy.

By 1867, Thomas's mental state had deteriorated to the point that he was declared *non compos mentis* and committed to the state asylum. His finances were in shambles, and the status of the Cherokee lands had to be unraveled through a series of lawsuits. In 1874, the courts ruled that the lands in question could only be held as security for the Cherokees' debts. It was also ruled that the remainder of the Removal and Subsistence Fund—set aside for the Indians in 1838 and made contingent upon their move to Oklahoma—should be released to them. From 1877 until his death in 1893, Thomas lived in and out of state mental institutions. However, Mooney's conclusion that "the East Cherokee of today owe their existence as a people" to Will Thomas is still valid.

Continue on U.S. 19 (Main Street) two blocks to Spring Street. On the right is a historical marker honoring Horace Kephart. As a young librarian in St. Louis, Kephart was captivated by Francis Parkman's accounts of life in the West, but he was disappointed that few others wrote as well as Parkman. "It is most unfortunate that there exists in American literature no intimate and vivid account of the western hunters and trappers," Kephart noted. "It is one thing to describe events; it is another to make the actors in those events live and speak in the reader's presence."

By 1904, Kephart was feeling hemmed in by obligations to his wife and family. He also had a serious problem with alcohol. Rather than heading to his beloved West, he came east to the Smokies to renew his health and "to enjoy the thrills of singlehanded adventure in a wild country." He later wrote, "Knowing nobody who had ever been here, I took a topographic map and picked out on it, by means of the contour lines and the blank spaces showing no settlement, what seemed to be the wildest part of this region; and there I went." His destination was the Smoky Mountains in North Carolina.

Kephart also noted before leaving St. Louis that "the most diligent research failed to discover as much as a magazine article, written within this generation, that described the land [around Bryson City] and its people.... Had I been going to Teneriffe or Timbuctu [*sic*], the libraries would have furnished information a-plenty; but about this housetop of eastern America they were strangely silent; it was terra incognita."

For three years, he lived on the site of an abandoned copper mine on the Little Fork of the Sugar Fork of Hazel Creek. He stayed comparatively sober and made himself a part of the community. Kephart then moved to the main hotel in Bryson City, the Cooper House. There, he established himself as such a celebrity among timbermen, salesmen, tourists, and traveling merchants that the structure was called "the Kephart Tavern."

He lived in Bryson City until 1931, when he was killed in a taxicab accident while returning from a bootlegger's with a visiting writer. Kephart left his legacy in two books. He became known as "the dean of American campers" and "the grand old man of the campfire and long trail" for his classic work, *Camping and Woodcraft*, published in 1906 and still in print. With its historical references to explorers, its trivia about everything from tepee building to cave exploring, and its practical information about survival in the wilderness, the book still makes wonderful reading. His second book, *Our Southern Highlanders*, published in 1913, is filled with anecdotes and folklore about the way of life in the Appalachians. Kephart neither satirized nor exploited the people he came to know so well. He is credited with preserving much that would otherwise have been lost.

Kephart's greatest contribution was probably the vision and energy he devoted to the formation of a national park out of the land he saw being destroyed by lumber interests. He was one of the principal forces behind Great Smoky Mountains National Park. Some 138,843 acres of land were officially dedicated the autumn after his death.

Continue straight up the hill to the cemetery overlooking Bryson City. After rounding the curve at the top of the hill, take an immediate right to reach the Bryson City Cemetery. Follow the higher road to go directly to the burying ground. Turn left on the one-way road circling the cemetery. A few yards from the turn, you will see stone steps. Follow those to the end of the area on the right surrounded by a stone wall to reach the 10-ton granite boulder marking Kephart's grave. It is said that from a groove in the top of the boulder, Mount Kephart, one of the highest peaks in the Smokies, is visible 30 miles north. For certain, you can look down on the town of Bryson City.

If you continue into the cemetery and walk up the hill to the left, you will see a large angel atop the monument for Fanny Everett Clancy's grave. Many scholars believe this angel is the statue described in Thomas Wolfe's *Look Homeward, Angel*. Others believe the angel Wolfe described is a composite of this one and another

View of Bryson City

in Hendersonville. Both were imported from Carrara, Italy, and sold at the Asheville tombstone shop owned by Wolfe's father in the early 1900s. The Hendersonville statue has the smile and the foot of the angel in the novel, while this figure holds the lily Wolfe described.

Return to Spring Street and turn left to follow U.S. 19 South, then make a quick left at the next stoplight to stay on U.S. 19. In 3.2 miles, U.S. 19 South makes a left turn and then a quick right to join U.S. 74 West. Follow this four-lane highway for 2.6 miles until it intersects N.C. 28. Continue straight on N.C. 28, following the signs for Fontana Dam. At 0.6 mile, the road crosses the Little Tennessee River. It is 2.4

The Look Homeward *Angel*

miles to where N.C. 28 turns right and becomes a two-lane road. After 0.9 mile, the road crosses the Nantahala River and a cove of Fontana Lake. It is 2.5 miles to the turnoff for Tsali Campground and Recreation Area. In addition to campsites, the recreation area provides a boat launch for Fontana Lake, stables, and a horse trail that follows the shoreline.

Next to the campground are the trailheads for Tsali Recreation Area, which contains nearly 40 miles of trails shared by hikers, mountain bikers, and equestrians. The site is considered one of the top destinations for mountain biking in the eastern United States. The forest service has come up with an alternating schedule that allows horseback riders and mountain bikers to use the trail system without conflict. Hikers can enjoy any of the trails on any day, but bikers and equestrians

Fontana Dam

need to consult the daily schedule to see which trails they can ride on the day they visit the recreation area.

Just after the turnoff to Tsali Campground and Recreation Area, N.C. 28 crosses from Swain County into Graham County. Formed in 1872, Graham County has been characterized as some of the most rugged, isolated, and inaccessible land in the eastern United States. The Snowbird, Unicoi, Cheoah, and Yellow Creek mountains virtually enclose the entire 299-square-mile county. Fugitive Eric Rudolph managed to evade capture for five years by hiding out in this area and the surrounding counties despite a $1 million reward for his capture. Rudolph, who eventually confessed responsibility for the bombing during the 1998 Summer Olympics, as well as attacks at abortion clinics around the South, was on the FBI's Ten Most Wanted list until his capture in Murphy in 2003.

The first white settlers didn't arrive in the area until the 1830s. The first road came in 1838, constructed for the purpose of removing the Cherokees. Today, almost 60 percent of the county is located in national forests.

It is 6 miles from Tsali Campground and Recreation Area to Stecoah, a picturesque farming community, then approximately 2.5 miles to a junction with N.C. 143, then another 6.2 miles on N.C. 28 to Cable Cove Recreation Area, on the right. The recreation area offers camping, hiking, and boating access to Fontana Lake. It is only 4 miles from Fontana Dam, the Appalachian Trail, and Great Smoky Mountains National Park. A 1-mile nature trail helps hikers identify trees, shrubs, and historical features.

It is 3.8 miles farther on N.C. 28 to an intersection. Turn right and follow the road to Fontana Dam, the highest dam in the eastern United States. The massive structure is 480 feet high and 376 feet wide at its base. It holds back the 29-mile-long, 10,640-acre Fontana Lake. The lake has a 240-mile shoreline at an elevation of 1,727 feet.

After the bombing of Pearl Harbor on December 7, 1941, the federal government ordered the construction of a gigantic hydroelectric dam on the Little Tennessee River for aid in the production of atomic energy. By January 1942, more than 6,000 workers converged on the site, and 24-hour, seven-day workweeks began. By January 1945, the first production unit was in operation. The world's fourth-largest hydroelectric dam was completed shortly thereafter.

After viewing the dam, return to the intersection with N.C. 28. Continue straight on N.C. 28. It is 2.5 miles to the entrance to Fontana Village, on the left. The village served as a lumber camp in 1890 when the Montvale Lumber Company logged this side of the Little Tennessee. Mrs. George Leidy Wood, the wife of a lumber-company executive, spent a great deal of time in the camp and fell in love with the area. She suggested the name Fontana, and it stuck.

The Montvale Lumber Company constructed a second village called Fontana farther up Eagle Creek in 1902. More than just a tent camp, it boasted the Fontana Hotel and the first Fontana post office. When Great Smoky Mountains National Park was established, the federal government drastically reduced the amount of forest available for logging. At that point, Fontana became a mining town.

The copper mines near Fontana operated three shifts daily and employed more than 100 miners. The Southern Railroad spur hauled carloads of ore to smelters in Copper Town, Tennessee, just over the state line. After the bombing of Pearl Harbor, the government ordered the mining terminated immediately, and the miners were directed to vacate their homes.

The 6,000 workers who came to build Fontana Dam lived across the river at a spot called Welch Cove. They built a new and modern Fontana, complete with large community and recreation buildings, cafeterias, a hospital, a school, a theater, churches, and modern houses. When the work on the dam was completed in 1945, the Tennessee Valley Authority, overseeing the project, asked that some "agency, public or private, assume the operation of the townsite of Fontana Village." There were no takers for a year. Finally, Government Services, Inc.—a private business with no connection to the government—turned it into a vacation resort.

Today, Fontana Village is a major resort with cottages and an inn to house vacationers. The village operates its own water- and sewage-treatment facilities and boasts extensive recreational opportunities. It offers organized activities during the summer that include concerts, movies, talent shows, and square dancing, in addition to disc golf, boating, horseback riding, hiking, swimming, and fishing.

It is 1.2 miles from the entrance to Fontana Village to the turnoff to the lower-level observation area for Fontana Dam. N.C. 28 follows the shoreline of Lake Cheoah, which was created by the damming of the Little Tennessee farther downriver. Cheoah Dam is on the left. On the right is Great Smoky Mountains National Park.

After 7.9 miles, you will reach an intersection with U.S. 129 at Deal's Gap on the Tennessee–North Carolina border. This is the western end of the national park. It is also the beginning of what motorcyclists call "the tail of the dragon." If you follow U.S. 129 into Tennessee, you will encounter 318 curves in 11 miles. This route is considered the number-one motorcycle and sports-car road in the East. Definitely take a side trip if you enjoy this kind of driving. You may have noticed that motels, service stations, and restaurants along this route have signs welcoming bikers, especially "dragonslayers." The motorcyclists and sports-car enthusiasts take driving this route very seriously, so if you happen to be in front of one of them, take advantage of the many pull-offs to allow everyone to have a more enjoyable drive.

A junction with Gregory Bald Trail is near Deal's Gap. A 6.6-mile hike on the trail leads to Gregory Bald, which the Cherokees called Tsistuyi, "the Rabbit Place." It was there that rabbits had their "town houses." Tsistuyi was also the home of the Great Rabbit, the chief of the rabbits, supposedly as large as a deer. Today, Gregory Bald, devoid of large trees, offers a spectacular view of the area.

Turn left onto U.S. 129. After 2 miles, the highway passes below Cheoah Dam and in front of its power plant. Around 1910, the Aluminum Company of America investigated the possibility of damming the Little Tennessee for the production of power to be used in the manufacture of aluminum. As war spread across Europe in 1915, the demand for aluminum increased. Concrete was poured for Cheoah Dam in March 1917, and the powerhouse began operation on April 6, 1919. At the time, the 225-foot structure was the highest overflow dam in the world, and its turbines were the world's largest. No other dam could exceed Cheoah's 150,000-volt transmission line or its 5,010-foot span across the river.

If you have seen the 1993 movie *The Fugitive* starring Harrison Ford and Tommy Lee Jones, you no doubt remember the scene in which Ford's character jumps off a dam. This is the dam used in that film.

The nearby community of Tapoco grew up to accommodate the 2,000 workers brought in to build the dam. The town was first called Cheoah, but the name was changed because a community by that name already existed on Sweetwater Creek. The name Tapoco was drawn from the Tallassee Power Company.

In 1930, that same power company completed Calderwood Dam farther downriver, across the Tennessee line. Part of the railroad between Tapoco and Calderwood was covered by the newly formed Calderwood Lake. The railroad

Cheoah Dam

bridge across the Little Tennessee below the mouth of the Cheoah River was transferred to the jurisdiction of the North Carolina Highway Commission. Along with the useable portions of the old railroad bed, it is now part of the road you are traveling. When the highway was finished in 1931, Tapoco began to develop as a tourist attraction.

Completed in 1930, the Tapoco Lodge served as Andrew Mellon's private lodge while his aluminum company's power projects were under construction. Several cottages were added later, and it wasn't long before tour buses began to make the journey from Asheville. After the construction subsided, the town shrank to 25 or 30 residents.

It is 0.8 mile to Tapoco. The brick Tapoco Lodge is on the right.

U.S. 129 now enters the gorge of the Cheoah River, which falls over a rocky bed for the next 7 miles. You will pass under a huge pipe that is part of the aqueduct from Lake Santeetlah to Lake Cheoah. A sign on the right 7 miles from Tapoco directs visitors to Horse Cove Campground and Joyce Kilmer Memorial Forest. Turn right onto Joyce Kilmer Road (S.R. 1147). After 0.5 mile, Joyce Kilmer Road makes a 90-degree turn across the river; Santeetlah Dam Road (S.R. 1134) continues straight to Santeetlah Dam.

As you continue on Joyce Kilmer Road, you will pass under the aqueduct tunnel again. It is 5.5 miles from the bridge to Horse Cove Campground, located on Little Santeetlah Creek. Just past the campground is an intersection with Santeetlah Road. If you turn right onto F.R. 53, it is a side trip of 4.5 miles to Maple Springs Observation Point, where an 0.5-mile loop trail designed for the handicapped provides a panorama of Lake Santeetlah and much of Nantahala National Forest. Great Smoky Mountains National Park is visible in the distance.

It is 0.9 mile straight ahead on F.R. 416 to the parking area at Joyce Kilmer Memorial Forest. One of the few remnants of virgin timber on the East Coast, the forest is left completely to nature's control; no plants or trees, living or dead, are supposed to be cut or removed.

In recent years, the hemlocks in western North Carolina have become infested with a non-native insect called the hemlock woolly adelgid. In 2005, forest managers began efforts to protect the hemlocks in Joyce Kilmer. Despite various treatments, many trees did not survive. As the limbs and even whole trees began to fall, the managers became worried about visitors' safety. In November 2010, they felled standing dead trees. Since this is a wilderness area, they tried to simulate the effects of wind or ice storms by using explosives to bring down the dead hemlocks, instead of using saws. The stumps and logs were left to decay naturally. The managers are continuing treatment of the remaining hemlocks. Visitors can still see the huge yellow poplars, as well as more than 100 other species of trees. Many specimens are over 300 years old. Some trees exceed 100 feet in height and 20 feet in circumference. The 3,800-acre forest was set aside in 1936 as a memorial to Joyce Kilmer, a soldier-poet who was killed in France during World War I and whose best-known poem is "Trees."

Memorial to Joyce Kilmer

The parking lot provides access to a 2-mile recreation trail that loops through the forest and passes through Poplar Cove. The more than 60 miles of hiking trails in Joyce Kilmer Memorial Forest and the adjoining 14,000-acre Slickrock Wilderness Area offer a true wilderness experience. Maps are available at the Cheoah Ranger Station, which you will pass later in the tour.

Return to the intersection near Horse Cove Campground and turn right onto Santeetlah Road (S.R. 1127). It is 0.4 mile to Rattler Ford Campground. From the campground entrance, it is 1.9 miles to the intersection with N.C. 143, better known as the Cherohala Skyway, at Santeetlah Gap, elevation 2,660 feet. The skyway, which travels along the ridges of the surrounding mountains for 40 miles from this intersection to Tellico Plains, Tennessee, is one of the most spectacular drives on the East Coast. It takes an hour and a half to two hours to go from here to Tellico Plains. More information about the skyway is in "The Chief Junaluska Tour," where it is incorporated as part of the tour.

From the left turn at the skyway intersection, it is 0.2 mile to the turnoff for Snowbird Mountain Lodge, on the right. The rustic mountain lodge, built of chestnut logs and native stone, has been in business since 1941. Each of the 15 guest rooms is paneled in a different wood harvested on the site in 1938. The dining room serves hearty breakfasts and gourmet dinners; picnic lunches are packed for guests. The lodge's flagstone terrace offers an excellent view of the Snowbird range.

Continue on Santeetlah Road for 2.6 miles to the turnoff to Blue Boar Lodge, on the left just before the bridge over Santeetlah Lake. This lodge was built by Fred Bruckmann, who organized and promoted boar hunts in the Snowbird Mountains,

Snowbird Mountain Lodge

a tradition that continues today. The wild boars are part of an interesting segment of local history.

In 1908, the Whiting Manufacturing Company of England purchased an extensive tract of land for logging purposes. The company hired George Gordon Moore of St. Clair, Michigan, to establish a European-style shooting preserve for the entertainment of wealthy clients on 1,600 acres of Hooper Bald, elevation 5,429 feet. Three years were spent in preparing the preserve. A 10-bedroom clubhouse and a four-room caretaker's cottage were built, a horse trail laid out, and telephone lines strung from the village of Marble in Cherokee County. A road was constructed to Hooper Bald, and 25 tons of barbed wire were hauled by wagon to fence in the game lots. A 600-acre enclosure with huge chestnut rails arranged nine high was to contain the wild boars. The buffalo enclosure was over a mile in circumference.

In 1912, animals began to arrive in Murphy and Andrews in wooden crates shipped by rail. Some were hauled to the bald by wagons pulled by oxen; later, the

Blue Boar Lodge

logging railroad from Andrews was used. The final inventory included eight buffalo, 14 young wild boars, 14 elk, six Colorado mule deer, and 34 bears, including nine huge Russian brown bears. Two hundred wild turkeys and 10,000 English ring-necked pheasant eggs were also brought in.

The hunting preserve was ill-fated. The bears quickly learned to climb out of their enclosure, while the boars learned to dig out of theirs. The location was so remote that the anticipated visitors never materialized. Local poachers killed off the wild turkeys. The buffalo did not fare well in their new environment, so they were sold; likewise, the elk were sold to start a herd at Mount Mitchell. By the 1920s, only the caretaker, Cotton McGuire, remained. The Whiting Manufacturing Company finally gave him full ownership and forgot its dream of a hunting lodge.

Of all the animals, only the wild boars flourished. They are supposedly descended from Russian wild boars—hence the nickname by which they are known locally, "Rooshians"—but their physical traits bear a stronger resemblance to those of the *wildschwein* (wild pigs) of the Harz Mountains of Germany. It is said that they can jump 20-foot obstacles and hit the ground running at full speed. They stand three feet high and weigh between 200 and 400 pounds. Hunters love them for their fighting spirit, speed, and stamina. Hunting dogs are probably less enthralled when they come into contact with the razor-sharp tusks. Naturalists don't care much for the wild boars either, since their rooting leaves a path of destruction.

The wild boars' reputation as game animals spread. Hunts were held year-round, many of them organized out of the Blue Boar Lodge. Today, the renovated lodge caters to a much more genteel crowd than its earlier hunting patrons.

Back on Santeetlah Road (now N.C. 143), it is 2.4 miles to the intersection with Snowbird Road. To the right, the road leads to the heart of the Snowbird community and the center of the settlement of the Snowbird Cherokees, descendants of the refugees allowed to stay after Tsali's surrender. Will Thomas purchased land in the Little Snowbird Mountain area for the Snowbird Cherokees. The land remains in their hands today.

Interesting evidence of the Cherokee influence in the area comes via the green road signs, many of which are bilingual, showing the road names in both English and Cherokee.

To the left, N.C. 143 East follows Snowbird Road. As you continue, the road skirts the shoreline of Lake Santeetlah. Begun in 1926, Santeetlah Dam first generated power in 1928. The lake covers more than 3,000 acres and enjoys a reputation as one of the best bass-fishing lakes in the area.

It is 2.2 miles from the Snowbird turnoff to the intersection with Massey Branch Road, on the left. Turn onto Massey Branch Road, which skirts the lake and leads to the Cheoah Ranger Station, on the left after 2.3 miles. Across the road is the historic site that was once the location of Camp Santeetlah, a Civilian Conservation Corps (CCC) camp. The CCC was formed to provide employment for men during the Depression. Enrollees had to be physically fit, unemployed, and unmarried, and they had to make allotments for their families. Each man received $30 per month, $25 of which was sent to his family; if he had no family, the sum

was held until his retirement. The CCC built bridges, fire towers, and trails, planted trees, fought fires, cleared land, stocked streams, and did just about any kind of public work connected with conserving and developing natural resources. Camp Santeetlah housed over 200 men in 1935 but was closed upon America's entry into World War II. A 20-minute interpretive trail takes visitors around the site of the former camp.

Follow Massey Branch Road for 1.4 miles to its intersection with U.S. 129. Turn right to reach Robbinsville. If you would like to continue past Robbinsville, take U.S. 129 to Topton; from there, you can turn left and follow U.S. 19 back to Bryson City or turn right and follow U.S. 129/19 into Andrews.

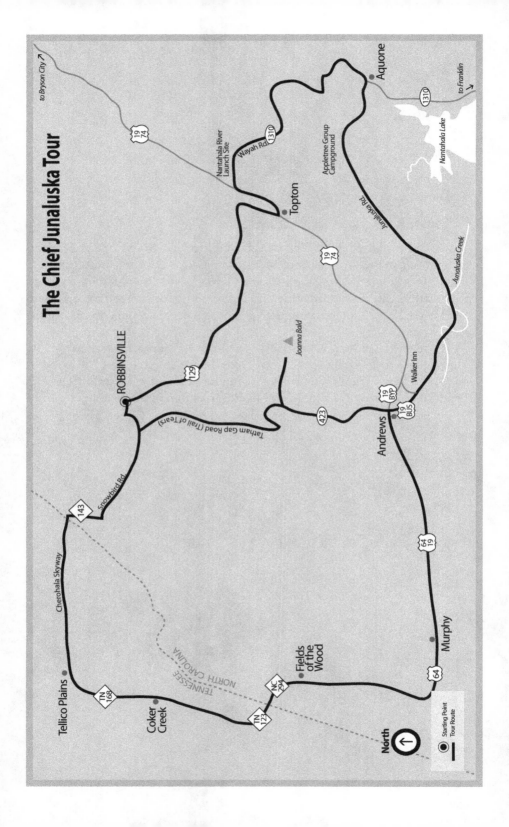

TOUR 2
The Chief Junaluska Tour

This tour begins in Robbinsville, the county seat of Graham County, at the grave site of the Cherokee chief Junaluska. It proceeds to Topton, then swings through the Nantahala Gorge and travels along Junaluska Creek on its way to Andrews. There, it picks up a segment of the historic Trail of Tears. It then takes the Cherohala Skyway to Tellico Plains, Tennessee, before traveling to Coker Creek and then on to Murphy.

Total mileage: approximately 150 miles

On a tour that includes part of the site of the Cherokee Nation's most sorrowful tragedy, it seems fitting to begin at the memorial to one of the tribe's greatest chiefs, Junaluska. From N.C. 129 in Robbinsville, drive on N.C. 143 (Main Street) past the Graham County Courthouse. Follow Main Street when it makes a 90-degree right turn. It is 0.2 mile to a sharp left turn up the hill to the Junaluska Memorial and Museum and the Traditional Medicine Trail.

In the War of 1812, the eloquent Shawnee chief Tecumseh forged an Indian confederacy to fight the white settlers along the frontier. According to Cherokee tradition, there was much support for Tecumseh and his cause among the tribe. Tecumseh supposedly journeyed to a Cherokee gathering at the Soco town house, near what is now Soco Gap, where he captivated the gathered chiefs until Junaluska, one of the influential patriarchs, convinced the Cherokees to remain neutral in Great Britain's fight against the Americans.

The Cherokees did not side with Tecumseh—who soon formed a pact with the British—but rather joined the American troops led by General Andrew Jackson. The Creek Nation split in its allegiances. The half that allied itself with Tecumseh became known as "the Red Stick Creeks."

In the Battle of Horseshoe Bend, fought March 27, 1814, on the banks of the Tallapoosa River in Alabama, it was the Cherokees who saved the day against the

Red Sticks. Jackson's troops were held at bay, unable to approach the fortress held by the Creeks because of the heavy crossfire. Junaluska led a Cherokee force that swam silently across the river to the enemy's rear, captured Creek canoes, and established a beachhead.

One story says that upon leaving to fight the Creeks, Junaluska had boasted that he would exterminate them. He returned a war hero but was forced to admit that some Creeks still lived. It was then that his friends awarded him the nickname by which he is remembered; Junaluska meant, "He tried repeatedly but failed." However, an examination of the muster rolls of the Cherokees at Horseshoe Bend lists Chunuloskee, so this story is most likely untrue.

The treaty of 1817 provided the Cherokee Nation with land in Arkansas for those who wanted to immigrate voluntarily. It also offered Cherokees an opportunity to remain in their homeland. If the head of a Cherokee family applied for United States citizenship, he would be allotted a 640-acre private reservation. But those who signed the treaty had to give up their citizenship in the Cherokee Nation. Indians who agreed to the treaty became known as "reservees."

In 1820, Robert Armstrong, a surveyor for the federal government, laid out several of the Cherokee reserves. Before he could finish, the state of North Carolina auctioned off the land recently acquired in the treaty. Most of the land claimed by the reservees was sold, resulting in conflicting claims. One Cherokee, Euchella, sued to regain his claim. See "The Nantahala Tour" for more about this lawsuit.

Under the treaty's terms, Junaluska took a reservation in what is now Macon County near Sugartown on Junaluska Creek. But he and his family were forced off their property when their land was sold at auction. Junaluska then moved around 1822 to Valley Town near what is now Andrews. After departing with a detachment on the Trail of Tears in 1838, he and his brother led a group of 50 in deserting and attempting to return to their homes. They were captured and forced to continue to Oklahoma. Upon his return from the War of 1812, Junaluska had been hailed as a hero for saving the life of Andrew Jackson. But his opinion of Jackson was considerably changed by the late 1830s. Old Hickory was by then president of the United States and an instrumental man in the implementation of the Cherokee Removal treaty. Junaluska reportedly said, "If I had known that Jackson would drive us from our homes, I would have killed him that day at the Horseshoe." It is little wonder that Junaluska came to harbor such bitterness, for his wife and other members of his family died on the Trail of Tears. (Junaluska remarried. A later wife, Nicie, is buried by his side.)

Around 1842, Junaluska returned from the West, walking the entire distance. He tried to reclaim his old home on Junaluska Creek, but the government would allow Indians to settle only in unoccupied places. He set up a new home in what is now Graham County. In 1847, the state made a tardy retribution by awarding Junaluska 337 acres in what is now Robbinsville, making him a citizen of North Carolina, and giving him the sum of $100. Junaluska was reportedly 71 years old at the time, and his anger had changed to a resigned grace. He spoke a few words of appreciation before both houses of the state legislature: "If I had as many as I am

Chief Junaluska's grave site

years old to devote to the service of North Carolina, I could not repay her for this great gift she has given me."

In 1910, the Daughters of the American Revolution unveiled the memorial that marks the graves of Junaluska and his third wife. It supposedly took 16 oxen to transport the boulder marking Junaluska's grave to its present site. The inscription reads, "Here lie the bodies of the Cherokee chief Junaluska, and Nicie, his wife. Together with his warriors, he saved the life of General Jackson, at the Battle of Horseshoe Bend, and for his bravery and faithfulness North Carolina made him a citizen and gave him land in Graham County. He died November 20, 1858, aged more than one hundred years." He is buried on the land he was granted by the state.

Today, the small park built around the grave site includes a short nature trail that focuses on plants that the Cherokees used for medicinal purposes. A small museum has exhibits about Junaluska and Cherokee history.

Retrace Main Street through the center of Robbinsville and head south on U.S. 129 for 12.7 miles through a flat farming valley surrounded by mountains. As the mountains open to the left, the Nantahala River Gorge is visible far below. At the community of Topton, also known as Red Marble Gap, U.S. 129 intersects U.S. 19/74. Turn left, heading toward Bryson City and into the gorge area on U.S. 19 North/74 East. It is 2.2 miles to Wayah Road (S.R. 1310) and the Nantahala River Launch Site, one of the main public access areas for the hundreds of rafters and kayakers who shoot the rapids of the Nantahala Gorge. Turn right onto Wayah Road and travel past the launch site.

On your immediate right is the Duke Energy Access Area for the trailhead for the Bartram Trail. For more about the Bartram Trail, see "The Nantahala Tour."

This part of the tour parallels the scenic Nantahala River. In his *Letters from the Alleghany Mountains*, Charles Lanman wrote, "The river Nan-ti-ha-lah, or the 'Woman's Bosom,' was so named on account of its undulating and narrow valley, and its own intrinsic purity and loveliness." Whether or not Nantahala really does mean "woman's bosom" in Cherokee is debatable, but the fact that the Cherokees also called the river canyon "Land of the Middle Sun" (some translate it as "Land of the Noonday Sun") seems perfectly logical. The gorge is so deep and its sides so sheer that the Indians believed only the noonday sun could penetrate its depths. The Cherokees' several legends about mythic creatures that dwelt in the isolated gorge are discussed in detail in "The Nantahala Tour."

Nantahala River

The drive beside the Nantahala River is one of the most scenic in western North Carolina. Cascades and small waterfalls are located all along the way. It is 9.7 miles from the launch site to a turnoff onto Junaluska Road, on the right. You will see a sign for Appletree Group Campground. It is easy to miss the turn, so watch for the campground sign.

Junaluska Road is unexpectedly straight for such mountainous terrain. You will pass Appletree Group Campground and signs for public boat-launch areas for Nantahala Lake. After crossing from Macon County into Cherokee County, the route parallels Junaluska Creek.

There are conflicting views about the exact place of Junaluska's birth, but it has been established that he was living on a farm about 0.25 mile below the bridge crossing Junaluska Creek in 1838, when he and the rest of his tribe were forced to move to Oklahoma.

After traveling 10 miles from the turnoff to Appletree Group Campground, you will see the Walker Inn on the right. In 1839, immediately after the Cherokee Removal, William Walker and his partner, Colonel John Waugh, were granted a tract of 295 acres in an area known as Old Valleytown. They supposedly dismantled Junaluska's home and transported the logs to a site farther down the valley, where they erected the first store in the area. In 1846, the local post office was moved to their store as well. The logs were burned for fuel in 1926, so nothing remains of the historic structure today.

In 1844, William Walker married Margaret Scott and built a two-story log

house that he soon expanded into the stately Colonial structure that survives as the Walker Inn. The inn became an important stopping place on the turnpike from Franklin to Murphy, serving many important visitors over the years. In 1845, Colonel Alan Davidson, a lawyer traveling the legal circuit, described it in this manner: "At Wm. Walkers at Old Valleytown, was one of the very best houses in Western North Carolina, the bill for man and horse was fifty cents." Another visitor, landscape architect Frederick Law Olmsted, described the inn in 1857 as "a house which the wealthy planters from the low country make a halting station on their journey to certain sulphur springs farther north and east."

The Civil War brought trouble to the Walkers. As in all accounts of Civil War action in the mountains, the facts are obscured by the subjectivity of the narrators. Margaret Walker's version of her husband's capture by "bushwhackers"—men called simply "Union soldiers" by other sources—is moving nonetheless. "On October 6, 1864," she wrote, "there came to my house at 11 A.M., twenty-seven drunken men. They had stopped at a still house and were nearly swearing drunk. Dinner was just set on the table, but they did not eat, as they were afraid they would be poisoned, but they broke dishes from the table, and went to my cupboards, and smashed my china and glassware." Despite his wife's pleas, William Walker, ill at the time, was taken away. Margaret followed the next day on horseback, accompanied by her sister for the first 15 miles, then on her own for another 6 upon entering an area where her sister feared to go.

Margaret's search was in vain. She returned home to find most of her belongings destroyed and to face the prospect of raising five sons alone. She continued to run the Walker Inn, winning a reputation for being the finest housekeeper in the mountains. Her search for her missing husband never ceased. She wrote, "I wept for three years and two pillows were so stiffened by salt tears that they crumbled to pieces." Margaret Walker deserves full credit for raising her sons and making the Walker Inn famous. She never found any trace of her husband. The inn is listed on the National Register of Historic Places.

Continue 0.4 mile past the inn to the intersection with U.S. 19 Business. Turn left and head toward the business district of the town of Andrews.

In 1890, the local railroad bypassed Valleytown, which had until then been the focal point of the area. The undeveloped tract near the proposed depot was quickly surveyed, platted, and sold, inaugurating the new town of Andrews. William Pitt Walker—one of the Walkers' five sons—was among the first to see the writing on the wall and relocate. He began the town's original mercantile business in 1891.

In 1897, the railroad also brought the first major industry to the area. The Kanawha Hardwood Company prospered by hauling timber from as far away as Graham County. It even built the Snowbird Valley Railway Company in 1905 for help in moving the wood down to Andrews. In 1899, a second industry—the F. P. Cover & Sons Tannery—came to town.

Andrews boomed in the early part of the 20th century, but the indiscriminate use of timber resources ultimately proved disastrous. With the timber gone, the industries left. Andrews survives as the second-largest town in Cherokee County, but the beautiful homes built by the Walkers and the Covers attest to better days. More information about one of these houses is in "The Cherokee County Tour."

After 0.4 mile on U.S. 19 Business, turn right onto Robbinsville Road. Watch closely for the road sign, as it is difficult to spot in the midst of commercial congestion. For the next 12 miles, you will travel the route of Tatham Gap Road, which constituted part of the infamous Trail of Tears. One note: The next 50 miles of the tour offer few opportunities to get gas, so you might want to fill up before leaving Andrews.

When elected president in 1828, Andrew Jackson put through Congress the Indian Removal Act, by which all Indians were to be led west of the Mississippi. The state of Georgia, spurred by the discovery of gold in the Dahlonega district in the Appalachians, passed a law confiscating all Cherokee lands. The pressure for removal intensified, though votes in Congress were close and the Indians did have

Entrance to
Tatham Gap Road

many white supporters. The 1835 Treaty of New Echota proved the final blow. With only 500 Cherokee signatures on the treaty supposedly representing the tribe of more than 16,000, preparations were made to move the Indians westward. The Cherokees would receive $5 million and land in what is now Oklahoma in exchange for their 7 million acres in the East.

By May 1838, only 2,000 Cherokees had moved voluntarily. General Winfield Scott and a force of 7,000 men were sent to evict the remaining Indians. The tragedy that transpired was poignantly described by James Mooney in his voluminous report to the Bureau of American Ethnology in 1898. It read in part,

> Under Scott's orders the troops were disposed at various points throughout the Cherokee country, where stockade forts were erected for gathering in and holding the Indians preparatory to removal. From these, squads of troops were sent out with rifle and bayonet to every small cabin hidden away in the coves or by the sides of the mountain streams, to seize and bring in as prisoners all the occupants, however or wherever they might be found. Families at dinner were startled by the sudden gleam of bayonets in the doorway and rose up to be driven with blows and oaths along the weary miles of trail that led to the stockade. Men were seized in their fields or going along the road, women were taken from their wheels and children from their play. In many cases, on turning for one last look as they crossed the ridge, they saw their homes in flames, fired by the lawless rabble that followed on the heels of the soldiers to loot and pillage. So keen were these outlaws on the scent that in some instances they were driving off the cattle and other stock of the Indians almost before the soldiers had fairly started the owners in the other direction. . . . A Georgia volunteer, afterwards a colonel in the Confederate service, said: "I fought through the Civil War and have seen men shot to pieces and slaughtered by thousands, but the Cherokee removal was the cruelest work I ever knew."
>
> To prevent escape the soldiers had been ordered to approach and surround each house, as far as possible, so as to come upon the occupants without warning. One old patriarch when thus surprised, calmly called his children and grandchildren around him, and kneeling down, bid them pray with him in their own language, while the astonished soldiers looked on in silence. A woman, on finding the house surrounded, went to the door and called up the chickens to be fed for the last time, after which, taking her infant on her back and her two other children by the hand, she followed her husband with the soldiers.

General Scott established his headquarters for the Removal at Fort Butler in what is now Murphy. He also established a series of outlying stockades to hold the captured Indians until they began their journey westward. There was no direct way to bring the Cherokees held at Fort Montgomery in what is now Robbinsville across the Snowbird Mountains, so General Scott hired James Tatham, a Valleytown resident, to lay out a road from Robbinsville to Andrews. Tatham staked out the route without the aid of a compass, and soldiers hacked it out of the virgin wilderness. The route from what is now Robbinsville to Andrews became one of several trails used by the soldiers to evacuate the Indians.

By October 1838, the main procession of the Removal was set to begin. Michael Frome described the trek in his book *Strangers in High Places*:

> The young, the sick, and the small, 14,000 of them, having stowed blankets, cook pots, and trifling remembrances in their six hundred wagons, bid adieu to their ancestral land, and marched across the Tennessee, across the Ohio, across the Mississippi in the dead of winter, averaging ten miles a day over the frozen earth, stopping to bury their dead who perished of disease, starvation, and exhaustion and to conduct Sabbath worship to the Great Spirit . . . while the new President, Martin Van Buren, advised Congress before Christmas that all had gone well, the Indians having moved to their new homes unrelunctantly. The whole movement was having the happiest effects, he so reported with sincere pleasure.

The name *Trail of Tears* actually encompasses several routes rather than one exact trail. Four detachments were removed along water routes from their homelands, while another 13 groups made their way overland along existing roads. The 1,200-mile trek to Oklahoma usually took about six months. Sources vary, but it is estimated that between 10 and 25 percent of the tribe died along the various routes. All of these journeys collectively came to be known as the Trail of Tears.

The white settlers who moved in after the Removal called the route that is traveled on this tour Tatham Gap Road, in honor of the man who laid it out. It survives as a gravel forest-service road today. Though it is frequently rough, its views are spectacular, and the dark history of the route remains eerily present—perhaps because the road has changed little since 1838.

Continue on Robbinsville Road across the four-lane U.S. 19 Bypass. It is 0.4 mile beyond the bypass to a stop sign. Turn right onto Stewart Road, then turn left at the first public road, Tatham Gap Road (S.R. 1391), and head toward the Snowbird Mountains. The road curves to the left. After 0.5 mile, you will come to a dead-end sign. Turn right onto the gravel F.R. 423. You have been following the original course of Tatham Gap Road ever since you left U.S. 19 Business, but it is only when you hit the gravel of F.R. 423 that you can begin to imagine the oppressiveness of the Cherokees' journey.

It is 4.3 miles to the sign identifying Tatham Gap. Turn right onto F.R. 423B for a short drive to Joanna Bald, which offers an impressive view of Cherokee and Graham counties. The Cherokees called Joanna Bald "the Lizard Place," after a great lizard with a glistening throat that was frequently seen sunning itself on the mountaintop.

From the intersection at Joanna Bald, F.R. 423 heads downhill for 3.3 miles. The road, now called Long Creek Road, is then paved for 2.6 miles to the outskirts of Robbinsville. The beginning of the original Tatham Gap Road is at the edge of the property that the state of North Carolina granted to Junaluska in his later years.

Turn left off Long Creek Road at the intersection with Snowbird Road. It is 4.1 miles to a turnoff on the left for the Snowbird community. The tour continues on what is now called Santeetlah Road (N.C. 143). It is 4.7 miles to Santeetlah Gap and the beginning of the Cherohala Skyway.

Dedicated in 1996, the skyway crosses through Cherokee and Nantahala national forests (thus the name Cherohala) and connects Tellico Plains, Tennessee, to Robbinsville, North Carolina. It took over 30 years to complete and cost $100 million, but the resulting highway is worth it all. The spectacular views have earned it a designation as a national scenic byway. The route winds up and over 5,400-foot mountains for nearly 18 miles in North Carolina and descends another 25 miles into Tennessee. Driving the entire route takes approximately two hours. The numerous scenic overlooks along the way offer astounding views.

On the North Carolina side of the skyway, it is 7.5 miles to the Hooper Bald trailhead, where a quarter-mile hike leads to the site of what was a hunting preserve in the early 1900s. From more information about the preserve, see "The Tour of the Lakes."

It is 3.5 miles farther to the Santeetlah Overlook. Located at an elevation of 5,390 feet, this is the highest overlook on the skyway.

Continue 5.3 miles to the Stratton Ridge Overlook. Stratton Bald was the home of John Stratton, who came to what is now Graham County from Tennessee in the 1830s and was probably one of the first white settlers in the vicinity. Stratton earned the nickname "Bacon John," the story goes, for catching 19 panthers—or "painters," as they were called in the mountains—and making their shoulders and hams into painter bacon. It is said that he arrived on Stratton Bald with nothing but his rifle, blanket, cooking utensils, and ammunition. In the 10 years he lived in the area, he made enough money from herding cattle and selling deer, bear hams, and hides to buy a farm in Tennessee.

It is another 1.3 miles to Unicoi Crest Overlook, located at the crest of the Unicoi Mountains at an elevation of 4,470 feet. This mountain range is part of the Blue Ridge section of the Appalachian Mountain chain. The name Unicoi comes from the Cherokee word *unega*, which means "white." It refers to the low-lying

View from Cherohala Skyway

clouds that often drape the mountains.

This overlook offers access to the Benton MacKaye Trail. Benton MacKaye (rhymes with "sky") was a Massachusetts forester and cofounder of the Wilderness Society. He was also the man whose vision inspired what is now the Appalachian Trail (AT). When the AT was being constructed, MacKaye selected a more westerly route, along the western crest of the Blue Ridge, than what the AT follows today. In 1980, the Benton MacKaye Trail Association was incorporated to build and maintain a trail that followed MacKaye's original concept. That route, which covers nearly 300 miles from Springer Mountain, Georgia, to Davenport Gap on the northern edge of Great Smoky Mountains National Park, officially opened in 2005.

From the overlook, it is 0.3 mile to the Tennessee line. At the state line, the skyway also becomes Tenn. 165. Continuing on the Cherohala Skyway, it is 9.8 miles to a turnoff on the right for F.R. 345, which leads to Indian Boundary Recreation Area, managed by the United States Forest Service. This site features campsites located around a 96-acre lake. The swimming area has a 400-foot beach and a fishing pier. Hiking and cycling trails are nearby.

Indian Boundary Recreation Area is near the border of Citico Creek Wilderness Area, which is accessible by continuing past the campground entrance on F.R. 365. Formally designated a wilderness in 1984, Citico Creek boasts nearly 60 miles of lightly used hiking trails that vary in elevation from 1,400 feet to 5,000 feet along the crest of the Unicoi Mountains. Blazes are nearly nonexistent on some trails, so hikers should be sure to take a topographical map and a GPS device. Citico Creek Wilderness Area adjoins North Carolina's Joyce Kilmer–Slickrock Creek Wilderness Area.

Citico Creek's original white owners were wealthy plantation families who used the area as a mineral investment. After the Civil War, the land went to Northern investors. During the late 1800s, George Peabody Wetmore, a wealthy United States senator from Rhode Island, owned Citico. The Babcock Land and Timber Company bought the land in 1922 and began logging operations. In 1925, a wildfire made worse by dry weather and logging burned over half the forest. Replacing the facilities needed for timber harvesting was cost prohibitive, so logging ceased in the upper elevations, though it continued along Doublecamp Branch until 1929. The forest service acquired the land in 1935.

If you look at the topographical map for Citico Creek Wilderness Area, you will notice that a great deal of the land bears the name Jeffrey's Hell. The *WPA Guide to Tennessee* records an amusing story of how this region received its name. Supposedly, a hunter named Jeffrey ventured too far from camp and wandered for two days without food. When he reached the headwaters of the Tellico River and was asked where he had been, he replied, "I don't know, but I have been in Hell." With that warning in mind, it bears repeating that those who venture into the wilderness area should have a map and compass or a GPS device.

It is 9.1 miles on the skyway to a turnoff on the left for F.R. 210, which leads to Bald River Falls. The 6-mile drive to the waterfall follows the Tellico River. The overhanging cliffs are close to the shoulder on this road. In some places, signs list

the maximum clearance for the rock overhang. The road, however, is paved, and the drive is scenic.

Even if the drive were not so pleasant, Bald River Falls would still be worth the trip. The falls are approximately 100 feet high. The road travels right over the bottom of the falls, where the Bald River enters the Tellico. You won't even have to get out of your car to see the falls, although you can park across the bridge and walk back for photos. A foot trail to the left of the parking area leads to the top of the falls.

Retrace your route to Tenn. 165 West and continue 4.2 miles to the intersection where the skyway ends at Tenn. 360. Turn left and follow Tenn. 360 South. It is 0.8 mile to the Cherohala Skyway Visitors' Center and the Charles Hall Museum, on the right. The museum features local historical treasures, including exhibits of old rifles, Indian arrowheads, antique telephones, and historical photographs. The visitors' center offers a good introduction to the skyway.

Continue south on Tenn. 360 through the business district of Tellico Plains. When Abraham Steiner and Frederick de Schweinitz volunteered to come to the Overhill Towns as Moravian missionaries in 1799, they recorded their impressions of the Cherokee village of Tellico:

> We emerged in the great Tellico Plain, through which we rode some distance in the midst of high grass. . . . In this plain we came upon a small hill, on which a flock of turkeys ran before us. Here we had a fine view. Before us and to the side [was] the beautiful plain, entirely clear of woods. . . . The plain has very fertile land, all bottom, many miles around, through which the small Tellico flows

on many windings. Around this plain the land rises gradually, on three sides in broken country and on the fourth in small hills that become larger and, at last, lose themselves in the Chillhowee [*sic*] Mountains, which can be seen at some distance.

Despite man's best efforts, you can still view what Steiner and de Schweinitz saw in 1799.

Tellico Plains was the site of one of the main Overhill Towns of the Cherokees. The Overhill Towns were the upper villages of the tribe, located along the Little Tennessee, Hiwassee, and Tellico rivers in Tennessee and the Cheoah River in western North Carolina. The white settlers referred to them as the Overhill Towns because they were across the mountains from the Carolina colonies.

The Cherokee village of Tellico enjoyed quite an interesting early history. One recorded reference to Tellico comes from Sir Alexander Cuming's visit to the Cherokees in 1730. It appears that Cuming was something of a con man. Upon his arrival in Charleston, South Carolina, he established a reputation as a rich man on the strength of borrowed money and bravado. It is not quite clear whether or not anyone actually granted him the authority to negotiate with the Native Americans, but under the pretense of journeying to Cherokee territory for scientific exploration, he took it upon himself to conduct a secret mission to persuade the Cherokees to maintain their alliance with the British. The end result was that Cuming convinced the Cherokees to submit to all the concessions desired by the British. Some accounts attribute Cuming's success to a keg of rum and a call to the chiefs to drink to King George's health. Others say he simply impressed them with his bold bearing. In his journal, Cuming related the following chain of events, writing of himself in the third person:

> The 29th [of March] he arriv'd at Great Telliquo. . . . Moytoy the head Warrior here, told him, that the Year before, the Nation design'd to have made him Head over all; but he said, that now it should be as Sir Alexander pleas'd. Here the great Conjurer declar'd the same, and both told him they would make him a present of their Crown.
>
> The 30th he arriv'd at Great Tannassie, 16 Miles up from Telliquo; the Path from Telliquo to this Place, was said to be lined with Enemies, but neither Sir Alexander nor Mr. Grant [Ludovick Grant, a local trader who accompanied Cuming], met with any Accident. This Day he made the King of Tannassie declare his Obedience on his Knee, and return'd to Telliquo the same Night.
>
> From thence he return'd to Nequassie [now Franklin, North Carolina], where the Kings, Princes, Warriors, Conjurers, and beloved Men, were all met, according to his Appointment, the 3d of April, most of which had come there the Day before. Here with great Solemnity Sir Alexander was placed in a Chair by Moytoy's Orders, Moytoy and the Conjurers standing about him, while Warriors stroak'd him with 13 Eagles Tails, and their Singers sung from Morning 'till Night, and, as their Custom is on solemn Occasions, they fasted the whole Day.

On that occasion, Cuming made a speech in which he required Moytoy and all the head warriors to pledge obedience to King George and to promise to "do whatever Sir Alexander should require of them." Cuming recorded that they all fell "on their Knees, calling upon every Thing that was terrible to them to destroy them, and that they might become no People, if they violated their Promise and Obedience." Cuming appointed Moytoy their leader—answerable, of course, only to Sir Alexander himself and King George.

The next day, Moytoy presented "The Crown" and "five Eagles Tails and four Scalps of their Enemies" to Cuming and asked that he lay them at His Majesty's feet. Ludovick Grant later wrote that the crown "resembles a wig and is made of Possum's hair Dyed Red or Yellow."

Cuming persuaded the Cherokees to send seven chiefs with him back to England. Moytoy declined the invitation because his wife was sick. Attakullakulla was one of the chiefs who accepted.

During their four months abroad, the Cherokee chiefs were the toast of London, going to the theater, inspecting ships, posing for a portrait by William Hogarth while wearing court costumes, and generally delighting the English with their painted faces and the feathers they wore in their hair. They presented the king with the scalps, eagle tails, and "crown." In return, they received a substantial quantity of guns, ammunition, and, most importantly, red paint. A treaty was signed in which the British pledged their friendship "as long as the mountains and rivers last, and the sun shines." The colonial governor of South Carolina reported that the Cherokee chiefs returned "in good health and mightily well satisfied with His Majesty's bounty to them."

Due to the collapse of his financial schemes and his exposure as a fraud in Charleston, Cuming chose not to return from England with the chiefs. But his legacy remained. Atakullakulla's visit to England played a prominent role in convincing him of the strength of the British. From that point, he always counseled friendship with the English and became one of their greatest allies.

Six years later, in 1736, Tellico became the site of another bizarre arrangement after the arrival of Christian Gottlieb Priber, said to be a Jesuit acting in the interest of France. Priber quickly learned the language, exchanged his continental clothing for Cherokee garb, and became a major influence on the Indian leaders. Dreaming of a new nation—a more perfect society—he drew up plans for his "Kingdom of Paradise."

In 1742, the Cherokees captured a Frenchman named Antoine Bonnefoy, who remained in their village for two months and recorded some of his conversations with Priber. Priber described his dream government as one in which "legality should be perfectly observed, as well as liberty, each would find what he needed, whether for subsistence, or the other needs of life; that each should contribute to the good of the society, as he could." According to Bonnefoy, Priber later elaborated that in his republic

there would be no superiority; that all should be equal there; that he would take the superintendence of it only for the honor of establishing it; that otherwise his condition would not be different from that of the other; that the lodging, furniture and clothing should be equal and uniform as well as the life; that all goods should be held in common, and that each should work according to his talents for the good of the republic; that women should live there with the same freedom as the men; that there should be no marriage contract, and that they should be free to change husbands every day; that the children who should be born should belong to the republic, and be cared for and instructed in all things that their genius might be capable of acquiring; that the law of nature should be established for the sole law, and that transgressions should be punished by their contrast.

The best part was the one exception to property ownership: "The individual was to have as his only property a chest of books and paper and ink."

British authorities began to worry about Priber's influence on the Cherokees. Fearing Priber would convince them to ally with the French, Governor James Glen of South Carolina sent Ludovick Grant to Tellico to arrest him. Priber was expecting Grant. He challenged Grant to lay a hand on him and simply laughed in his face. Governor Glen was not amused.

Several years after coming to the Cherokees, Priber was seized by English traders while on his way to Fort Toulouse in Alabama. He was imprisoned in Georgia at Fort Frederica. Among his papers that were seized was a manuscript for a dictionary of the Cherokee language. The papers he worked on until his death shortly after his confinement were evidently destroyed by prison authorities.

Priber's observations of the Cherokees during this era would be invaluable today. His political theories were far ahead of their time. The Cherokees at Tellico followed his advice about controlling their own destiny, holding out for years in not granting the English exclusive rights to their friendship.

One other note of interest: When the Cherokee Nation relocated its council ground to Oklahoma, the new seat of government was called Tahlequah, a name taken from the town of Tellico.

At the intersection of Tenn. 360 and Tenn. 68 about 0.4 mile from the visitors' center, turn left onto Tenn. 68. It is 10.5 miles to signs designating the Coker Creek community.

This section of highway parallels the route of the Unicoi Turnpike, which was built with the permission of the Cherokees in a treaty signed in 1813. The road generally followed an old Indian trading path that ran from Chota to Charleston, South Carolina; from Chota, the route went through Cane Creek to Tellico Plains, Coker Creek, Unicoi Gap, and Murphy, North Carolina. The route was used when cannons were brought across the mountains to Fort Loudoun. It is also the route for most of the rest of this tour. You can travel another part of the turnpike's route in "The Cherokee County Tour."

A toll was collected at the Tennessee–North Carolina line. Records show that

for every man and horse twelve and one-half cents was charged; for every lead horse not in a drove, six and one-fourth cents; for every loose horse in a drove, four cents; for every foot man, six and one-fourth cents; for every wagon and team, one dollar; for every coach or chariot, or other four wheel carriage of pleasure, one dollar and twenty-five cents; for every two wheel carriage of pleasure, seventy-five cents; for every head of cattle, two cents; for each head of sheep, goats and lambs, one cent; for each head of hogs, one cent.

It is 1.2 miles to the Coker Creek Village Adventure and Retreat Center in the middle of Coker Creek. This village and campground complex is in the historic gold district of Coker Creek.

Coker Creek was the second area in the United States where gold was discovered, an event that took place almost 25 years before the California gold rush. Legend says that whites inadvertently learned of the gold when a soldier noticed a large nugget hanging around the neck of an attractive Indian woman. He inquired about the nugget's source and was told it came from Coqua Creek. The settlers eventually corrupted the Indian name into Coker.

In 1826, the Indians complained to authorities that white settlers were violating treaty provisions and stealing their gold. A garrison of soldiers was sent to protect the rights of the Native Americans. However, Girard Troast, Tennessee's first state geologist, visited Coqua Creek in the late 1820s and reported that hundreds of white men were working the gold fields on Indian land, despite the nearby garrison.

In 1828, gold was discovered in nearby Dahlonega, Georgia. By 1838, the United States set up a branch mint in Dahlonega because so much gold was coming from the area. This desire for gold probably played a major role in sealing the Cherokees' fate and forcing their removal to Oklahoma.

In its 23 years, the mint in Dahlonega coined over $6 million. Although records disagree on how much of the gold came from the Coker Creek region, more than 1,000 people were reportedly working the local mines and panning the creek when the Civil War broke out. The war brought roving outlaw bands to the region, which interrupted the mining. After the war, mining resumed. It was largely discontinued when surveys showed the Coker Creek area could not be mined profitably because the gold was too fine and too hard to separate from its ore.

It is 9 miles from Coker Creek to the Hiwassee River. Continue 3.9 miles to the intersection with Tenn. 123, turn left, and drive 1.2 miles to the North Carolina line, where the road becomes N.C. 294.

It is 4.7 miles from the state line to Fields of the Wood, on the left. A complete description of this interesting site is in "The Cherokee County Tour." If you are not too tired, it is worth a stop now.

From Fields of the Wood, it is 8.8 miles to the junction with U.S. 64. Turn left and travel the 5 miles into Murphy, where the tour ends.

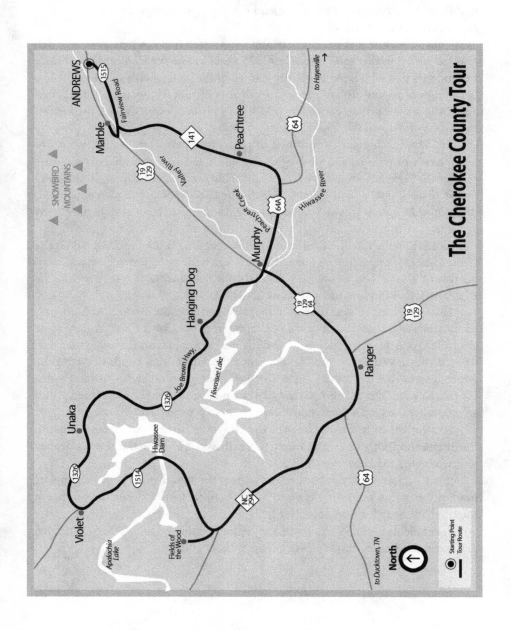

The Cherokee County Tour

TOUR **3**

The Cherokee County Tour

This tour travels through Cherokee County, the westernmost county in North Carolina. It begins in the town of Andrews and follows the Valley River to the once-prosperous community of Marble and the ancient Indian site at Peachtree. From there, it follows the Hiwassee River through Murphy, past Hanging Dog, and around Hiwassee Lake and its Tennessee Valley Authority (TVA) dam. The tour then goes to Fields of the Wood before returning to Murphy.

Total mileage: approximately 73 miles

The tour begins in Andrews. From U.S. 19 Bypass, take U.S. 19 Business toward the downtown area. You are on Main Street, which is also Second Street. When the street makes a sharp left turn, note that Fairview Road goes off to the right; you will return to this intersection. Continue for two blocks to the intersection with Chestnut Street. Turn left onto Chestnut and go one block. Straight ahead is the Franklin Pierce Cover house. The Queen Anne–style brick house with gable dormers and a three-story tower was built around 1900. It is said that the bricklayers brought to Andrews to build this home came from Virginia, which makes sense, since Franklin Pierce Cover was a successful tanner in Virginia before coming to Andrews in 1898. In Andrews, he founded the F. P. Cover & Sons Tannery, one the industries responsible for the town's growth at the turn of the 20th century.

Continue on Chestnut Street as it crosses the railroad tracks, then turn left onto Wilson Street. Go one block and turn left back onto Main Street. Continue one block and turn right onto Fairview Road, heading out of town.

After a mile through a residential area, you will enter a beautiful river valley; you are paralleling the Valley River, to the right. On old maps, the Valley River was identified by a variety of Indian names, including Gunahita (meaning "long") and Konehete (meaning "valley"). As recently as the 1930s, maps referred to the old flood plains, which had spread to a width of about 2 miles, as the Konnaheeta Valley. Today, those flood plains are known as the valley of the Valley River—a nice tongue twister, the Valley River Valley.

When George Featherstonhaugh recounted his trip through the area in his 1837 book, *A Canoe Trip up the Minnary Sotor*, he described the prosperous river country as "a valley enlarging to a mile of rich bottom land surrounded by lofty and picturesque hills covered with fine woods. This was the Paradise of the Cherokees, their wigwams built on graceful knolls rising above the level of the river bottoms, each of them having its patch of Indian corn with beans climbing to the top of each plant, and squashes and pumpkins growing on the ground."

Though the Cherokees were living in log cabins by Featherstonhaugh's day, the author was correct in his assessment of the area's fertility. Approximately 10 miles long, the valley offers the most level land in the entire county. The bottoms contain practically three-fourths of the cleared land in Cherokee County and are the heart of its agriculture. The valley is surrounded by the Snowbird Mountains on the right (or north) and the Valley River Mountains on the left (or south).

In 1858, the editor of the *Asheville Spectator* described a scene similar to the one visible from Fairview Road today: "The valley . . . is one of the most beautiful I have ever seen; and, in fertility, it does not deceive its looks. Not only is the soil fertile, but there is, in the hillsides and valleys, a mineral wealth perfectly inexhaustible. . . . I could stand and gaze at it,—beautiful even in its not half cultivated state,—and my heart swells with pride, when I think that all this beauty is within my own glorious Carolina."

After 5.8 miles, Fairview Road ends at N.C. 141. Turn right. It is 0.4 mile to the four-lane U.S. 19/23. Cross the highway, stay on Marble Springs Church Road, and continue past the Marble post office to a stop sign across from the railroad tracks. This is the center of the Marble community.

Henry Moss, the first white settler in the area, arrived in 1842. Marble's period of prosperity started with the exploitation of its mineral resources. Iron ore was dug around 1845. In 1861, an English company opened a successful gold mine that operated until 1896. But it took the most extensive marble deposits in North Carolina to assure the area's economic success and supply the name for the resulting town.

The marble deposits were of very high quality and had an estimated thickness of 500 feet. The Columbia Marble Company's product—high-grade marble of regal blue and sterling gray, colors that lent themselves to intricate carving and polishing—dominated the local mining industry. Regal blue marble is found only in

Marble community

this valley. Some 90 percent of the marble was used for monuments and buildings. Area people were especially proud when their marble was selected for Arlington National Cemetery.

Getting a block of marble out of the quarry required seven men. Once out, it was sawed into slabs by means of blades with diamond bits. Sawing a single block into slabs required from 52 to 56 man-hours.

The town of Marble hit its height in the early 1900s. Incorporated in 1914, it saw three of its iron-ore mines reopened during World War I. But the boom period was brief. By 1940, the town was no longer incorporated. Unlike so many boom towns in the mountains, some of Marble's original one- and two-story commercial buildings can still be seen along the railroad tracks. They offer mute evidence of what the community once was.

After viewing what remains of Marble, retrace your route, continuing south on N.C. 141 past the intersection with Fairview Road. It is 6.6 miles to the elementary school in the community of Peachtree. In 1735, the once-powerful Natchez Indian tribe was uprooted from its homeland in Mississippi by the French. The Natchez Indians established a village just above Peachtree Creek and eventually merged with the Cherokees. By 1820, the area that is now the Valley River Valley had been established as a center for Baptist missionary work among the Indians.

From Peachtree, it is 1.8 miles to an intersection with U.S. 64. Turn right, heading west toward Murphy. The Hiwassee River is a scenic presence on the left. Some early maps gave the river's name as Owassa, which means "main river" in Cherokee. Others claim that Hiwassee means "savannah" or "meadow." In his 1849 account of his travels, Charles Lanman described the river in this manner: "The Owassa is a tributary of the noble Tennessee, and is as clear, beautiful, rapid and

Peachtree Mound and Village Site

picturesque a mountain river as I have ever seen." Since Lanman's journey had taken him all over western North Carolina, that was quite a statement.

The area the tour now passes through holds the beginnings of Cherokee County's long history of settlement. At the place where Peachtree Creek flows into the Hiwassee from the right stand the remains of the Peachtree Mound and Village Site. The site has proven to be of considerable interest to historians and archaeologists because of the information it has revealed about early settlement.

Although no exact route has been established for the expedition led by Hernando De Soto in 1540, some evidence suggests that the Spaniards passed through this area. De Soto's search for gold took him all the way to the Mississippi River in 1541. Details of his journey were recorded in several journals kept by members of the expedition, but it has proven difficult to match current locations with the descriptions in those journals. Thus, considerable controversy exists over De Soto's exact route.

An unscientific exploration of the Indian mound was conducted in 1885. Considerable archaeological material was removed to Richmond, Virginia, where it is now housed in the Valentine Museum. In 1933, the Smithsonian Institution sponsored and organized a more thorough investigation, which arrived at several interesting conclusions. Smithsonian investigators placed the earliest occupation of the site during the Archaic period (from 8000 to 1000 B.C.) and agreed that it was continuously occupied until historic times. They came to believe that the site was the ancient Cherokee village of Guasili, mentioned by three chroniclers of De Soto's 1540 expedition. The chroniclers wrote that they were kindly received and hospitably entertained by the Indians in Guasili. Among other foodstuffs, the Spaniards received 300 dogs, which the Indians bred for eating purposes at that time. They also provided corn for the Spaniards' horses. The officers of the expedition were lodged in the town house on top of the mound. De Soto left without finding gold. Another Spaniard, Juan Pardo, arrived in 1567, also searching for gold. It is believed that after Pardo's expedition, the Spaniards mined the area for more than a century.

The Smithsonian investigators described the mound in their report:

> It may be said that the Peachtree site consisted of an artifactually rich and extensive habitation site. . . . Upon this village site was built a hard packed area which later became the floor of a ceremonial structure of stone and wood. This was covered by a small round-topped mound, about 60 feet in diameter. Over this mound, and separated from it by a sand strata, was a larger secondary mound which underwent at least two major periods of construction and several minor additions. The secondary mound had upon it three ceremonial buildings, as evidenced by three superimposed floors.

The report estimated that 250,000 pieces of Indian pottery were found at the site. It also mentioned the discovery of 68 burial sites, including some stone-lined graves.

It is approximately 3.8 miles from the Peachtree Mound and Village Site to the intersection where the road you are now on (U.S. 64 Alternate) merges with U.S. 64 coming from the other side of the river. Turn right onto what is now U.S. 64. Almost immediately, you will intersect U.S. 19/74/129. Continue straight across this four-lane. The road you are traveling becomes Peachtree Street and passes into the center of Murphy, the county seat of Cherokee County. Ironically, Murphy is nearer to the capitals of seven other states—Kentucky, Georgia, Tennessee, Alabama, South Carolina, Florida, and West Virginia—than it is to its own.

During the Cherokee settlement of the area, the village where the Hiwassee and Valley rivers meet—the present site of Murphy—was called Tlanusiyi, "the Leech Place." In his report to the Bureau of American Ethnology in 1898, James Mooney recorded the following legend:

> Just above the junction is a deep hole in Valley river, and above it is a ledge of rock running across the stream, over which people used to go as on a bridge. . . . One day some men going along the trail saw a great red object, full as large as a house, lying on the rock ledge in the middle of the stream below them. As they stood wondering what it could be they saw it unroll—and then they knew it was alive—and stretch itself out along the rock until it looked like a great leech with red and white stripes along its body. It rolled up into a ball and again stretched out at full length, and at last crawled down the rock and was out of sight in the deep water. The water began to boil and foam, and a great column of white spray was thrown high in the air and came down like a waterspout upon the very spot where the men had been standing, and would have swept them all into the water but that they saw it in time and ran from the place.

Mooney reported that this was one of the best-known myths of the Cherokees.

He also corrected an 1849 report by Charles Lanman, who had said that Tlanusiyi meant "large turtle." Both men wrote of the Cherokee belief that, as Lanman put it, "there is a subterranean communication between this immense hole in Owassa and the river Notely [Nottely], which is some two miles distant. . . . The testimony adduced in proof of this theory is, that a certain log was once marked on the Notely, which log was subsequently found floating in the pool of the Deep Hole in the Owassa."

As white settlement proceeded westward and forced the Indians to spread out, the Cherokee tribe divided into distinct groups. While the factions living in South Carolina, Georgia, and Tennessee were quick to assimilate the white man's culture, those in certain villages west of the Blue Ridge tended to be more conservative and traditional. They became known as Middle or Valley Cherokees and their villages as Middle or Valley towns. The Peachtree-Murphy area was the center for those villages.

In 1813, giving in to pressure from their white neighbors, the Cherokees allowed part of a new road connecting Tennessee and Georgia to be built through their land. The Unicoi Turnpike passed alongside the Hiwassee River and spawned several inns run by mixed-blood members of the Cherokee Nation. Sometime around 1828, A. R. S. Hunter, the first white man to settle in the area, built an Indian trading post across the Hiwassee from the present site of Murphy. The small settlement was later called Huntington.

Not long before that time, gold had been discovered in Cherokee territory in what is now Georgia. The Cherokees had adopted the white man's ways more readily than any other tribe, yet the lure of gold made prejudice rear its ugly head. Whites began to pressure the Cherokees to accept land west of the Arkansas River in exchange for their Eastern territory.

Though the Cherokees were divided over accepting the government's offer, the great majority opposed the Removal plan. The question grew so serious that by 1820 the Cherokee Nation passed a law declaring that entering into any negotiation for the sale of tribal lands without the consent of the national council would be considered treason, punishable by death.

The Cherokees had already learned some hard lessons about the white man's democracy. When they found their lands and rights threatened, they sent a delegation to Washington. It was led by John Ross, the head of the upper house of the tribe's bicameral legislature. Ross's presentation to Congress, excerpted here, was an eloquent statement underscoring the hypocrisy of the federal government in its dealings with the Cherokees:

> Happy under the parental guardianship of the United States, [the Cherokees] applied themselves assiduously and successfully to learn the lessons of civilization and peace, which, in the prosecution of a humane and Christian policy, the United States caused to be taught them. Of the advances they have made under the influence of this benevolent system, they might a few years ago have been tempted to speak with pride and satisfaction and with grateful hearts to those who have been their instructors. . . . But now each of these blessings has been

made to them an instrument of the keenest torture. Cupidity has fastened its eye upon their lands and their homes, and is seeking by force and by every variety of oppression and wrong to expel them from their lands and their homes and to tear them from all that has become endeared to them.... Having failed in their efforts to obtain relief elsewhere, [they] now appeal to Congress, and respectfully pray that your honorable bodies will look into their whole case, and that such measure may be adopted as will give them redress and security.

John Ross received his answer with a new treaty proposed in 1835. While an Indian council representing fewer than 500 members of a population of more than 16,000 Cherokees met at New Echota, Georgia, Ross was held prisoner in Washington without a charge against him. Signed that same year, the treaty was proclaimed in 1836. President Martin Van Buren proposed a two-year extension to give the Cherokees time to move to Oklahoma.

Fort Butler was built in Huntington. It became one of six fortifications in North Carolina established for the purpose of gathering the Cherokees for removal. It soon became obvious, however, that the majority—especially the traditional Indians from the Valley Towns—had no intention of moving voluntarily. In the spring of 1838, a force under General Winfield Scott occupied Fort Butler as its headquarters, and the forced evacuation of the Cherokees began in earnest. In describing the Removal, James Mooney wrote that it "may well exceed in weight of grief and pathos any other passage in American history." Historical records seem to bear him out. More details on the Removal are in "The Tour of the Lakes" and "The Chief Junaluska Tour."

The intersection of Peachtree and Hiwassee streets is the center of Murphy. Turn left onto Hiwassee Street and head downhill. Just after crossing the river, turn right onto Lakeside Drive in front of the fire department, then take an immediate left onto Hunter Street, which curves to the left. It is 0.5 mile to a right turn onto Fort Butler Street. A small park that includes a stone monument marks the location for Fort Butler.

Retrace your route down the hill and across the river to the intersection of Hiwassee and Tennessee streets. Turn left onto Tennessee Street and head out of town. A more detailed discussion of some of the buildings in downtown Murphy is in "The Standing Indian Tour."

Tennessee Street turns into Joe Brown Highway leaving Murphy. It is 2.6 miles to the signs identifying the community of Hanging Dog and another 1.5 miles to Hanging Dog Campground. Formerly referred to as "the Old Mill" when it was

Fort Butler monument

owned by Nathan Dockery, the campground property was condemned and purchased by the TVA when it was planning Hiwassee Dam; it is now part of Nantahala National Forest.

On May 6, 1865, Hanging Dog was the site of one of the last battles of the Civil War east of the Mississippi. Confederate forces claimed that Union renegades raided and burned the Cherokee County Courthouse in an effort to destroy court claims against themselves. Confederate forces stationed in the community of Valleytown chased the raiders and caught up with them at Hanging Dog, precipitating the skirmish.

The tale that accounts for Hanging Dog's name is an excellent example of mountain folklore. Due to crop failure, a Cherokee village found itself facing starvation during one of the most bitterly cold winters in memory. A man called Deer Killer was the only Cherokee able to find game that year, thanks to his expert hunting dog. After a whole day of maneuvering a large buck for his master to kill, the dog was able to chase the quarry into range. When Deer Killer's arrow struck but failed to kill the prey, the deer broke for the nearby creek, closely followed by dog and master. While swimming the creek in pursuit, the dog became entangled in a mass of logs, vines, and debris. Seeing his beloved dog in danger of drowning, Deer Killer jumped into the icy water and freed him. The two then continued across the creek and resumed their chase. When they brought deer meat back to the village, there was enough to share with everyone. Deer Killer told of his dog's brush with death. From that time, the Indians took to calling the creek where the dog had been hung up in debris Hanging Dog Creek.

Joe Brown Highway winds among the coves of Hiwassee Lake. For the next 17 miles, continue on Joe Brown Highway whenever you come to an intersection. You are following the same route as the Unicoi Turnpike. The earliest European maps of the area noted the route as a connector between the Cherokee territories

View of Hiwassee Lake

and the ports of Charleston and Savannah. In 1756, the British hauled weapons and supplies across this trail to establish Fort Loudoun. In the early 1800s, the trail was converted into a toll road and turnpike, on which drovers herded millions of head of livestock to market. In 1838, it became part of the Trail of Tears as 3,000 Cherokees were moved via the turnpike toward Oklahoma.

The route now passes through the small communities of Grape Creek and Unaka. It is 6.9 miles from Hanging Dog Campground to Ogreeta Baptist Church, on the right, and Shooks Boat Dock, on the left, then 8.5 miles from this intersection to a fork in the road. Joe Brown Highway takes the lower fork on the left, heading downhill. After 1.5 miles, Joe Brown Highway ends. If you were to turn right onto the gravel road heading toward Tellico Plains, you would continue on the Unicoi Turnpike. Instead, turn left onto Hiwassee Dam Road, heading toward Violet Baptist Church. After 4.7 miles, you will reach the Hiwassee Dam visitors' overlook, located just before the dam itself.

In 1935, Congress authorized the TVA to build a dam on the Hiwassee River for flood control and the generation of electricity. Over 1,600 men were employed. Hiwassee Lake is the reservoir created by the dam.

The overlook provides an excellent opportunity to see the top of the dam. A sidewalk parallels the road along the top. Built of concrete, the dam is 307 feet high and more than 0.25 mile long. It is the highest overspill dam in the United States. In 1954–55, the first integrated pump-turbine used in an American power plant was installed here. Water flows from Hiwassee Lake to the dam, where the turbine generates power during peak hours of demand. Downriver to the west are Apalachia (yes, that spelling is correct) Dam and Lake, where the used water is dumped.

Hiwassee Dam

Fields of the Wood

During the night, when demand for power drops, the Hiwassee unit functions as a pump, drawing water out of Apalachia Lake, lifting it 205 feet, and putting it back into Hiwassee Lake for use the next morning during peak hours.

It is 0.6 mile from the Hiwassee Dam overlook to the visitors' reception center, on the right, where you can see the famous pump-turbine in action.

Continue on Hiwassee Dam Road for 5.4 miles from the dam to the junction with N.C. 294. Turn right, following the signs for 0.7 mile to Fields of the Wood.

In *A Traveler's Guide to the Smoky Mountains Region*, Jeff Bradley characterized Fields of the Wood as "one of those things that future civilizations will ponder over." An official brochure describes it as a "Bible-theme park developed on more than 200 acres." After driving through the gates (and pleasantly discovering there is no admission charge), you will see dozens of religious monuments on two adjacent slopes. The park is owned and maintained by the Church of God of Prophecy, and many of the church's affiliates have donated monuments. Among the attractions are the world's largest cross (150 feet tall and 115 feet wide), a replica of Christ's sepulcher, prayer monuments along a giant stairway, an electric Star of Bethlehem, and the main attraction—the world's largest representation of the Ten Commandments. The grass "tablet," 300 feet square, is laid out on a mountainside; the letters spelling out the Ten Commandments are five feet high and four feet wide. A 24-foot-tall, 34-foot-wide statue commemorating the New Testament stands at the top of the mountain. You can walk to the platform on top of the statue for a panoramic view of the Ten Commandments below. Or you can drive to the observation overlook at the top by following the road to the right as you face the tablets. Taking photographs is encouraged. A building with a lounge and a gift shop is nearby. The area is billed as one of the "Biblical Wonders of the Twentieth Century," and there is little doubt that it probably is.

Leaving Fields of the Wood, turn left onto N.C. 294, heading toward Murphy. It is 8.8 miles to a junction with U.S. 64. Turn left and complete the tour by traveling the 5 miles into Murphy.

The Standing Indian Tour

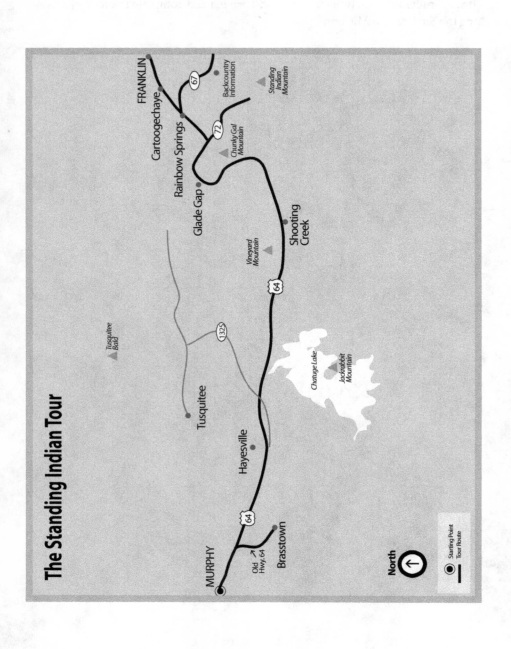

TOUR 4
The Standing Indian Tour

This tour begins in Murphy, the county seat of Cherokee County. It travels to Brasstown and the John C. Campbell Folk School, then to Hayesville, the county seat of Clay County. From there, it climbs over Chunky Gal Mountain to Standing Indian Mountain, then through Winding Stair Gap and into Franklin, the county seat of Macon County.

Total mileage: approximately 75 miles

The intersection of Peachtree and Hiwassee streets marks the center of downtown Murphy. On the other side of the intersection, Peachtree becomes Tennessee Street. If you head south, driving downhill on Hiwassee Street, the name changes to Valley River Avenue. The site of Fort Butler is located on the hillside across the river. Fort Butler was one of the temporary stockades built to house captured Cherokees until they could be removed to Oklahoma in 1838. Fort Butler's role in Murphy's early history is discussed more thoroughly in "The Cherokee County Tour." If you look north on Hiwassee Street, you can see the distinctive Murphy United Methodist Church, with its large central dome flanked by projecting gables. The church was built in 1922.

However, to begin this tour, head east on Peachtree Street to the impressive Cherokee County Courthouse, located one block from the town square. The present structure is actually the county's fifth courthouse. It is listed on the National Register of Historic Places.

Soon after the Cherokee Indians were moved to Oklahoma, Cherokee County was created and opened for white settlement. Legislation was passed in 1838 designating a county seat and naming it after Archibald D. Murphey, whose efforts had resulted in the formation of North Carolina's public-school system. An error in spelling dropped the e in Murphey's name, and it was never restored. A petition was started to name the new county seat after Junaluska, a Cherokee chief who many believe was born near here, but the movement never gained the necessary momentum.

Murphy United Methodist Church

By 1844, Murphy had its first permanent courthouse. The building remained standing until May 1865, when, shortly after the surrender at Appomattox, Union sympathizers raided Murphy and burned the courthouse. Confederates claimed the act was an effort to destroy records, since most of the Union renegades responsible had cases pending against them, with papers on file inside the building. That may be a one-sided view, but it is no doubt the one that prevailed during the pursuit of the culprits. Confederate forces finally caught the Union renegades at Hanging Dog, and the May 6 encounter is believed to have been one of the last battles of the Civil War east of the Mississippi.

Owing to financial circumstances following the war, the community decided to rebuild the courthouse using the old bricks. After erecting a one-story structure, the builders discovered they still had enough bricks for a second story, which they completed in 1868. The second courthouse was replaced in 1891 by a commodious building erected one block from the town square and its predecessor, at the site of the present courthouse. That building burned in 1895. Murphy had to build again. The 1896 version was a Romanesque brick structure featuring two towers in front, the larger of which contained a belfry and an enormous clock. But Murphy seemed to have a problem with fires. The fourth building burned in 1926.

The present courthouse was completed in 1927. A Neoclassical structure, it was built of beautiful, unpolished regal blue marble from the nearby marble works. Its tower, including the flagstaff, is 132 feet high. It contains a bell and clocks facing in each of the four directions. A bronze eagle with wings spread for flight is mounted atop the flagpole.

Next to the courthouse is the old Carnegie Library building, constructed in 1922. It now houses the Cherokee County Historical Museum, which contains one of the most eclectic collections in western North

Cherokee County Courthouse in Murphy

Carolina. The collection began with a man named Arthur Palmer—the owner and operator of a filling station in Marble—and grew to encompass over 2,000 relics gathered over a 70-year period. The collection was donated to the local historical society in 1977 by Herman West. The exhibits include displays of native rocks and minerals; Indian artifacts such as pottery, war instruments, jewelry, baskets, tools, and toys; artifacts left by Spanish explorers; old guns, powder horns, and swords; and even some stuffed animals. A display of particular interest features fairy crosses, which are framed and displayed on one of the museum's walls. The legend of the fairy crosses is explained later in the tour.

In addition, the building houses an interpretive center for the Cherokee County segment of the Trail of Tears; the interpretive center acts as a hub for the Cherokee Heritage Trail. Visitors can also see an exhibit on the Unicoi Turnpike National Millennium Flagship Trail, which follows the old Unicoi Turnpike. That turnpike is discussed in "The Chief Junaluska Tour" and "The Cherokee County Tour."

Across the street from the museum is the Church of the Messiah, an Episcopal

church built in 1896. Miss Lucy Morgan is remembered for her work with the Penland School near Burnsville (see "The Overmountain Victory Trail Tour"). Her mother was one of the principals behind the movement to build the Church of the Messiah. Remembering how her mother canvassed the area for contributions by sending cards with holes the size of quarters stamped out of them, Miss Lucy speculated, "I imagine a great part of the church was built with the quarters returned in Mama's cards." Since only two Episcopal families lived in Murphy at the time, she was

Church of the Messiah

probably right. The church's stained-glass window is from Tiffany's in New York.

Continue east on Peachtree Street, which becomes U.S. 64 when it leaves the business district. Continue straight across U.S. 19/64/129. Almost immediately after crossing the four-lane and before the bridge over the river, turn left on U.S. 64 Alternate. For the next 3.8 miles, the route follows the Hiwassee River, on the right, to its confluence with Peachtree Creek, coming in from the left. This is the location of the Peachtree Mound and Village Site, described in "The Cherokee County Tour."

It is about 1.3 miles farther on U.S. 64 Alternate to the intersection with U.S. 64 just past Tri-County Community College and the Murphy Medical Center. Proceed straight across and follow Old Highway 64 for 1.4 miles to the Brasstown Volunteer Fire Department and the large "Welcome to Brasstown" sign.

You may have seen the exhibit of fairy crosses at the Cherokee County Historical Museum. At first glance, the tiny stone crosses appear to be man-made. They used to be abundant in certain fields near Brasstown. No one knows their exact origin, but the Cherokees offer a legendary explanation. Stories of the Yunwi Tsunsdi, or "Little People," appear frequently in early Cherokee mythology. The Cherokees believed that several locations in the Appalachians were occupied by Little People, tiny, fairylike spirits who were as kind and helpful as they were comely. They were noted for finding lost people—especially children—and guiding them home. They often lived underwater and were known to help local fishermen, but they were wary of people and usually made themselves invisible when human beings were around. The Little People should not be confused with the Nunnehi, another Cherokee race of spirits discussed later in this tour. Little People hardly reached a man's knee.

The Cherokees tell that the Little People were gathered for singing and dancing near Brasstown one day when a messenger arrived from a distant land. When he spoke of Christ's death on the cross, the Little People wept. Their tears fell upon the earth and turned into small crosses. They left without noticing that the ground

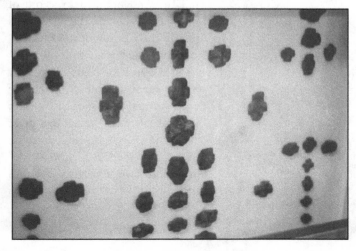

Fairy crosses

was covered with the precious product of their grief. Most of the crosses have been collected over the centuries, but those lucky enough to find one will supposedly have good fortune.

Today, Brasstown is known for a different type of artistry, thanks to the John C. Campbell Folk School. Follow the signs to the school. Turn right onto Brasstown Road; straight ahead is the campus. The best place to get information about the school is the Keith House. Follow Brasstown Road past the first road on the left to where the road curves left. There, you will see signs for the Keith House and the History Center, on the left.

During his lifetime, John C. Campbell was considered the preeminent authority on economic and social conditions in the Appalachians. He and his wife, Olive Dame Campbell, were intrigued by the possibility that Danish-style folk schools might serve as an alternative to the schools they saw in the mountains. Free of traditional forms and methods, Danish folk schools directed education toward preserving the integrity and developing the native intelligence of area people. Implicit in the folk-school theory was the use of "all that is native and fine" in local culture.

John C. Campbell died in 1919, before his dream of a folk school in western North Carolina became a reality. In 1925, after returning from over a year's worth of study of folk schools in Denmark, Olive Campbell and her friend Marguerite Butler founded the John C. Campbell Folk School in Brasstown on 25 acres donated by a local family. According to a school brochure, the school was inaugurated as "a progressive social experiment centered around adult education, cooperative agriculture, and community service." Young men learned modern farming and husbandry methods, while girls received instruction in home economics and revived mountain crafts such as weaving. The folk school also aided the community

Campus of John C. Campbell Folk School

in 1926 by founding a credit union and in 1938 by funding a loan system for help-ing local students buy their own homes and farms.

In 1930, Mrs. Campbell arranged the first woodcarving course at the school. By 1933, the school boasted 36 carvers, ranging from an 11-year-old to grandfa-thers. They came to form the nucleus of the world-famous Brasstown Carvers, the best known of the school's craftsmen. Though they began by carving animals, the carvers grew equally famous for fashioning everything from museum crèches to napkin rings. For years, they came to the folk school every Friday to sell the work they had done the past week and to pick up blocks for carving new figures. The school sanded and applied coats of preservative to the figures before selling them to customers from all over the country through the John C. Campbell Folk School Craft Shop.

Today, the school offers over 800 weekend, week-long, and two-week courses in traditional and contemporary crafts, art, dance, cooking, nature studies, photog-raphy, writing, and numerous other disciplines that attract thousands of students from all over the map.

The famous craft shop is located next to the Keith House. Information about the school and its course offerings is also available there. The campus covers over 300 acres on both sides of the road. Many of the unique stone buildings were de-signed and built in the late 1920s and the 1930s under the direction of Leon Des-champs, a Belgian engineer who worked for the school.

After visiting the folk school, return to the "Welcome to Brasstown" sign. Be-fore retracing your route to U.S. 64, you might want to visit the artisan shops in the community of Brasstown that have sprung up around the folk school.

Return to U.S. 64 and turn right, heading toward Hayesville. It is approximate-ly 1 mile to the intersection with Mission Road. On the left, you will see a roadside exhibit just before the intersection. Immediately northwest of the marker is the location of Mission Farms, the site of the Valley Towns Baptist Mission, which operated from 1820 to 1836. This boarding school for Cherokee children became the center for Cherokee scholarship and political activism prior to the Removal. Students gained vocational as well as academic training, thanks to the mission's model farm, gristmill, and blacksmith shop.

Evan Jones, a Baptist missionary, was the pastor and main teacher here. After their initial failure with English-only instruction, the teachers adopted Cherokee in their classrooms, which led to the Valley Towns Baptist Mission becoming the most successful Protestant mission in the Cherokee Nation. The school housed 50 students. Hundreds attended during its 16-year existence. Several students went on to become political leaders in the resistance movement against the Treaty of New Echota, which resulted in the Removal.

In 1836, the United States Army expelled Jones from the Valley Towns for his efforts against the Removal. When the last group of Cherokees began their trek to Oklahoma, Jones accompanied them. In Oklahoma, he helped reestablish and expand Baptist churches in the new location.

Continue on U.S. 64 through a long, scenic river valley with mountains lining the edges. It is 9.4 miles to a stoplight at the intersection with N.C. 69. Turn left, or north, to visit Hayesville, the county seat of Clay County.

Clay County is the least populated of North Carolina's mountain counties, primarily because Nantahala National Forest occupies 65,560 acres of land, or 50 percent of the entire county. Miles of trails—including the Appalachian, Rim, Fires Creek, and Chunky Gal trails—make the national forest a prime spot for hikers who are serious about escaping the crowds.

Clay County was formed as the result of a campaign promise made by George Hayes when he ran for the state legislature in 1860. Hayes was having an uphill fight in his home territory, Cherokee County. But he stumbled upon a lively issue when he traveled to the southeastern section of the county to campaign. Local constituents were angered that they could not travel to their county seat, Murphy, and return home in a day. They favored the formation of a new county with a seat of government closer to home. Hayes knew a good thing when he saw it. His promise to introduce legislation to form a new county became the focal point of his campaign. He captured the southeastern part of the county and won the election, then kept his promise in 1861. The seat of the new county was named Hayesville in his honor.

Due primarily to the disruption caused by the Civil War, the Clay County government was not organized until 1868. A courthouse was built in 1888, and the Old Jail was constructed in 1912.

Follow N.C. 69 to the traffic circle. Go three-fourths of the way around the circle and turn onto Herbert Street heading toward the town square. In the center of the square sits the courthouse, a well-preserved example of vernacular Italianate architecture that is listed on the National Register of Historic Places. A marker designates the location of Fort Hembree, another of the stockades used to hold the Cherokees before the Removal in 1838.

When Charles Lanman traveled in the area in 1849, he had this to say about

Scenic valley near Brasstown

*Clay County Courthouse
in Hayesville*

what was left of Fort Hembree: "The only evidences that there ever was a fortification here are a breastwork of timber, a lot of demolished pickets, and two or three block-houses, which are now in a dilapidated condition. The site is a commanding one, and takes in some of the grandest mountain outlines that I have ever seen."

Once you have driven around the square, return to Herbert Street. As you retrace the route you took to the square, you will see the Old Jail straight ahead. This structure now houses the Clay County Historical and Arts Center. Drive past the former jail back to the traffic circle and turn right. Go one-quarter of the way around the circle to return to N.C. 69. Drive south back to the intersection with U.S. 64 and turn left, heading east.

Chatuge Lake, billed as "the crown jewel of the TVA lakes," is on the right after 0.8 mile. Constructed in 1941–42, it boasts over 130 miles of shoreline. Chatuge Dam is 144 feet high. Extensive camping facilities are located nearby at Clay County Recreation Park, to the right.

Clay County Historical and Arts Center in the Old Jail

It is 1.4 miles on U.S. 64 from Chatuge Dam and Clay County Recreation Park to the turnoff for Tusquitee. A creek, a community, a chain of mountains, and a bald—all named Tusquitee—are in the general area on the left. In his report to the Bureau of American Ethnology in 1898, James Mooney recorded a curious legend about Tusquitee Bald. The Cherokee name for the area translates as "where the waterdogs laughed." Waterdogs—or mudpuppies, as they are often called— are salamanders noted for the way they muddy river waters. "A hunter once crossing over the mountain in a very dry season, heard voices," Mooney recorded, "and creeping silently toward the place from which the sound proceeded, peeped over a rock and saw two water-dogs walking together on their hind legs along the trail and talking as they went. Their pond had dried up and they were on the way over to Nantahala River. As he listened one said to the other, 'Where's the water? I'm so thirsty that my apron [gills] hangs down,' and then both water-dogs laughed." The tale apparently lost something in translation, but it obviously made an impression on the Cherokees, as they named the prominent bald after the incident.

After 2.5 miles, you will pass an intersection with N.C. 175 and a turnoff to Jackrabbit Mountain Recreation Area. This camping facility is located on a peninsula wooded with pines and surrounded by Chatuge Lake. It has over 100 campsites, a swimming beach with shower facilities, hiking trails, picnic areas, and a launching ramp for boats.

Stay on U.S. 64. The peak on the left is Vineyard Mountain. Local tradition says that an Englishman once set out a good many grapevines here but later gave up his enterprise and returned to his native land. The vineyard is remembered even if the man's name is forgotten.

Continue another 2.3 miles to the community of Shooting Creek. If you happen to get out of your car within earshot of the creek, be sure to listen with the utmost attention, as Shooting Creek is quite literally a babbling brook. *North Carolina: A Guide to the Old North State*, compiled by the Work Projects Administration in 1939, recorded that "the people of an Indian town on the Hiwassee River, near its confluence with Shooting Creek, prayed and fasted that they might see the Nunnehi [a race of supernatural beings]. At the end of seven days the Nunnehi came and took them under the water. There they still reside and on a warm summer day when the wind ripples the surface those who listen well can hear them talking below."

View from Glade Gap on
Chunky Gal Mountain

Drive 7.6 miles past Shooting Creek on U.S. 64 to Glade Gap (elevation 3,679 feet), the route over Chunky Gal Mountain. A scenic overlook is on the left at the top of the gap. In *These Storied Mountains*, John Parris wrote that this peak received its name when a buxom Cherokee maiden eloped with a Wayah brave. The girl's father caught up with the two as they paused to refresh themselves at the big spring in the gap in the mountains. The girl was forced to return home without her lover, and the other village maidens, envious of her well-endowed body, took to calling her "Chunky Gal." It is doubtful that "Chunky Gal" was part of the Cherokee vocabulary in its exact translated form, but the name does seem to fit the high ridge that this route follows.

It is another 4.3 miles to a brown forest-service sign noting that F.R. 72 and Deep Gap are to the right. It takes 20 to 30 minutes to drive the 5 miles to the parking area at Deep Gap. There, you can gain access to an extensive system of hiking trails, including the Appalachian Trail. The parking area at Deep Gap is also the closest you can drive to Standing Indian Mountain.

Standing Indian Mountain, elevation 5,498 feet, has been called "the grandstand of the southern Appalachians." It dominates Standing Indian Basin, a horseshoe-shaped area formed by the Nantahala and Blue Ridge mountains and bisected by the Nantahala River. Several prominent peaks over 5,000 feet high are along the rim. Though you may not be able to pick out anything that looks like a standing Indian in the jumble of rocks, you will undoubtedly enjoy the spectacular view from the treeless bald.

The Cherokee name for Standing Indian Mountain translates as "where the man stands." According to legend, the area was once terrorized by a huge bird that would swoop out of the skies and carry off children. To defend against such raids, the Cherokees cleared the mountaintops to make them better lookout points, then posted sentries.

The beast's lair was finally discovered in the cliffs atop what is now Standing Indian Mountain. The cliffs were inaccessible, so the Cherokees prayed to the Great Spirit for assistance. Their prayers were answered. The Great Spirit sent lightning to destroy the bird and its home. The Indian sentry stationed nearby was so frightened by the lightning that he tried to flee the mountaintop. He was turned to rock for deserting his post, and his stone figure has kept vigil ever since. According to early accounts, the likeness used to be more easily recognizable, but erosion has taken its toll over the years. The cliffs where the great bird lived, however, are still very much in evidence.

Continue 2.7 miles on U.S. 64 to Rainbow Springs, which was the base of the Ritter Lumber Company's logging operations in the early 1900s. Practically all of Standing Indian Basin has been logged at least once. The Ritter Lumber Company used the selective-cut system, taking all good timber more than 15 inches in diameter and leaving small trees, large defective trees, and poor lumber species. The United States Forest Service purchased the land in 1920, but the area's virgin timber has been lost forever.

Signs on the right direct travelers to Standing Indian Campground, the site of Ritter's main logging camp at one point. Near the campground is a bulletin board that provides information about the complex system of hiking trails in the backcountry area. Hikes are available to suit almost every type of visitor. There are also designated trails for horseback riders, as well as several longer and more difficult hikes that connect with the Appalachian Trail and the trails to Standing Indian Mountain used by back-country campers.

Continue east on U.S. 64 for 1.8 miles to Winding Stair Gap, elevation 3,820 feet, where the highway was literally carved through a mountain. It is another 0.5 mile to a scenic overlook that provides a panoramic view of Macon County, the town of Franklin, and the Little Tennessee River Valley.

As U.S. 64 descends the Nantahala Mountains, it enters the Cartoogechaye Creek area. In 1818, two white settlers, Jacob Siler and William Brittain, entered Indian territory and set about building a shelter for their horses. The Cherokee chief Santeetlah suddenly appeared on their third morning in the area and told them, "Be gone to your own house." Brittain moved on, but Siler insisted he had

View from Winding Stair Gap

come to stay. He convinced his three brothers—William, Jesse, and John—to join him. They settled in the valley. It was through the efforts of William Siler that the Sand Town branch of the Cherokees was allowed to remain in North Carolina during the Removal. Since the Sand Town Indians—or any other Indians, for that matter—were not permitted to own land, William Siler provided them with a tract on Cartoogechaye Creek near Muskrat Creek. Though isolated from the other Cherokees for years, they eventually merged with Indians in the Qualla area or joined their kinsmen in Oklahoma.

It is 9.8 miles from the scenic overlook to Franklin. In 1849, Charles Lanman wrote, "The little village of Franklin is romantically situated on the little Tennessee. It is surrounded with mountains, and as quiet and pretty a hamlet as I have yet seen among the Alleghanies." The town was established in 1855, though its historic tradition began centuries before that.

Entering Franklin, U.S. 64 runs conjunctively with U.S. 441. Leave the four-lane at the exit for U.S. 64 East/N.C. 28; the signs designate Highlands and Franklin. At the bottom of the exit ramp, turn left onto Highlands Road, heading into Franklin. It is 1.4 miles to the junction with U.S. 441 Business. Turn left onto U.S. 441 Business, which is also East Main Street. It is 0.2 mile to a large mound of grass-covered earth on the left just across the Little Tennessee River. This is the Nikwasi Indian Mound. It may be difficult to see at first because of the commercial congestion; just look for the grassy mound.

Nikwasi was among the oldest Cherokee settlements and an important ceremonial center. It was one of the few towns in Cherokee country that possessed the "everlasting fire" important in religious ceremonies. Even in the 1890s, older Cherokees claimed that the sacred fire continued to burn in the Nikwasi Indian Mound. Destroyed and rebuilt twice, Nikwasi was continuously occupied until the land was sold in 1891. In 1947, residents of Macon County, including many schoolchildren, raised money to purchase the mound and save it from developers and entrepreneurs.

According to Cherokee tradition, the mound was the town house where the Nunnehi lived. In Cherokee, Nunnehi means "people who live anywhere." Some translations make it "people who live forever," which explains why the Nunnehi were also called "the Immortals." Not to be confused with the Little People, who populated other areas of the mountains, the Nunnehi looked like average Cherokees—whenever they allowed themselves to be seen, that is. Usually, they remained invisible and reclusive. Like the Little People, the Nunnehi loved music and dancing. Their drums could often be heard echoing through the hills. Both groups were generally friendly and were noted for helping lost Cherokees find their way home.

James Mooney recorded one traditional Cherokee story about the Nunnehi at Nikwasi. Years before white men came to the area, local Indians faced certain defeat at the hands of an invading tribe that had just finished plundering Cherokee towns in South Carolina. The men of Nikwasi met the opposition on the town's outskirts, when, according to Mooney, "suddenly a stranger stood among them and shouted to the chief to call off his men and he himself would drive back the enemy." The Nikwasi warriors assumed the stranger to be a chief who had come with reinforcements from the Overhill settlements in Tennessee. They fell back as ordered, and it wasn't long before they saw a great company of warriors coming out of the side of the mound. "The Nunne'hi poured out by hundreds, armed and painted for the fight, and the most curious thing about it all was that they became invisible as soon as they were fairly outside of the settlement, so that although the enemy saw the glancing arrow or the rushing tomahawk, and felt the stroke, he could not see who sent it." Nikwasi was saved, thanks to the Nunnehi. The Cherokees then knew that the Immortals lived inside the mound.

Mooney also reported that the Cherokees believed the Nunnehi resided in the mound as late as the Civil War. A surprise attack on a Confederate stronghold at Franklin was canceled when Union soldiers saw a large contingent of soldiers, presumably Nunnehi, guarding the town as they approached.

After visiting the Nikwasi Indian Mound and the town of Franklin, you can continue on U.S. 441/23 to Dillsboro and Asheville, or you can return to the stoplight and follow U.S. 64 East/28 South to Highlands. For more information about the Franklin area, see "The Nantahala Tour." For information about Highlands, see "The Highlands Tour."

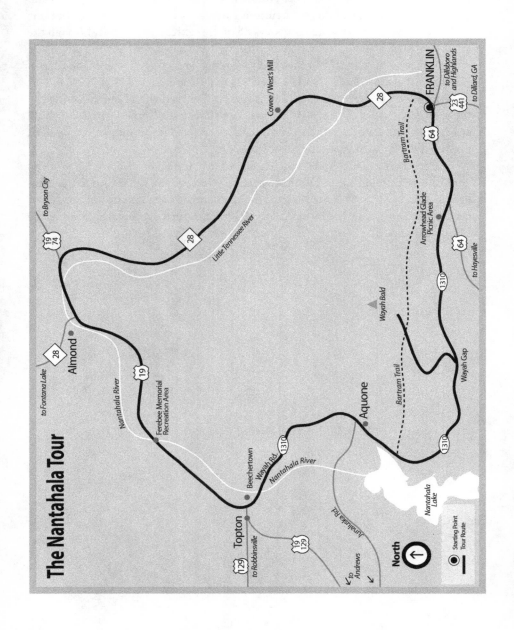

The Nantahala Tour

TOUR 5

The Nantahala Tour

This tour begins in the town of Franklin and follows the Little Tennessee River to Cowee Valley. It then follows the Nantahala River through its famous gorge, passing Nantahala Lake and Wayah Bald before returning to Franklin.

Total mileage: approximately 85 miles

The tour begins at the Nikwasi Indian Mound in Franklin, which marks the site of an ancient Cherokee village. To reach the mound from U.S. 64/N.C. 28, take the Highlands exit and drive toward Franklin. It is 1.4 miles to the junction with U.S. 441 Business. Turn left onto U.S. 441 Business (East Main Street). The mound is on the left after 0.2 mile, just across the Little Tennessee River. It may be difficult to see because of the commercial buildings; look for the grassy hill. "The Standing Indian Tour" explains the Cherokee legends about the Nunnehi, or "the Immortals," who supposedly lived inside the mound and kept the sacred ceremonial fire burning.

In later years, the same mound played an important role in the relations between Indians and whites. In 1721, the British-appointed governor of South Carolina met with Cherokee chiefs representing 37 towns to sign a treaty establishing the first boundary line between Indian lands and English settlements. Between 1721 and 1730, however, the French became increasingly influential among the various Indian tribes. The Cherokees grew so disillusioned with the British and their promises that they, too, began to consider an alliance with the French. Then, in 1730, Sir Alexander Cuming came to Nikwasi and pulled off one of the biggest diplomatic coups in frontier history. More information about Cuming's exploits is in "The Chief Junaluska Tour."

After viewing the site of Cuming's historic encounter, turn right onto Depot

Nikwasi Indian Mound in Franklin

Street, which becomes Riverview Street. You are following N.C. 28 along the Little Tennessee River.

Much of the area covered in this tour was Cherokee territory, so it saw a lot of the warfare between the tribe and early white settlers. Some historical background may help to understand how the relationship between the two groups disintegrated so badly.

By the time hostilities between the French and the British began around 1756, the Cherokees—regardless of Sir Alexander Cuming's earlier efforts—were growing dissatisfied with their treatment at the hands of the British. Several unfortunate incidents only served to escalate the bitterness, despite the pleas of the more level-headed leaders on both sides.

In February 1756, a group of Cherokees accompanied a British expedition against the Shawano tribe. Not only were the Cherokees treated with contempt by the British forces, they had to endure a march through the snow, during which they lost all their provisions. On the journey home, they were forced to kill their own horses for food. Upon finding some horses running loose on the range, the Cherokees confiscated them. The white owners interpreted the act as horse stealing and killed a number of Indians, mutilating their bodies and taking the scalps to a local settlement to collect the regular price for French Indian scalps. Young Cherokee warriors were prepared to take revenge, but their elders convinced them to seek satisfaction through legal channels.

Next, some men from Fort Prince George, located in what is now Pickens County, South Carolina, "committed an unpardonable outrage at the neighbor-

Mooney. The Cherokees retaliated by attacking back-country white settlements.

Several Cherokee chiefs seemed on the verge of bringing the situation under control again when South Carolina governor William Henry Lyttleton demanded the surrender and execution of some Indians known to have killed colonists. The Cherokees sent a delegation headed by a chief named Oconostota to discuss a peace arrangement. Lyttleton ordered the entire delegation (some sources say 25 men, others say 32) held as hostages until the Cherokee "murderers" were surrendered. The chiefs were imprisoned in a room hardly large enough for half their number. Atakullakulla, one of the chiefs who had accompanied Cuming to England and become a friend of the English, interceded and gained the release of Oconostota and several other chiefs.

Oconostota, however, wanted his disgrace revenged. He led a siege of Fort Prince George in February 1760, after Lyttleton had left thinking everything was under control. Saying he wanted to talk peace, Oconostota summoned the commanding officer, then shot him. The soldiers inside the fort retaliated by killing the rest of the still-imprisoned chiefs.

Colonel Archibald Montgomery's British force of 1,600 men, fresh from Indian warfare in western Pennsylvania and New York, arrived to reinforce Fort Prince George. After burning five Indian towns in lower South Carolina by June 1, Montgomery decided to attack the Middle Towns farther north. On June 27, his men entered "a plain covered with wood and brush so thick that one could scarce see three yards distance with an ugly muddy river in the middle of it, overlooked on one side by a high mountain, and on the other by hilly uneven ground," according to one source. More than 600 Cherokees lay in ambush there. The British were forced to retreat to Fort Prince George.

Montgomery's defeat sealed the fate of Fort Loudoun, located near what is now Knoxville, Tennessee. The forces there had held out under siege by eating horses and dogs, aided by the kindness of some Cherokee women who smuggled food to their sweethearts among the white soldiers. But by August 8, Captain Demeré and his men were forced to surrender. After the British left, the Indians discovered that ammunition had been buried or thrown into the river, counter to the surrender settlement. Enraged at this duplicity, the Cherokees attacked and killed Demeré and his men.

In June 1761, Colonel James Grant arrived with a large force. The Cherokees attacked on June 10 at a site about 2 miles south of their battle with Montgomery. This time, they were unable to inflict heavy casualties. The British marched on to Nikwasi. During the next two weeks, Grant burned local Indian towns and the crops and orchards of all the Middle Towns of the Cherokees. The Indians quickly sued for peace—a peace that was to be short-lived, as detailed later in the tour.

Approximately 7 miles from Franklin (after crossing the Little Tennessee River), you will reach Cowee Baptist Church, Cowee Creek Road, and the community of West's Mill. Turn right onto Cowee Creek Road (S.R. 1341), where you will see a sign noting the Cowee/West's Mill Historic District. In 1820, William West took title to land along Cowee Creek and built the gristmill that gave the community its name. On the right is the restored T. M. Rickman General Store, now used as a community building. Take the fork to the left in front of the general store, then turn left again onto West's Mill Road to get back on N.C. 28. You will see several old buildings in various states of repair. These were the stores and churches used by the community in the 19th and early 20th centuries. The Cowee School was built by Civilian Conservation Corps employees, whose camp was nearby. It is still used as a school today. As you turn onto West's Mill Road heading toward N.C. 28, you will see an information board that tells the history of these and other buildings in the designated historic district.

T.M. Rickman General Store in Cowee

The Cowee Valley was also known as "the Valley of Rubies." Though people in the area had known about the red stones in the creek bed for years, it wasn't until Dr. George Frederick Kunz of Tiffany's in New York made an official report about the Cowee Valley rubies in 1893 that their value was realized. Alerted to the stones' worth, area landowners began mailing their stones to Tiffany's for cutting. Word got out, and in 1895 the American Prospecting and Mining Company of New York bought out old claims and began work under the supervision of W. E. Hidden. It's main goal was to find the source of the rubies so abundant in the gravel creek bed. The American Prospecting and Mining Company and others began to sink shafts and test holes.

In 1912, Joseph H. Pratt and Joseph V. Lewis conducted a geological survey for the state of North Carolina. Their work revealed that there was indeed an occurrence of corundum in the Cowee Valley. Corundum is a gem species second in hardness only to diamonds. Its colored varieties are rubies and sapphires. It was valuable not only for its decorative qualities but also for its use in watch movements, abrasives, and the manufacture of bearings for electrical equipment. Pratt and Lewis compared the Cowee Valley with the Mogok Valley in Burma, the world's premier ruby field.

It turned out that the percentage of marketable stones, though consistent, was too low to cover the high labor costs. The main source was never discovered, and commercial mining was finally abandoned in 1914.

The work done by the mining companies was primarily exploratory, so the creek's gravel bed remains intact. Today, the area has several ruby mines open to

View of Cowee Valley

the public. For a nominal fee, tourists and rock collectors can buy panning privi-leges in the nearby creek—as well as the use of screens and stools—to search for fabulous gems. Most of the mines have exhibits or posted records of gems found at the sites to inspire rock hounds.

Where West's Mill Road intersects N.C. 28, you will see a historical marker reading, "Pottery Clay." It seems that this area was blessed with natural resources of all types. In the early 1760s, Andrew Duché, a potter from Savannah, Georgia, learned that clay similar to that used in Chinese porcelain could be found in Cher-okee territory. He traveled into the wilderness, located a source of kaolin, and ne-gotiated with the Cherokee chiefs for the right to mine their clay.

In 1767, British pottery manufacturer Josiah Wedgwood sent South Carolina planter Thomas Griffiths to make similar arrangements. The Indians, quickly learn-ing the game, set a high price for the clay that the whites wanted so badly. The traders who supplied the packhorses did likewise. Nonetheless, Griffiths managed to ship several tons of the white clay to England. It was made into the inaugural Queen's Ware, for which Josiah Wedgwood and his company were to become famous. A dinner service fashioned for Catherine the Great came from Macon County clay. Wedgwood later found a more economical source for his clay. Those early place settings are now museum pieces.

Turn right onto N.C. 28. After 0.8 mile, you will see a historical marker desig-nating the site of Cowee, the chief town of the Middle Cherokees.

Little Tennessee River

In 1773, Dr. John Fothergill, one of London's leading physicians, commissioned William Bartram of Philadelphia to explore the South in order "to collect and send me all the curious plants and seeds and other natural productions." For four years, Bartram traveled all over the Southeast, gathering specimens and keeping a journal that has become an invaluable source of historical information and a classic work in its own right. In 1775, Bartram visited the Cowee area and recorded his observations:

> I arrived at Cowe [*sic*] about noon. This settlement is esteemed the capital town: it is situated on the bases of the hills on both sides of the river, near to its bank, and here terminates the great vale of Cowe, exhibiting one of the most charming mountainous landscapes perhaps anywhere to be seen; ridges of hills rising grand and sublimely one above and beyond another, some boldly and majestically advancing into the verdant plain, their feet bathed with the silver flood of the Tanase [the Little Tennessee], whilst others far distant, veiled in blue mists, sublimely mounting aloft with yet greater majesty lift up their pompous crests, and overlook vast regions.

Bartram went on to note that Cowee consisted of 100 homes and was dominated by a great town house built on a 20-foot mound. He described the town house as "a large rotunda" that could easily accommodate most of the town's residents. A year after Bartram's visit, the town was destroyed in another series of confrontations between the Cherokees and white settlers.

When the Revolutionary War began, the Cherokees sided with the British. The newly formed state governments of North Carolina, South Carolina, and Virginia decided to join in a concerted military effort to punish the Indians for attacking settlements on their frontiers.

On September 1, 1776, General Griffith Rutherford and an army of 2,500 left what is now Old Fort and crossed Swannanoa Gap heading for the Cherokee Middle Towns, where they planned to rendezvous with Colonel Andrew Williamson and his South Carolina army.

Williamson reached the Little Tennessee and the Middle Town of Watauga on September 8. He found the town deserted. Rutherford arrived the next day, but Williamson had gone. The general sent a detachment to look for him. The rest of his army set about destroying the Cherokee towns along the Little Tennessee, including Nikwasi and Cowee. Rutherford then decided to leave some of his troops to wait for Williamson. He took 1,200 men across Wallace Gap with the intention of destroying the Cherokee towns along the Hiwassee River in Clay and Cherokee counties.

Meanwhile, Williamson arrived in Nikwasi, only to learn that Rutherford had gone on to the Cherokee Valley Towns. He camped at Cowee on September 18, then headed across the mountains at Indian Grave Gap. A large contingent of Cherokees was gathered there, and the opposing forces fought for over two hours. Williamson's men were able to hold the field. They continued their march through what is now Nantahala Gorge. Their trip was so arduous that it took them four days to cover the approximately 20 miles to what is now Topton. Before meeting Rutherford in Murphy, they destroyed most of the Cherokee towns along the Valley River. Rutherford and Williamson succeeded in devastating most of the Middle and Valley towns during this campaign.

In more recent times, the Cowee Mound, once a Cherokee ceremonial center and part of the village destroyed in Rutherford's campaign, has been recognized as one of the most important archaeological sites in western North Carolina. In 1965, archaeologists working the site of the former town collected prehistoric ceramics that dated the mound to 600 A.D.

In 2007, the Eastern Band of the Cherokee Indians, working with the Land Trust for the Little Tennessee, acquired 71 acres including the mound. The Ralph Preston Historic Cowee Mound is now protected for future generations.

Another part of the area that the Cherokees acquired included the historic farm of Euchella. According to treaties made in 1817 and 1819, each head of a Cherokee family who wished to become a citizen of the United States was granted a life reservation of 640 acres with a reversion in fee simple to his children. The claim registered in 1819 by a Cherokee named Euchella included much of historical Cowee Town. White settlers moved into the area and claimed some of the same territory. Rather than protecting the rights of the Indians, North Carolina sold some of their lands to the whites. A white man named Joseph Welch bought 299 acres of Euchella's land in a state sale in 1821. Euchella sued—which shows just how assimilated the Cherokees were becoming to the white man's culture. The case went all the way to the North Carolina Supreme Court, where it was decided in Euchella's favor. The state admitted its error and upheld the rights of the Cherokees. In cases where Indians had already been deprived of their property, the state compensated them with land elsewhere in the area. The decision handed down in

Euchella v. Welch became an integral part of legal precedence on several later issues involving the Cherokees.

Although the court found for Euchella, the claim was invalidated on a technicality about signatures. Euchella vacated his land and moved to Euchella Cove near the Nantahala River. As detailed in "The Tour of the Lakes," Euchella later played an even more important role in Cherokee history when he led the group that captured Tsali in exchange for a grant of immunity from removal. He became the head of the Wolf Clan in the Qualla settlement, which went on to form the Eastern Band of the Cherokees.

The tour continues for 11 miles on N.C. 28 along the Little Tennessee River. A turnout on the left allows a good view of the river valley below with the mountains in the background.

From the turnout, it is 1.9 miles to the intersection with U.S. 19/74. Turn left onto U.S. 19/74/N.C. 28 as all three highways travel conjunctively on a four-lane. Continue on U.S. 19/74 when N.C. 28 splits off. After an additional 3 miles, the route enters the steep Nantahala Gorge, following the Nantahala River. A visitors' center is on the left just past the sign announcing the gorge area.

Ahead is one of the most impressive scenic drives in western North Carolina. The gorge is so deep and its sides so sheer that the Cherokees called it "the Land of the Middle Sun," referring to the fact that direct sunlight is shut out until nearly noon.

Naturally, such a place would figure to be inspiration for legends. The Cherokees believed the gorge to be the home of Uktena, "a great snake as large around as a tree trunk with horns on its head and a bright, blazing crest like a diamond on its forehead, and scales glittering and flashing like sparks of fire," as transcribed by

Nantahala Outdoor Center

James Mooney. Uktena could not be wounded except by being shot "in the seventh spot from the head because under this spot are its heart and its life." The diamond on its forehead was called Ulunsuti, which translates as "transparent." If anyone could detach it, that person would see the future. Many tried to capture the talisman, but those who looked upon Uktena were so dazed by the diamond's light that they were drawn toward it, to certain death. One hunter was finally able to shoot the serpent on the seventh spot while it slept. It is said that the Cherokees still keep the large, transparent crystal with the blood-red streak through its center in a secret cave high in the mountains.

The stretch of the Nantahala River you are following is widely recognized as world-class whitewater. Continuous rapids and moderately high water during the summer offer a challenge for whitewater enthusiasts; periodic releases from the power company's dam provide the fast water needed for rafting or paddling. An entire outfitting industry has developed here.

You will reach the Nantahala Outdoor Center (NOC) complex 4 miles from the visitors' center. Founded in 1972, the NOC operates rafting trips on seven rivers in the Appalachians. Approaching the buildings, you will see a public access area that is jammed in the summer. If you can find a parking space, this is the place to get a good photograph of rafters as they shoot the rapids right in front of the NOC.

Continue 7.4 miles from the NOC to the Nantahala River Launch Site. All along the route are picnic tables and areas where travelers can pull over to watch adventurers running the river. Ferebee Memorial Recreation Area is a particularly scenic spot.

At the launch site, turn left onto Wayah Road (S.R. 1310). The small community centered around the power plant is known as Beechertown.

In the parking area for the launch site are a chimney and some informational signs. One tells about Colonel Nimrod S. Jarrett, who ran a railroad through the gorge and owned Jarrett's Station, located 1.5 miles downriver. The sign notes that Jarrett was 72 when he was murdered by a drifter named Bayles Henderson in 1871. Henderson became the first man hanged in Macon County.

Another section of the sign mentions that two chimneys located across the river mark the site of a house built by Matthew Cole in 1890. Cole Fields may have been one of North Carolina's earliest wineries. The Cole homestead had over 800 apple trees, as well as grapevines that produced over 2,000 gallons of wine a year.

You will also notice a historical marker indicating that William Bartram met the Cherokee chief Atakullakulla near this spot in May 1776.

After Bartram left the village of Cowee, he tried to convince his white guide to lead him over the Nantahala Mountains to the Overhill Towns. The guide refused because the area was not considered safe for whites at that time. Bartram went on alone. When he arrived at what is now Beechertown, he met a band of Indians led by Atakullakulla, who was known among the Cherokees as "the wily savage" and "the Indian capable of enthusiasm for good and evil." Such designations would not seem a good omen for Bartram. As a token of respect, he yielded the trail to the

Nantahala Lake

chief. "His highness with a gracious and cheerful smile came up to me," Bartram wrote, "and clapping his hand on his breast, offered it to me, saying, I am Ata-cul-culla; and heartily shook hands with me, and asked if I knew it." Bartram identified himself as a Quaker from Pennsylvania and then proceeded to stretch the truth in the interest of self-preservation by informing the chief that "the name Ata-cul-culla was dear to his white brothers of Pennsylvania." The two passed a few more pleasantries. Impressed that he was known so far away, Atakullakulla welcomed Bartram "to their country as a friend and brother, and then shaking hands heartily bid me farewell."

Though Bartram enjoyed astounding luck in his encounter with Atakullakulla, the experience must have unsettled him, for he soon decided to turn back for the security of Cowee. The incident suggests what a resourceful man this scholarly naturalist proved to be in the wilderness.

The launch site marks the beginning of Class II and III whitewater rafting on the Nantahala River. Across the road is a trailhead for the Bartram Trail, which follows the route Bartram took through the Southeast from 1773 to 1777. His vivid descriptions of what he saw were later published as *Bartram's Travels*, still in print today.

Follow Wayah Road as it winds alongside the Nantahala River for 10.5 miles to where Nantahala Lake is visible on the right. You will reach a marker indicating another trailhead for the Bartram Trail 0.4 mile later. Hikers can follow the trail from the Nantahala Gorge across Wayah Bald and into Franklin.

It is another 8.2 miles to F.R. 69. Wayah Gap is at the crest of the ridge. You will see signs for the Appalachian Trail, which crosses the road here. The Wayah Crest Picnic Ground is on the right.

Turn left onto F.R. 69, which travels to the top of Wayah Bald, elevation 5,335 feet. The 4.5-mile drive on a gravel road takes approximately 15 minutes. It is 1.4 miles on F.R. 69 to the Wilson Lick Ranger Station, on the left. Built in 1913, this was the first ranger station in Nantahala National Forest. You will also pass Wine Spring Bald and another sign for the Bartram Trail. It is approximately 2 more miles to the parking area at Wayah Bald, then a five-minute walk to the fire lookout tower.

Evidence indicates that Indians used this bald as a hunting ground as early as 300 B.C. The Cherokees gave it the name Wayah, meaning "wolf," because of the large number of wolves in the vicinity. During the 1850s and 1860s, there was a bounty on wolves in Macon County, which soon eradicated them from the area.

Another name the Cherokees had for Wayah Gap was Atahita, or "the Shouting Place," because of its role in the destruction of Ulagu, "the Great Yellow Jacket." The giant insect was said to be as large as a house. It would swoop down from its secret hiding place and carry off children from a village on the Nantahala River. In order to track the insect to its hiding place, the Cherokees killed a deer and tied a long white string to it. When Ulagu carried off its bounty, it found the load so heavy that it had to fly slowly, thus enabling the Indians to follow the string. At Wayah Gap, they saw Ulagu's nest in a large cave in the rocks on the other side of the valley. They gave a shout of excitement, and the site came to be known as "the Shouting Place" from that day. The Indians built fires around the entrance to the cave and smothered the insect with smoke. Some smaller yellow jackets escaped from the cave. Their descendants are still found in the area's forests.

After the Treaty of Washington established a boundary between whites and Indians along the crest of the Nantahala Mountains in 1819, it became apparent

*Wayah Bald
fire tower*

that it was only a matter of time before the Indians would be pushed completely out of the territory. In 1820, the town of Franklin was surveyed. In 1856, a toll turnpike was built from Asheville to the Tennessee line, and mail and passengers traveled through Wayah Gap on a daily basis. The bald, used primarily as pasture, then became a popular place for summer picnics as well.

The United States Forest Service took over management of the bald in 1913. The Civilian Conservation Corps improved Wayah Road in 1933–34 and began constructing Wayah Bald's rock fire tower in 1935. Completed in 1937 and dedicated to John B. Byrne, a well-loved national-forest supervisor, the tower was 60 feet tall. The second of its three floors was an observation level with 12 windows and an outside deck. The top floor housed two fire lookout men.

Unfortunately, there was a flaw in the mortar work. Water seeped in. In 1947, a contractor was hired to tear down the tower because it was unsafe. He removed the top two floors and built a new rock staircase on the outside of the south wall. In 1983, a new roof of hemlock beams and cedar shakes was constructed. The forest service removed many of the scrub trees that had grown up around the bald and pruned some of the azaleas there.

In September 2009, several young men were charged with possession of weapons of mass destruction for repeated acts of throwing homemade explosive devices into the lower level of the lookout tower. They were first suspected when police found a damaged forest-service padlock in their car at a road checkpoint. They then discovered bomb-making materials in the trunk of the vehicle. As it turned out, the men had thrown explosive devices at the fire tower on at least six occasions. The best part was that they had videotaped their escapades and put them on YouTube. The video camera, which was confiscated, even recorded the dates of the incidents.

Even without such senseless vandalism, the tower had been deteriorating. Fortunately, some American Recovery and Reinvestment Act funds were allotted to restore the tower, so people will be able to enjoy the view for years to come.

The bald is an excellent observation point during May and June, when the azaleas, rhododendrons, and wildflowers are in full bloom. Now back in service, the lookout tower provides an incredible view of the surrounding mountains any time of year.

After enjoying the view atop Wayah Bald, retrace F.R. 69 to Wayah Road (S.R. 1310) and turn left. It is 5.7 miles—most of it downhill—to the LBJ Civilian Conservation Center, on the right, and Arrowhead Glade Picnic Area, on the left. You will reach an intersection after another 3.1 miles; a store is on the right. Turn right. It is less than a mile to an intersection with U.S. 64. Turn left and drive about 4 miles into Franklin.

After exploring the Cowee Valley, you might want to stop off at the Franklin Gem and Mineral Museum, housed in a 150-year-old former jail downtown. The free museum features a 49-pound corundum crystal found at the Corundum Hill Mine in Macon County in 1886. Fossils, gems, and minerals from all over the world are exhibited. The museum also offers a display of Indian artifacts from the

Little Tennessee River area and around the country.

Follow U.S. 441 Business as it becomes Main Street leading into downtown Franklin. The museum is located in the center of town at 25 Phillips Street near the corner of Main Street; it is next to the statue on the right. This completes the tour.

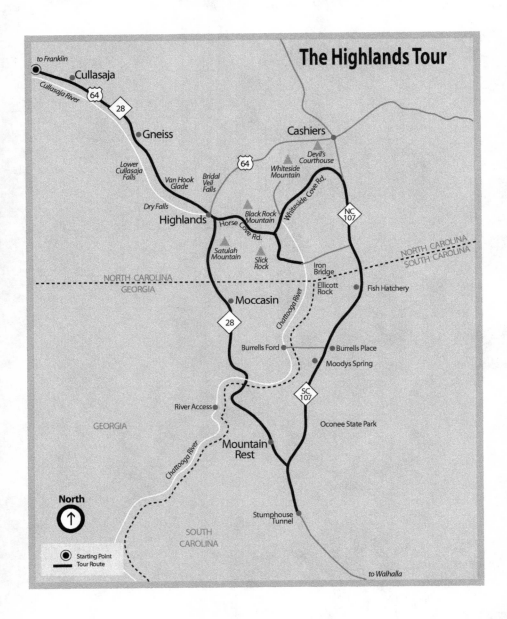

TOUR 6
The Highlands Tour

This tour begins in Franklin and travels through the Cullasaja Gorge to the town of Highlands. From there, it heads south along the Chattooga River to Stumphouse Tunnel Park and Issaqueena Falls. It then travels north to Whiteside and Horse coves before returning to Highlands.

Total mileage: approximately 86 miles

To begin the tour, drive east on U.S. 64/N.C. 28 from Franklin toward Highlands. It is 4.4 miles through a farming valley intersected by the Cullasaja River to the community of Cullasaja. The water from the Cullasaja River flows 1,500 miles via the Little Tennessee, Tennessee, Ohio, and Mississippi rivers to empty into the Gulf of Mexico. On the North Carolina portion of the journey, it flows through some of the most picturesque areas of the state.

Several sources from the early 1800s claimed that *Cullasaja* was the anglicized version of the Cherokee word for "sugar water." James Mooney corrected that misconception in his 1898 report to the Bureau of American Ethnology after learning that it came from the Cherokee word *Kulsetsiyi*, meaning "honey locust place." The honey locust tree was a religious symbol equated with the gods of thunder and lightning. According to Cherokee mythology, there was a throne made of honey locust in the home of the Thunder Man. The Indians believed in a connection between the pinnated leaves of the tree and lightning. The confusion started when white traders arrived with their sugar, for which the Cherokees had no name. The closest they could come was their word for honey. The traders further confused matters when they started to call any location featuring the Cherokees' revered honey locust "Sugartown." One such settlement was near what is now Cullasaja. The place where the Little Tennessee River flows into the Cullasaja was once known as Sugar Fork. Topographical maps still show a Sugar Fork along Ellijay Creek, which feeds into the Cullasaja.

In 1934, the Smithsonian Institution undertook the challenge of tracing the

1540 expedition of Hernando De Soto, the Spanish explorer who ventured into the mountains in search of gold. With the help of descriptions from the journals of several men who accompanied the expedition, the Smithsonian used landmarks to verify the route. Arriving from South Carolina, De Soto and his men left what is now Highlands and followed the Cullasaja River to the Cherokee village of Nikwasi, located where Franklin stands today. The area apparently didn't manage to hold De Soto's interest, because by 1541 he had reached the Mississippi River. Numerous historical markers all over the vicinity commemorate his visit.

It is 3.7 miles from Cullasaja to another small community, Gneiss. Just past Gneiss is a sign noting the entrance to the Cullasaja Gorge. The next 7.5 miles constitute not only one of the most scenic routes in western North Carolina but an amazing engineering feat as well.

In their 1883 book, *The Heart of the Alleghanies*, Wilbur Zeigler and Ben Grosscup described an older version of the route as "one possessing panoramic grandeur to an extent equalled by but few highways in the Alleghanies. . . . A series of picturesque rapids and cascades enlivens the way; and, in a deep gorge, where, on one precipitous side the turnpike clings, and the other rises abruptly across the void, tumbles the lower Sugar Fork falls [Lower Cullasaja Falls]."

In 1929, local people started lobbying for a good road through the gorge between Franklin and Highlands. North Carolina officials were reluctant to begin the project, knowing how difficult it would prove to complete. The federal government further complicated matters by denying aid, since the proposed course was not the most direct or the least expensive.

When construction finally began, the first task was to blast away parts of the solid granite mountains to allow space for the road. Workers were lowered from the tops of the cliffs in rope slings tied to trees; gazing at the cliffs today, it doesn't take much of an imagination to envision what a popular job that must have been. The workers drilled holes in the granite and placed dynamite in the holes. They were then hauled back to the top, and the charges were set. The steel rods used to drill the holes were 10 feet long—meaning that only a 10-foot width of rock could be cleared at a time—so several trips down the face of the cliffs were required at each blasting site. The first load of gravel was laid in May 1931. The road was partially paved by 1932. Built on a granite shelf 250 feet above the river, it literally hangs on the rock wall.

The river drops 2,000 feet in the 7.5-mile gorge. Cascades and waterfalls are abundant. The first is Lower Cullasaja Falls, which is actually a dramatic series of cascades falling more that 250 feet in 0.25 mile. The waterfall is 0.6 mile from the sign announcing the entrance to Cullasaja Gorge. In 1993, this section of the route was designated part of the National Forest Service's Mountain Waters Scenic Byway.

The falls deserve a look, though stopping is tricky. Since the roadbed between the rock wall and the gorge barely allows space for two lanes, little room is available for a turnout for tourists to stop and gawk or take photos. Stone parapets only a few feet high have been built on the edge of the gorge, and there is a small area where

Above: *Lower Cullasaja Falls*
Right: *Dry Falls*

a few cars can pull over; it is not marked, so keep a sharp lookout. Many visitors find it easier to drive past the falls, park, and walk back, though the absence of a designated pedestrian path means that they have to walk close to the rock wall or out in the highway. If you decide to try to park at the pull-off, you will find the view well worth the effort.

The road continues to parallel the Cullasaja River, though the drop-off becomes a little less dramatic and unsettling. It is 4.6 miles to the entrance to Cliffside Lake Recreation Area, on the left. If you want to take a brief side trip, it is a 1.5-mile drive to picturesque Cliffside Lake and its swimming and fishing facilities; be sure to note that cold mountain lakes will make the adrenalin flow. The campground, the lake, the picnic area, and the several trails in the area are all part of Nantahala National Forest.

From the entrance to Cliffside Lake Recreation Area, it is 0.1 mile on U.S. 64/N.C. 28 to Van Hook Glade Campground. Continue 0.8 mile to a parking area on the right for the popular Dry Falls. A short paved path with rails leads behind the 75-foot falls; the name for the waterfall comes from the fact that visitors can walk behind it without getting wet. Looking out through the falls toward the river is a unique perspective. An excellent photo opportunity, Dry Falls is well worth the stop.

It is another 0.8 mile to Bridal Veil Falls, where tourists can actually drive behind a 120-foot waterfall. Before the road was rerouted, motorists had no choice but to drive behind the falls, a startling experience for first-timers and those traveling at night. They now have the option of staying on the main road or making the slight detour. Either way, photos are usually in order. Legend says Indian maidens

Bridal Veil Falls

believed that if they passed behind the falls in the spring, they would wed before the first snowfall.

For the next 0.5 mile, the highway parallels a series of 18 small falls known as the Kalakaleskies. At the head of the falls is Sequoyah Dam, built in 1927. Only 28 feet high and 175 feet wide, the dam nonetheless produces a scenic overflow of water from the 76-acre lake behind it. Both the lake and the dam were named for Sequoyah, who invented the Cherokee alphabet around 1821, ultimately enabling thousands of Cherokees to read and write in their own language. Thus, much of their culture has been preserved.

Approaching Sequoyah Dam, you will see a sign announcing the town of Highlands. At 4,118 feet, Highlands was recognized as the highest town east of the Mississippi until 1981, when the community of Beech Mountain, at 5,005 feet, was incorporated.

In March 1874, an article appeared in *Scribner's Monthly* magazine describing the area around what is now Highlands. "For some time we had felt the exhilarating effects of the keen, rarified air, and had noticed the exquisite atmospheric effects peculiar to these regions," the article stated. "The land is of surprising fertility . . . and there are numerous quartz veins running through the hills, indicating the presence of gold in large quantities."

It was inevitable that someone would develop the region, and soon. Two land developers, Samuel T. Kelsey and C. C. Hutchinson, were intrigued. Tradition has it that they studied a map of the United States and drew a line between the major population centers of Chicago and Savannah, then another one between New Orleans and Baltimore. Their theory was that the intersection of the lines would one day mark the center of population of eastern America. When they saw that the

Sequoyah Dam in Highlands

lines met near what is now Highlands, they were on their way.

Kelsey and Hutchinson purchased 839 acres and began promoting their new town, Kelsey's Plateau. They soon changed the name to Highlands. In 1876, they produced their first promotional brochure, which proclaimed there was "no better climate in the world for health, comfort and enjoyment" than that at Highlands. The advertisement went on to boast that "there are a dozen mountain peaks within a radius of as many miles. Almost to the very tops of these highest mountain peaks are beautiful coves and dells where gigantic forest trees stand guard over perennial springs of purest, softest waters, which send their cooling rills down the mountain's side."

Kelsey sent the brochures all over the country. Before long, he began attracting permanent residents. By 1883, Highlands boasted a population of 300 people from 18 states. The town's first inn was the Smith Hotel—now the Highlands Inn—built in 1879. The hotel's 1884 advertisement in the *Blue Ridge Enterprise* read, "Highlands is unsurpassed for equable climate, pure, invigorating air, pure, cold spring water and grand mountain scenery. All who try our very long, cool and delightful summers . . . pronounce this the best place east of the Rockies for those who seek health and natural scenery." The advertisement also pointed out that there were no mosquitoes and few flies in the area.

By 1887, Kelsey produced a second set of brochures focusing on the town's growing reputation as a health resort. Highlands was proclaimed a curative for consumption, ague, and yellow fever, to name only a few. Kelsey's brochures even supplied 24 testimonials to support his claims. Many who traveled to Highlands for their health ended up staying. Today, the town's wintertime population of approximately 900 explodes to between 12,000 and 20,000 during the summer months.

In 1885, Highlands was the site of a Western-style shootout. Just across the

Highlands Inn

Georgia line in Rabun County, four brothers named Billingsley lived in the township of Moccasin. The brothers were well known in the area for their moonshining activities. When two of their associates were arrested by federal agents for selling moonshine, the Billingsleys set out to free them. Since the area had no jail, the prisoners were confined in a room in the Smith Hotel in nearby Highlands while they awaited trial. When the Billingsley forces arrived, they laid siege to the hotel. What followed was a classic showdown.

The federal agents, apparently assisted by townspeople, armed and barricaded themselves within and behind the Smith Hotel, while the 18 members of the Billingsley gang took up positions across the street. The two sides proceeded to exchange gunfire over the course of three days. The mayor of Highlands was even forced to temporarily declare martial law. When a man named Tom Ford finally climbed to the top of the hotel and killed one of the Moccasin gunfighters, the Georgians withdrew from Highlands.

Several days passed before the Billingsley gang sent a messenger with news that they intended to blockade the main road from Highlands to Walhalla, South Carolina, and kill any man from Highlands who attempted to pass. Since that route was one of the main arteries to the South Carolina Low Country, the blockade proved a great inconvenience to Highlands residents.

The Moccasin War, as it is called in some local histories, ended rather uneventfully. A local teamster named Joel Lovin finally decided to test the blockade. The story goes that he rode right past the Billingsley brothers, who made no attempt to stop him. The "war" was over.

Upon reaching the center of the Highlands business district, you will see the Highlands Inn on the left. On the right is the Old Edwards Inn, built in 1878 as the first boardinghouse in Highlands. Originally called Central House, it stood next to The Stone Store House; that rock structure was made into a post office in 1893 and was later used as a grocery store. In 1925, a two-story addition was built onto Central House. Only the lobby and foundation of the stone store were kept and incorporated into a new brick-and-rock hotel that opened in 1935 as Hotel Edwards. Today, the entire complex is part of the Old Edwards Inn and Spa, a world-class resort.

Follow N.C. 28 as it turns right beside the Old Edwards Inn and heads south toward Walhalla, tracing the old route blockaded by the so-called Army of Moc-

Old Edwards Inn

casin. As you start the descent from the plateau about 3.6 miles from the center of Highlands, you will notice a large rock formation on the left. Known as Satulah Mountain, it has an elevation of 4,560 feet. An overlook on the right offers a beautiful view of the Piedmont region and the high, narrow waterfall known as Lower Satulah Falls or Clear Creek Falls below.

This section of the route is known as the Walhalla Road. Constructed in 1920, it was preceded by four other roads between Highlands and Walhalla. The Walhalla Road saw regular runs of passengers, mail, and supplies as early as 1895, but the route was so often muddy that the round trip of 64 miles took at least three days. One passenger on the ride north from Walhalla wrote, "Up in the clouds we certainly were. As we approached Satulah exclamations of delight were heard at the grandeur of the scenery, mingled with screams and clutches at whatever was within reach to cling to." Though the trip now takes considerably less than three days, the sublime views and the hair-raising curves have changed little since the turn of the 20th century.

The next 20 miles of serpentine road pass through three states. It is approximately 5 miles from Highlands to Sassafras Gap and then another mile to the Georgia border. It is then 1.4 miles to the beginning of the Moccasin precinct, home of the Billingsleys and their gang. Travel another 6.3 miles to a bridge that crosses the Chattooga River, where the road enters South Carolina at Oconee County. Parking areas beside the bridge allow whitewater rafting access.

After an additional 1.1 miles, you will see a historical marker for Chattooga Town. The marker notes that this was the site of one of the Cherokee "Lower Towns" that existed in what is now Upstate South Carolina during the 17th and early 18th centuries. In 1721, the British conducted a census of all the Cherokee Lower Towns and recorded that this was the smallest, claiming only 90 inhabitants.

Informational signs describe this location as the site of the Russell Farmstead,

Satulah Mountain

Lower Satulah Falls

listed on the National Register of Historic Places. It is said that William Ganaway Russell drove a herd of cattle west to California during the gold rush. He sold meat to miners near Sacramento and sewed the coins he took in exchange into his vest for his return home. He purchased land near the Chattooga River, where in 1867 he built a small house, a structure that was enlarged three times over the next 40 years and served as an inn for travelers making the stagecoach trip from Walhalla to Highlands. Russell's inn reportedly housed as many as 80 visitors. Still others camped in tents on the grounds when the Chattooga River was too deep to cross. The inn sometimes hosted enough guests to consume 20 turkeys at one meal. Woodrow Wilson supposedly stayed there before he was elected president. Russell's wife, Jane Nicholson Russell, bore 15 children in addition to serving as midwife, postmistress, and cook-hostess for the inn. Some of the 10 outbuildings are still visible, but fire destroyed the inn in 1988. Russell and his wife are buried nearby.

It is another 0.6 mile to a river access area for what is called Floating Section II of the Chattooga. In 1974, Congress designated the Chattooga as a Wild and Scenic River. That designation is reserved for rivers possessing not only outstanding scenery but recreational, wildlife, geological, and cultural value as well. The Chattooga begins in the mountains of North Carolina and forms the boundary between Sumter National Forest in South Carolina and Chattahoochee National Forest in Georgia for almost 40 miles. The lower 31 miles are open for boating and constitute some of the best whitewater in the Southeast. Visitors who enter the river at the access area can enjoy a 6-mile float to Earls Ford. This section of the Chattooga offers a challenge for beginning whitewater boaters and is open for tubers—those riding inner tubes—as well. The largest of the 20 rapids in the area is Big Shoals, a

Class III rapid that can be portaged on an island in the middle of the river. Depending on the water level, two to four hours are required to negotiate this section by canoe, and an extra hour by raft or tube.

Continue 3.1 miles to the community of Mountain Rest. After 4.3 miles, you will see S.C. 107 coming in from the left; make note, as you will backtrack to this turn later in the tour. It is 2.9 miles farther on S.C. 28 to the Stumphouse Ranger Station, on the left, than an additional 0.4 mile to the entrance to Stumphouse Tunnel Park. Turn left at the park entrance and drive 0.5 mile to the parking lot and picnic area. The top of Issaqueena Falls is to the right of the picnic area. Stumphouse Tunnel is a short drive to the left.

Russell Farmstead

Stumphouse Tunnel was the longest of three tunnels proposed to complete South Carolina's portion of the Blue Ridge Railroad, which was to run from Charleston, South Carolina, to Cincinnati, Ohio. Work began in the 1850s. Irish immigrants housed in a town named Tunnel Hill atop Stumphouse Mountain provided most of the labor. They worked 12 hours a day for six days a week, pounding their way through the granite with sledgehammers, hand drills, and blasting powder.

Tunnel Hill supposedly had more saloons than churches. In 1854, Father Jeremiah Joseph O'Connell came to town. Dismayed by the lack of sobriety and the

Stumphouse Tunnel

lawlessness he found, the priest convinced the railroad company to fire anyone who could not stay sober.

Stumphouse Tunnel was to be 5,863 feet long. Due to the scope of the project, all work was dropped on the other two tunnels and concentrated on Stumphouse by 1857. The tunnel was to run 236 feet below the highest point of the mountain. Four vertical shafts were sunk to tunnel level, then dug horizontally toward each other. That way, work could proceed from a total of 10 different surfaces. At the peak of the operation, the men were able to tunnel 200 feet a month.

The work on shafts #1 and #4 did manage to connect with the tunneling from the outside, but the two middle tunnels were never completed. The company overseeing the work ran out of money, and the Civil War broke out before new funds could be raised.

The north end of Stumphouse Tunnel is now underwater, but the 1,600-foot section at the south end is open to the public. The temperature in the tunnel is 50 degrees year-round, and the humidity is always 90 percent. Thanks to the humidity, it is perpetually raining at the base of the vertical shaft that rises to the top of the mountain. Be sure to heed the warning about not wearing shoes you have used in other caves, so you don't unintentionally spread the white-nose syndrome that is proving so deadly to bats in America.

The iron gate near the entrance to the tunnel and the brick wall past the vertical shaft were added in the 1950s by Clemson University. Clemson used the tunnel for experimentation in the manufacture of blue cheese. Since the temperature and humidity matched that of caves in France where blue cheese was aged, the university converted the tunnel and used it successfully for several years. Studies on the aging process were finally moved to the Clemson campus after the construction of a suitable building in 1956.

The mountain received the name Stumphouse sometime in the 1850s. Various stories have emerged explaining the name's origin. Most seem to involve a one-room cabin located near the present tunnel. One version centers around four large chestnut trees. The story goes that three of the trees were ideally suited to provide walls for the cabin, so they were cut down to stumps. A section of the fourth tree was cut to form the remaining wall. Though the cabin disappeared long ago, its unusual architecture apparently impressed travelers enough to name the mountain in its honor.

Numerous legends surround nearby Issaqueena Falls (frequently spelled Isaqueena). According to one of the most frequently told accounts, Captain James Francis and his two sons, Allan and Henry, established a Cherokee trading post sometime between 1730 and 1750 near what is now the community of Ninety Six in Greenwood County, South Carolina. Through his business dealings with the Cherokee chief Karuga, Allan Francis met and fell in love with a young maiden named Issaqueena, a captive Choctaw or Creek Indian (depending upon the version) who was living as Karuga's slave in the village of Keowee near what is now Lake Keowee in Pickens County, South Carolina.

When Issaqueena learned that Karuga planned to attack the white traders, she set out to warn her lover. The legend attributes various South Carolina place names—including Six Mile; Twelve Miles River; Eighteen, Three, and Twenty creeks; and even Issaqueena's destination, Ninety Six—to mileage points along her route. (The names actually indicate distances along an old trading path that ran the 96 or so miles between Keowee and the fort and settlement at Ninety Six, but it still makes a good story.) Issaqueena completed her escape from her Cherokee captors at the falls at Stumphouse Mountain. She leapt from the falls, landed on a ledge, and hid behind the falling water until the Cherokees left. Some versions say she had a baby in her arms when she accomplished this amazing feat.

Issaqueena Falls

One of the welcome improvements since the second edition of this book is a paved path to the right of the top of the falls that offers a walk of less than 200 yards to a viewing stand where visitors can take photographs without endangering their lives. To the left of the falls is a well-maintained path with steps that lead to the bottom of the falls, where travelers can see the ledge where Issaqueena supposedly landed. The falls are about 200 feet high, but the flow of water depends on rainfall. At times, the falls are so skimpy that it is hard to believe anyone could hide behind them. Healthy skepticism aside, it must be admitted that the falls provide a great spot for a picnic at the tables provided near the parking area.

When you are ready to leave Stumphouse Tunnel Park, retrace your route to S.C. 28, turn right, and head north for 3.3 miles to the intersection with S.C. 107 noted earlier. Turn right and drive 2.3 miles to the entrance to Oconee State Park, on the right. This 1,165-acre park is centered around a 20-acre mountain lake ideal for swimming and fishing. The park offers fully furnished rental cabins, family campsites, and a restaurant. This is also the southern trailhead for the Foothills Trail, described in "The Cashiers Tour."

As you round the curve from Oconee State Park on S.C. 107, you will see a pullover on the left. This is the location of historic Moodys Spring. Visitors can still use the spring where Wade Hampton II, hero of the Battle of New Orleans and the Mexican War, often stopped while traveling to his summer home at High Hampton. More information about Wade Hampton is in "The Cashiers Tour."

After another 1.4 miles, turn left onto Burrells Ford Road (F.R. 708). It is about 2 miles to Burrells Ford on the Chattooga River. A trail southeast of Burrells Ford leads 0.5 mile to King Creek Falls. It is an easy 20-minute walk to the 70-foot falls. An easy 15-minute walk leads north to the 60-foot Spoonauger Falls.

Retrace the route to S.C. 107 and continue in your original direction. It is

0.5 mile to Burrells Place Campground, located on the right just past the overlook. Continue another 1 mile to the road leading to the Chattooga Picnic Area. A 1.9-mile side trip on a paved road leads to the picnic area and the Walhalla State Fish Hatchery, where you can see large numbers of trout being raised in pools. The best time to visit is fall, when you can view more stages in the life cycle of trout. The first trout release from the hatchery occurred around 1937. Many of the buildings here were built by the Civilian Conservation Corps during the Depression. Both Burrells Place Campground and the Chattooga Picnic Area are good sites for picnics.

Continue up S.C. 107, which becomes N.C. 107 when it crosses the state line. It is 8.8 miles from the turnoff to the Chattooga Picnic Area to the Wade Hampton Golf Club.

Drive 0.6 mile to the Zachary-Tolbert House, on the left. This Greek Revival structure was built between 1842 and 1852 by Mordecai Zachary, a skilled carpenter. Because the house has been owned by only four families and has never been modernized with plumbing or electricity, it is a pristine example of a rural antebellum structure. When Zachary departed the area in 1873, he left behind much of the furniture he had built, which was passed along with the deed each time the house was sold, making it the largest known collection of Southern plain-style furniture by a single, identifiable furniture maker. The home stands next to the Cashiers Historical Society and is open to the public.

Just past the Zachary-Tolbert House, turn left on Whiteside Cove Road (S.R. 1107). Almost immediately, you will begin catching glimpses of the impressive stone face of Whiteside Mountain and its neighbor, Devil's Courthouse. This area was settled in 1827 when Barak Norton arrived from Virginia and built a cabin at

Whiteside Mountain

the foot of Whiteside Mountain. Zeigler and Grosscup wrote an excellent description of the scene:

> We came out before the massive front of a peculiar mountain. Whiteside, or in literal translation of the Cherokee title, Unakakanoos, White-mountain, is the largest exposure of perpendicular, bare rock east of the Rockies. It is connected, without deeply-marked intervening gaps, with its neighboring peaks of the Blue Ridge; but from some points of observation it appears isolated—a majestic, solitary, dome-shaped monument, differing from all other mountains of the Alleghanies in its aspect and form. The top line of its precipitous front is 1,600 feet above its point of conjunction with the crest of the green hill, which slopes to the Chatooga [*sic*], 800 feet lower. The face of the mountain is gray, not white; but is seared by long rifts, running horizontal across it, of white rock.

More information about Whiteside Mountain and the Devil's Courthouse is in "The Cashiers Tour."

Continue 3.8 miles to one of the most stunning views in the area. At the base of Whiteside Mountain is a lake that reflects the sheer 1,800-foot white precipice.

Just past a private parking area beside the lake is the restored Grimshawes post office, on the right. Billed as the smallest post office in the United States, it measures six feet by eight feet. Established in 1875, it did not bear the Grimshawes name until 1909.

The pavement ends 1.3 miles past the old post office but resumes again after 1.7 miles. It is a total of 3.7 miles from the post office to an intersection with Bull Pen Road, which is well marked with mileages to various points. You may elect to turn left (or east) onto Bull Pen Road (S.R. 1603) for a popular side trip. Although some of the side trip is on paved roads, be forewarned that much of it follows gravel forest-service roads.

*Grimshawes
post office*

After 0.7 mile on Bull Pen Road, you will reach the Slick Rock Trail, on the right, which leads to the Slick Rock Vista and its view of the entire area. Continuing on Bull Pen Road, it is 0.6 mile to Ammons Branch Campground, on the right. A trailhead for the Ellicott Rock Trail is on the right 0.4 mile from the campground. This marked trail leads into the 3,030-acre Ellicott Rock Wilderness Area, a rugged tract on the Chattooga River that encompasses parts of three states. The 7-mile round-trip hike to Ellicott Rock is moderately difficult. When you reach the Chattooga, ford the river and go downstream approximately 0.1 mile. Commissioner Rock, 10 feet downstream from Ellicott Rock, is now recognized as the boundary shared by North Carolina, South Carolina, and Georgia, though Ellicott Rock once held that distinction. Commissioner Rock bears the inscription, "LAT 35 AD 1813 NC + SC," while Ellicott Rock has a simple "NC" chiseled into it.

The pavement soon resumes on Bull Pen Road. It is 1.3 miles to an old iron bridge on the Chattooga. A well-kept forest trail along the river and a waterfall make this a popular place to hike or picnic.

If you prefer to travel to Cashiers rather than return to Highlands, continue on Bull Pen Road for 5.3 miles to N.C. 107. Turn left and drive 6.9 miles to Cashiers. Otherwise, if you prefer to return to Highlands, retrace your route to the intersection with Whiteside Cove Road to complete the side trip. From the intersection, head west on Horse Cove Road.

The area you are driving through, Horse Cove, offers dramatic views of the sheer sides of the mountains to the right. The name Horse Cove has a number of explanations. Some say Indians used the area as pasture for their horses, while others say General William T. Sherman hid his horses in the cove one winter during the Civil War. Still others say it was Revolutionary War general Andrew Pickens who pastured his horses here. Regardless of the origin of the name, the scenic cove remains much as Zeigler and Grosscup found it in 1883: "Black Rock, with bold, stony, treeless front, looms up on one border, and on another, Satoola [Satulah],

Trout fishing at the iron bridge

with precipitous slope, wood-covered, forms a sheltering wall for the 600 acres of fertile, level land below."

Horse Cove was settled soon after the Cherokees agreed to move out of the area in 1819. Its chief claim to fame is that Woodrow Wilson spent several weeks here with his mother and other relatives during the summer of 1879, just after he graduated from college.

Traveling through Horse Cove, you will notice Black Rock Mountain looming on the right. It was once believed that black lichens were responsible for the mountain's distinctive character, much as white lichens were credited for the appearance of nearby landmark Whiteside Mountain.

A little over 3 miles from the intersection with Whiteside Cove Road, Horse Cove Road begins its climb up the mountain. Zeigler and Grosscup wrote that "the road . . . leads up the Blue Ridge, in zigzag course, through the forested aisles. . . . Three miles and a half is the distance from its base to the hamlet of Highlands. The engineering of the road is so perfect that, in spite of the precipitousness of the mountain, the ascent is gradual." The ascent does not seem quite so gradual today, for the road winds through 37 curves over the next 2 miles. The crest, however, offers a rewarding view of Horse Cove and the surrounding countryside.

It is 4.1 miles from the intersection of Whiteside Cove and Horse Cove roads to Highlands Nature Center, on the right. Travelers can park on the left side of the street and follow the gravel road on the right side of the parking area to Sunset Rock. It is an easy 1.2-mile round trip to a spectacular view overlooking Horse Cove and Highlands.

Continue an additional 0.5 mile to the intersection with U.S. 64 and N.C. 28 near the center of Highlands. This completes the tour.

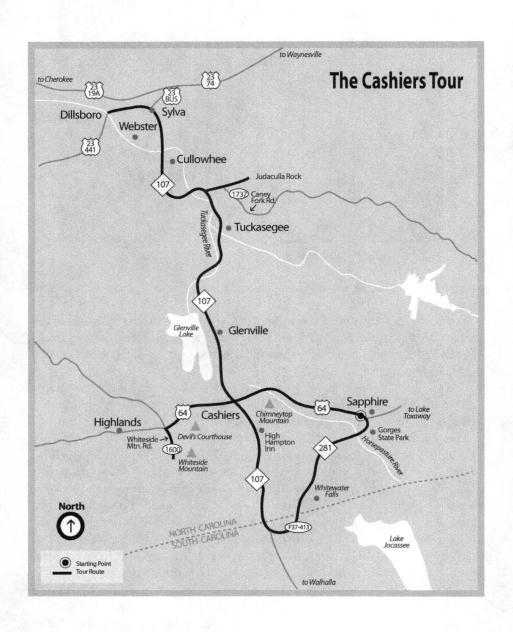

TOUR 7

The Cashiers Tour

This tour begins in Sapphire and travels to nearby Gorges State Park, then heads south to Whitewater Falls. It then turns north to the town of Cashiers. From there, it takes a side trip to Whiteside Mountain before continuing north to Glenville Lake and following the Tuckasegee River to Judaculla Rock. The tour passes through Cullowhee and Sylva and ends in Dillsboro.

Total mileage: approximately 60 miles

The tour begins at the intersection of U.S. 64 and N.C. 281 in the community of Sapphire.

In 1892, the Sapphire Valley Mining Company began digging for corundum at the Burnt Rock Mine, located 7 miles northeast of town. The company built a plant on the Horsepasture River that processed 400 tons of corundum in 1892. It also constructed the 14-room Sapphire Inn as its headquarters. The mining town included a large store, several houses, shacks for the miners, and a 12-foot-high dam that created a mile-long lake. Though the Sapphire Valley Mining Company built a railroad spur to nearby Toxaway to shorten the haul to Hendersonville, it worked the mines for only a year. The Sapphire Inn was remodeled for the benefit of summer visitors in 1899 but burned down in 1906.

In 1916, when the dam containing Lake Toxaway broke, a record amount of water gushed downriver, destroying communities in its path. After the flood, local citizens sold large tracts of land in the Jocassee Gorges area of Transylvania County to the Singer Sewing Machine Company, which logged most of the land. In the 1940s and 1950s, Singer sold the land to Duke Power. The corporation purchased the land because of its steep topography (the elevation rises 2,000 feet in only 4 miles) and high rainfall (over 80 inches a year). Those characteristics offered opportunities for developing hydropower projects. Crescent Land and Timber Corporation, a subsidiary of Duke Power, managed the land.

In the late 1990s, the company now named Duke Energy determined that it no longer needed large portions of the gorges area and offered the land for sale to natural resources agencies in North and South Carolina. In 1999, the North Carolina Wildlife Resources Commission purchased 10,000 acres, 7,500 of which now form Gorges State Park.

The park is currently undergoing extensive improvements. A new visitors' center is scheduled for completion in June 2012. Once the center opens, travelers will turn off U.S. 64 onto N.C. 281 and drive 1 mile to the park entrance, on the left. This is the Grassy Ridge Access for the western part of the park. Until the visitors' center opens, a temporary office is located on U.S. 64 in Sapphire in a small strip of offices across from the intersection where N.C. 281 goes south. Be sure to stop there before beginning this tour to get up-to-date information about the park's offerings. You can also learn about hiking and camping possibilities on the eastern side of the park via the Frozen Creek Access, which is not on the tour route.

In 1986, some 4.5 miles of the Horsepasture River Gorge—which is 2 miles wide and 800 feet deep in places—were designated part of the National Wild and Scenic River System. This stretch creates several spectacular waterfalls as it drops 2,000 feet. The area was threatened when a private corporation revealed its plan to build a hydroelectric dam on the river, but local conservationists calling themselves FROTH (Friends of the Horsepasture) launched a grass-roots campaign that saved the falls.

One of the most popular waterfalls on the Horsepasture is Rainbow Falls. Although the waterfall is actually in Pisgah National Forest and not inside the park boundary, access to it is one of the main attractions of the new facility; visitors can park and hike 3 miles round-trip from the access area. Rainbow Falls thunders 150 feet into a deep pool, spraying mist against the canyon walls that forms a rainbow when the sun is right. It is said that if the river is up during a full moon, rare moonbows arch over the falls at night. The trail continues for 200 yards to Turtleback Falls. Before the state park was formed, people used to park on N.C. 281 and hike down the waterfalls beginning with Drift Falls—which was also called "Bust Your Butt Falls" because people used to slide down the rocks. However, that land is now privately owned, and the owners will prosecute trespassers.

Trails will eventually lead from the access area to Upper Bearwallow Falls and two overlooks. One overlook is handicapped-accessible and has an observation deck visitors can drive to; it gives a view of Lake Jocassee and Upstate South Carolina. The Bearwallow Overlook observation deck, located at a higher elevation, offers a breathtaking view of the Bearwallow Valley and Lake Jocassee from a different perspective. On clear days, visitors can see as far as Lake Keowee.

Stairway Falls, a waterfall on the Horsepasture that is not accessible by trail at this time, has an unsettling story about the wife of a previous owner. In 1879, a woman named Eliza Dodgen died mysteriously. Her body was discovered in the fireplace of her home along the Toxaway River. A coroner's inquest ruled that "the deceased Eliza Dodgen came to her death by falling into the fire from some unknown cause and burnt to death." A few months later, her husband, Adam Dodgen, purchased the land containing the stairstep falls, which for many years were called Adam Shoals. Eliza Dodgen is buried on the ridge east of the falls.

The Horsepasture River area is home to the rare and beautiful plant called shortia. Shortia is believed to occur naturally in the United States in only six counties, all in this immediate area. It blooms around the end of March or the beginning of April. Its leaves closely resemble galax, but shortia bears only a single large blossom—white or pink—on a slender stem. The plant was discovered by André Michaux when he was combing the Appalachians to collect specimens for the Royal Botanical Gardens in France. In 1787, Michaux placed a specimen in his collection and noted that he had found it in "les hautes montagnes de Caroline" (the high mountains of Carolina). In 1842, Asa Gray, a well-known Harvard botanist, stumbled upon the plant in Michaux's collection and named it *Shortia glacifolia*. Gray was intrigued because the specimen was identical to a plant previously found only in Japan. He made trips to the mountains in 1838 and 1843 in search of shortia but did not manage to find it, though a few plants were collected by others in the following years. In 1886, Professor C. S. Sargeant located what was probably the site of Michaux's discovery, in South Carolina just across the border from Jackson County. After the exact location in the "high mountains" was ascertained, acres of the plant were found near an old Indian path along the Horsepasture River. Shortia has since been carried away by the wagonload, but it can still be sighted near the river on occasion.

Head south on N.C. 281 for 6.2 miles to the turnoff for Whitewater Falls Scenic Area, on the left. It is an easy five-minute walk from the parking lot to the overlook for Whitewater Falls. The falls measure 411 feet, making them the highest east of the Rockies. In the 1880s, William Gilmore Simms described them in the journal he kept while traveling in the area: "The upper Fall is that of the White Water, which from the distance at which we behold it, is a galaxy, scintillating in the sunshine, with a perfect torrent of starlight.... [The river] darts over a cliff, and continues its headlong tumble for nearly three hundred yards, in a foamy and fearful conflict, with the great boulders and the fractured masses, through which it has torn itself a way."

It is another 0.2 mile on N.C. 281 to the South Carolina line. Just before the state line is a trailhead for the Foothills Trail, a backpacking and hiking trail that runs for 80 miles along the

Whitewater Falls

Blue Ridge Escarpment from Oconee State Park to Table Rock State Park in South Carolina. The Blue Ridge Escarpment is the geological phenomenon where the southern Appalachian Mountains suddenly end and the Piedmont begins. The dramatic 2,000-foot drop in elevation gives the area the nickname "the Blue Wall."

The road now becomes S.C. 130. On the left is an overlook that offers a vista encompassing Lake Jocassee and the South Carolina Piedmont. The Keowee River once had its origin here, where the Whitewater and Toxaway rivers merged just below the North Carolina–South Carolina line near the Cherokee village of Jocassee. The entire area is now covered by Lake Jocassee, one of two adjoining lakes created by Duke Power. The 7,500-acre Lake Jocassee boasts 75 miles of shoreline. It has established a reputation as one of the South's finest trout lakes.

According to legend, Jocassee was a Cherokee princess whose name signified "a full bosom" or "a fertile field," but she died before she fulfilled the promise of that name. In his journal, William Gilmore Simms wrote that Jocassee's lover was a man called Toxaway. When Toxaway died at the hands of Jocassee's brother, Chief Oconee, Jocassee disappeared from a canoe while crossing the river. The story goes that she leapt overboard when she saw the outstretched arms of her slain lover beckoning her to join him beneath the waters. Simms wrote, "She rose not once to the surface. The stream from that moment, lost the name of Sarratay, and both whites and Indians, to this day, know it only as the river of Jocassee." Toxaway, Oconee, and Jocassee survive in the names of various parks, waterfalls, lakes, and communities in the area.

Continue on S.C. 130 for 1 mile, then turn right onto Wiginton Road (F.R. 37-413) to connect to N.C. 107 leading to Cashiers. Drive 0.8 mile to S.C. 107. As the road crosses the state line, it becomes N.C. 107. About 4.2 miles from where the route joined S.C. 107, you will see a trailhead for the Silver Run Falls Access. It is about 250 yards to the waterfall, which cascades about 25 feet into a tree-lined pool. The waterfall has a sandy beach. You will have to either wade across the Whitewater River or cross on a fallen tree to reach the falls. The area can be crowded in summer.

It is 2.5 miles to the entrance to High Hampton Inn, on the right. The McKee family purchased the Hampton estate in 1924 and constructed a small inn on the property, but it was destroyed by fire in 1932. The present rustic inn, with its exposed beams and bark-covered exterior, was erected in 1933 and still operates as one of western North Carolina's most exclusive resorts. It is located at the foot of 4,625-foot Chimneytop Mountain, another sheer-faced peak. Chimneytop will remain in view on the right on the drive north into Cashiers (pronounced Cash-ers), elevation 3,486 feet.

Several explanations have been offered for the naming of the Cashiers Valley. The name may have come from a horse called Cash owned by Senator John C. Calhoun, who had a plantation near what is now Clemson, South Carolina; this version says that Cash wandered off to a valley pasture and that a search party yelled, "Cash's here!" upon finding him. Or the name may have come from another horse called Cash, whose considerable earnings from racing entitled him to spend his winters in the sheltered valley, as he preferred, rather than migrating to South Carolina with the rest of the stock. Or it may have originated with Cassius, one of the prize bulls owned by General Wade Hampton, who summered in the area. The least romantic explanation is perhaps the most likely one—Cashiers was named for an old hermit who lived in the Whiteside Cove area long before other white settlers arrived.

In their 1883 book, *The Heart of the Alleghanies,* Wilber Zeigler and Ben Grosscup described the Cashiers Valley as "a mountain plateau of the Blue Ridge, 3,400 feet in altitude, from four to five miles long and a mile and a half wide. Attracted by its climate, freedom from dampness, its utter isolation from the populated haunts of man, the rugged character of its scenery, and deer and bear infested wildwoods, years since, wealthy planters of South Carolina drifted in here with each recurring summer."

One of the most famous of those South Carolinians was Wade Hampton II, who as a colonel in the Battle of New Orleans in 1814 was selected by General Andrew Jackson to deliver the report of victory to President James Madison. Hampton supposedly rode the 1,200 miles from New Orleans to Washington in 10 days, using only one horse, to announce the message. He later set up a summer estate, Hampton Place, in the Cashiers Valley. The estate included a two-story, seven-bedroom cottage, a kitchen building, servants' quarters, and assorted outbuildings.

His son, General Wade Hampton III, continued the tradition at Hampton Place. General Hampton was one of South Carolina's favorite sons and an important Civil War figure. After the death of J. E. B. Stuart, he was given command of the Confederate infantry and cavalry unit that came to be known as the Hampton Legion. It was Hampton who ordered the evacuation of Columbia, South Carolina, upon Sherman's approach. Sherman later accused him of burning his own city. Hampton went on to become governor of South Carolina; he was at Hampton Place when he learned of his election. He later served in the United States Senate. He continued to spend his summers in Cashiers until his death in 1902.

At the intersection of N.C. 107 and U.S. 64, turn left, heading toward Highlands. As you climb the mountain for the next 4.7 miles, you will see a huge rock formation looming on the left. As the road curves sharply at the crest, the view opens up, but don't stop to look. The tour returns this way later.

After crossing the Jackson County line, you will see the entrance to Wildcat Cliffs Country Club on the left. Turn onto Whiteside Mountain Road. It is approximately 1 mile to a parking area from which you can hike all or part of the 2-mile loop trail that goes to the top of Whiteside Mountain. The summit provides magnificent views of the Chattooga River Valley, Black Rock Mountain, and at least 26 other peaks in the area. The trail follows the edge of the 400- to 600-foot cliffs for 1.1 miles to another overlook, then descends to the parking lot. Be sure to honor all signs that restrict hiking in order to preserve peregrine falcon nesting areas. A small fee is charged for use of the trail; it is paid by the honor system at the trailhead.

Situated on the Eastern Continental Divide, Whiteside Mountain rises 2,100

Whiteside Mountain

feet from the valley floor. Its summit has an elevation of 4,930 feet. Both the north and south faces feature stunning sheer cliffs ranging from 400 to 750 feet in height. The cliffs are comprised of Whiteside granite, which contains a high content of feldspar, quartz, and mica. The south side of the mountain has little vegetation. Its blue-gray color comes from the rock showing through. The white streaks on the south face are feldspar and quartz. The north side has a darker appearance because of the mosses and lichens that grow there.

Though visitors can reach the top of the mountain with relative ease today, that was not the case in 1880, when Rebecca H. Davis described her trip to White-side for *Harper's Magazine*. "When the top is reached, after a short stretch of nearly perpendicular climbing," she wrote, "the traveler finds himself on the edge of a sheer white wall of rock, over which, clinging for life to a protecting hand, he can look, if he chooses, two thousand feet down into the dim valley below."

Thrill seeking seems to have been the order of the day. Zeigler and Grosscup described a similar experience: "As the observer to secure a fair view lies flat on the ground with part of his head projected over a space of dread nothingness . . . the pure, apparently tangible air of the void, and the soft moss-like bed of the deep-down forest bordered by a silver stream, have an irresistible fascination, especially over one troubled with ennui. Get the guide to hold your feet when you crawl to the verge."

According to James Mooney's 1898 report to the Bureau of American Ethnology, the Indians compared the cliffs to a sheet of ice. From Mooney's and other 19th-century accounts, it appears that the two separate peaks known as Whiteside Mountain and the Devil's Courthouse were once a single long ridge. The area adjoining Whiteside Mountain called Wildcat Cliffs is covered with lavish summer homes today. It was formerly known as "the Sitting Down Place," since Indians using the trail that came up from what is now Whiteside Cove often camped at the nearby spring.

Mooney recorded an interesting Indian legend about the area. The Cherokees believed Whiteside Mountain to be part of an enormous bridge that Utlunta, better known as Spearfinger, was building across the mountains. A terrible ogress, Spearfinger subsisted on livers plucked from the bodies of Indian children. Because Spearfinger could take on any appearance that suited her purposes, the Cherokees could never tell when she was around. She frequently disguised herself as an old woman. In her natural form, her body was covered with a skin as hard as rock. Her most distinctive characteristic was a long, stony forefinger shaped like a spear, which she used to stab children through their hearts or the backs of their necks preparatory to stealing their livers.

Legend has it that Spearfinger could lift huge boulders and cement them together by striking them against each other. Using that technique, she began building her bridge at Tree Rock—a rock resembling a tree trunk—on the west side of the Hiwassee River about 4 miles from Hayesville, near the Georgia line. Spearfinger intended to extend the bridge all the way to Whiteside Mountain, but lightning destroyed it and scattered rock fragments along the entire ridge, where they can still be seen today.

The Cherokees eventually rid themselves of Spearfinger by digging a deep pit across a trail they knew she would use. Once she was trapped in the pit, they tried to shoot her, but their arrows were repulsed by her rock skin until a chickadee perched on her finger, alerting the Indians to her vulnerable spot. Upon shooting her finger, they managed to reach her heart, and Spearfinger fell dead.

Accounts from the 1800s use Whiteside Mountain and the Devil's Courthouse interchangeably. They often refer to a cave on Whiteside Mountain as the place where the devil kept his throne. Another Devil's Courthouse is located in the Balsam Mountains just off the Blue Ridge Parkway (see "The Cradle of Forestry Tour"). The one at Whiteside Mountain has been called the "supreme" courthouse to distinguish it from its lesser sibling. Zeigler and Grosscup noted that old Indian ladders—trees trimmed to stub branches—probably provided access to the cave.

Not only Indians and mythological beings left their imprint on the cliffs. Over 150 years ago, early settlers in the area discovered a Spanish inscription at the Devil's Courthouse. It was all but forgotten until developers explored the area in the 1950s. The letters are two inches high and carved a quarter-inch deep. The inscription reads, " 'T. T.' Un Luego Santa Ala Memoria." Many believe it was left by one of Hernando De Soto's men in 1540. Researchers are fairly certain that De Soto's expedition followed the old Indian path that ascended Whiteside Mountain from Whiteside Cove. But the meaning of the words remains a mystery.

Return to U.S. 64 and turn right. As you round the curve after crossing the Jackson County line, drive slowly so you can park on the left side of the road and enjoy what is aptly known as "the Big View." This is probably one of the most-photographed vistas in the vicinity, thanks to its excellent view of Whiteside Mountain and the surrounding area.

The Big View

Continue on U.S. 64 to the intersection with N.C. 107 in Cashiers. Turn left, heading north. After 3.5 miles, the road begins to parallel the shoreline of Lake Glenville, formerly called Thorpe Lake.

In the late 1920s, the Aluminum Company of America (ALCOA) needed to expand its generating capacity to produce more aluminum. In 1929, it secured a charter that allowed the Nantahala Power and Light Company to develop power-production sites on the Little Tennessee, Nantahala, and Tuckasegee rivers. ALCOA's primary site was Fontana (see "The Tour of the Lakes"), a location desired by the Tennessee Valley Authority (TVA) as well. A compromise was worked out that allowed the TVA to build at Fontana and Nantahala Power to build on the Tuckasegee. Nantahala Power constructed a dam at Glenville in 1941, a small dam for the Thorpe power plant in 1950, and other projects along the Tuckasegee in the 1950s. The lake formed by the dam at Glenville was first called Glenville Lake, but in 1951 it was renamed Thorpe Reservoir for J. E. S. Thorpe, Nantahala Power's first president. In 2002, the community of Glenville expressed its desire to address the inconsistency; most travel brochures and maps called it Lake Glenville, and the tourists were getting confused. The USGS Board of Geographic Names, which has the jurisdiction to change place names, heard the case and agreed to the change when it was supported by everyone from the county commissioners to the Eastern Band of the Cherokees. It is now known simply as Lake Glenville.

The lake is 4.5 miles long and covers almost 1,500 acres. The construction of dams along the Tuckasegee meant the loss of several well-known scenic landmarks, including High Falls, described in the book *Scenic Resources of the Tennessee Valley* as being "among [the] three or four most impressive and beautiful cataracts in the Tennessee Valley region."

It is 1.5 miles to the Glenville post office. One thing you may notice as you

drive the backroads is that a sign will announce you are entering a certain community. Several miles later, you will see a second sign saying you are finally leaving that community. In most cases, the boundaries of these "communities" follow the districts for the volunteer fire departments, so they extend for miles.

After another 1.7 miles, the route begins a steep ascent that continues for 3 miles. Just before the road levels off, it passes a dam and power plant. You will then drive 7 miles alongside the river through a prosperous farming area to the community of Tuckasegee. You may notice as you drive the area the numerous ways to spell Tuckasegee. For consistency's sake, this book will use the simplest spelling.

At the time that whites arrived in the area, Tuckasegee (Tsiksi'tsi) was one of the largest of the Cherokee Middle Towns. When the Cherokees backed the English during the Revolutionary War, North Carolina forces under General Griffith Rutherford marched to squelch them. Rutherford left Old Fort in September 1776 and headed through Swannanoa Gap, following an old Indian trail that

Tuckasegee River

later became known as Rutherford Trace or the War Road. Rutherford initially by-passed the Tuckasegee settlements and headed for Macon County. Later, he sent Captain William Moore and 100 horsemen back to the area. Captain Moore re-corded, "We took a Blind path which led us Down to the Tuckyseige [Tuckasegee] river through a Very Mountainous bad way. Came upon a Very plain path, Very Much used by Indians Driving in from the Middle Settlement." Moore and his men destroyed a deserted village before departing.

The war was not over for the Cherokees. By March 1781, Colonel John Sevier—one of the leaders of the Tennessee forces that marched over the mountains to aid in the American victory at Kings Mountain—had returned home. After leading several raids that helped end the war on the frontier, Sevier and 150 select horse-men made a daring raid into Cherokee territory. James Mooney wrote that Sevier

> started to cross the Great Smoky mountains over trails never before attempted by white men, and so rough in places that it was hardly possible to lead horses. Falling unexpectedly upon Tuckasegee . . . he took the town completely by sur-prise, killing several warriors and capturing a number of women and children. Two other principal towns and three smaller settlements were taken in the same way . . . the Indians being entirely off their guard and unprepared to make any ef-fective resistance. Having spread destruction through the middle towns, with the loss to himself of only one man killed and another wounded, he was off again as suddenly as he had come.

The raid helped Sevier—nicknamed "Nolichucky Jack"—establish the reputa-tion that eventually carried him to the governorship of Tennessee.

By 1802, Return J. Meigs and Thomas Freeman had surveyed a treaty line to separate Indian settlements from white farmsteads. The Meigs-Freeman line roughly paralleled the north bank of the Tuckasegee River. It served as a boundary for 17 years.

Though a few early trading posts were in the area, most white settlement in the Tuckasegee Valley began around 1850. Cultivation of the valley proved a prosper-ous enterprise, as a high percentage of farmers produced more grain than their families needed. They began to sell the excess to drovers en route with their herds to markets in South Carolina and Georgia. Soon, local families were raising and marketing their own herds.

It is 3.5 miles to an interesting roadside monument overlooking the river; a bridge crosses the Tuckasegee at Moody Bridge Road just before the curve where the monument is located.

The bronze plaque on its massive slab of granite denotes "the boyhood home of Dr. John R. Brinkley and his Aunt Sally." Orphaned at age 11, John Brinkley was taken in by his aunt, who lived on a nearby farm. A month after Sally's death, Brink-ley struck out westward to make his fortune—and make it he did. It all started while he was practicing medicine in a small Kansas town. One day when a farmer complained of sexual problems, Brinkley remarked that the farmer ought to take his example from goats. When the farmer suggested that Brinkley actually transplant goat glands into his body, an entrepreneurial light clicked on in Brinkley's head.

History has not recorded exactly which organs Brinkley used (though one can guess) and exactly where he put them in the farmer's body, but it's clear that the operation was a success. When people heard that Brinkley's goat-gland operation could create marvels of sexual potency, patients flocked to his office. He constructed a hospital, then decided to build a radio station—one of the most powerful in the country—to advertise his services. Over the years, Brinkley performed his operation and used a subsequent nonsurgical treatment on more than 16,000 people, at a

John Brinkley's monument to Aunt Sally

fee of $750 each. He also paid druggists a commission to act as agents for his products. It is believed that Brinkley netted $10,000 a week for 13 years. He owned a fleet of Cadillacs, including a 16-cylinder model with his monogram on the doors. He owned three yachts, a palatial Texas estate where he raised his goats, and a big blue plane, the *Romancer*.

But Brinkley's lasting contributions to American culture came when he decided to run as a write-in candidate for the governorship of Kansas. He revolutionized political campaigning with the introduction of radio, sound trucks, and airplanes. He also changed campaign strategies with the use of bands, bluegrass music, lollipops, bumper stickers, buttons, and banners—anything that would get his name before the public. Brinkley's billboard campaign was widespread. His radio station plugged his candidacy constantly. He promised free schoolbooks, free auto tags, and free medicine for the poor, as well as lower taxes, old-age assistance, and a lake in every county in the state. His radio slogan was, "Let's pasture the goats on the statehouse lawn."

Though he sent out legions of cheerleaders to teach voters how to mark write-in ballots, he did not employ experienced poll watchers. Many think that Brinkley ballots were intentionally lost. The Democratic candidate won 217,171 votes and the Republican 216,914, while Brinkley amassed 183,278. He ran again in 1932 but lost to Alf Landon. He tried once more in 1934, but his heart didn't seem to be in it, as he hardly campaigned.

When the medical community and the government began harassing him,

Brinkley moved his radio operation to Mexico and started a famous border station. He knew his world was crumbling. He died bankrupt before the government had a chance to bring him to trial for tax evasion. But thanks to the monument alongside N.C. 107, Jackson County at least has a memorial to the man nicknamed "the Goat-gland King" and "the Ponce de Leon of Kansas."

Continue 0.7 mile on N.C. 107 to an intersection with Caney Fork Road (S.R. 1737). Turn right, drive 2.5 miles, and turn left onto Judaculla Road, where signs will direct you through a farm to Judaculla Rock, a large soapstone slab covered with rude carvings that have never been translated. A wooden walkway allows visitors to view the rock without causing erosion to the area. Future plans include a hiking path from the creek through the meadow, so visitors will be able to approach the rock the way earlier visitors viewed it.

The Cherokees believe that the carvings were made by the fearful giant Judaculla (or Tsulkalu, meaning "slanting eyes") when he leapt from his mountain farm—located on Tanasee Bald where Haywood, Jackson, and Transylvania counties meet—and landed at the creek near the rock. The markings predate recorded Cherokee history. Various theories suggest that they are a memorial to a peace treaty, a commemoration of a battle, or a boundary marker. Most people, however, like to think it's Judaculla's footprint on the rock.

Return to N.C. 107 and continue north for 3 miles to Cullowhee and the campus of Western Carolina University. Begun in 1889 as a small school for mountain children, it is now a comprehensive university that is part of the University of North Carolina system. An Indian mound on the campus was excavated in 1898. Most of the artifacts recovered are housed in the Valentine Museum in Richmond,

Judaculla Rock

Old Jackson County Courthouse in Sylva

Virginia. The mound was leveled in an expansion project in 1956.

It is 9 miles from Cullowhee to a junction with N.C. 116, which leads to the town of Webster, the original seat of Jackson County and the area's commercial center until the building of the Western North Carolina Railroad in the 1880s. Most local people wanted and expected the railroad to go through Webster, but a shorter route was plotted along Scotts Creek to Dillsboro. The traditional story goes that a county representative known to enjoy an occasional drink was taken aside at a crucial moment and given a sufficient quantity of alcohol to convince him to route the railroad to Dillsboro. Meanwhile, the town of Sylva, also on the railroad some 2 miles east of Dillsboro, was emerging as the county's new industrial and trade center. The rivalry between Sylva and Webster culminated in a 1913 vote that moved the county seat to Sylva, where it remains.

Stay on N.C. 107. You will reach Sylva after approximately 2 miles. The beautiful old Jackson County Courthouse, built in 1914, has been converted into a community center connected to the new Jackson County Public Library. It sits atop a hill in the center of town and is visible for miles. If you're looking for exercise, you can reach the courthouse by climbing a 108-step staircase.

Turn left onto U.S. 23 Business and travel into town, where the streets are one-way; you are on Mill Street. Just before reaching the courthouse, turn left and go one block to Main Street. The visitors' center is housed in the historic Hooper House, built around 1905. This classic example of Queen Anne/Victorian architecture was the home of Dr. Delos Dexter Hooper, one of the first medical doctors in the county.

Interestingly, the house was built from plans acquired from Sears, Roebuck

Sylva Visitors' Center in the Hooper House

and Co. Sears once promoted itself as "the largest home building organization in the world." It produced handsome catalogs with numerous floor plans and illustrations of interiors and exteriors. Supposedly, over 100,000 "kit" houses were built in the United States between 1908 and 1940. Expanding upon its forays into building materials and house plans, one of which was probably used for the Hooper House, Sears entered the market for complete kit houses in 1908. After ordering directly from a catalog, buyers received all the necessary supplies in shipments by rail car (a typical house could fit into two boxcars) for assembly by the new homeowner or a local contractor. Following the stock-market crash in 1929, construction of the houses declined. Sears printed its last such catalog in 1940.

Drive along Main Street to enjoy the town's shops and restaurants. At the end of the downtown district, turn back onto Mill Street and retrace your previous route. This time, continue past the courthouse for 2 miles to the community of Dillsboro.

Dillsboro dates to 1882, when William Allen Dills built what are known today as the Riverwood Shops. Dills's home, adjacent to the Mount Beulah Hotel, was constructed in 1884. The inn was renamed the Jarrett Springs Hotel in 1894, when R. H. Jarrett bought it and noted the sulphur spring at the rear of the property.

The railroad took the lead in promoting tourism in the area. In 1886, Dillsboro welcomed its first summer vacationers—two women from Edenton, North Carolina, who shocked everyone by smoking in public. By 1888, Dillsboro had become an important town boasting two sawmills, lumberyards, two clay mines, a corundum-crushing plant, two livery stables, six general stores, and a shoemaker's shop.

In 1975, Dillsboro residents began a successful effort to restore their town to

its original appearance. The community has since become a marketing center for area craftsmen. The Jarrett Springs Hotel survives as the Jarrett House, a 22-room inn noted for its family-style meals. The Riverwood Shops are across the Tuckasegee River from the Jarrett House. The craft and gift shops feature work by members of the Southern Highland Craft Guild, whose artisans are known for the quality of their crafts. Dillsboro also offers a number of fine souvenir and food shops.

This completes the tour. You can take U.S. 23/441 south to Franklin, U.S. 23 north to Waynesville, or U.S. 19A to Cherokee.

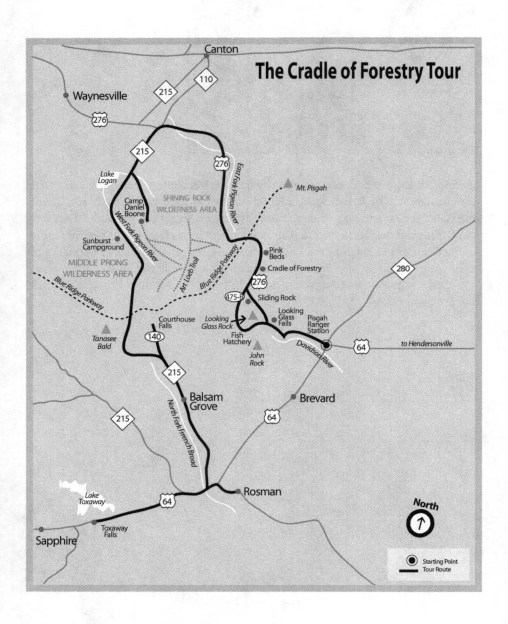

TOUR **8**

The Cradle of Forestry Tour

This tour begins in the community of Pisgah Forest and follows the Forest Heritage National Scenic Byway past Looking Glass Falls, Sliding Rock, the Looking Glass Scenic Area, and the Cradle of Forestry in America. It proceeds to an intersection with the Blue Ridge Parkway near Mount Pisgah before traveling downhill along Shining Rock Wilderness Area and the East Fork of the Pigeon River. The route then travels along the West Fork of the Pigeon River as it climbs to Tanasee Bald. Next, it heads downhill and picks up the North Fork of the French Broad River. It ends at the Lake Toxaway community.

Total mileage: approximately 90 miles

The tour begins at the intersection of U.S. 64 and U.S. 280 just east of Brevard in the community of Pisgah Forest. Turn onto U.S. 276, following the signs to the Cradle of Forestry. You will see the entrance to the Forest Heritage National Scenic Byway, which you will travel for most of the tour. In 1989, thanks to the efforts of state and local agencies working in partnership with the United States Forest Service, the byway was dedicated to promote public enjoyment of outstanding scenic attractions in Pisgah National Forest. It became the first national forest scenic byway in North Carolina.

Most of the tour travels through Pisgah National Forest. In 1889, George Vanderbilt, the grandson of railroad baron Cornelius Vanderbilt, began buying property at the confluence of the Swannanoa and French Broad rivers near Asheville. Vanderbilt planned to build a reproduction of a 16th-century French château and surround it with a large game preserve. He purchased about 60 local farms and hired Frederick Law Olmsted, America's first landscape architect and the man behind New York City's Central Park, to plan his model farm. Part of Olmsted's master plan involved the restoration of exploited forestland. He hired Gifford Pinchot—the son of one of his friends—to develop the first managed forest in the United States.

Upon his arrival, Pinchot was struck by the abuse the land had suffered. He recorded that destructive logging "had been done with an eye single to immediate returns and wholly without regard for the safety of the forests, and fires had been permitted to burn unchecked. There had been much injudicious clearing of upper slopes, which, after a few years of unprofitable cultivation, were generally abandoned to erosion."

Pinchot began a systematic mapping of the 7,280 acres of the Biltmore Estate. His plan was to harvest old trees so that young growth would have room to develop. He trained local men in the way to cut trees so the least harm would be done to the forest. A sawmill was soon in operation.

Vanderbilt then sent Pinchot in search of land higher in the mountains to serve as a game preserve. This led to the purchase of the 20,000-acre parcel called "the Pink Beds." Vanderbilt later added 80,000 adjoining acres on Pinchot's recommendation and named the entire tract Pisgah Forest, honoring the biblical mountain from which Moses viewed the Promised Land.

Pinchot went on to found the United States Forest Service under President Theodore Roosevelt. He was replaced at the Biltmore Estate by a German forester, Dr. Carl A. Schenck. Since America had no accepted forestry standards at that time, Schenck was free to experiment. Forestry apprentices came to Biltmore to work under his guidance, many without remuneration.

In 1912, Vanderbilt sold the rights to "all timber, wood and bark standing and down" on over 69,000 acres of Pisgah Forest to Louis Carr for $12 an acre. Carr had 20 years to cut the timber. He generally took everything over 14 to 16 inches in diameter at the stump. Carr also built rail lines along the creeks to bring out the timber.

After Vanderbilt's death in 1914, the forest service bought over 78,000 acres from his estate. In 1915, the land became the first national game preserve east of the Mississippi River. In 1916, it was made part of Pisgah National Forest, the first national forest in the country created from purchased land. Today, Pisgah National Forest covers 480,000 acres.

It is 0.5 mile from the forest entrance to Davidson River Campground, on the left. This is one of the largest family campgrounds in Pisgah National Forest. Signs direct visitors to the English Chapel. In 1860, A. F. English founded this church after paying five dollars for a half-acre on which to build it. By 1940, the chapel was in sad disrepair. Volunteers pitched in and built the current structure from rock collected from the nearby river.

Continue on U.S. 276. It is 0.5 mile to a visitors' center/ranger station on the right. Information, exhibits, a gift shop, restrooms, and nature and exercise trails are offered here. If you are interested in hiking in the area, visit the interactive kiosks designed to hook you up with trails that meet your specific requirements for difficulty and distance.

As you continue driving the byway, the route parallels the Davidson River. After the Revolutionary War, Benjamin Davidson moved alongside what was then known as the Rolling River. His 640-acre land grant, given for his service during the war, was made official in 1797. Davidson built a mill and dug ditches to drain the bottom lands so he could grow crops. It wasn't long before Rolling River became known as Davidson's Creek, and later Davidson's River. At the time the Buncombe County Courthouse was built in Morristown (now Asheville), the main road from the communities in the southern part of the county still traveled along the river.

It is 3.7 miles to F.R. 475. Turn left and drive 1.3 miles to the Pisgah Center for Wildlife Education and the Bobby N. Setzer State Fish Hatchery. You will pass a popular trailhead, located on the right 0.4 mile down the road. A 6.2-mile round-trip hike leads to the 3,969-foot summit of Looking Glass Rock, which offers a beautiful view of the Pink Beds and the surrounding area. During wet springs or winters when the water freezes on Looking Glass Rock, the rock acts as a giant mirror, reflecting the sheer cliffs. The Cherokees called it "the Devil's Looking Glass," since it is located so close to the Devil's Courthouse. Looking Glass Rock offers some of the best rock climbing in the South, so you may see climbers on its face. Several other trailheads for hikes to Looking Glass Rock are mentioned on the upcoming side trip, but be sure to check with the rangers because restrictions due to nesting peregrine falcons may be in effect.

It is another 0.9 mile to the wildlife center and fish hatchery. North Carolina has 4,000 miles of stocked trout streams, more than any other state in the Southeast. This hatchery, run by the North Carolina Wildlife Resources Commission, is the largest in the state. It raises 60,000 trout annually. Trout eggs are placed in large incubator trays, where water flows over them continuously, supplying oxygen until the eggs hatch in 50 days. When the trout grow to fingerling size (two or three inches), they are placed in a series of 54 outdoor raceways, which channel 3,500 gallons per minute of cold mountain water. They are later taken to hatchery-supported streams and released.

Camp John Rock

The wildlife center offers many educational programs including fly-fishing instruction, hunter education, and outdoor photography classes. The hatchery, located at the foot of John Rock Scenic Area, is a popular place to bring children, who especially like to see the feeding frenzies of the trout.

Upon entering the parking lot for the wildlife center, you will see a statue dedicated to the young men who served in the Civilian Conservation Corps (CCC) here at Camp John Rock from 1933 to 1941. During the Great Depression, 3 million unemployed young men were given work by the CCC. Known as "the Tree Army," these workers planted trees, built roads, bridges, and schools, and made lasting improvements to federal and state forests, parks, and agricultural lands.

Leaving the parking area, you have two choices.

If you are not inclined to travel gravel forest-service roads with washboard switchbacks, turn right and retrace your route to U.S. 276. Turn left to continue on U.S. 276.

If you're feeling adventurous, you can take a side trip that loops around Looking Glass Rock. Leaving the parking area, turn left, then take an almost immediate right up the gravel road marked F.R. 475-B, which heads up the hill. As you ascend, you will see John Rock on the left. It is approximately 2 miles to a pull-off, where a trail on the right leads to Slick Rock Falls, so named because of the moss that covers the rocks on the brink. Several deer carcasses have been found below the falls, which should serve as a grim reminder to visitors of the tricky footing along the top.

As you continue on F.R. 475-B, Looking Glass Rock is in view on the right. It is a little over 1 mile to a pull-off on the right, where a trail along an old logging road leads to Looking Glass Rock. F.R. 475-B circles Looking Glass Rock for another 3.5 miles until it intersects U.S. 276 just below the Cradle of Forestry entrance. If you took the side trip, you will double up on this next leg of the trip—but you will also get a completely different view from the other side of the road, so it's worth the effort. Turn right and travel approximately 5 miles back to the intersection with F.R. 475 to complete the side trip and rejoin the tour route.

It is 0.3 mile on U.S. 276 to Looking Glass Falls, on the right. A parking area is in front of the falls, which are 30 feet wide and drop unbroken more than 60 feet

Looking Glass Rock

down a rock cliff. Because Looking Glass Falls is so accessible from the highway, lots of tourists stop to take photographs during the summer months.

Continuing on U.S. 276, it is 1 mile to the Moore Cove Trail, on the right. Visitors can park on either side of the stone bridge and follow the steps to the trailhead. The 0.7-mile trail leads along an old railroad grade to Moore Creek Falls, where the creek drops 50 feet over a granite wall. Visitors can walk behind the falls.

It is another 1.2 miles on U.S. 276 to Sliding Rock Recreation Area, on the left.

Sliding Rock is one of the hundreds of waterfalls in Transylvania County, nicknamed "the Land of Waterfalls." Transylvania County has one of the greatest variations in elevation of any county in the eastern United States, ranging from 6,025 feet atop Chestnut Bald to 2,220 feet where the Toxaway River crosses the South Carolina border. The county averages over 80 inches of rainfall annually, ensuring that each of its acres is provided more than 2 million gallons of water per year. The rainfall also ensures the continued existence of the waterfalls.

Sliding Rock is unusual as waterfalls go. Visitors can slide down it. The granite incline provides a natural 60-foot water slide. Eleven thousand gallons of water per minute glide into a six-foot-deep pool at the bottom. Bathers have enjoyed Sliding Rock since Dr. Carl A. Schenck brought his students here in 1898. What has been called "the fastest 60 feet in the mountains" was rediscovered in the 1950s.

Sliding Rock

The United States Forest Service constructed a bathhouse and a parking lot to accommodate summer visitors. A lifeguard is even provided from Memorial Day to Labor Day.

Continue 2.7 miles to the intersection with F.R. 475-B, which brought you back to U.S. 276 if you took the earlier side trip. It is 0.9 mile to the entrance of the Cradle of Forestry in America, a national historic site commemorating the birthplace of scientific forestry and forestry education in America.

In 1898, Dr. Carl A. Schenck, the German who succeeded Gifford Pinchot in supervising George Vanderbilt's vast forest holdings, founded a school that he hoped would satisfy his questioning apprentices. The Biltmore Forest School was the first forestry school in America. Winter classes were held at the Biltmore Estate, while summer sessions were conducted in Pisgah Forest. Some of the students operated a trout hatchery and bred pheasants for the Vanderbilt game preserve. Students were told to find their own places to stay, and the campus soon encompassed several abandoned cabins and farmhouses with such descriptive names as Hell Hole, Little Bohemia, the Palace, and Rest for the Wicked. Schenck built several lodges, imitating architecture used in the Black Forest of Germany. He distributed the lodges to privately hired rangers, who watched for game violators and unauthorized timber cutters.

Schenck worked tirelessly to teach private owners that they could ensure future production of salable timber by means of proper management, including replanting and selective cutting. Pisgah Forest served as a demonstration site. In 1908, Schenck invited businessmen, lumbermen, educators, and politicians to a three-day Biltmore Forest Fair. There, he showed them what practical forestry

could do. Evidently, his demonstrations were successful, since many adopted his
principles.

Vanderbilt discharged Schenck in 1909 in what was the beginning of an interesting feud between the two. Schenck described it in his book, *The Birth of Forestry in America*. His students remained loyal, and the Biltmore Forest School lived on, moving with Schenck to Germany; to Cadillac, Michigan; and finally to Sunburst, discussed later in this tour. Schenck had a friend and admirer in Reuben Robertson of the Champion Fibre Company (formerly the Champion Coated Paper Company). Robertson offered Schenck the use of facilities at his newly built logging village, which was unoccupied because logging operations hadn't yet started in that area. The Biltmore Forest School was headquartered in Sunburst until it graduated its last class in 1913. In 16 years, the school produced 367 graduates, who went on to become practicing professional foresters throughout the United States.

In 1968, Congress designated 6,500 acres of Pisgah National Forest as the Cradle of Forestry in America. Today, the site offers a gift shop, a snack bar, a visitors' center with exhibits and a film, and interpretive trails. One trail leads through restored and reconstructed buildings that depict the life of the first forestry students. Another duplicates the tour Schenck gave visitors to the Biltmore Forest Fair in 1908. A small fee is charged at the gate for entrance to the area. It is worth the cost, if only to ride the fire-fighting helicopter simulator over a forest fire and to enjoy the other hands-on exhibits.

Almost next door is the Pink Beds Picnic Area. The Pink Beds are an unusual forested upland bog at an average altitude of 3,250 feet. The name most likely came from the dense growth of pink rhododendron and mountain laurel that blooms in late spring and early summer.

It is 3.5 miles uphill to an intersection with the Blue Ridge Parkway. If you exit U.S. 276 and drive north on the parkway, it is a side trip of 3 miles to Mount Pisgah. According to tradition, the 5,721-foot peak was named for the biblical mountain by the Reverend James Hall, an Indian-fighting chaplain who accompanied General Griffith Rutherford on his march through the area in 1776. Rutherford was on an expedition to subdue the Cherokees. George Vanderbilt later applied the name to his entire forest.

U.S. 276 continues straight downhill for the next 14.2 miles. Upon reaching the bottom of the descent from the parkway, you will cross the East Fork of the Pigeon River. On the left is the Big East Fork parking area for trailheads entering Shining Rock Wilderness Area.

One of the first national wilderness areas in the East, Shining Rock is accessible only by trail. Its first 13,400 acres were among the original components of the National Wilderness Preservation System, passed in 1964. It now includes over 18,000 acres, making it the largest wilderness area in North Carolina. The steep, rugged terrain includes five peaks above 6,000 feet. The wilderness area was named for the white quartz that caps 6,000-foot Shining Rock. The highest peak in the area is Cold Mountain, elevation 6,030 feet.

The Big East Fork parking area is one of the popular trailheads for access to

Shining Rock and the Art Loeb Trail System, but be advised that it offers no comforts such as water spigots, shelters, or picnic tables. The wilderness-area designation also means that trail markings are not allowed, though the trails are heavily used. Often, a location will have several worn paths, leading to confusion about which one to take. Hikers are advised to bring GPS devices, trail guidebooks, compasses, and topographical maps. Rather than starting from Big East Fork, most hikers prefer the trailhead at the Black Balsam Knob parking area, located just west of Milepost 420 on the Blue Ridge Parkway. A trailhead for the western section is detailed later in this tour. Look at a trail guidebook to help you decide which section of trail suits you best. Whichever you choose, the views are spectacular.

U.S. 276 now follows the East Fork of the Pigeon River. The route passes through a stretch of small farms and homes before opening into a scenic valley that is becoming fairly developed. After traveling through virtually deserted national-forest lands, you may find the area congested.

When you reach a stop sign, turn left and follow N.C. 215. It is 2.3 miles from the stop sign to a sign for Camp Daniel Boone, a Boy Scout camp. Turn left onto Little East Fork Road (S.R. 1129) and go 3.8 miles upstream to the camp. At the parking area at the south edge of the camp is a trailhead for the Art Loeb Trail System. Loeb was a hiking enthusiast and the leader of the Carolina Mountain Club. The system, which includes over 30 rugged miles of trails, was dedicated to his memory and designated a national recreation trail in 1979. Many experienced hikers feel that the system, which includes some of the longest and most challenging trails in Pisgah National Forest, provides the most beautiful hiking in the area. The trail beginning at Camp Daniel Boone ascends 2,926 feet into the heart of Shining Rock Wilderness Area and provides the closest access to Cold Mountain.

Return to N.C. 215 and continue in your original direction. In less than a mile, you will begin to notice that tall pine trees in symmetrical rows almost form a canopy over the road. Unfortunately, many of those trees are dying from the hemlock woolly adelgid infestation. This Asian pest, introduced to the United States in the 1950s, has spread rapidly, especially in the last 10 years. Various efforts are being used to control the damage, including the release of predator beetles that feast on the adelgids. Nonetheless, many large hemlocks in the wild will be lost in the next few years.

It will become obvious that you are riding through a resort area when a lake appears on the right. Lake Logan is a beautiful, private mountain lake built in 1932 as a water supply for Champion's mills. Prior to the damming of the river, the community of Sunburst was located here. Sunburst was once the center for 10 of Champion's logging camps.

Peter G. Thomson started the Champion Coated Paper Company in Ohio in 1896. His process of making paper and coating it on both sides in one operation was very profitable, but he owned no forests and was forced to buy wood from his competitors. Needing to make his own pulp, he built a plant at Canton, North Carolina. Champion then began logging the fine hardwood forests of the area.

In 1906, Thomson sent his son-in-law, Reuben Robertson, on a 50-day assign-

ment to improve the company's operations. Robertson set out to make Sunburst a model logging town. He accomplished his task, and he and his wife ended up staying for over 50 years.

At the time of Champion's arrival, 400 people lived in Canton. By 1916, the population had grown to around 6,000, with another 2,000 living in the surrounding area. Business boomed so much that Champion employed over 1,000 men and shipped 15 carloads of products from Canton daily. The large sawmill in Sunburst operated until the mid-1920s, when it was destroyed by fire. The railroad into the area was abandoned soon afterward.

It is 2.8 miles from Lake Logan to the Sunburst Campground. The campground is actually located on the former site of the town of Spruce, which boasted a large band mill. Today, the Sunburst Campground provides an ideal base camp for hikes into the Middle Prong Wilderness Area.

As you ascend N.C. 215 for the next 8.6 miles to the Blue Ridge Parkway, the area to the right is the Middle Prong Wilderness Area. Designated in 1984, the 7,900-acre tract is part of North Carolina's wilderness system. N.C. 215 is the boundary between this wilderness area and Shining Rock Wilderness Area. Much of the area was logged by Champion in the early 1900s, but the forest has grown back to the point where man's imprint is virtually unnoticeable, save for occasional evidence of abandoned logging roads and railroad grades.

The tour now follows the West Fork of the Pigeon River, which forms several cascades. As you ascend, drive slowly whenever the road crosses a small bridge, in order to see the waterfall that usually comes down the hillside on the right. If the

Waterfall in the Middle Prong Wilderness Area

leaves are off the trees, you will also see numerous waterfalls on the left as the river heads into the gorge.

As N.C. 215 climbs to the crest of the mountain at Beech Gap, you will see a prominent mountain bald. This is Tanasee (or Tennessee) Bald. According to Cherokee legend, it was near here that the giant Tsulkalu (anglicized to Judaculla and translated as "slanting eyes") had his 100-acre farm; it is said that because he cleared his fields, the area has remained bald to this day. It was also from this point—where Jackson, Haywood, and Transylvania counties meet—that Judaculla made his famous jump. He landed near Caney Fork in the valley below, and the scratches left where his foot hit are still visible on Judaculla Rock (see "The Cashiers Tour").

This area is also called the Devil's Old Fields. Cherokee legend tells of an occasion when some Indians intruded on Judaculla here. The slant-eyed devil-giant must not have cared for their visit, because he turned himself into a snake and swallowed all 50 of them in a single gulp.

Nearby is the 5,462-foot summit known as the Devil's Courthouse. The Cherokees believed that Judaculla had a courtroom in a cave there.

At Beech Gap, N.C. 215 intersects the Blue Ridge Parkway before making a steep ascent. If you are interested in a nice hike to a waterfall, it is 6.5 miles to F.R. 140. Right after you cross a bridge, a gravel road turns to the left and goes uphill along Courthouse Creek. The creek leads to the source of the French Broad River, located at the base of the west wall of the Devil's Courthouse. It is 3.1 miles on the gravel road to small parking pullovers on both sides just past a bridge with a warning that it has an eight-ton limit. On the left is a marked trailhead for a moderately difficult 0.6-mile route to Courthouse Falls. At 0.2 mile on the left is a narrow path with sections of steps that descend 0.1 mile to Courthouse Falls, where the creek plummets 50 feet into a round basin carved from solid granite. Retrace your route to N.C. 215 to complete the side trip.

Views of Tanasee Bald

It is 1.7 miles on N.C. 215 past the forest road to the Balsam Grove post office, then another 2.5 miles to an intersection with Macedonia Church Road (S.R. 1326), on the right. At one time, this road led to the Rosman Research Center. Because the mountains are relatively free of electronic interference, the National Aeronautics and Space Administration built two dish-shaped antennas 85 feet in diameter at the research center. The facility, once used to track satellites, is now called the Pisgah Astronomical Research Institute. Since 1999, it has hosted research and study programs from several area universities.

The route now follows the North Fork of the French Broad River. The river was named by 18th-century explorers and hunters who discovered that it differed from other rivers they knew in that it eventually turned west and flowed toward lands claimed by the French. They named it the French Broad to distinguish it from the rivers that flowed toward English settlements along the Atlantic Ocean. The Cherokees called it "Long Man" and its tributaries "Chattering Children." They called some of the faster-moving parts Tahkeeostee, meaning "racing waters." Little has changed today.

After traveling 4.3 miles past Macedonia Church Road, you will see an interesting rock formation hanging over the left lane of the highway. It is easy to see why it was named Alligator Rock.

Just after passing the formation, the route leaves Pisgah National Forest. It is 1.6 miles to an intersection with U.S. 64. The turnoff for Rosman is 1.6 miles to the left.

From 1905 through the 1930s, Rosman was the most prosperous community in Transylvania County. It was built where four prongs of the French Broad River—the North Fork, the West Fork, the East Fork, and the Middle Fork—come together. The location had proven itself a good site for fording the river as far back as the days when the ancient Indian trading path called the Estatoe Trail ran nearby. A white settlement formed there in the early 1800s but didn't begin to prosper until the coming of the Henderson-Brevard Railroad shortly after the turn of the 20th century.

About the time the railroad made its appearance, Joseph Silversteen arrived from Pennsylvania and began his experimental tanning and tanning extract operations. The settlement was called Jeptha at that time but was incorporated as Toxaway in 1901. When the Lake Toxaway resort opened, its developers asked that the town's name be changed to avoid confusion. In 1903, the town became known as Estatoe, an unpopular choice that survived only two years. In 1905, it was called Rosman, a combination of the names of a couple of Joseph Silversteen's associates.

In 1910, Silversteen acquired 30,000 acres of forestland from George Vanderbilt. He built a lumbermill and a company store for his 300 workers. Silversteen's band mill sawed 26,000 board feet of lumber daily. Two trains a day hauled logs out of what is now Pisgah National Forest. Silversteen's tanning operations were suspended in 1956, and the lumbermill closed in 1966.

The tour continues by turning west onto U.S. 64. It is 7.7 miles to where the highway crosses the top of Toxaway Falls. You will most likely zip right over the falls and never see them. However, if you watch the mileage carefully, you can pull over just before the dam and take a short walk across the road to look down on the falls—a great, bare expanse of rock more than 300 feet wide with a steady stream of water dropping 300 feet to the bottom. This is a well-traveled highway, so be very careful.

The dam and the lake it created, Lake Toxaway, have an interesting history. In 1896, Pittsburgh entrepreneur E. H. Jennings formed the Lake Toxaway Company to build "a high class resort with the best of service in every particular," as one of the company's early brochures described the project. Following the construction of the dam and the formation of the 640-acre Lake Toxaway, with its 14 miles of shoreline, the mountainous setting lived up to its billing as "America's Switzerland."

The setting was not the only attraction that brought visitors to this isolated area. The year 1903 saw the opening of a lavish five-story wooden hotel with curving verandas overlooking the lake. It contained over 500 rooms, each with a view of the lake and the mountains. The rooms had tongue-and-groove woodwork of walnut, cherry, chestnut, oak, pine, poplar, and beech. The hotel boasted electric lighting, refrigeration machinery, elevators, and steam heat. It was even "equipped with baths" and had "Western Union and long distance telephones." Guests could dine on the finest of French cuisine, served in the chandeliered dining room with china, linen, crystal, and silver accompaniments. An orchestra played daily concerts. There was a ballroom for dancing. The hotel also offered tennis, boating, fishing, and hunting. A livery stable was available for drives and horseback rides, and a steam launch provided tours of the lake. A spring on the property was available for those who wished to take a mineral bath.

The railroad reached Lake Toxaway in 1903. Six passenger trains ran daily, some pulling private cars. Guests at the hotel included Henry Ford, the Wanamakers, the Dukes, and Thomas Edison. One guest who fell in love with the area was Lucy Camp Armstrong from Savannah, Georgia. In 1912, when land became available, she purchased 40 acres. In 1915, the home on her estate was completed.

The good times began to wane in July 1916, when a great flood devastated much of the mountain region. It did not cause the dam to break but probably hastened its demise. When the dam gave way in August, water washed away livestock and property along the Toxaway River all the way into South Carolina. The railroad ran extra trains so sightseers could see the destruction and collect stranded fish in the drained lake.

Facing numerous settlements, the Lake Toxaway Company closed the hotel and abandoned the property. The hotel was torn down in 1948, but a new Lake Toxaway Company began to resurrect the property in 1960. Another dam was built. Lucy Armstrong's five-story home was restored and is now part of The Greystone Inn in the heart of Lake Toxaway Country Club and its surrounding residential resort community. The community is private, but lodging is available at the upscale inn. The entrance to the country club is on the right just past the dam.

The tour ends here. You can continue on U.S. 64 for 11 miles to Cashiers or 22 miles to Highlands or return approximately 20 miles on U.S. 64 to Brevard.

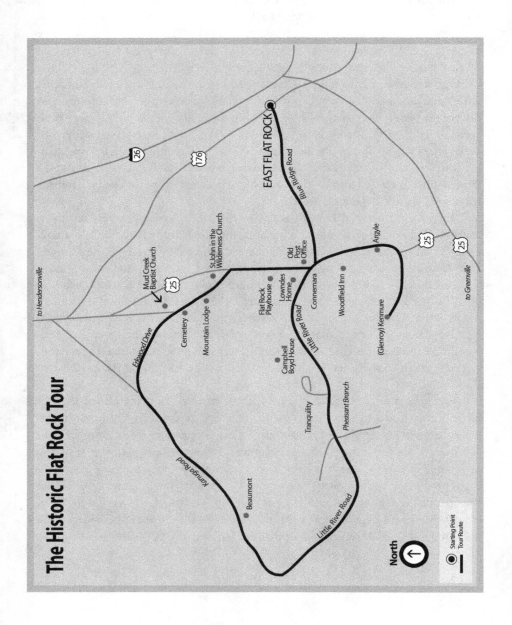

The Historic Flat Rock Tour

The Historic Flat Rock Tour

This tour makes a complete circle around the community of Flat Rock, once the summer social mecca for the Southern antebellum aristocracy. Although the tour covers a shorter distance than the others in the book, Flat Rock's wealth of history and legend certainly deserves a concentrated tour of its own. Those who desire a longer trip may combine this with "The Hunting Country Tour."

Total mileage: approximately 35 miles

Flat Rock is located approximately 3 miles south of Hendersonville off I-26. Take Exit 53 and drive 1.2 miles west on Upward Road (which may be unmarked) to the intersection with U.S. 25/176. Turn left onto that road and drive 0.9 mile to East Flat Rock.

The area's first railroad was routed through the middle of a forest 2 miles from Flat Rock, which was already a popular resort. Passengers wishing to visit Flat Rock were deposited in the woods at a location that eventually became known as East Flat Rock. They then had to walk or arrange transportation into town. If no passengers were alighting, the mail was simply thrown off the train. The small community of East Flat Rock grew up to accommodate rail passengers.

Turn left onto West Blue Ridge Road. East Flat Rock School is on the left at the stoplight. East Flat Rock United Methodist Church is on the right. For the next 1.8 miles, you will follow the route used by railroad passengers traveling to Flat Rock in the 1830s.

Before white settlers moved into the area, the land between Knoxville, Tennessee, and the Watauga settlement in North Carolina, as well as that between the Watauga settlement and Greenville, South Carolina, was known on maps simply as "the Wilderness." One Wilderness landmark—a large, flat rock—marked the location where Cherokee Indians held their annual hunting ceremonies. Some accounts also suggest that the rock marked the site of a camp from which Cherokee braves departed to attack the Block House in Tryon in 1776 (see "The Hunting Country Tour"). When frontiersmen retaliated by burning Indian settlements in the Smoky Mountains, the Cherokee families at the site of the flat rock turned their temporary settlement into a permanent camp that lasted until the early 1800s.

Once the Cherokees sided with the British during the Revolutionary War, it was only a matter of time before the victorious Americans pushed them farther west. Following the opening of new roads, settlers from South Carolina were quick to move into this area. By 1827, the Buncombe Turnpike had opened the way for travel from Charleston, South Carolina, all the way to Tennessee and Kentucky.

Most settlements grew up for economic reasons, but Flat Rock was a summer haven for the rich almost from its inception. The story of Flat Rock starts with Charles Baring, a prominent Englishman associated with a banking firm in London. Baring was sent to Charleston on behalf of his cousin, Lord Ashburton, to arrange Ashburton's marriage to Susan Heyward, the widow of a wealthy rice planter. Fortunately for Flat Rock, Baring neglected his assignment and married Susan himself.

Although no one at the time understood what caused the dreaded summer outbreaks of yellow fever, Baring knew that he needed to protect his precious wife and her wealth in Low Country plantations. Susan was already past middle age when she married Baring, her sixth husband, and she was in ill health during the first years of their union.

Bolstered by his personal theory that infertile soil at high altitudes made for healthy living, Baring set out to find the ideal place for a baronial estate for his wife. Though his theory was right for the wrong reason, his judgment in selecting Flat Rock proved thoroughly sound. Baring lived to the age of 92 and his wife to the age of 83.

After purchasing several hundred acres, Baring built a replica of an English estate in 1827 and named it Mountain Lodge. The residence was considered the patriarch of Flat Rock's many grand dwellings. The Baring estate included a deer park, a billiard house, a gatekeeper's cottage, and a private chapel.

The Barings were soon joined by their friend Mitchell King, a lawyer, probate judge, and export merchant from Charleston. Judge King had become interested in the area upon touring it as a member of a survey team evaluating possible railroad routes. He purchased 900 acres in 1830 and began construction on Flat Rock's second great mansion. His first wife, Susan, and the wife he took after Susan's death, Margaret, were sisters. They were descended from Lord Campbell, Scotland's Duke of Argyle, so Judge King settled upon Argyle as the name for his new home. Since King had 18 children, the arrival of his entourage each summer was a big event in Flat Rock.

King and Baring bought surrounding land until they owned over 11,000 acres. Judge King donated the tract that eventually became the county seat, Hendersonville. His slaves laid out the town's main street. It is ironic that Hendersonville now dwarfs Flat Rock, its older neighbor.

Flat Rock's founding families began spreading the word about their wonderful mountain summers to other members of the South Carolina aristocracy. The social season began with the two-week trek up from Charleston in May and lasted until October. It was one party after another. Since they had plenty of slaves to care for their needs and maintain their estates, Flat Rock's wealthy enjoyed summers that epitomized gracious antebellum life.

The climax of the social season was Susan Baring's birthday party; she always came attired in royal purple and covered in diamond jewelry, with a headdress of flowing plumes. Her flair for the dramatic continued her entire life. When she was close to death, Susan declared that no one in nearby Greenville, South Carolina, knew how to conduct a proper funeral. She then ordered a hearse and carriages driven up to Flat Rock, decorated the horses' heads with plumes, and supervised the dress rehearsal for her upcoming service from her window.

The Barings were instrumental in making Flat Rock a social mecca, but they were by no means the only important people to spend their summers here. So many Low Country planters established mountain estates that Flat Rock became known as "the little Charleston of the mountains." The list of local landowners reads like a who's who of South Carolina society. It included the families of four signers of the Declaration of Independence, two members of George Washington's State Department, two secretaries of the treasury of the Confederacy, the French consul at Charleston, and the British consul at Savannah. The families that built the famous Magnolia and Middleton gardens in Charleston joined the fraternity. In more recent years, poet Carl Sandburg selected Flat Rock as his home. Since so many historical figures inhabited such a small area, touring Flat Rock today is like taking a step back in time. Though a number of the large estates cannot be seen from the highway because of long entrance drives cut through forests, several may be viewed.

The intersection of Blue Ridge Road (formerly known as Depot Road) and U.S. 25 marks downtown Flat Rock. On the right, facing north, is the old post office; the current incarnation is across the street. The town received its first post office in 1829; the preserved "old" post office dates from 1847.

Follow Little River Road (and the signs for the Carl Sandburg Home and the Flat Rock Playhouse) as it splits off to the left next to the new post office. The grounds of the Flat Rock Playhouse are almost immediately on the right. The playhouse is the State Theatre of North Carolina. Performances run throughout the summer. In front of the playhouse is the huge

Old Flat Rock post office

outcropping of gray granite that gave Flat Rock its name. The nearby house, built by the Lowndes family in 1885, serves as the playhouse's offices. It is said that while staying at Flat Rock, the Lowndes family raised the first Confederate flag in North Carolina.

Across Little River Road from the playhouse is the parking area for the Carl Sandburg Home National Historic Site. The white columns of the home, which is known as Connemara, are visible atop a hill overlooking a lake.

The home's original owner, Christopher Gustavus Memminger, christened the structure as Rock Hill in 1838. An orphan born in Germany, Memminger was raised by Thomas Bennett, who later became governor of South Carolina. Memminger was such a success as a lawyer that he amassed the funds to build Rock Hill by the age of 35. When the Civil War broke out, he chaired the committee that drafted the Confederacy's constitution. Jefferson Davis appointed him secretary of the treasury, a position from which Memminger organized the entire financial

Connemara—Carl Sandburg Home National Historic Site

structure of the new country. But such responsibilities took their toll. After three years on the job, Memminger was forced to resign because of poor health. He retired to Rock Hill but kept in touch with his colleagues. When it appeared that Richmond, Virginia, was in danger, he wrote several leaders suggesting that they move the Confederate capital to Flat Rock, which could be defended more easily. Legend has it that Jefferson Davis sent the Provisional Seal of the Confederacy to Memminger in Flat Rock when it became evident that Richmond would fall. The seal has never been found. Some say Memminger buried it on Glassy Mountain behind Rock Hill.

In 1945, Carl Sandburg moved here with his wife, Paula, the sister of famous photographer Edward Steichen. Paula ran the farm and raised prize-winning goats while Carl wrote. During his 22 years in Flat Rock, Sandburg penned several volumes of poetry, his only novel, *Remembrance Rock*, and several children's books. While here, he also won his second Pulitzer Prize and a Grammy Award. His former house is one of the best-preserved writer's homes in America. It is open to the public.

Leaving the national historic site, continue on Little River Road for 0.2 mile to the Campbell Boyd home, on the right. The original "house" was actually the two Saluda Cottages, built in 1836 by Count Joseph Marie Gabriel St. Xavier de Choiseul. The count's family was active in court circles in France and Austria. It was his uncle who, as emissary of Louis XV to the court of Marie Theresa of Austria, arranged the marriage of Marie Antoinette to Louis XVI. The count himself was a former governor of Corsica and a cousin of Louis Philippe, the Duke of Orleans. He discovered Flat Rock while acting as French consul to Savannah and Charleston and was so taken with the social season that he settled his family here. The family members became so attached to Southern society that the count's son, Charles, joined the Confederate army. Charles was killed while fighting in Virginia in 1862 and is buried in Flat Rock.

Campbell Boyd home, formerly the Saluda Cottages

In the late 1880s, Rudolph Seigling, the owner of the *Charleston News & Courier*, purchased the cottages, added the Victorian-style story and tower, and renamed the house San Souci. That is the home visible today.

If you look back over your shoulder as you continue on Little River Road, you will see the stone face of Glassy Mountain.

Little River Road winds for 0.9 mile through the valley as it passes the gates of a residential development called Tranquility. The development is named for the Gay Nineties home that Christopher Memminger's son, Edward, built for his bride. The house still stands atop the hill. You may be able to glimpse the home, but it is not easily seen from the road. It was supposedly on this land that four Union soldiers hid after escaping from a Confederate prison. One of the soldiers, J. V. Hadley, wrote an account of his escapades entitled *Seven Months a Prisoner*. Hadley told how he and his cohorts were hidden by the daughters of tenants on the Memminger estate until they were able to make their escape to Knoxville. The fact that they accomplished their feat in such a Confederate stronghold is remarkable.

It is 1.3 miles to a development called Teneriffe. The original Teneriffe was a Gothic-style home built by Dr. J. G. Schoolbred in 1852. After the Civil War, the house was remodeled with a blend of Neoclassical and Tudor influences. Until recently, it was a bed-and-breakfast.

After another 0.8 mile, you will pass a small creek called Pheasant Branch. In the days before the members of Charleston society built homes around Flat Rock, a man named Abraham Kuykendall—already advanced in age—moved to the area, purchased more than 1,000 acres of land, and opened a tavern. A shrewd businessman, he made his patrons pay in gold or silver. The area was still untamed, and as the years rolled by Kuykendall began to worry about the safety of his money. Legend has it that one night he transferred his gold and silver to a large wash pot made of black iron, blindfolded two slaves, and instructed them to carry the pot. He led them into the forest, removed the blindfolds, ordered them to bury the treasure, and blindfolded them again for the return trip. He warned the slaves never to reveal what they had seen that night.

During Kuykendall's 104th year, the story goes, he found himself in need of money, so he set out to dig up his cache. That was the last time he was seen alive. His body was subsequently found facedown in Pheasant Branch. The only light the two slaves could shed on the mystery was that they had buried the treasure under a stooping white oak near a clear stream. Given the location of the body, it was generally believed that the coins had to be somewhere near Pheasant Branch.

Soon after Kuykendall's death, night travelers on Little River Road began to tell of seeing an old man digging frantically in the moonlight. Others spoke of seeing a wagon driven by an old man with a wash pot by his side; when the travelers came upon the wagon, it disappeared.

Those who drive the road today may be moving too quickly to see ghosts. To this day, the treasure has never been found.

A little over 1 mile later, Little River Road intersects Kanuga Road. Turn right. After 0.8 mile, you will pass the entrance to another residential development—Beaumont Estates—that sprang up around one of the old Flat Rock mansions. In

1839, a wealthy rice planter named Andrew Johnstone brought a small army of slaves to the area, cut a large quantity of gray, mica-flecked granite from a quarry on Glassy Mountain, and constructed a home called Beaumont. When the Low Country was occupied by Union troops during the Civil War, Johnstone moved his family to Beaumont, thinking the area would be safe. Ironically, he was shot in his own dining room at Beaumont after feeding some deserters who had demanded a meal. As his father lay dying, 11-year-old Elliott Johnstone shot one of the unwelcome guests. That soldier was buried on the lawn at Beaumont, his grave marked by a stone bearing a devil's head. The original Beaumont is visible on the hillside just before the entrance.

After another 2.2 miles, turn right at the stoplight onto Erkwood Drive. It is 0.9 mile to Rutledge Drive. The huge Mud Creek Baptist Church, dating from 1805, is straight ahead. The old graveyard where Abraham Kuykendall is buried is on the right as you approach Rutledge Drive.

Turn right onto Rutledge Drive. Mountain Lodge—the Baring estate—sits atop a knoll behind huge pine trees about 0.4 mile down Rutledge Drive, where Trenholm Road goes to the right. Kuykendall's tavern was also located along this section of the road.

The Church of St. John in the Wilderness is on the left 0.4 mile later, just before the intersection with U.S. 25. The Barings built the church as a private chapel and turned it over to the Episcopal Diocese of North Carolina in 1836. Nestled on a pine-clad knoll, it is considered one of the best examples of 19th-century Renaissance-style architecture in the nation.

A path ascends from the parking lot to a terraced walkway. The gray granite steps and the walls of the terraced burial plots surrounding the church blend with the old brick of the tower and the main structure. The bricks, imported from England, have aged to a soft yellow color. The sanctuary and the chancel were built in 1836. The nave was added in 1853. The interior copies traditional English country churches in its floor, its altar, and its posts supporting arches that converge in a pointed roof, all made of hand-hewn pine. The pews, also pine, each bear a family nameplate.

The driveway up the forested hill connects with a yellow

Church of St. John in the Wilderness

brick walkway at the crest. This old carriage entrance is the subject of a story that gives an indication of the strong influence the Barings had over Flat Rock. On Sunday morning, Susan Baring, dressed all in white, would ride with her husband in their bright yellow carriage with its coat of arms—a carriage drawn by perfectly groomed horses harnessed with silver buckles and rings. The other members of their party would follow. Upon arriving at the carriage entrance, Susan would have her door opened by a footman, who waited for her to lay her prayer book and Bible on a velvet pillow he held ready. Another attendant would be sent to notify the rector that Susan was at the church door. Susan and her party would then enter, followed by a maid in a white turban bearing the velvet cushion with the prayer book and Bible. The maid would also carry a large turkey-tail fan, which she used to cool her mistress during the service. Only when the Barings were seated would the service begin.

The Barings lie in a vault under the pews opposite the side door, beneath the spot where their large, square pew once sat. In the church cemetery are the graves of a number of Flat Rock's most illustrious citizens—Christopher Memminger, the wife and son of the Count de Choiseul, the Reverend John Grimké Drayton (the man who created Charleston's Magnolia Gardens), and people with such historically important South Carolina names as Rutledge, Middleton, Laurens, and Haywood. Just outside the side entrance to the church is the grave of James Brown, a trumpeter in the Royal Scots Greys at the Battle of Waterloo and a charter member of the first congregation at the Church of St. John in the Wilderness. Some stories suggest that Brown was Susan Baring's coachman, while others maintain he was the family's butler. It is said that on certain sultry nights when summer lightning flashes across the sky, a trumpet can be heard sounding a battle charge.

Church of St. John in the Wilderness Cemetery

When you are ready to leave the church and graveyard, turn right (or south) onto U.S. 25. You will pass the old parsonage, built around 1853, then the Flat Rock Playhouse and the Lowndes home again, this time from a different direction. The old post office is now on the left. Continue straight on U.S. 25 South.

It is 0.5 mile from the post office to the entrance to the Woodfield Inn, on the right. In 1847, several of the most prominent men in Flat Rock banded together to establish what they hoped would be "a good, commodious tavern on or near the Main Saluda Road." That tavern became known as the Flat Rock Hotel. The following year, Squire Henry T. Farmer bought the men out, changed the name, and began the long tradition of the Farmer Hotel.

Squire Farmer and his three brothers and three sisters were relatives of Susan Baring's and became wards of the Barings upon their father's death. As an adult, Squire Farmer proved to be a shrewd businessman. Having worked as a building contractor before buying the hotel, he decided to make some of the furnishings for his new establishment himself. The black walnut rockers made by Squire Farmer for the porch of his hotel became famous throughout the area. Known as Flat Rock Rockers, they were unique in that they did not creep across the floor when they were rocked. They became so popular that Farmer opened a furniture factory to meet the demand. Unfortunately, the factory closed during the Civil War. Without Squire Farmer's mold, the chairs have never been duplicated. Though rockers are on the huge porch of the inn and restaurant known today as the Woodfield Inn, they are only imitations.

Continue on U.S. 25 through an area lined with tall white pines. It is easy to imagine how grand the Buncombe Turnpike must have been when Flat Rock was in its prime. You may be able to glimpse some of the old homes behind the trees and shrubbery.

On the right 1 mile from the Woodfield Inn is the entrance to a plush golf course surrounded by an exclusive residential development. The course and its environs were once part of the estate of Dr. Mitchell Campbell King, the son of Judge King. Dr. King was a beloved and highly respected physician not only in Flat Rock but throughout the entire area. Numerous stories about his life survive.

While pursuing postgraduate studies at the University of Göttingen in what is now Germany, Dr. King formed a friendship with a fellow student named Otto von Bismarck. It is said that one night during a discussion of politics, Dr. King bet Bismarck a case of champagne that Prussia would never become the most powerful nation on earth. Forty years later, finding himself one of the preeminent men in the world, Bismarck wrote Dr. King to remind him of their bet. Dr. King supposedly paid up, though that is not known for certain. It *is* known that the two men corresponded for many years. The letters Dr. King received from Bismarck are now housed in the Library of Congress in Washington.

It is also said that when one of the worst yellow-fever epidemics in memory struck Florida during the summer of 1888, Dr. King convinced the local commissioners to invite Florida residents to seek refuge in the Flat Rock–Hendersonville area. On his journeys throughout the world, Dr. King had observed some hard

Woodfield Inn

evidence that served to refine Charles Baring's simplistic early theory—namely, he had seen that yellow fever never occurred in high elevations, only in tropical climates. Dr. King had also noted that the fever did not spread once its victims fled to high altitudes.

Train after train brought an estimated total of 10,000 refugees. People in Georgia and South Carolina were so frightened by the epidemic that they sent armed groups to ensure that the trains passed through their states without stopping. The summers that followed also brought refugees. No one in the area ever contracted the disease. Though Dr. King did not know the cause of yellow fever, his observations about its spread were correct. His efforts may be partly responsible for the large number of Floridians who continued to come to the area long after the threat of disease disappeared.

When Dr. King decided to make Flat Rock his permanent home, he built an elaborate mansion named Glenroy across from his father's summer home. The McCabe family purchased the home in 1924 and changed the name to Kenmure. Today, Dr. King's home is the centerpiece of the golf course and residential development that bear the latter name. The mansion sits atop a hill overlooking the course and serves as the resort's clubhouse, complete with pro shop, dining rooms, and offices. Unfortunately, it is open only to members except for the Thanksgiving and Easter buffets, when the general public can dine here.

Retrace U.S. 25 when you leave Kenmure. About 0.2 mile north of Kenmure is the entrance to Argyle, the home of Judge King. An old wrought-iron mailbox marked with the Argyle name is near the two stone pillars on either side of the dirt road. Built around 1830, the large white Colonial home is sometimes visible from the highway.

It is less that 1 mile to the Flat Rock post office. There, you may either continue north on U.S. 25 to Hendersonville or turn right onto Blue Ridge Road and

follow the signs to I-26. At the junction of I-26 and U.S. 176, you have the option of extending your drive by turning right and embarking on "The Hunting Country Tour."

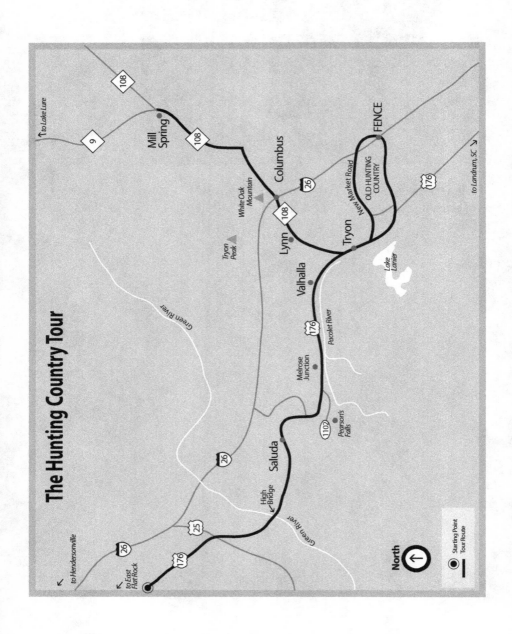

The Hunting Country Tour

TOUR 10
The Hunting Country Tour

This tour travels from East Flat Rock to the community of Saluda. It follows the famous Saluda railroad grade, which parallels the Pacolet River, into Tryon. It then circles town, passing through the Old Hunting Country before ending on the outskirts of Tryon.

Total mileage: approximately 50 miles

The tour begins at Exit 54 off I-26, where the interstate intersects U.S. 25/176. About 1.3 miles west of the exit, take Exit 7 off U.S. 25 and follow the signs to U.S. 176 East. Turn left to head east on U.S. 176 toward Saluda. Over the next 3 miles, the road descends through a series of sharp, steep curves to a bridge spanning the Green River.

An abandoned bridge is next to the one over which the highway now travels. The U.S. 176 bridge crosses 200 feet above the river. The older bridge was known locally as "the High Bridge," though that is something of a misnomer. The original bridge across the river was constructed by Peter Guice around 1820; it was located out of sight from where U.S. 176 lies today. When the first U.S. 176 bridge was built across the Green River, it earned the title of "High Bridge" in comparison to Guice's span, which was much lower. That title was rendered inaccurate in 1972 with the opening of the 220-foot-high bridge carrying I-26 across the river. Built near the site of Guice's original span, the new interstate bridge was appropriately named the Peter Guice Bridge. It remains one of the highest spans east of the Mississippi.

You can park at either end of the High Bridge and walk to the center. Though the brush in the gorge is thick, the Green River is still visible flowing far below.

Just beyond the bridge, U.S. 176 passes under a trestle and begins paralleling the railroad for the 2.7-mile stretch into Saluda. The road curves sharply and crosses a bridge over the railroad tracks before heading straight into downtown.

The tracks pass through the center of Saluda. The quaint shops—highlighted by a restored depot on the left as you enter town—line the street across from the tracks. All around is evidence that this once-thriving community has undergone a renewal.

Old "High Bridge"

In the early 1800s, the area around what is now Saluda was known primarily as a crossroads. Two well-traveled trading paths intersected here—Winding Stair Road led to Greenville, South Carolina, and Georgia, while Howard Gap Road led to Spartanburg, South Carolina, and the Low Country. Local commerce had its beginnings when a family named Pace built an inn to serve the drovers who brought their livestock herds across the mountains to the South Carolina markets. The Pace family raised a fence around the inn's yard so the drovers' stock could be penned up during their stay. The area soon became known as Pace's Gap.

Shortly after the Civil War, an engineer named Charles William Pearson was commissioned to locate a route for a railroad to be built from Spartanburg to Tryon and up the mountain to Hendersonville and Asheville. The obvious route followed Howard Gap Road around Warrior Mountain, but it had a shifting roadbed caused by underground springs. Pearson settled upon a much steeper route following the gorge along the Pacolet River—and thus the famous Saluda grade was born.

One of the first things to greet visitors in Saluda today is a historical marker across from the depot. It reveals that the steepest standard-gauge railroad grade in the United States crested here. Boasting high fills, deep cuts, and a total of 50 curves, the 3-mile stretch from Saluda to Melrose Junction had a grade that varied from 4 to 7 percent, with an overall grade of 6 percent—considered very steep even today. Construction moved slowly in the early stages. Logs felled from the virgin forest were sometimes greater in girth than the mules and oxen that had to drag them away. The construction crew had to clear the way through hills of granite, often using unstable blasting powder. The cuts they made tended to fill with water, while the fills they made tended to sink. Cold weather impeded progress, and the workers suffered poor living conditions. The problems seemed insurmountable until the North Carolina legislature finally sent convicts to help build the grade. Three months later, on July 4, 1878, the first passenger train made the trip from Spartanburg to Saluda.

The completion of the railroad did not end its problems. By 1903, some 27 men had been killed by engines that went out of control on the downhill trip and jumped the tracks on the sharp curves. One 10-degree bend was so notorious that it earned the nickname "Slaughterhouse Curve." The Southern Railroad Company

Saluda depot

was about to abandon the route when Pitt Bellew, an engineer who had been in-jured in a wreck on the Saluda grade, came up with a solution. He recommended a system of side tracks that would route runaway trains off the main route and onto dead-end lines running up the steep mountain. The system was built. If a train was under control, the engineer blew his whistle and the switchman gave him the main line. If a train was out of control, a different whistle let it be known that the train should be sent up a safety track, where gravity brought it to a halt.

The trains also experienced difficulty traveling uphill. The problem of supply-ing enough power to get them up the grade was solved by the introduction of a pusher engine known as "the Helper." Built for traction, the Helper would be con-nected to the rear end of a train in Melrose Junction. It would push while the main engine in front pulled. Once the grade was attained, the Helper would be discon-nected, to return on its own to Melrose Junction to await the next westbound train.

The arrival of the Carolina Special became the center of local activities. The westbound train came from the Low Country in the mornings, and the eastbound train returned in the afternoons. The trains were met by boys carrying trays of fried chicken, coleslaw, and lemonade to sell to the passengers. As the community's rep-utation as a resort increased, so did the number of inns and hotels. At the height of local popularity, 37 hostelries were in town.

By 1881, Pace's Gap had grown so prosperous that it was chartered as the town of Saluda. The name came from the nearby Saluda Mountains and Saluda River. Saluda was supposedly the white man's phonetic spelling of a Cherokee chief's name that translated as "corn river."

In the early 1900s, the town was both the height of fashion and a haven for suf-ferers of tuberculosis. But as highways were improved, train travel had less allure,

and Saluda lost much of its vitality. Fortunately, signs of new life are evident in the town today. The entire downtown area is listed on the National Register of Historic Places.

Continue on U.S. 176, which parallels the Saluda grade and the valley of the Pacolet River. After about 1 mile, you will see the entrance to the Orchard Inn on the right. Now a bed-and-breakfast, the inn was built in 1926 as a vacation retreat for the Brotherhood of Railway Clerks.

After another 2 miles, you will see a sign for Pearson's Falls. Turn right onto Pearson's Falls Road. Another sign notes a trailhead for the Palmetto Trail. This is the Poinsett Reservoir Passage for the trail, which is planned as a 425-plus-mile recreational trail across South Carolina. It begins at Oconee State Park in the west and will eventually connect all the way to Charleston.

Continue driving Pearson's Falls Road, following the signs for 1 mile.

When Charles Pearson was surveying the area around the Pacolet River for a railroad route, he became so taken that he purchased a large tract between Tryon and Saluda that included one of the area's most beautiful waterfalls. In June 1930, naturalist Donald C. Peattie wrote to the Tryon Garden Club asking that Pearson's prize spot be rescued from lumber operations. The club raised enough money to purchase the falls, which it named in honor of Pearson. The club still owns the tract and has set the land aside as a preserve for native flora and fauna. The preserve attracts naturalists from all over America, who come to study mountain plant life. Others can visit the park for a reasonable fee. An easy 0.25-mile trail leads to the 90-foot Pearson's Falls, at the foot of which is a great tablelike rock. En route, the trail passes more than 200 species of ferns, as well as various species of mosses, trilliums, and orchids. The garden club has done a remarkable job of placing rails, benches, and picnic tables along the trail in ways that blend perfectly with the surrounding habitat.

Return to U.S. 176 and continue in your original direction down the mountain for 0.1 mile to Melrose Junction, the community from which the Helper began pushing trains up the Saluda grade. Traveling this scenic route in the summer, you may notice the prolific kudzu vines so well known to native Southerners. Kudzu was introduced to this country from Asia in 1876. It burst into prominence in the South through the soil-conservation programs of FDR's New Deal. Kudzu adapted so well to the Southern environment that it soon became a formidable pest. It grows so rapidly that it completely covers trees, abandoned buildings, and anything else that stands still long enough.

If you travel through the Pacolet River Valley in early spring, you will notice the prevalence of a distinctive tree bearing purple flowers. It is the paulownia, or princess tree. Locals know it as "the coffee tree." A Dutch botanist named it after Anna Pavlovna, daughter of Czar Paul of Russia and granddaughter of Catherine the Great. Native to Japan and China, the tree was once the exclusive property of the Japanese imperial family. The crest of the empress of Japan featured three leaves surmounted by an equal number of blossoms from the paulownia. The ruling family was so possessive of the paulownia that if a tree was found growing outside the

Pearson's Falls

imperial forest, it was removed and its owner beheaded. Since each of the paulownia's pods produces 2,000 winged seeds, the executioner must have been a busy man.

Introduced in this area when it was planted in the gardens of George Vanderbilt's Biltmore Estate in Asheville, the paulownia found its way to the Pacolet River Valley as early as the 1890s. Blue and violet are rare colors for tree blossoms, so the dense clusters, sometimes a foot in length, are easy to spot. The paulownia is also conspicuous in winter, since its seed balls remain after most local trees have lost their foliage.

Kudzu vines and paulownia trees reflect a phenomenon that has given the Pacolet River Valley an unusual climate. The region's mountain slopes surround a thermal belt in which there are no frosts or freezes like those at slightly higher altitudes. Nineteenth-century visitors like R. H. Edmonds of Baltimore wrote glowing descriptions of Polk County's climate: "The peculiarity of this circling mountain range gives to this country a protection from cold, and adds to the wonderful charm of the climate throughout this far-famed mountain section a freedom from coldness and dampness that can only be appreciated by those who have felt its exhilarating influence."

By the 1880s, new residents who had come because of the thermal-belt climate began to plant apple and peach orchards and vineyards. A little over 1.5 miles from Melrose Junction, U.S. 176 passes through the community of Valhalla. Some of the area's earliest vineyards were established on the slopes of nearby Little Warrior Mountain, on the left.

George Edward Morton arrived in the area in 1886 after his physicians had given him less that a month to live. He recovered and prospered for another 30 years. In addition to founding the *Tryon Bee*, nearby Tryon's first newspaper, Morton was a pioneer in growing the famous Tryon grapes at his Valhalla Fruit Farm. W. T. Lindsey started a nearby vineyard in 1893. He even sent his fruit to the New York State Fair. On the east side of nearby Piney Mountain was the Doubleday vineyard, started by the son of poet Sidney Lanier and the son of General Ulysses Doubleday of Civil War fame. Around 1890, Doubleday supposedly brought Alexis La Morte, a French-Swiss grape grower, to Tryon to improve his vineyard.

The reputation of the Tryon grapes spread. A story is told that all trains stopped in town except the Carolina Special, the main train between Charleston and Chicago in those days. The citizens of Tryon flagged down the Carolina Special one day and served Tryon wine to all on board. From that date, the train never failed to stop. In 1896, Polk County made its first commercial shipment of grapes. A hundred thousand pounds were marketed that year. But by the 1950s, the vineyards were abandoned and the clearings overgrown.

About 1 mile later, U.S. 176 passes a small parking area on the left for Norman Wilder Forest; the parking area is just past Tau Rock Vineyard Road, where there is also a parking area for the forest's trail system. Tau Rock Vineyard was one of the many vineyards that grew up in this area in the early 1900s. Norman Wilder Forest was opened to the public in 2001. Owned by the Pacolet Area Conservancy, it consists of 185 protected acres of mixed hardwood forest located on the slopes of Little Warrior Mountain. The trailhead gives access to 2 to 3 miles of moderate hiking.

It is 2.8 miles from Valhalla to the Tryon city limits. In 1730, representatives of the English colonial government met with leading Cherokee chiefs and drew up what was supposed to be a perpetual treaty of peace. A lucrative trade developed between coastal settlements in South Carolina and the Indians of western North Carolina. Villages and trading posts appeared along the frontier until the French and Indian War broke the peace. When Indians attacked upcountry settlements around 1756, whites built forts to protect the frontier. These included Earle's Fort near what is now Landrum, South Carolina, the Block House near Tryon, and Young's Fort near what is now Mill Spring.

After the war, conflicts between white settlers and Indians grew so numerous that William Tryon, the royal governor of the colony of North Carolina, came west in 1767 to negotiate a new boundary line. He met with John Stuart—an agent trusted by the Indians—and a group of Cherokees led by Ustenaka. On June 4, a survey was begun from the Reedy River near what is now Greenville, South Carolina, northward to "a Spanish oak standing on the top of a mountain called by us Tryon Mountain, on the headwaters of White Oak and Packolato Creeks," as described in the treaty. The landmark cited as Tryon Mountain was actually the highest peak on what is now White Oak Mountain. Now known as Tryon Peak, it dominates the landscape for miles. (If you were approaching from the south on I-26, Tryon Peak would come prominently into view directly ahead at the boundary between North and South Carolina. I-26 passes just to the left, or west, of the peak at Howard Gap.) By 1839, a frontier post office at the foot of the peak bore

Governor Tryon's name as well. The community eventually grew into the town of Tryon.

The efforts of Governor Tryon and the boundary team were futile. White settlers continued to encroach upon Cherokee lands, and ill feelings frequently erupted into violence. When the Revolutionary War began, the Cherokees sided with the English. In the spring of 1776, a group of Indian braves gathered on the side of what is now Warrior Mountain near the future site of Tryon. They planned to attack the Block House and then descend upon Earle's and Young's forts. Their plan might have succeeded save for a traitor in their midst. An Indian named Skyuka made his way to Captain Thomas Howard, who had assembled a small band of American Patriots at the Block House. Legend says that Howard had once saved Skyuka's life after Skyuka was bitten by a rattlesnake. Whatever the case, Skyuka led Howard through a gap in the mountains to the rear of the Cherokee forces. Howard and his men overwhelmed the surprised Indians in the Battle of Round Mountain, which ended Cherokee dominance in the area. The trail Skyuka showed Howard became known as Howard Gap Road.

The coming of the railroad in the 1870s transformed Tryon into a popular tourist resort. With the tourists came a whole new class of settlers, who proceeded to leave their distinctive mark. As you drive U.S. 176 (Trade Street) through downtown Tryon today, you will see their influence everywhere. Most of the old inns have disappeared, but the depot on the hill to the right has been restored. Around

Tryon depot

Lanier Library

Wooden horse in Tryon

the corner from the depot at the intersection of Melrose Avenue and Chestnut Street is the Lanier Library, a tribute to the literary interests of Tryon's residents. The Lanier Club was organized in 1890. Its weekly meetings were directed toward procuring a library for the town. What it achieved was not only a fine example of a small-town library but a social center for the community as well.

At the main intersection in town—the junction of Trade and Pacolet streets—stands a large wooden horse, a Tryon landmark since 1928. The horse, 22 hands high, was designed by Eleanor Vance, who moved into a cottage on the Biltmore Estate with Charlotte Yale in 1901. The classes they conducted in woodcarving, weaving, and various other crafts evolved into what is known today as the Biltmore Industries. In 1915, they moved to Tryon and opened the Tryon Toymakers and Woodcarvers Shop, which became famous across the country for its hand-carved toys.

Just before crossing the railroad tracks, turn left off Trade Street onto New Market Road, following the signs for the Pine Crest Inn. A sign on the left at the top of the hill indicates the entrance to the inn.

In 1918, Carter P. Brown, owner of a hotel in Michigan, transformed a former tuberculosis sanatorium into the Pine Crest Inn, still known for its rustic charm. Seven years later, Brown played an instrumental role in forming the Tryon Riding and Hunt Club, the organization that accounts for much of Tryon's present reputation. Most people who have heard of Tryon equate it with horses. It was Brown and the guests at the Pine Crest Inn who began mounting their horses and following hounds across an area between the Pacolet River and Landrum, South Carolina. That area is now known as "the Old Hunting

Pine Crest Inn

Country." Though the original hunts were informally organized, regular drag hunts were being scheduled by 1926. In a drag hunt, participants rode over a course after a fox scent had been dragged along the trails. Thanks to frequent jumps, a drag hunt resembled a steeplechase. In 1935, a local club known as the Tryon Hounds was recognized by the Masters of Foxhounds Association of America. Hunts are still held today. The Tryon Hounds and the Tryon Riding and Hunt Club are responsible for the steeplechases held in April and October. Both events have turned into social occasions well attended by spectators from all over the Carolinas.

Continue past the entrance to the Pine Crest Inn. Stay on New Market Road as it winds through a residential area for 1.6 miles until it reaches a stop sign. Turn left onto Hunting Country Road. As you turn, you will see the Block House beyond the fields on the right.

After its days of service as a fort, the Block House became a popular stop for drovers. It later served as a hideout for deserters during the Civil War. In its original location, the building touched two states and three counties. Its unusual geographical site made it a natural choice for such illegal activities as cockfighting and whiskey manufacture. Depending upon whose laws were being violated, participants could walk a few feet to a neighboring county or state and avoid officers appearing from any direction. The building was later moved to its present location.

Carter Brown saved the Block House when he bought and restored it for a family that wanted a home near Tryon. The new owners, the Plamondons, invited local riders to run a steeplechase over their property. The Block House Steeplechase, held in April, was conducted here until its steady growth in popularity led it to be moved to a larger facility. That steeplechase, which has run continuously since 1947, draws crowds of 18,000 to 20,000 spectators.

Hunting Country Road passes one large horse farm after another. It is 2.7 miles to Morgan Chapel Baptist Church, on the right immediately after I-26. Continue for 0.6 mile to the Foothills Equestrian Nature Center (FENCE) properties, the site where horse shows, horse trials, and steeplechases are now held. In addition to riding trails and courses, FENCE has nature trails for hikers.

The road makes a sharp uphill curve approximately 0.2 mile past the Kidd Barn on the FENCE property. Take the road to the right in the middle of the curve

Block House

and go a few hundred yards to Columbus Avenue. Turn right onto Columbus Avenue and go 0.6 mile, then turn right onto Greenwood Road. Drive 2.2 miles, then turn right onto Block House Road, located just before the junction with U.S. 176. You are now traveling along the backside of the Block House property. In front of the house is a large stone that marked the 1772 dividing line between North and South Carolina.

Follow Block House Road for 0.6 mile to another intersection with U.S. 176. Turn right and head back through downtown Tryon. After driving 1.6 miles through the downtown area, follow U.S. 108 East when the road splits. It is 1 mile to the Mill Farm Inn, located on the left where Harmon Field Road comes into U.S. 108.

Built in 1939 on the site of an old gristmill, the inn was designed by Chicago architect Russell Walcott for Frances Nevins Williams. Williams had operated a boardinghouse for students at Harvard University and lived for a time in the Provence region of France. Her inn of blue granite was intended to evoke a French farmhouse. From 1939 to 1948, Williams ran an establishment that catered to many well-to-do literary and artistic visitors from New York and other Northern cities. The site, which was listed on the National Register of Historic Places in 2009, is once again operated as an inn.

Continue 1.4 miles to the community of Lynn and the first of its two historic landmarks. On the right is the Mimosa Inn, which can lay claim to 200 years of history. In the 18th century, King George of England granted 90,000 acres of mountain land to a man named John Mills. The trading trail that later became Howard Gap Road passed by Mills's inn. He and his son, Columbus, became widely known for their hospitality. After the Civil War, the inn was sold to Dr. Leland McAboy, a Presbyterian minister from Pennsylvania. The McAboy House continued the fine tradition. The township of Lynn, established before either Tryon or Columbus, was named for McAboy's son. Aaron French and David Stearns bought the property in 1903 and changed the name to the Mimosa Inn. They installed new

Mill Farm Inn

plumbing, heating, and lighting equipment—even a hydraulic elevator. They also built a casino with billiard tables and a bowling alley in the rear. Each room at the inn had hot and cold running water, steam heat, gaslights, and call bells. Each floor boasted men's and women's bathrooms—progressive accommodations in those days. The Mimosa Inn quickly became one of the most popular resort hotels in the South. When it burned in 1916, Stea-

Mimosa Inn

rns rebuilt the former casino. He created 12 bedrooms with baths, a dining room with seating for 100 guests, and a nine-hole golf course.

Across the road is the former home of Lemuel Wilcox. Built in 1869, it became a landmark when Sidney Lanier, a Southern poet, died in an upstairs bedroom. Lanier suffered a long, severe illness after spending five months in a Union prison camp during the Civil War. He came to the area seeking relief from his tuberculosis. When he and his wife arrived in Lynn in 1881, the McAboy House was full, so Dr. McAboy sent them across the road to his son-in-law's home. Lanier was never to leave. Best known for his poems "The Symphony" and "The Marshes of Glynn," Lanier left an indelible stamp on the area. After his death, his family moved to Tryon and resided for years on Lanier Street. His son started a vineyard, as described earlier in the tour. The Lanier Club, the Lanier Library, and Lake Lanier all serve as testimony to Tryon's devotion to his memory.

Though the Mimosa Inn contributed greatly to local prosperity, Lynn's fate was sealed when the new road from Tryon to Saluda bypassed the town. In 1965, the North Carolina legislature passed a bill repealing Lynn's articles of incorporation.

This ends the tour. You can follow U.S. 108 for 2.2 miles to reach the intersection with I-26 in the town of Columbus.

Lemuel Wilcox House

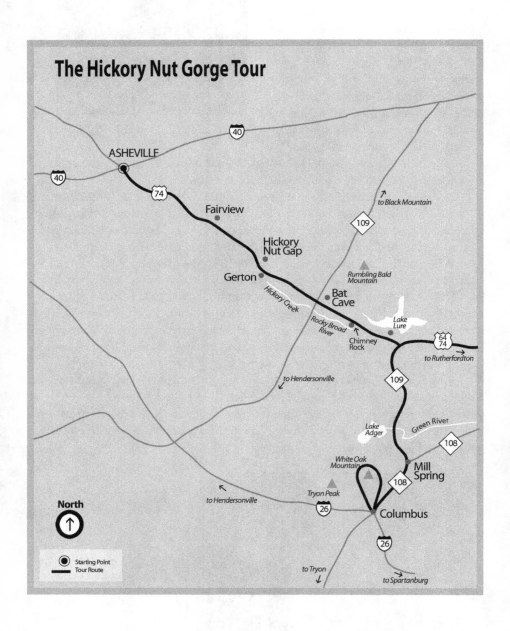

The Hickory Nut Gorge Tour

ASHEVILLE

40

40

74

Fairview

Hickory
Nut Gap

Gerton

Hickory Creek

Rocky Broad
River

Bat
Cave

109

to Black Mountain

Rumbling Bald
Mountain

Lake
Lure

Chimney
Rock

64
74

to Rutherfordton

to Hendersonville

109

Lake
Adger

Green River

108

White Oak
Mountain

Mill
Spring

108

North

Tryon Peak

to Hendersonville

26

Columbus

26

Starting Point

Tour Route

to Tryon

to Spartanburg

TOUR 11
The Hickory Nut Gorge Tour

This tour begins near Asheville, travels through Hickory Nut Gap to Bat Cave, then follows the Rocky Broad River to Chimney Rock and Lake Lure. It then travels to Columbus before ending at I-26.

Total mileage: approximately 46 miles

To begin the tour, take Exit 53A off I-40 just east of Asheville. After approximately 3 miles on U.S. 74 East, you will pass through the community of Fairview. Another 5.2 miles will bring you into a scenic valley that extends to the foot of a chain of mountains that opens at Hickory Nut Gap.

After another mile, just before the road ascends through a series of corkscrew curves, you will see a sign on the left for Hickory Nut Gap Farm. In the fall, signs advertise the farm's apple orchard. This is the first of many such orchards you will see, since a great deal of the tour travels through Henderson County, which claims to rank seventh among American counties in the production of apples. Henderson is responsible for 70 percent of North Carolina's apple crop.

At 0.8 mile, in the middle of the series of curves climbing through the gap, you will see a historical marker for Sherrill's Inn on the right. The renovated version of the inn is visible on the hillside behind the marker. Today, it is a private residence.

Bedford Sherrill held the contract to haul the mail from Salisbury via Lincolnton and Rutherfordton to Asheville. In 1834, he purchased property at Hickory Nut Gap and expanded the existing house there into a tavern, which served as a well-known stopping place until 1909. One Civil War–era story about Sherrill's Inn concerns a Union cavalry unit that stayed the night when crossing through Hickory Nut Gap. It is said that Mrs. Sherrill, a Southern sympathizer, emptied the dirt from her shoes onto the eggs she was forced to fry for the Union soldiers' breakfast the next morning. That was certainly not the type of hospitality for

Sherrill's Inn

which Sherrill's Inn was famous, especially for guests including Millard Fillmore and Andrew Johnson.

It is 2.6 miles to the Gerton post office, originally called the Pump post office in 1883. According to volume 3 of Frank FitzSimons's *From the Banks of the Oklawaha*, the name came from a spot near a local water pump. If a person left a quarter or a half dollar on the spot, he would find a jar of liquid the color of water in its place upon his return. The liquid was unlike water in that "it had a bead and was much more potent." Such was the way the moonshine business operated in the mountains.

FitzSimons also related the story of how the post office's original name came into disfavor. It seems that a cancellation stamp issued by the government to be used by the local postmaster was discovered to read "Rump, N.C." It was then that the people of Pump decided a name change was in order. They chose to honor Gertrude Freeman, a local teacher. Though justifiably flattered, Mrs. Freeman thought that a post office named Gertrude would be unbecoming for a lady. When the name Gerton was offered as a compromise, everyone was happy.

After 4.8 miles, U.S. 74 East merges with N.C. 9 and U.S. 64 where the Broad River comes into Hickory Creek from the left. Continue on U.S. 74/64/N.C. 9. The Broad River—also known as the Rocky Broad River to avoid confusing it with the French Broad River—now becomes the primary waterway through the gorge.

The tour next enters the community of Bat Cave. On the right is Bat Cave Mountain. The name comes from a huge, dark cave near the top of the mountain that runs hundreds of feet back under the hillside. For generations, the cave has been a refuge for a huge colony of bats.

It is 4.3 miles to the Bat Cave Apple House, on the right. A suspension bridge behind the apple house crosses the Rocky Broad River to a trail that ascends to Bat Cave. In 1981, Margaret Flinsch began making gifts of land in the Bat Cave area to The Nature Conservancy, which now completely owns the property. The Flinsch family had owned it since the 1920s.

Bat Cave is the largest known granite fissure cave in North America. The main chamber is a dark cathedral more than 300 feet long and approximately 85 feet high. The conservancy is trying to reestablish the critically endangered Indian bat in its former habitat, so the cave is closed to visitation at all times. The preserve is closed from October to mid-April to allow the bats to hibernate undisturbed. In the summer, the conservancy leads occasional hikes through the area.

Across the road from the apple house are the remnants of the turnpike that once ran through the gorge. The tollgate was located near the boundary between Hen-

Suspension bridge over the Rocky Broad River leading to the actual Bat Cave

derson and Rutherford counties in an area known as Parris Gap. It was run by a man named Joe Williams, who charged 25 cents for a wagon pulled by two horses or a yoke of oxen and five cents a head for the herds of cattle, horses, mules, sheep, and hogs that traveled the route. People on foot or horseback were allowed to go around the tollgate without charge.

There is a ghost story about the area near the old tollgate. In 1830, Christopher Bechtler and his son August came to Rutherford County from the grand duchy of Baden in what is now Germany. They established a private mint in Rutherfordton for the coinage of gold—the only private mint in the Southeast recognized by the United States government. The Bechtlers operated their mint for nine years, turning out approximately $2,250,000 in one-dollar, two-dollar, and five-dollar gold pieces. Legend has it that late one afternoon in 1840, Christopher Bechtler was returning from business in Asheville by way of the turnpike. He passed through Joe Williams's tollgate—and that was the last time he was seen alive. Bechtler's smashed buggy was later found on the river rocks below the turnpike. It was said that he had been carrying a large sum of gold at the time. Neither the gold nor Bechtler's body was ever discovered. For years after the disappearance, people reported hearing a buggy along the Rocky Broad River on moonlit nights. No one ever claimed to have seen the buggy itself.

Continue 0.9 mile to the Esmeralda Inn, which sits atop a hillside on the left. The original inn, built by Colonel Tom Turner, opened in the spring of 1892. After a fire destroyed the main building in 1917, the inn was rebuilt on the original foundation. Colonel Turner named the Esmeralda for the book of the same name by Frances Hodgson Burnett, who also wrote *Little Lord Fauntleroy* and *The Secret*

Garden. Burnett penned *Esmeralda* while staying in the area.

In 1915, the motion-picture industry discovered Hickory Nut Gorge. Several silent movies were made in the vicinity of the Esmeralda Inn. Stars like Mary Pickford, Gloria Swanson, Douglas Fairbanks, William S. Hart, and Clark Gable stayed at the inn while filming. Author Lew Wallace finished the script for the Broadway production of his *Ben Hur* while staying in Room 9.

It was a custom for Esmeralda visitors to write their comments in the register. Colonel Bob Ingersoll took the opportunity to wax eloquent on the subject of Colonel Turner's "Mountain Dew":

> Col. Turner's moonshine is the most wonderful whiskey which ever drove a skeleton from the feast or painted landscapes in the brain of man. It is the mingled soul of corn and rye. In it you will find the sunshine and the shadows that chase each other over the billowy fields; the breath of June; the carol of the lark; the dews of night; the wealth of summer and autumn's content—all golden with imprisoned life. Drink it and you will hear the voices of men and maidens singing the harvest home; mingled with it is the laughter of children; drink and you will feel within your blood the scarlet dawns; the dreamy, tawny memory of many perfect days. For many years this liquid has been within the happy staves of oak, longing to touch the lips of man and maiden.

In 1997, the Broad River flooded many businesses and homes in the area. For months, the Esmeralda Inn served as a place where locals could stay, get fresh water, or shower. Just as things began to return to normal, a devastating fire burned the inn to the ground. It was rebuilt but maintains its original historic character. While the inn makes no pretense of being able to duplicate the extraordinary beverage described by Colonel Ingersoll, it continues to offer hospitality and fine food today.

While traveling this route, it is impossible not to notice the high cliffs and the cascading Rocky Broad River. Travelers have remarked upon the scenery for generations. Little has changed. In 1859, Henry E. Colton wrote in his book *Mountain Scenery* that "the road . . . winds upon the banks of the Broad River, the contortions of whose troubled waters are beyond description. They curvet and lash around each rock, as if caressing it, then scornfully, seemingly with coquettish glee, dash on, singing a wild song, as if murmuring at the barriers which nature has put in its course."

Of course, any natural phenomenon that could inspire such lofty thoughts would also figure to inspire legends about its origin. The Hickory Nut Gorge is no exception.

Rocky Broad River

In his 1849 book, *Letters from the Alleghany Mountains*, Charles Lanman preserved the Cherokees' explanation for the appearance of the gorge, as told to him by Chief Flying Squirrel, also known as "All Bones." Flying Squirrel spoke of a time when the Cherokees found themselves without their beloved *Tso-lungh*, or tobacco weed. Many became sick and died. The Cherokees knew that tobacco grew to the east, but the gateway to that country was closely guarded by a group of malicious spirits known as the Little People. (These should not be confused with the Yunwi Tsunsdi, a kindly band of Little People who lived in another region of the Cherokees' territory, as discussed in "The Standing Indian Tour.") Anyone who tried to travel along the river near the gateway found the Little People raining rocks upon him from the high cliffs.

A young warrior was sent to bring back tobacco from the lands to the east. When he failed to return, a magician arose and offered his services. On his first attempt, the magician turned himself into a mole and tried to burrow past the Little People, but they spotted him, and he was forced to return. The magician found more success when he turned himself into a hummingbird, though he was able to bring back only a small amount of tobacco. Finally, he turned himself into a whirlwind and "stripped the mountains of their vegetation, and scattered huge rocks in every part of the narrow valley." The Little People scurried away in fear. The magician returned with a load of the fragrant weed to save his people. Tobacco still grows abundantly in the area, though the cliffs remain barren of growth, thanks to the magician's heroics.

It is 1 mile from the Esmeralda Inn to Chimney Rock, the area's most striking landmark. Chimney Rock, too, has inspired abundant praise from travelers over the decades. Charles Lanman wrote,

> The highest bluff is on the south side . . . and midway up its front stands an isolated rock, looming against the sky, which is of a circular form, and resembles the principal turret of a stupendous castle. The entire mountain is composed of granite, and a large proportion of the bluff in question positively hangs over the abyss beneath, and as smooth as it could possibly be made by the rains of uncounted centuries. Over one portion of this superb cliff, falling far down into some undiscovered, and apparently unattainable pool, is a stream of water, which seems to be the offspring of the clouds.

During the late 1800s, the entire area between the Rocky Broad River and the top of the mountain was owned by Jerome B. "Rome" Freeman. The mountain was covered by giant virgin black walnut trees. A London firm contracted with Freeman to cut and deliver the logs to the railroad in Hendersonville. After the timber was cleared, Freeman recognized the possibility of developing the chimneylike rock standing apart from the mountain into a tourist attraction. He opened a trail from the village at the base and began charging a fee for guided tours to the top. The reputation of the view spread, and Chimney Rock was soon known all over the Southeast.

Lucius Morse was a physician from St. Louis who, like so many others, came to the area seeking a favorable climate. In 1902, he purchased 64 acres of the mountain from Freeman. Dr. Morse replaced the trail with a well-graded, hard-surfaced road that allowed automobiles to drive to the top. Norman Gregg operated the attraction for the Morse family. Gregg had a 196-foot tunnel cut along the bottom

View from Chimney Rock

of Chimney Rock and a 258-foot shaft chiseled to the top, for a total of 454 feet through solid granite and quartz. The tunnel and the elevator shaft were finished in 1949. Eighteen months, 50,000 man-hours, and more than eight tons of dynamite were required to complete the project.

In 2007, the Morse family sold the land to the state of North Carolina to be used for a state park in Hickory Nut Gorge. The former private park will join land acquired by local conservancies to form the new state park. During the winter of 2010–11, the upper trails from the parking lot to the chimney area were closed for improvements. Future projects will necessitate the closing of the park's elevator and the Sky Lounge facility, but admission fees will be reduced. Inside the park, visitors can see the dramatic, 404-foot

Chimney Rock

Hickory Nut Falls at the foot of the mountain. Those who pay the park entrance fee have access to trails leading to the top and bottom of the waterfall, which was used in one of the scenes in the 1992 movie *The Last of the Mohicans.*

Chimney Rock was in the newspapers long before Rome Freeman arrived in the area. On July 31, 1806, a widow named Patsey Reaves reported that she and her two children had seen a "very numerous crowd of beings" atop Chimney Rock. She went on to say that the beings were clad in brilliant white raiments and that they seemed to rise in unison. Though the Cherokees would have dismissed it as a gathering of the Little People, the sighting managed to create quite a stir in western North Carolina.

Other witnesses came forward to report similar hilltop gatherings, but things were relatively quiet until September 1811, when a husband and wife who lived below Chimney Rock spotted two opposing armies of men riding winged horses high in the air. It was obvious that they were readying for combat atop Chimney Rock. The couple reported that when the preparations were over, the two armies dashed into each other, cutting, thrusting, and hacking. The wife distinctly "heard the ring of their swords and saw the glitter of their blades flashing in the sun's rays." Newspaper accounts of the sighting created so much excitement that a public meeting was held and a delegation with a magistrate and a clerk was appointed to visit the couple and take their affidavits. The delegation also reviewed the testimony of three other locals who witnessed similar cavalry gatherings on subsequent evenings.

In 1878, Silas McDowell, a well-known farmer, scientific observer, and man of letters in the area, came forward with the explanation he found most plausible. "In autumn," McDowell proclaimed, "when the atmosphere is clear, before a change in weather, the lower atmosphere in the ravine is surcharged with vapor, and to all objects in the upper atmosphere, seen through this medium, this vapor acts with telescopic effect and swells in size a bunch of gnats when at play in the sun's rays to the appearance of a squadron of winged-horse." Regardless of how much credence one gives McDowell's theory of the gnats, it is fun to look up at Chimney Rock around twilight during the fall and imagine a ghostly cavalry fight.

Another legend concerns Round Top, the mountain opposite and just north of Chimney Rock that forms one wall of the valley. In the 1700s, some Englishmen who owned a mine farther north were on their way to the coast with a load of gold when they were attacked by Indians. The Englishmen retreated to a nearby cave and tried to fight. All but one of them died. The lone survivor managed to reach the coast and sail back to England. He intended to return to America for his gold, but a loss of eyesight forced him to dictate a map showing the location of the cave as he remembered it. A search party was dispatched to look for the treasure. Subsequent parties were organized over the years, but no gold was ever found. Rumors circulated that a copy of the Englishman's map was on file in the Library of Congress. So many requests were made for the map that the library finally issued an official explanation: "From time to time the Division of Maps has received requests for a manuscript showing the location of a cave near Chimney Rock, N.C., where gold is said to have been hidden by a party of Englishmen in the 18th century, but we have never located such a map. The statement that the map is in the Library of Congress is said to have been printed in the 1890s and has been copied repeatedly since, but without basis so far as we have been able to ascertain." So don't write the library and ask.

Continue 1.1 miles to the heart of the Lake Lure community. In 1927, the Morse family—the developers of Chimney Rock—drastically changed what was a cross-shaped agricultural valley by building a dam 115 feet high and 600 feet wide across the Rocky Broad River. The resulting lake—Lake Lure—covers 720 acres and has 27 miles of shoreline and depths of up to 100 feet. Lake Lure has been described as one of the most beautiful man-made lakes in the world. The resort community that grew up around it covers an estimated 88 square miles, making it one of the largest towns in North Carolina in area.

Across from the lake's sandy beach is the Lake Lure Inn and Spa, built in 1927. The upscale inn underwent a complete restoration in 2005. Through the years, its guests have included F. Scott Fitzgerald, Franklin D. Roosevelt, Calvin Coolidge, and of course Patrick Swayze and Jennifer Grey while they filmed the 1987 film *Dirty Dancing* in the area.

If you stop in front of the inn, you can look across the lake to Rumbling Bald Mountain, some sections of which will be included in the new state park.

From January 3, 1874, to the early summer of that year, the mountain shook with such force that it "rattled plates on pantry shelves in the cabins in the valley [and] shook windows to pieces in their sashes," in the words of one local resident. The series of shocks dislodged huge boulders and opened a fissure in the mountainside. Another resident noted that "dust, smoke, and weird noises" issued from the fissure. One writer claimed that the rumbling steadily increased in intensity to the point that inhabitants began fleeing the area, thinking they were one step ahead

Lake Lure Inn and Spa

of a lava flow. Another source put his finger on what was perhaps the only positive result of all the geological activity—namely, that residents who remained had to send "ten miles for an itinerant preacher who conducted so successful a revival that twenty-five new members connected themselves with the Baptist Church." The rumblings continued, though they were not as severe as those from the six-month period in 1874.

In July 1940, the National Speleological Society sent a team of scientists from Washington, D.C., to try to discover the cause of the noise. The scientists found that the rumblings were caused by boulders breaking loose from the tops of subterranean crevices and thundering down to the bottoms of caves inside the mountain. The shape of several caves was such that they served to amplify the sound.

Of course, less scientific explanations have been put forward as well. According to one legend, a family that lived on Rumbling Bald Mountain was known for the size and strength of the father and his several sons. The family was an argumentative bunch. Their constant quarrels often ended in physical fights.

After attending a logrolling one day, the father and one of his sons did not return. A search found no trace of them. Years passed. An urgent request finally

Rumbling Bald, with Lake Lure in the foreground

arrived from the long-lost son, who was on his deathbed out west. His brothers hurried to his side in time to hear his confession. The long-lost brother said that he and his father had quarreled violently the day of the logrolling. The ensuing fight had left the father dead. The son piled logs on the body and attempted to destroy the evidence of his crime, but the smoke rose to the top of Rumbling Bald and transformed the rock into the profile of his late father.

Though the brothers had never noticed before, they clearly saw their father's face on the mountain upon their return to North Carolina. When the rumbling started in 1874, local people familiar with the tale said that the brothers were still fighting inside the mountain.

Across from the Lake Lure Inn are signs for the Bottomless Pools, another of the area's main attractions. Visitors can enter the park for a fee. Water has carved three pools into Henderson granite gneiss, one of the oldest rocks on earth. The Bottomless Pools form a most unusual "pothole." They were featured in a "Ripley's Believe It or Not" cartoon on June 29, 1939. The Lower Pool has circular walls and a strong whirlpool. Sticks and other floating objects revolve for hours under the force of the current. They rarely escape. The pools are estimated to be between 25,000 and 100,000 years old.

Continue east for 3.5 miles, then turn right to follow N.C. 9 toward Tryon. After 5.3 miles, you will see the Green River on the left. On the right are the Lake Adger power plant and dam. You will also see entrances to several developments that have grown up around the lake.

It is 3 miles to Mill Spring. In the 1740s, Young's Fort, located in Mill Spring, protected local settlers against Indian attacks. Ambrose Mills moved to the area in 1766 and established a trading post and a sawmill near two springs in a natural basin chiseled from granite. The vicinity soon became known as Mills Springs. In recent years, a postmaster with illegible handwriting caused the terminal *s* to be dropped from each word in the name.

Turn right here onto N.C. 108, heading south. Drive 3.5 miles to the Columbus city limits.

Columbus is the county seat of Polk County, which had a rather difficult beginning as a governmental unit. The North Carolina legislature approved the formation of Polk County in 1847, but there was so much squabbling over where a county seat should be built that the matter was not settled until 1855. Even then, it took a specially appointed commission of three men from outside the new county to make the final site selection. Instructed to choose a site as near the center of the county as possible, the committee purchased 100 acres of wilderness in an area known as Foster's Racepath.

One man who worked especially hard to see Polk County become a reality was Dr. Columbus Mills, the great-great-grandson of Ambrose Mills. Ambrose Mills showed bad judgment in siding with the English in the Revolutionary War and was hanged as a Tory traitor shortly after the American victory at Kings Mountain. Columbus Mills's father exercised better judgment, serving on the American side as a colonel in the War of 1812. Upon his death, he left his land along the Pacolet River to Columbus. As a North Carolina legislator, Columbus Mills fought to settle the dispute over the Polk County seat. His efforts were rewarded when the legislature stipulated that the new town be named for him, not for Schuywicker, also called Skyuka, the Indian hero of the Battle of Round Mountain, as had originally been proposed. The story of Skyuka is in "The Hunting Country Tour."

Mills served the Confederate cause during the Civil War. It is ironic that when he returned to Polk County at the end of the war hoping to find peace, he instead discovered himself a prime target for raiding by renegades, since he was one of the area's most affluent landowners. After the repeated plundering of his plantation—which stood on the site now occupied by the Mimosa Inn (further described in "The Hunting Country Tour")—Mills was forced to flee in the middle of the night. He escaped to Cabarrus County, sold his plantation, and never returned to Polk County, despite having campaigned so hard for its creation.

Mills at least stayed long enough to see the town of Columbus become a reality. The Greek Revival courthouse, completed in 1859, was built by slaves using bricks of native clay baked near the site. The bell housed in the graceful white belfry has since rung every day Polk County Court has been in session. Citizens once feared that the wood in the belfry was rotting and that the bell might fall, but it turned out they had little cause for alarm. Upon investigation, it was discovered that over 100 years' worth of bird droppings had encased and completely preserved the wood.

A second man who greatly influenced the development of Columbus arrived in 1888. Frank Stearns had made a fortune with his grindstone quarry in the village of Berea, Ohio, just outside Cleveland. He learned of Columbus because of its thermal-belt climate. So convinced was Stearns of the area's potential for commercial development that by 1912 he purchased 3,000 acres, including much of what is now Columbus, land on Tryon Peak, and the multiple peaks of White Oak Mountain.

Immediately after his arrival, Stearns went to work on a development on White Oak Mountain that he called Spring Mountain Park. He advertised it as "the coming sanitorium and Switzerland of America." To make Spring Mountain Park easily accessible, Stearns built what he called a "serpentine drive" all the way to the 3,102-foot summit. He bragged that the grade was "so easy that a horse could trot all the way up." On the summit, he constructed the Log Cabin Inn, which soon established itself as an elite mountain resort. In 1894, Stearns's brother David and a man named Aaron French added a large, four-story frame structure they named the Skyuka Hotel. David Stearns and Aaron French later remodeled what was formerly the McAboy House to create the Mimosa Inn.

Drive 4.4 miles from Mill Spring into Columbus. The Polk County Courthouse is on the left. Stearns Park—formerly the Stearns School, a testament to Frank Stearns's commitment to education—is on the right. On the corner in front of the former school building, directly across from the courthouse, is a large obelisk called "the Warrior Monument." Erected in 1909 by the Daughters of the American Revolution, the monument commemorates the Battle of Round Mountain, which is discussed in detail in "The Hunting Country Tour." When some of the

Above: *Polk County Courthouse in Columbus*
Right: *Warrior Monument*

old Howard Gap Road was incorporated into I-26, the state removed the Warrior Monument and stored the stones. It relocated the monument upon the completion of I-26 in 1967. In 2007, the Polk County Historical Association moved it to this spot.

In front of the courthouse is a historical marker commemorating the birthplace of Old Bill Williams, christened William Sherley Williams in 1787. Until the age of eight, Old Bill lived near where Horse Creek flows into the Pacolet River. After his family moved to St. Louis, he went on to become, in the words of Albert Pike of Pikes Peak fame, "the bravest and most fearless mountaineer of them all." Thanks largely to the literary exaggerations of Frederick Ruxton, Old Bill established a legendary reputation as a drinker, a trapper, and a guide in the West from the early 1800s through the middle of the century.

Many tales of Old Bill's exploits survive. One of the best concerns an encounter with three Blackfoot braves who ambushed him while he was trapping alone. Bill took an arrow in the leg but managed to escape. After cutting the arrow out, he tracked the Indians for four days without the aid of rifle, horse, or pack, surviving mainly on berries. Bill slit the throats of two of the Indians while they slept, then kicked the third awake and sent him fleeing. Asked later why he spared one brave, Bill retorted that if he had dispatched them all, the Blackfeet would never have known who killed them.

Old Bill Williams died in an Indian attack in 1849. In Arizona, a 9,000-foot mountain and a nearby stream bear his name.

After viewing the courthouse and Stearns Park, turn right at the next light onto Houston Road. A half-mile from the stoplight, the road forks after passing under the I-26 bridge. Note this location, where Skyuka Mountain Road goes to the left, as you will return here. For now, bear right, following Houston Road. Turn left at the second road, which is White Oak Mountain Drive. The first road to the left is the entrance for the White Oak development. All of this area was once part of Spring Mountain Park.

In following the paved White Oak Mountain Drive to the top of White Oak Mountain, you will trace the route of the "serpentine drive" Frank Stearns constructed to the Log Cabin Inn. En route, you will pass an impressive 150-foot waterfall on the right immediately next to the road. There is no shoulder, but you can drive to a pull-off on the left and walk back. The waterfall was known as Horse Creek Falls until 1891, when Stearns changed the name to Shunkawauken Falls to honor an Indian chief. The current name is one of the few remaining imprints of Stearns, a man who once controlled the entire area.

Shunkawauken Falls

It is 0.7 mile from the falls to an overlook where I-26 is visible curving up from the Piedmont through Howard Gap. Continue on White Oak Mountain Drive as it goes over the peak. You will come to an overlook at Sunset Rock. Although the overlook is on private property, the owners have placed a sign welcoming people to enjoy the view; please express your gratitude by not leaving any trash.

When you are ready to leave the overlook, follow White Oak Mountain Drive until it intersects Skyuka Mountain Road. Turn left and follow Skyuka Mountain Road back to the intersection with Houston Road noted earlier. The entire loop around White Oak Mountain takes about 45 minutes—or longer if you get out to enjoy the view. Continue straight into Columbus and turn right on N.C. 108.

The tour ends at the junction with I-26. You can continue on N.C. 108 to Tryon, or you can go north on I-26 to Hendersonville and Asheville or south to Spartanburg, South Carolina.

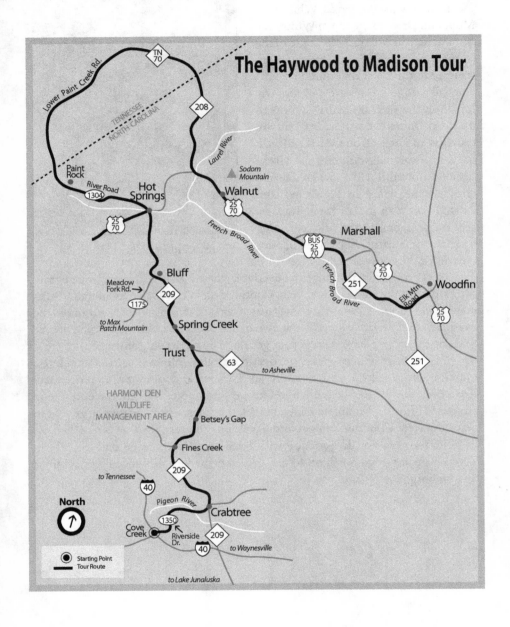

The Haywood to Madison Tour

TOUR 12

The Haywood to Madison Tour

This tour begins at Cove Creek in Haywood County, near the old Cataloochee Trail. It follows the Pigeon River, then travels northeast to Madison County. It heads to Hot Springs, circles around Paint Rock, comes back into Marshall, and follows the French Broad River before ending in Woodfin.

Total mileage: approximately 97 miles

Take Exit 20 off I-40—the exit for U.S. 276 and Maggie Valley—west of Lake Junaluska and Clyde. When you reach the stop sign at the end of the ramp, head straight across onto Rabbit Skin Road.

If you were to follow the signs for U.S. 276, you would see a historical marker on the other side of I-40 for the famous Cataloochee Trail. Across from the sign is Little Cove Road, which follows a path similar to that of the old trail. You are in the vicinity of the Cove Creek community.

Cataloochee is the anglicized version of the Cherokee *Ga-da-lu-sti,* which means "standing up in a row," according to James Mooney in his 1898 report to the Bureau of American Ethnology. It apparently referred to the high mountain ranges in the area, now within the boundaries of Great Smoky Mountains National Park, a few miles north of Exit 20. The Indians first used the Cataloochee Trail as a route across the mountains into what is now Tennessee. White settlers later followed it in driving their cattle to the good rangeland atop the peaks. Cattle were brought to the peaks in the spring and allowed to graze until late fall, when their owners returned for the roundup.

One early traveler along the trail was Francis Asbury, who arrived in America in 1771 and became the first bishop of the Methodist Church in this country in 1784. In the 45 years after his arrival, Asbury traveled an estimated 275,000 miles in an effort to save the new settlers' souls from wickedness and whiskey. Though he had covered other areas in the mountains, it wasn't until 1810, and the age of 65, that he followed the Cataloochee Trail from East Tennessee. Asbury's description of the journey is preserved in his journal, which reads in part, "Friday, our troubles began at the foaming, roaring stream which hid the rocks. At Catahouche [Cataloochee] I walked over a log. But O, the mountain—height after height, and five miles over! After crossing other streams, and losing ourselves in the woods, we came in, about nine o'clock at night, to Vater Shuck's. [Located near what is now Clyde, Shook's Campground was a well-known site for camp meetings.] What an awful day."

Asbury passed near the location of Exit 20 on that "awful day." If you have a desire to follow in his footsteps, you can hike the 7-mile Francis Asbury Trail, located inside Great Smoky Mountains National Park. If you are not up to the hike, take comfort in the fact that you will cross paths with Bishop Asbury again on this tour.

Follow Rabbit Skin Road, which travels through the Iron Duff community. The name has an interesting history. One of the early white settlers in the area was a Scot named Aaron McDuff. He must have been a popular man, as the territory was known as Aaron Duff's Bend until 1873, when the first local post office was established. The name Aaron Duff was suggested in the petition sent to Washington, but the Western Union telegraph operator sending the petition transcribed *Aaron* as *Iron*. Anyone who has heard a person with a mountain accent pronounce Aaron will have no problem understanding why the township accepted the new name as a matter of fate.

At least Iron Duff doesn't carry a negative connotation like Rabbit Skin, the locals' name for an area within the township. The latter name supposedly arose one day when a village wag remarked, "Looky here, fellers, at this pore, rotten thin soil—hit's as rotten an' thin as a rabbit's skin." The analogy must have been a good one, because the name stuck.

After 3.4 miles on Rabbit Skin Road, you will round a curve and see the Pigeon River flowing beside you. The river's name had a much less imaginative origin—the large flocks of pigeons that once lived along its banks. They are no longer in evidence.

Approximately 0.3 mile after your first look at the Pigeon River, you will see a bridge on the left. Turn onto the bridge. (If you had continued straight, you would have passed the point where the name changes from Rabbit Skin Road to Iron Duff Road.) After crossing the river, turn right onto the scenic route known locally as Riverside Drive.

It is 2.3 miles along the Pigeon River to an intersection with N.C. 209 at the community of Crabtree. (If you wish to shorten the tour, you can begin it at this point by taking N.C. 209 North from Lake Junaluska or from I-40.) Turn left and begin a drive through scenic farmland.

It is 5.2 miles to where N.C. 209 makes a sharp right turn at the Ferguson Supply Store. This is Fines Creek Township, which received its name in the early 1790s when white settlers along the Holston River in what is now Tennessee found it necessary to send raiding parties eastward to retaliate against the attacking Cherokees. The story goes that one such party, led by Captain Peter Fine, came through this area searching for a more direct route into Tennessee. Fine had followed some fleeing Cherokees into North Carolina, and his brother was killed in a resulting skirmish. The ground was too frozen to dig a grave, so the party decided to break the ice in a nearby creek and submerge the body at a still place. They reasoned that the broken ice would refreeze and that the body would be preserved until their return. The body was never found, but Fine's name stuck.

The Fines Creek area was once part of a 60,000-acre tract called the Boudinot Boundary. A man named Daniel Huger obtained the original grant in 1795, but it was Elias Boudinot who left his name on the area. A native of Philadelphia, Boudinot is remembered as much for the way he appended his signature—"Ph.D. and Curator of the Mint"—as for anything else. The tract went through several owners until it was finally divided in 1876. Harmon Den Wildlife Management Area, located several miles north of Fines Creek, is managed by the federal government. It covers a large segment of the original Boudinot Boundary.

N.C. 209 now climbs to Betsey's Gap, elevation 5,895 feet. It is approximately 4 miles from the turn at the Ferguson Supply Store to the Madison County line at the crest of the range, which offers an incredible view of the surrounding peaks. Continue 6.1 miles to the community of Trust, which has a substantial general store and a café. N.C. 209 intersects N.C. 63, which leads to Asheville. Turn left and continue on N.C. 209 toward Hot Springs. The route follows Spring Creek; the landscape opens into a scenic valley. It is 4.4 miles—past a volunteer fire department, a former school that now serves as a community center, and a Methodist church, all named Spring Creek—to the sign for the actual community of Spring Creek.

Drive another 3.1 miles to a sign indicating that Max Patch Mountain is 10 miles to the left on Meadow Fork Road. Standing 4,629 feet, Max Patch Mountain is located near the boundary of Harmon Den Wildlife Management Area. The Appalachian Trail crosses the top of the mountain's grassy bald. Some have called Max Patch Mountain "the crown jewel of the Appalachian Trail" because of the panoramic view from its summit.

It is 0.7 mile past the turnoff to the mountain to the community of Bluff, whose name is easily understood, as the route immediately begins climbing the bluffs overlooking Spring Creek. A drive of 3.4 miles leads to Rocky Bluff

Spring Creek Community Center

Recreation Area, which offers camping, picnicking, and trailheads for hiking.

Continue 1.9 miles to the outskirts of Hot Springs. In 1778, two men named Henry Reynolds and Thomas Morgan were acting as advance scouts, watching for Indian movements. Spotting some stolen horses on the other side of the French Broad River, they left their own mounts on the bank and waded across. While doing so, they noticed that the water was unusually warm. It turned out that the site was fed by an underground natural hot spring. Reynolds and Morgan spread the word when they returned to their settlement. Soon thereafter, invalids began journeying to the area to take the waters in the hope that they would be healed.

But it was a completely different phenomenon that put the town originally called Warm Springs (the name was changed to Hot Springs in 1886) on the map. At the turn of the 19th century, drovers from Kentucky and Tennessee began taking their herds of cattle, hogs, and horses to markets in South Carolina and Georgia. The most popular route ran from Greeneville, Tennessee, through Warm Springs, along the French Broad River, past what is now Asheville, and on to Greenville, South Carolina. In the fall months, a steady stream of livestock moved south along the French Broad. Estimates suggest that between 150,000 and 200,000 hogs were driven along the route every year.

In the early days, the drovers simply slept on the ground at night. But as the number of herds increased, stock stands—places where drovers could contain and feed their animals for the night and enjoy some rest and relaxation of their own—sprang up. It was not uncommon for 10 to 12 herds numbering from 300 to 1,000 or 2,000 animals apiece to stop overnight and feed at the stands. Each drove had an individual lot to itself. Wagons drove through the lots bearing 10 or 12 men who scattered enough corn to literally cover the ground. The facilities at the stock stands were little better than sleeping on the ground. There was usually a large room with an immense fireplace. The men were given a blanket or two each. They formed a semicircle, their feet to the fire, and slept on the bare floor. Several communities that grew up around stock stands will be pointed out on this tour.

The year 1828 saw the opening of the Buncombe Turnpike, a toll road that ran from Saluda Gap near the South Carolina line through Asheville and Warm Springs to the Tennessee line. It was a considerable improvement over the previous route. One description of conditions on the earlier road came from Bishop Asbury, who journeyed into this area in the autumn of 1800. "My roan horse . . . reeled and fell over, taking the chaise with him," he wrote. "I was called back, when I beheld the poor beast and the carriage, bottom up, lodged and wedged against a sapling, which alone prevented them both being precipitated into the river." Neither did the bishop write favorably of the people of Warm Springs: "My company was not agreeable here—there were too many subjects of the two great potentates of this Western World, whisky, brandy. My mind was greatly distressed."

The Buncombe Turnpike brought regular stagecoach traffic, as well as private carriages. In 1831, James Patton and his son John bought the drovers' stand in Warm Springs and began to upgrade its accommodations. The place burned in 1838, but the Pattons rebuilt. This time, they constructed a masterpiece. The principal structure was a 250-foot-long brick building. Two stories high, it had a piazza fronting the river studded with 13 columns 20 feet high, representing the original states. The hotel could accommodate 500 guests, and the dining room seated 240. A bar, a ballroom, a large stable, and the therapeutic baths were a few of the attractions.

Charles Lanman discussed the springs in his 1848 *Letters from the Alleghany Mountains.* "The water is clear as crystal, and so heavy that even a child may be thrown into it with little danger of being drowned," he wrote. "As a beverage, the water is quite palatable, and it is said that some people can drink a number of quarts per day, and yet experience none but beneficial effects. The diseases which it is thought to cure are palsy, rheumatism, and cutaneous affections.... The Warm Springs are annually visited by a large number of fashionable and sickly people from all the Southern States.... As a resort, especially for the latter part of summer, it has no superior in any State."

The hotel's brochure claimed that the waters could "bring bloom back to the cheek, the lustre to the eye, tone to the languid pulse, strength to the jaded nerves, and vigor to the wasted frame."

When the Civil War began in 1861, tourism in Warm Springs dropped considerably. In 1862, the hotel was purchased by James Rumbough, the operator of a stagecoach company that ran between Greeneville, Tennessee, and Greenville, South Carolina. Rumbough and his wife, Carrie, were Confederate sympathizers, and their move to Warm Springs was inspired by the uncomfortable conditions in Unionist Greeneville, Tennessee. The story is told that Rumbough was captured while in active service with the Confederates in 1865 and that Carrie, pregnant at the time, rode to Morristown, Tennessee, to beg for his release. She succeeded, and Rumbough returned to Warm Springs to operate the hotel. The property saw its golden years under his ownership.

In 1875, the Rumboughs' oldest daughter, Bessie, married Andrew Johnson Jr., son of the Unionist who became president of the United States after Abraham Lincoln's assassination. Though Bessie's father had been a Confederate colonel and her mother had burned the bridge in Warm Springs upon hearing of the approach of Union troops, no record exists of any objections to the marriage.

The following year, Rumbough's hotel received an unexpected and highly profitable endorsement from a popular novel. *"The Land of the Sky"; Or, Adventures in Mountain By-Ways* was a travel tale based on an actual excursion taken around 1874. Its author was Frances Christine Fisher Tiernan, writing under the nom de plume Christian Reid. Manly Wade Wellman described Reid's novel in *The Kingdom of Madison*: "In it, a socially elegant party visits the North Carolina mountains, exclaiming over the scenery and carrying on flirtatious exchanges in terms that ... seem cumbersomely self-conscious." Though it may be difficult to understand the popularity of *"The Land of the Sky"* today, Christian Reid's descriptions of Warm Springs and Rumbough's hotel brought guests flocking.

Rumbough used most of his profits to improve the hotel. He added a pair of three-story wings and hundreds of feet of porches. As many as 1,000 guests were frequently accommodated. By that time, 16 springs had been discovered, varying in temperature from 98 to 117 degrees. Guests could bathe in a shower of warm water, or they could choose an enclosed tile tub whose water was piped in from the springs. They could also use the large outdoor pool, where the water ran directly out of the springs. Hunting, horseback riding, fishing, hiking, billiards, bowling, tennis, carriage rides, and balls were other popular activities.

By January 1882, the Western North Carolina Railroad was completed all the way to Paint Rock outside Warm Springs. From there, the new line connected with the East Tennessee Railroad, which brought passengers from the Midwest. Thanks to the new means of transportation, business increased even more.

The hotel burned in 1884. Rumbough lacked the funds to rebuild, so he sold the property to a group of New York investors, who changed the name of the town to Hot Springs and built a new inn called the Mountain Park Hotel. Their resort had steam heat, electricity, and approximately a quarter-mile of broad porches enclosed by glass. It also boasted a modern bathhouse with 16 marble pools measuring nine feet by six feet each, with depths of up to six feet. The investors overextended themselves and were forced to sell to pay their bills. Rumbough bought the property back and took over the operation as before. In 1875, the first golf course in the Southeast was built on the grounds.

Upon the outbreak of World War I, business slowed at the Mountain Park Hotel. Rumbough negotiated with the federal government to house 2,700 officers and crew members of German merchant vessels captured in New York Harbor at the declaration of war. Although barbed wire was strung up around the hotel grounds, security was relatively relaxed, since the prisoners were noncombatants. Only one escaped; he reportedly wrote from New Mexico that things were better in Hot Springs. Tents were pitched for the enlisted men, while officers were housed in the hotel itself. The prisoners requested and were granted materials to build a more substantial community of shelters resembling the inn's chalet style. On Sunday afternoons, the band from the ship *Vadderland* gave concerts for the townspeople. When the armistice was announced, the band played all night. Most prisoners and townspeople had only fond memories of each other.

After the war, renovations were started on the hotel, only to be halted by another disastrous fire in 1920. The property passed through several owners but never regained its former grandeur. The last remaining part of the hotel burned in 1976. When a new interstate through the mountains was being discussed, locals had some hope of reviving the area as a resort. But the plans died when I-40 passed west of Hot Springs, leaving it off the beaten path. In recent years, the mineral baths have reopened. Although no resort hotel exists today, a campground is located across the street from the baths and cabins, and a small inn with suites is nearby.

Entering Hot Springs, N.C. 209 (Lance Avenue) merges with U.S. 25/70 to become Bridge Street. On the right at the corner of Lance Avenue and Walnut Street is a historical marker commemorating the work of musical scholar Cecil Sharp, who visited the area in 1916 to collect mountain folk songs. On the hill beside the marker is the former home of Jane Gentry, who supplied many of the songs Sharp collected.

Across from the marker, turn left and follow U.S. 25/70 (Bridge Street) as it

heads up the hill. At the top, you will pass a large stone monument whose inscription says it was built "in loving memory of Robert E. Lee." It also marks the route of the Dixie Highway, planned in 1914 as a "National Auto Trail" system that would connect the Midwest with the South. Constructed from 1915 to 1927, the trail was more a small network of paved roads than a single highway. In the late 1920s, the United Daughters of the Confederacy placed bronze plaques on granite pillars like this one to mark the route and honor Lee.

Behind the monument is a stately home constructed around 1902. In the 1950s, it became a Jesuit residence. By the 1970s, it was a retreat center. The Jesuit House of Prayer is still run for that purpose. The staff maintains the Hikers' Hostel, used frequently by hikers on the Appalachian Trail.

Follow U.S. 25/70 for 0.9 mile past the monument, then turn right onto Lookout Loop, a section of the old road that gives access to a home atop the high bluff overlooking the French Broad River Valley. The owners of the home were considerate enough to construct an overlook for those who wish to view the scenery.

In her book *The French Broad,* Wilma Dykeman explained how the river received its name. Some of the first white men to explore the region were long hunters, who spent extended periods in the wilderness on hunting expeditions. Those hunters named the river. Dykeman wrote,

> The rivers must have impressed them by their width for they named them First and Second and English Broad. And when at last a party of these trail break-

Monument to Dixie Highway and Robert E. Lee

Jesuit House of Prayer

ers climbed the Ridge and stood in a gap facing toward the unknown western land under control of France by way of the Mississippi, they looked at the new river they found in the valley just beyond the Blue Ridge and called it the French Broad. It flowed toward the lands and rivers owned by France; when a Long Hunter had gulped from a spring on the far side of the dividing mountains, he could say he had drunk of the French waters.

Retrace the route to Bridge Street and turn left. On the left in the first block is Dorland Memorial Presbyterian Church, built in 1900. Dr. Luke Dorland came to Hot Springs in 1887 and opened a school under the auspices of the Presbyterian Church. Many guests at the hotel contributed to the school, and its campus spread around the town. In 1918, the Dorland Institute merged with the Bell Institute, founded in nearby Jewel Hill. The Dorland-Bell Institute subsequently merged with the Asheville Farm School in 1942 to become Warren Wilson College, located in Swannanoa. Many of the buildings still standing in Hot Springs served as dormitories or classrooms for the original Dorland Institute.

At the post office, turn left onto Spring Street. It is approximately 100 yards to a gravel road leading to Mountain Magnolia Inn, a beautifully restored bed-and-breakfast. When this magnificent Italianate Victorian mansion was built in 1868 for James and Carrie Rumbough, the owners of Mountain Park Hotel, it was known as Rutland. The restored home has been featured in *Southern Living* and *This Old House* and is well worth a side trip.

Return to Bridge Street and continue across the railroad tracks. On the left between the tracks and the French Broad River is a large sign for Hot Springs Resort and Spa, located on the former site of the Mountain Park Hotel. The building at the end of

Dorland Memorial Presbyterian Church

the drive is where visitors can arrange mineral baths and/or spa treatments.

Continue across the bridge over the river. On the left is a historical marker for Paint Rock. Turn left just before the marker onto River Road, or Paint Rock Road (S.R. 1304). Circle back under the bridge. You will soon see signs for Nantahala Outdoor Center. Just past an area where rafters prepare to depart on the French Broad are signs for the Appalachian Trail and the Silvermine trailhead. The Silvermine Trail is a 1.6-mile loop that goes to an imposing rock bluff called Lover's Leap.

Retrace your route under the bridge. On the left is a sign noting that this route was part of the Buncombe Turnpike. Continue straight on River Road, following the signs to Paint Rock. The scenic road parallels the French Broad. In 3.3 miles, the pavement ends. It is 1.1 miles to Murray Branch Recreation Area, which has picnic tables, restrooms, viewing stands along the river, and a trailhead across the road for the 1.3-mile River Ridge Loop Trail.

Continue 2.2 miles alongside the French Broad to one of the area's best-known landmarks.

In 1799, a commission was appointed to establish the boundary between North Carolina and Tennessee once and for all. David Vance, Joseph McDowell, and Mussendine Matthews assembled at the Virginia border that May with surveyors James Strother and Robert Henry. The men worked their way south. Strother kept a daily journal that provides some of the best material available about early frontier life. On June 28, the men dropped a plumb line from the top of Paint

Hot Springs Resort

Rock and established its height as 107 feet, three inches. Strother reported that Paint Rock "rather projects out," and that "the face of the rock bears but few traces of its having formerly been painted, owing to its being smoked by pine knots and other wood from a place at its base where travellers have frequently camped. In the year 1790 it was not much smoked, the picture of some humans, wild beasts, fish and fowls were to be seen plainly made with red paint, some of them 20 and 30 feet from its base." Strother also put to rest the argument voiced by some Tennesseans that the "painted rock" referred to in the Act of Cession—the act by which North Carolina ceded its western land for the creation of a new

Paint Rock

state, as detailed in "The Mars Hill to Burnsville Tour"—was farther downstream. Strother wrote that Paint Rock "has, ever since the River F. Broad was explored by white men, been a place of Publick Notoriety."

Continue just past Paint Rock to where the pavement begins again. You are now in Tennessee and have gone from Pisgah National Forest into Cherokee National Forest. After rounding Paint Rock and crossing the creek, you will reach a fork. Take Lower Paint Creek Road (F.R. 41), to the right. For the next 5 miles, the paved one-lane road follows the creek. Several camping and picnic areas are along the way. You will also see numerous fishermen during trout season, since the creek is stocked. The road is also called "the Paint Creek Corridor." It follows the former Paint Mountain Turnpike, which 19th-century travelers used for their 14-hour journey between Asheville and Greeneville, Tennessee. During the early 1900s, the Patterson Lumber Company logged this area. The lumber company converted 4 miles of Paint Creek into flumes that carried logs to the French Broad River.

A picnic area and campground are located at the intersection with Hurricane Gap Road at the entrance to the corridor. Turn left and travel 1.7 miles to Rollins Chapel Road. Turn right and go 1.3 miles to the intersection with Asheville Highway (Tenn. 70). Turn right, heading back toward North Carolina. It is 3.3 miles to the state line, where the highway becomes N.C. 208 entering Madison County.

Continue 3.1 miles to a historical marker on the right. Early in the 19th century, a man named Allan kept a stand here where drovers could spend the night while driving their stock from Tennessee to the South Carolina and Georgia markets.

The historical marker notes the Frances Goodrich Home, located across the road. From 1879 to 1882, Frances Goodrich studied art and painting at the Yale School of Fine Arts, the first art school at an American university and the first part of Yale to admit women. She later went to New York to be an artist. Sometime in the late 1880s, she decided to change her focus to social service.

In 1890, Goodrich came to the region as an unpaid assistant to a teacher sent by the Presbyterian Church to educate and convert the mountain people. She

loved the nickname given to her by the locals—"the Woman Who Runs Things." Soon after arriving at Brittain's Cove, she organized a meeting of local women at "The Library," one of the small buildings she paid to have built. At one of these "mothers' meetings," as they were called, a local woman gave Goodrich a gift of a double-bowknot coverlet. She took the coverlet north to confirm what she suspected (that a large potential market existed for handmade quilts and coverlets). On a subsequent trip to Greeneville, Tennessee, to attend a presbytery meeting, Goodrich and her fellow travelers passed through Allanstand, named for the old drovers' station. She had heard that it was possible to identify the local folk by the distinctive homespun red clothes they wore. Here was evidence that the old-time weaving tradition was still alive.

Goodrich had been searching for a way to help the mountain people without injuring their pride. By the end of 1897, she opened a school and a cottage, which quickly needed to be expanded. There, she began supervising the making of quilts and coverlets by local women. The first exhibition of the crafts of the Cottage Industries Guild was held in 1899. By 1908, Goodrich's operation was called Allanstand Industries and had a shop in Asheville.

In 1931, to ensure that Allanstand would continue after her death, Goodrich gave her business to the recently formed Southern Mountain Handicraft Guild. The guild, still thriving today as the Southern Highland Craft Guild, sells its members' wares in several locations in the area.

It is 2.8 miles to where N.C. 208 intersects N.C. 212. A historical marker here commemorates the Shelton Laurel Massacre and notes that the graves of the victims are located 8 miles east. The story behind the event sheds light on why this section of Madison County was given the nickname "Bloody Madison" during the Civil War.

The communities near Laurel River and Laurel Creek are called Rich Laurel, Big Laurel, Little Laurel, Sodom Laurel, Wolf Laurel, and Shelton Laurel. They served as a center for Unionist activities. A shortage of salt in the winter of

1862–63 brought matters to a head. Shopkeepers in the town of Marshall tended to be Southern sympathizers. They frequently denied salt to Union supporters. In January 1863, some 50 armed men from Shelton Laurel traveled to Marshall and plundered the town's salt depot and stores.

A company under Confederate lieutenant colonel James Keith was dispatched to round up the culprits. Fifteen men and boys were captured on the first sweep. They were quartered in a cabin and denied food while the search continued. Another 13 suspected culprits were then captured. Thirteen of the 28 prisoners were subsequently marched to a field near Shelton Laurel Creek. They were ordered to their knees and told to pray, and then they were shot. Their bodies were thrown into a nearby sinkhole. Four women who had followed to see what happened to their loved ones protested. One of them was stripped bare and flogged. The other three were tied to trees with ropes around their necks.

The local militia leader wrote Zebulon Vance, the governor of North Carolina, that 12 "Tories" had been killed and another 20, including the four women, had been captured. Vance ordered his friend Augustus Merrimon, the solicitor for the Eighth Judicial District, to visit the scene and send him a report. Merrimon submitted a horrified account that read in part, "Such savage and barbarous cruelty is without a parallel in the State and I hope in every other." He charged that, without any semblance of a trial, Keith had ordered the captives to kneel and then shot them without warning. Merrimon also estimated that "probably eight of the thirteen" who were executed were not in the band of looters.

Ultimately, only four prisoners—not 20—were brought in alive. Governor Vance pronounced the incident "a horror disgraceful to civilization" and demanded that court-martial proceedings be brought against Keith. Others found it difficult to blame Keith for his reaction to the hot resistance he had encountered from snipers in Shelton Laurel. He was finally allowed to resign without facing a court-martial. The relatives of the slain swore revenge.

Turn right to stay on N.C. 208 for the next 3.5 miles. The route parallels Big Laurel Creek on the scenic drive to the intersection with U.S. 25/70. Here, too, you will see dozens of anglers along the creek during fishing season.

Turn left onto U.S. 25/70. It is approximately 4 miles to the turnoff for the community of Walnut.

During the days of the stock stands, this area was known as Jewel Hill. When a bill was introduced in 1850 to establish Madison County, disagreement arose over whether the county seat should be located at Jewel Hill or Lapland, another stock-stand community. While the dispute was being ironed out, court sessions were held in Jewel Hill.

Augustus Merrimon, the man later sent by Governor Vance to investigate the Shelton Laurel Massacre, was in those days a young attorney. He attended a court session in Jewel Hill in 1853 and recorded his observations in his diary. The son of a Methodist minister, Merrimon was a bit shocked by what he saw. He recorded that Judge David T. Caldwell "opened court in a verry [sic] bad house—open without seats fit to sit in and without any place to do business. . . . Some twenty or thirty women were present and most of them drunk, or partially so, and the majority of the men were drunk.—I do not know any rival of this place in regard to drunkenness, ignorance, superstition and the most brutal debauchery." The next day, he further noted that he had seldom seen "such a drunken crowd. . . . As I passed along to my lodgins [sic] I saw several persons so drunk they could not walk, and their friends were dragging them along to their homes."

Merrimon returned in 1854 and found that things had not improved. "Women sell themselves to prostitution of the basest character not infrequently for whisky," he lamented. "O wretched state of morals." Jewel Hill was obviously not one of Merrimon's favorite stops on the judicial circuit.

Two popular stock stands near Jewel Hill have frequently been cited as the location of a notorious robbery-murder conspiracy. Some tales say that Sam Chunn's tavern was the site, while others lay the burden on William Barnett's stand. The story goes that a drover staying at a stock stand overheard screams during the night—screams that, the next morning, the owners of the establishment denied having heard. Shortly after continuing on his journey, the drover was ambushed by a man with a blackened face. The drover killed his attacker and ran to the tavern to report what had happened. When he announced the news to the owner's wife, she screamed that he had killed her husband. She then fled, never to be seen again. An investigation discovered that the couple had been ambushing travelers and killing boarders, then robbing them and disposing of their bodies down a long chute that ran from an upstairs room in the inn to the French Broad.

The version centered around Barnett's stock stand says that the drover began to suspect something was up when the tavern owner showed him to his room and locked the door behind him. The drover saw blood on the floor and discovered a body under his bed. He placed the body in the bed and hid behind the door when the murderers came in later that night. He escaped while they were committing on the hapless corpse the crime intended for him. By the time the drover returned with help, the tavern owners had fled. It was then that searchers discovered the chute to the river.

The story of the murderous innkeeper is an archetypal gothic tale known around the world. Truth be told, Sam Chunn and William Barnett both died of natural causes, and their establishments were reputable places during their lifetimes. Chunn served in the North Carolina General Assembly in 1846. His tavern operated profitably until 1904. Barnett sold his stand in 1857 and lived in Madison County until his death in 1863. Neither man fit the description of the murderous innkeeper. Still, the legend persists.

Approximately 5 miles past the turnoff to Walnut, turn onto U.S. 25/70 Business and head into Marshall. Formerly known as Lapland, the town was Jewel Hill's rival for the distinction of becoming the county seat of Madison County. Marshall won the dispute after an election in 1855. Wilbur Zeigler and Ben Grosscup described the town in *The Heart of the Alleghanies*:

> Its situation is decidedly Alpine in character. Its growth is stunted in a most emphatic manner by these apparently soulless conspirators—the river, mountain and railroad. The three seem to have joined hands in a determination regarding the village which might read well this way: "So large shalt thou grow, and no larger!" It is sung by the river, roared by the train and echoed by the mountain. . . . Such a location is unfavorable for a man whose gait is unsteady; for a chance mis-step might precipitate him out of his front yard, with a broken neck.

In the Work Projects Administration's *North Carolina: A Guide to the Old North State*, Marshall was depicted as "one mile long, one street wide, and sky high." It hasn't changed much since that description was written in 1939. Local folklorist John Parris reported that the town was so geographically confined that cobblers found it impossible to stretch their thread to arm's length, so they were forced to use wooden pegs in their shoes instead of sewn soles. Indeed, there is so little space in Marshall between the mountains and the French Broad that the local high school was built on Blannahassett (also spelled Blennerhassett and various other ways) Island in the middle of the river. Today, the structure serves as a community arts center. In 2008, it won an award for historic preservation.

David Vance was the father of North Carolina governor Zebulon Vance and the brother of the former congressman killed in the famous duel described in "The Overmountain Victory Trail Tour." During the days of the stock drives, Vance kept

Marshall

a tavern at the upper end of Marshall that was reportedly 150 feet long. It is said that he fed 90,000 hogs during one month in 1826. Hezekiah Barnard, another proprietor, claimed to have fed 110,000 hogs over the same period. A historical marker in front of the Madison County Courthouse indicates that Vance's stand was located a few yards east. The courthouse was designed by Englishman Richard Sharp Smith, the resident architect at the Biltmore House and the designer of Biltmore Village.

Continue approximately 2 miles on U.S. 25/70 Business from the courthouse to the Ivy River bridge. Follow N.C. 251 instead of continuing on U.S. 25/70, which turns left. The route parallels the French Broad River. In his 1859 book, *Mountain Scenery*, Henry Colton quoted from a *Southern Quarterly Review* article that described a trip along a similar course: "In the vague and misty twilight the first flashings of the foaming torrent rose in sight; and, as the opposite shores could not be distinguished at that early hour, and in consequence of the heavy mist which overhung them, the illusion was perfect which persuaded us that we were once more on the borders of the great Atlantic Sea." Several roadside picnic areas maintained by Buncombe County offer similar views.

It is 9.8 miles from the Ivy River bridge to Ledges Whitewater River Park, where the water breaking over the rock ledges resembles whitecaps on an ocean. This is a choice spot for a picnic. The park serves as an access area for boaters on the French Broad River.

After another 4 miles, you will pass the large compound of Pace Analytical Services, on the left. On the right is Riverside Business Park. Turn left across from the business park onto Elk Mountain Road heading into Woodfin. Continue to the intersection with U.S. 19/23, which is also U.S. 70 and I-26. This ends the tour. A left turn leads north to Mars Hill and on to Tennessee. A right turn leads south into Asheville.

Madison County Courthouse in Marshall

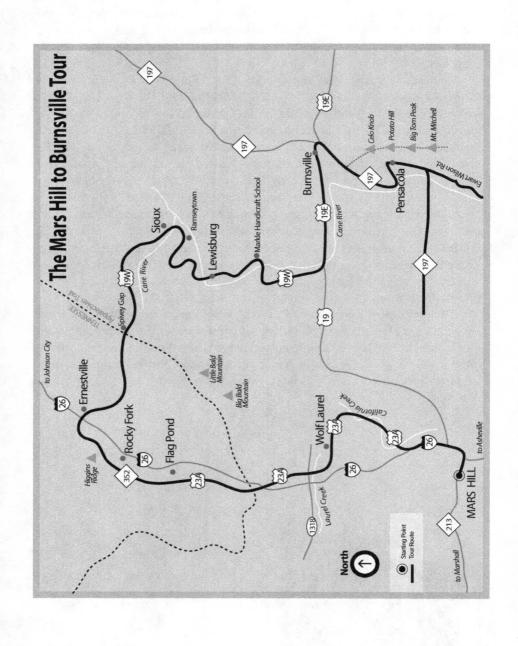

TOUR 13
The Mars Hill to Burnsville Tour

This tour begins in Mars Hill, goes over Sam's Gap to Flag Pond in Tennessee, then proceeds to Ernestville, where it turns south to travel through Spivey Gap. It then follows the Cane River into Burnsville. An optional side trip goes to Pensacola to the old Big Tom Wilson Motor Road near Mount Mitchell.

Total mileage: approximately 90 miles

The tour begins at Exit 11 off I-26/U.S. 19/23 leading to the town of Mars Hill. Take N.C. 213 (Carl Eller Road, which becomes Cascade Street) to the downtown area and the campus of Mars Hill College.

The life of this community has always centered around Mars Hill College, a Baptist liberal-arts school founded in 1856. In 2006, the 20 original buildings on campus joined the National Register of Historic Places as the Mars Hill College Historic District. Founders Hall, built in 1892, is the oldest academic building in western North Carolina.

Local landowner Edward Carter wanted his children educated and instructed in the Baptist Church, so he began the school as the French Broad Baptist Institute. (The name was changed in 1859.) Upon the completion of the first building on campus, local fundraisers found themselves $1,100 short of the needed sum. The sheriff supposedly seized a man called Old Joe, the slave of one of the trustees, J. W. Anderson. Joe was held as security until the debt was paid. The required funds were subsequently raised. A street at the bottom of Cascade Street that was formerly known as Dormitory Drive was renamed Joe Anderson Drive. It leads to Joe's grave-site memorial.

On Cascade Street in front of Cornwell Hall is a historical marker noting that Bascom Lamar Lunsford, "the minstrel of Appalachia," was born here. Lunsford collected hundreds of folk songs for the Library of Congress. In 1928, he organized

*Campus of
Mars Hill College*

the Mountain Dance and Folk Festival in Asheville, which gave him the platform to showcase the Southern style of buck dancing, also known as clogging. It survives as one of the oldest folk festivals in the United States. Lunsford himself buckdanced for such luminaries as Franklin Roosevelt and King George VI and Queen Elizabeth.

Return to I-26/U.S. 19/23 and turn north on the four-lane. Take the next exit, Exit 9. Turn right at the end of the ramp, then take an immediate left onto U.S. 23-A North (California Creek Road). After 2.8 miles, you will see a distinctive church on the right. This church, added to the National Register in 1984, has undergone several incarnations ranging from a restaurant to a wedding venue.

You are now traveling through the valley created by California Creek. The route passes through or near several communities with the word *laurel* in their names—Upper Laurel, Wolf Laurel, Bright Hope Laurel. The name comes from Laurel Creek, which flows through the area.

A little over 4 miles from the historic church, a large sign indicates a turn onto Laurel Valley Road to reach Wolf Ridge Ski Resort. It is another 1.4 miles to Little Creek Road, which leads through the territory of the Union sympathizers involved in the Shelton Laurel Massacre, described in "The Haywood to Madison Tour."

Church on California Creek

Continue on U.S. 23-A. Just past Little Creek, the road begins to climb dramatically until it reaches the crest at Sam's Gap, elevation 3,760 feet. You will see a parking area on the left just before U.S. 23-A goes under I-26. This area is frequently used by hikers on the Appalachian Trail, the longest continuous marked trail in the world. The trail extends from Mount Katahdin in northern Maine to Springer Mountain in Georgia, the southern terminus of the Blue Ridge Mountains. For 2,000 miles, it winds through the most scenic areas in the eastern United States, crossing privately and publicly owned lands that include eight national forests, two national parks, and numerous state parks.

One popular trek from Sam's Gap is the 6.5-mile hike to Big Bald Mountain, elevation 5,516 feet. Big Bald Mountain was also known as Greer's Bald because it was once home to an interesting character named David Greer. Greer came to the mountains in 1798 and worked for David Vance, who had a farm near what is now Weaverville. Vance was the grandfather of Zebulon Vance, governor of North Carolina during the Civil War. Greer fell in love with David Vance's daughter, but his affections were not returned. Some believe that being spurned left Greer crazed. In any event, he fled to the wilderness and the summit of Big Bald Mountain in 1802. He converted a cave into living quarters and remained undisturbed until the appearance of settlers.

An educated man, Greer declared himself the sovereign of *his* mountain. He wrote his own articles of government, along with a code of laws that postulated that every man had the right to take executive power into his own hands. He also wrote a tract on his religious views that revealed him to be a deist. Unfortunately, his notebooks were lost several years ago in a house fire.

One story about Greer centers on the time the sheriff of Burke County climbed Big Bald Mountain to collect an unpaid tax. When Greer refused to pay, he was summoned to court. He appeared with a loaded gun and ordered the judge, the sheriff, and others outside while he proceeded to break all the windows in the courthouse. The case was eventually dropped because it was decided Greer lived in Tennessee, not North Carolina.

He frequently shot at people who ventured into his domain and mutilated cattle that grazed on his land. In a quarrel with a neighbor named Holland Higgins over the ownership of a cherry orchard, Greer ambushed and killed Higgins while the latter was on his way to Jonesborough, Tennessee, to check his claim. Brought to trial, Greer was acquitted on the grounds that he was insane. He was so incensed at being judged insane that he published a pamphlet defending his action and sold it to anyone he could interest in his side of the story.

In 1834, he took some farming tools to the blacksmith shop of George Tompkins for repairs. Unfortunately, the tools were not ready upon Greer's return to the shop, and he grew furious. When Greer left, Tompkins's other customers warned the blacksmith that he had just signed his death warrant, as Greer had been seen building a blind in the bushes outside the shop. The customers took a gun, put Tompkins's hat on it, and stuck it out the door. When the hat flew across the shop with a bullet hole in it, Tompkins was convinced. Assuming he had killed Tompkins, Greer left his blind and headed up the road. Tompkins seized the opportunity and shot him in the back. No one ever complained that Tompkins wasn't brought to trial. Greer's 32-year reign of terror had come to an end.

For years, hundreds of small mounds of earth dotted the top of Big Bald. Inside were rocks—anywhere from a single large one to several small, round ones. Scientific studies attempted to explain the phenomenon, but the best story involves Greer, sometimes called "Hog Greer"—behind his back, undoubtedly—because he raised hogs and lived like one, too. At any rate, terrified neighbors spread the story that after planting several potato hills, Hog Greer discovered stones, not potatoes, inside them at digging time. Regardless of whether a deity seeking justice or neighbors seeking revenge were behind the stones, local people took to calling the mounds "Greer's Potato Hills."

After passing under I-26, continue on U.S. 23-A as it begins a dramatic descent through dozens of switchbacks into Tennessee; the road is called Flag Pond Road. It is 5.5 miles to the community of Flag Pond. Continue 2.2 miles to an intersection with Tenn. 352 as the road crosses South Indian Creek. Turn right onto Tenn. 352 East and cross Rocky Fork Creek. You are paralleling South Indian Creek. The tall peaks on the left comprise Higgins Ridge. This area was once part of the short-lived State of Franklin.

In 1784, North Carolina ceded its western lands (which now constitute the state of Tennessee) to the federal government, an action repealed later that same year. Many settlers in the ceded area were dissatisfied with the shoddy military protection they received and with the inconvenience of traveling long distances over the mountains to resolve judicial matters. They met in what is now Jonesborough, Tennessee, organized their own state, Franklin, and elected John Sevier their first governor. Political infighting led to the state's collapse in 1787. By 1790, North Carolina was prepared to cede its western lands again. The region was finally admitted to the union as Tennessee in 1796.

During that chaotic time, area settlers were having trouble with the Cherokee and Chickamauga Indians. In January 1789, Sevier learned that a large body of warriors was gathered at Flint Ridge and that they planned to venture forth in small groups to raid isolated cabins and settlements. Sevier gathered a force and marched up South Indian Creek, while another force entered the opposite side of the gorge from Devil's Fork Creek.

Sevier's official report to the privy council of the State of Franklin gave insight into the frontiersmen's side of the battle: "Our loss is very inconsiderable; it consists of five dead, and 16 wounded; amongst the latter is the brave Gen. M'Carter, who, while taking off the scalp of an Indian, was tomahawked by another whom he afterward killed with his own hand. I am in hopes this brave and good man will survive. . . . We suffer most for the want of whiskey." The battle proved one of the last engagements with Indians in the area. It occurred near the community of Rocky Fork.

It is almost 5 miles to Ernestville, located just past where the road crosses under I-26 again. Granny Lewis Creek is about a mile from Ernestville. In 1793, the Lewis family was the victim of a bizarre turn of events. According to historian Pat Alderman, the Cherokees meant to destroy John Sevier's family. They sent out three bands of braves on a mission. One band of 28 mistakenly found the isolated property of William Lewis, whose cabin and barn were located on South Indian

Creek near the mouth of Granny Lewis Creek. Lewis was away from home when his family was attacked. His wife and five of his children were killed. One son managed to escape to report the massacre. One daughter was taken captive. Folklore says Lewis tracked the Indians down and exchanged a gun for his daughter.

This region was also home to a colorful character named Kan (short for Kennedy) Foster. At one time or another, Kan owned most of the land in the area. He and his first wife, Mary, owned 5,000 acres along Spivey and Coffee ridges. When Mary died, Kan divided his land among his nine children and moved to Higgins Ridge. When he married a second wife, they

Illustration of Kan Foster from Harper's New Monthly Magazine

settled in the Devil's Creek section near the mouth of Granny Lewis Creek and raised seven more children.

Kan Foster was immortalized in a totally unexpected way. In January 1858, an illustration of him appeared in *Harper's New Monthly Magazine*. The image is often used when anyone wants an old-fashioned etching of an early mountain man. David Strother, the chief illustrator for *Harper's New Monthly*, was on a field trip, sketching for some writers preparing stories about the Southern mountains. Coming down the Tennessee side of Big Bald Mountain, Strother and his party lost their way—and their horses. Luckily, they stumbled upon Kan's home, then located near Spivey Creek. Kan and his oldest son spent the following day finding and returning the horses. While father and son were searching for the horses,

Illustration of David Strother's mountainside tumble from Harper's New Monthly Magazine

Strother sketched Kan's family, water mill, and neighbors. Later, he sketched Kan himself. Strother also sketched the adventure of tumbling down the mountainside the day before. That sketch, too, has been reproduced many times.

At Ernestville, turn right onto U.S. 19W South. The road follows Spivey Creek on the climb to Spivey Gap, elevation 3,252 feet. It is 4.3 miles from Ernestville to a primitive turnout that offers a view of an impressive waterfall, then 2.1 miles from the waterfall to the Tennessee–North Carolina line. Continue a mile farther to Spivey Gap Recreation Area, located 0.25 mile north of another intersection with the Appalachian Trail. From the recreation area, the road descends quickly, paralleling Big Creek. It is 5.1 miles to the community of Sioux, where several white clapboard storefronts are close to the highway.

Approximately 0.8 mile beyond Sioux, Big Creek flows into the Cane River, which the route will parallel for the next 15 miles as it passes through the communities of Ramseytown, Egypt, Lewisburg, and Higgins. From the bridge where the route begins following Cane River, it is 6.3 miles to where it crosses another bridge and turns left, following the river as it bends.

In her 1913 book, *The Carolina Mountains*, Margaret Morley described the valley: "There is no more romantically beautiful valley in the mountains than that of Cane River, which, in its upper part, is over three thousand feet high, and nowhere falls below twenty-five hundred feet. . . . From it one sees round-pointed mountains delightfully grouped in the landscape, and quaint houses placed in a superb setting of mountains and streams." The river was supposedly named for the heavy canebrakes in places along its banks. The canes were used for fishing poles, pipestems, and reeds for looms. One interesting feature of the valley is the large number of footbridges that span the river, connecting the houses with the highway.

Site of the Markle Handicraft School

It is 2.9 miles to some distinctive stone buildings on the left in the community of Higgins. The buildings were once the site of the Markle Handicraft School, which was established to preserve traditional native crafts. The school was funded by the John and Mary R. Markle Foundation, formed in 1927 by John Markle, a retired mining engineer who had made his fortune in coal. He and his wife had no children, so the bulk of their fortune went to the foundation. When he died in 1933, Markle endowed $15 million in grants to "promote the general good of mankind." The school was overseen by the Presbyterian Church and was a member of the Southern Highland Craft Guild. When the foundation changed its focus, the project was abandoned.

Continue 5.8 miles to where U.S. 19W ends. Turn left and head toward Burnsville on Old U.S. 19E for 2.1 miles to where it ends at U.S. 19E. Turn left and travel 3.2 miles to a stoplight just past a McDonald's. Turn left onto South Main Street and travel one block to the town square in the center of Burnsville.

Except for the courthouse, the scene has changed little since Charles Dudley Warner described it in his 1888 book, *On Horseback*: "Burnsville is not only mildly picturesque, but very pleasing. . . . [It] is more like a New England village than any hitherto seen. Most of the houses stand about a square, which contains a shabby court-house; around it are two small churches, a jail, an inviting tavern, with a long veranda, and a couple of stores. . . . The elevation of Burnsville gives it a delightful summer climate, the gentle undulations of the country are agreeable, the views noble, the air is good and it is altogether a 'liveable' and attractive place."

The shabby courthouse was replaced by a 1908 building that now houses the police department. An attractive Neocolonial structure built in 1965 serves as the courthouse today. The inviting tavern is now the well-known Nu-Wray Inn. Con-

Burnsville town square with statue of Otway Burns

structed in 1833, the same year Yancey County was formed, the inn is one of the oldest in the region.

An addition to the town square since Warner's visit is a statue of Otway Burns, the man for whom the town is named. Burns won fame in the War of 1812 by building one of the fastest sailing vessels of the time, the *Snap Dragon*. With his ship's speed and his extensive knowledge of the North Carolina coast, Burns set out to capture and destroy English vessels. Atop his home in Beaufort, he built an observatory that commanded an extensive view of the ocean. Lookouts notified the crew of the *Snap Dragon* whenever English ships were in sight of the coast.

Burns caused so much damage that the British offered £50,000 for him, dead or alive. They even went so far as to construct a special vessel to capture him. The *Snap Dragon* was finally taken in 1814, but Burns, shore-bound that particular voyage due to a bout of rheumatism, escaped.

Statue of Otway Burns

His life after the War of 1812 proved unexciting by comparison. He managed to spend most of the fortune he had amassed during the war. While serving in the North Carolina legislature, he cast the tie-breaking vote that led to the creation of Yancey County. He was rewarded when the county seat was named for him.

Later, his friend Andrew Jackson appointed him keeper of the Brant Island Shoal Light, where Burns "sank into his anecdotage, fond of his bright naval uniform, his cocked hat, good whiskey, and a good fight," according to the Work Projects Administration's *North Carolina: A Guide to the Old North State*. The cocked hat is a notable feature of the statue standing in the Burnsville town square. It gives the statue an unusual look. A story is told that a visitor at the unveiling remarked, "I didn't know he was an Indian."

According to court reports, Yancey County's early days were wild and woolly. Many blamed the easy availability of mountain moonshine for the full docket of cases involving drinking, fighting, and murder. Today, the area is attractive to tourists because of its 18 peaks above 6,300 feet. The most famous is Mount Mitchell, at 6,684 feet the highest peak east of the Black Hills of South Dakota.

Before leaving the downtown area, stop by the Yancey County Chamber of Commerce, located one block off the square on West Main Street—yes, the four streets leading off the square are all named Main Street. If you plan to take the

Pensacola side trip later in this tour, stop at the chamber to ask about the current status of the Ray Mine.

As you travel many of the counties in western North Carolina, you will observe colorful quilt blocks painted on the sides of barns, houses, and even some franchise restaurants. Early in 2007, the Toe River Arts Council was inspired by projects in neighboring states that combined the artwork of quilt patterns with trails through the local scenery. That year, the council, with support from Handmade in America and the Blue Ridge Heritage Area, launched the creation of a series of paintings of individual quilt-square designs. The project started in Yancey and Mitchell counties, where you will see the greatest rep-

Quilt square on Yancey County barn

resentation, though quilt blocks are also displayed in several other mountain counties. Since the program's inception, visitors have taken to the trails as an excuse for driving the countryside. The occupants or owners of the buildings where the quilt squares are placed select the prints. Each selection is linked to a story. A pattern might be part of a beloved family quilt, or it might be just an artistic favorite. The chamber of commerce houses a gift shop devoted to the quilt trails. There, you can view and/or purchase maps of different tours.

You can either end the tour here or add a side trip that travels along the backside of the Black Mountains. If you decide to continue, head east on U.S. 19E for approximately 1 mile from the Burnsville town square. Turn right onto N.C. 197, heading south. After 0.8 mile on N.C. 197, turn left onto Bolens (or Bowlens) Creek Road. Travel 1.3 miles and turn left onto Ray Mine Road just before Bowlens Creek Church. Park at the end of the road and follow the trail for an easy 0.5-mile hike to the former mica mine.

In recent years, the forest service threatened to close this site for safety reasons and to protect the threatened bats that live in the deserted mine shafts. Following an outcry from rock-hunting enthusiasts, the two sides found a compromise. Three of the four shafts will be filled in, the fourth will have a grate over the entrance to allow the bats to remain undisturbed, and a specific area away from the creek will be designated for those who wish to search for minerals. Please obey the restrictions so the area can remain open, the creek bed can be saved from destruction, and the bats can survive. For more about the Ray Mine, see "The Overmountain Victory Trail Tour."

Return to N.C. 197 to continue the side trip. The scenic route follows the Cane River for 8.4 miles to the community of Pensacola. Another 1.5 miles along the river through a valley rimmed with steep peaks leads to a place where N.C. 197 makes a right-angle turn. Instead of turning right, continue straight on S.R. 1100 (Ewart Wilson Road), which follows the same course along the river as Big Tom Wilson Motor Road in the 1920s and 1930s.

It is believed that in 1789, French botanist André Michaux became the first white man to set foot in the Black Mountains. But it was not until Dr. Elisha Mitchell arrived in 1827 that anyone had much of an idea how tall the Blacks really were.

Dr. Mitchell became a professor at the University of North Carolina in 1818. In those days, the university had only three faculty members and 92 students. Mitchell's initial appointment was in mathematics and natural philosophy, a discipline that included botany, zoology, and some of the physical sciences. He later took the university's other science professorship in chemistry, geology, and mineralogy. Mitchell also acted as bursar for the university and superintendent of its buildings and grounds. An ordained Presbyterian minister, he even preached regularly. Mitchell was a well-rounded individual, to say the least.

In 1825, he took charge of the North Carolina Geological Survey, the first statewide survey in the nation. In the course of fulfilling his duties, he made his first visits to the western part of the state. In an 1829 geological report, Mitchell stated his belief that the Black Mountains contained the highest land between the Gulf of Mexico and the White Mountains of New Hampshire. He returned to the Blacks in 1835 to take measurements. The first peak he climbed was Celo Knob, elevation 5,946 feet. There, he noted "peaks considerably more elevated farther South." Mitchell took measurements of barometric pressure and temperature and compared them to measurements taken at his base in Morganton. He then used a formula to determine that the peak that later became known as Mount Mitchell stood 6,476 feet above sea level. He proclaimed it "the Highest Peak of the Black."

Mitchell returned to Chapel Hill and made his revelations public in a lengthy article that appeared in the *Raleigh Register* on November 3, 1835. "The Black Mountain [range]," he noted, "has some Peaks of greater elevation than any point that has hitherto been measured in North-America, East of the Rocky Mountains, and is believed to be the highest Mountain in the United States." Mount Mitchell turned out to be 208 feet higher than Mitchell's figure. Had he correctly measured Morganton's elevation, he would have missed by only six feet.

He returned in 1844 to try to erase the doubts in his mind that he had actually found the highest peak in the chain. General Thomas L. Clingman, a member of Congress and a man of scientific tastes, was taking measurements in the area at that same time. Clingman published a statement claiming that he had found a peak higher than the one measured by Mitchell. Though it was agreed that the peak Clingman measured was the highest, controversy lingered as to whether that peak might be the same one measured previously by Mitchell.

Dr. Mitchell returned again in 1857 to settle the matter. He set out alone. He was scheduled to meet with his son during the course of his travels, and when he failed to do so, a search party was organized. Ten days later, the frustrated group enlisted the aid of Big Tom Wilson, a legendary hunter and tracker who lived in the Cane River area at the foot of the Blacks. Charles Dudley Warner described Big Tom Wilson as "six feet and two inches tall, very spare and muscular, with sandy hair, long gray beard, and honest blue eyes. He has a reputation for great strength and endurance; a man of native simplicity and mild manners."

The searchers eventually agreed to let Wilson take the lead. Following seemingly invisible clues—broken limbs and faint impressions in the earth—Big Tom brought the group to a 50-foot waterfall. There, in a pool at the foot, was the perfectly preserved body of Dr. Mitchell. It was surmised that he must have become lost in the fog and plummeted over the falls while following the stream. His body was buried in Asheville and later moved to the top of the peak that now bears his name.

Big Tom Wilson's tracking ability was soon known far and wide. By the time he retired from bear hunting several years later, Big Tom supposedly had 113 black bears to his credit. Upon visiting Big Tom, Warner wrote, "His backwoods figure loomed larger and larger in our imagination, and he seemed strangely familiar. At length it came over us where we had met him before. It was in Cooper's novels. He was the Leather-Stocking exactly. And yet he was an original; for he assured us that he had never read the Leather-Stocking Tales."

Warner was so impressed with Wilson that he couldn't resist investigating what tales Big Tom might tell from his Civil War days. "What a figure, I was thinking, he must have made in the late war! Such a shot, such a splendid physique, such iron endurance! . . . Yes, he was in the war, he was sixteen months in the Confederate army, this Homeric man. In what rank? 'Oh, I was a fifer'!"

Another story is told of Big Tom's eloquence at a banquet in Asheville given in his honor after his retirement. When asked to say a few words, Big Tom remarked, "I'm glad I seed you, because if I hadn't seed you I wouldn't have knowed you."

Wilson was hired by K. M. and David Murchison to watch for game poachers and keep foraging cattle off the 13,000 acres they owned—a tract known as the Murchison Boundary, which included most of Mount Mitchell. Wilson raised 10 children on the land and became so revered throughout the area that the government designated his home territory on the Cane River as "Big Tom Wilson's" on topographical maps. In 1946, a nearby peak only 77 feet shorter than Mount Mitchell was officially named Big Tom.

Tourists discovered Mount Mitchell in the early 1850s. Accommodations were built on and near the mountain. Most visitors approached the peak from the southern slope. In 1915, the Perley and Crockett Logging Company adapted its logging railroad to provide passenger service to the top of Mount Mitchell. Despite the popularity of the service, the company halted the operation in 1919 to devote the railroad exclusively to removing timber. In 1922, Perley and Crockett terminated its logging. The tracks were taken up, and the grade was realigned to create the toll road known as the Mount Mitchell Motor Road.

Not to be outdone, Ewart Wilson, Big Tom's grandson, constructed another

B. B. Wilson store in Pensacola

toll road along one of the logging-railroad grades on the Cane River side of the Blacks. Completed in 1925, it was named Big Tom Wilson Motor Road. Since it hooked into the Mount Mitchell Motor Road, motorists could take both roads and make a complete loop through Burnsville and Mars Hill back to Asheville.

When the local section of the Blue Ridge Parkway opened in 1939, the state of North Carolina fulfilled its promise to keep roads free of tolls by taking over the Mount Mitchell Motor Road. As a consequence, the continued operation of Big Tom Wilson Motor Road was not economically feasible. The road no longer exists, though travelers can drive the old route for 1.5 miles along the river on S.R. 1100. At that point, state maintenance ends and the road becomes private property.

Big Tom's family continued to operate Camp Wilson at the entrance to Mount Mitchell State Park until 1960. Park officials considered the camp an eyesore and finally acquired its land in 1962. But Tom Wilson's legacy lives on in area landmarks. For more about Mount Mitchell, see "The Overmountain Victory Trail Tour."

Historically, logging has been an important industry in the Black Mountains. The Murchison Lumber Company (also known as the Brown Brothers Lumber Company) was headquartered in nearby Eskota, while the Carolina Spruce Company had a 5,200-acre tract with headquarters in Pensacola. Logging operations boomed during World War I. When the labor shortage grew critical, about 400 Italian and Austrian workers were brought into the Cane River Valley. Pensacola grew into a thriving community, complete with a department store, a grocery store, a hardware store, a drugstore, a feed-and-seed store, and a barbershop. It even had a makeshift theater where movies were shown every Friday and Saturday night. Business decreased after the war, and the railroad tracks between Eskota and Burnsville were finally removed in 1933.

After touring Big Tom Wilson's former domain, retrace your route to U.S. 19E outside Burnsville. You can turn left on U.S. 19E for a 13-mile drive to I-26/U.S. 19/23 near Mars Hill. The interstate leads 20 miles south to Asheville or 30 miles north to Johnson City, Tennessee.

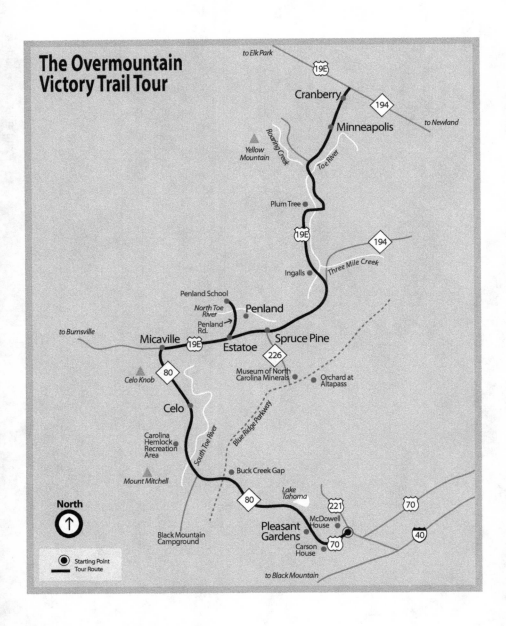

The Overmountain Victory Trail Tour

to Elk Park

19E

Cranberry

194

Minneapolis

to Newland

Roaring Creek

Yellow Mountain

Toe River

Plum Tree

19E

194

Ingalls

Three Mile Creek

Penland School

North Toe River

Penland

Penland Rd.

Spruce Pine

to Burnsville

Micaville

19E

Estatoe

226

Celo Knob

80

Museum of North Carolina Minerals

Orchard at Altapass

Celo

Blue Ridge Parkway

Carolina Hemlock Recreation Area

South Toe River

Mount Mitchell

Buck Creek Gap

Lake Tahoma

80

221

70

McDowell House

Black Mountain Campground

Pleasant Gardens

Carson House

70

40

to Black Mountain

North

Starting Point
Tour Route

TOUR 14

The Overmountain Victory Trail Tour

This tour begins at Pleasant Gardens near Marion, the county seat of McDowell County. It follows Buck Creek to the Blue Ridge Parkway near Mount Mitchell, then follows the Toe River to Micaville. It visits the Penland School of Crafts, travels to Spruce Pine, and picks up the Overmountain Victory National Historic Trail through Plum Tree, Minneapolis, and Cranberry in Avery County.

Total mileage: approximately 87 miles

To begin the tour, take Exit 85 off I-40 onto U.S. 221 North near Marion. After driving 1.7 miles, turn left onto U.S. 221 North/N.C. 226. After 5.3 miles, turn left at the stoplight onto U.S. 70.

One of the earliest white settlers in what is now McDowell County was Hunting John McDowell. It is believed McDowell came to the area in the 1760s and earned his nickname because of his considerable prowess as a hunter. In *Reminiscences and Memoirs of North Carolina and Eminent North Carolinians*, John H. Wheeler described Hunting John McDowell this way: "To a late period of his life, he could be seen on his way to the mountains, with four large bear traps tied behind him on his horse, with his trusty rifle on his shoulder. On these excursions he would go alone, and be absent for a month or more."

McDowell purchased land near the Catawba River and named his tract Pleasant Gardens. He also found time to marry and raise four children. One of his sons, Joseph, became a Revolutionary War hero for his leadership during a skirmish at Cowan's Ford on Cane Creek in what is now McDowell County and for his roles at the Battles of Kings Mountain and Cowpens. When McDowell County was formed in 1843, the citizens chose to honor their hero by naming the new county after him.

Colonel Joseph McDowell constructed the stately white frame McDowell

McDowell House

House, located on the right as you turn onto U.S. 70 at the stoplight. This area is heavily commercialized, but you should be able to pick out the home. The McDowell House was built in the 1780s of hand-hewn beams and lumber and of bricks that were probably made by slaves in the kiln near the home. It has seen better days, but its former grandeur is still apparent.

In 1780, American forces were not doing well in the battle to gain independence from Britain. Major Patrick Ferguson, commander of the British forces in the South, was convinced that the rebellion in his territory could be quickly squelched. That's where he made his big mistake. Ferguson sent word to Colonel Isaac Shelby, one of the American commanders in the area, that if Shelby and his fellow leaders "did not desist from their opposition to the British Arms," he would march his army over the mountains, "hang their leaders, and lay waste to the country with fire and sword."

Shelby relayed Ferguson's sentiments to John Sevier in what is now Tennessee, William Campbell in Virginia, and Benjamin Cleveland in the Watauga settlements. In September, those leaders rendezvoused for a battle against Ferguson. Since the majority of the 2,000 men who marched to the battle site came across the mountains, they became known as "the Overmountain Men." Their victory at Kings Mountain proved a turning point in the war. Ironically, Major Ferguson, who had promised to hang the leaders of the rebellious forces, was killed in the battle.

In September and October 1975, several hundred participants retraced the route across the mountains as part of the nation's bicentennial celebration. It was christened the Overmountain Victory National Historic Trail. Although this tour travels in the direction opposite that taken by the Overmountain Men, its second half follows much of the route of Sevier's men, who marched from Sycamore Shoals, Tennessee. Since Colonel Joseph McDowell led troops from Burke and Rutherford counties into the decisive battle, it seems appropriate to begin at Pleasant Gardens.

Approximately 1.5 miles from the turn onto U.S. 70 is a historical marker for the Carson House, built in 1780 by Colonel John Carson. The house was constructed of 12-inch walnut logs covered with white clapboards. John Carson had an interesting marital history. His first wife, Rachel, was a daughter of Hunting John McDowell. She bore him seven children. Carson later married the widow of Joseph McDowell, Mary Moffitt McDowell, who also happened to be his sister-in-law. She bore him five children.

Unlike the McDowell House, its sister home, the Carson House is still beautifully landscaped. It now serves as a museum and research library. In former days, it was a stagecoach stop and an inn for travelers between Asheville and Salisbury. The Carson House served as the seat of local government from the time of McDowell County's organization until a courthouse was built two years later. During the Civil War, the Carsons conducted a private school for young women in their home. The women and girls were terrified when Major General George Stoneman's Union raiders swept through the area and confiscated supplies, but the house itself was left unscathed.

Samuel Price Carson, one of John Carson's sons by his second marriage, was a United States senator who was involved in a scandalous duel. In 1827, Carson was running for reelection against a former friend, Dr. Robert B. Vance, a member of a well-known western North Carolina political family; Robert Vance was the uncle of future governor Zebulon Vance. Accusations were exchanged between the two opponents. Soon, family reputations were dragged into the matter. In the climate of the times, the only honorable way to settle the dispute was a duel. Since North Carolina law forbade dueling, Vance and Carson met at Saluda Gap, just across the South Carolina border, on November 5. Carson shot Vance, and the wound proved fatal. Davy Crockett, a friend of the Carsons who was present at the duel, rode to the Carson House to deliver the news of the outcome. Carson was not prosecuted for his actions—a fact that sheds light on the prevailing attitude toward dueling. He later moved to Texas, where he served as the first secretary of state during the time when Texas was an independent republic.

The Carson House and the entire valley still possess much of the beauty that

Carson House

Wilbur Zeigler and Ben Grosscup described in 1883 in *The Heart of the Alleghanies*:

> Bursting from a twilight wood, I beheld lying before me a valley scene of striking beauty. A broad and level tract of farming land, covered with meadows, corn and pea-fields, stretched away from the forested skirts of hill-sides. . . . On the right lay low hills. On the left [were] the summits of a lofty line of peaks, behind which the sun was sinking. . . . That night I stopped in Pleasant Gardens, one of the richest and most beautiful valleys to be found in any land. . . . The large, frame house [the Carson House] and surroundings . . . showed evidence of thrift and neatness, and withal a certain ancestral air, one that only appears with age.

Continue 0.2 mile on U.S. 70 to the intersection with N.C. 80 (Lake Tahoma Road), which follows Buck Creek through the valley. Turn right. It is 2.6 miles to the dam that forms Lake Tahoma. The dam's spillway creates a scenic waterfall visible on the right. The lake was formed in 1924 for the purpose of promoting the sale of real estate along its shore. When developers began the enterprise, they sponsored a contest to name the new lake. Tahoma supposedly translates as "mountain lake of God" or "God's mountain lake" in some unknown Indian dialect. A large casino constructed of rock was built over the water. Big-name bands such as those of Kay Kyser, Hal Kemp, and Jan Garber played there for weekend dances. The development proceeded nicely until the stock-market crash of 1929. Work on a 40-room hotel was abandoned; only the foundation is left. The property has passed through several owners and is now controlled by a small number of stockholders. It still provides a scenic interlude as the road begins its climb to Hazelnut, or Buck Creek Gap.

It is 20 miles to the Yancey County line at the crest of the mountain. The road winds through dozens of hairpin curves before reaching the overlook at Buck Creek Gap just below the Blue Ridge Parkway. The view from the overlook is worth the drive through the treacherous curves.

Lake Tahoma

View of the
Black Mountains

If you care to take a side trip, head south on the Blue Ridge Parkway for 11.3 miles to N.C. 128, which serves as the main entrance to Mount Mitchell State Park. It is 5 miles from the parkway to the parking lot near the summit of Mount Mitchell.

If you prefer to avoid the crowds and approach Mount Mitchell on foot, good trails are available. Continue on N.C. 80 past the Blue Ridge Parkway. It is 2.3 miles to F.R. 472 (South Toe River Road). Turn left and drive 3 miles to Black Mountain Campground, located at the foot of Mount Mitchell. A 5.2-mile trail to the top of the mountain and a trailhead for the Black Mountain Crest Trail, which reaches almost to Burnsville, are available in addition to the camping facilities.

Mount Mitchell State Park was established in 1916 as the first state park in North Carolina and one of the first in the South. But the mountain actually began attracting tourists as early as the 1850s, when relative prosperity and improved transportation led to an interest in the scenic attractions of western North Carolina. Word filtered out through newspaper and magazine articles.

A Charlestonian named William Patton got things started by purchasing land in the area. In 1851, he erected a two-story cabin at an altitude of 5,200 feet and called it Mountain House. To reach Mountain House from his lower cabins, Patton constructed a 2-mile horse trail, which made access to the high peaks relatively easy. Others followed suit in building tourist accommodations. Talk began circulating about constructing a turnpike.

The Civil War brought a temporary halt to such ideas, but the creation of the Mount Mitchell Railroad from a logging railroad in 1915 changed the mountain forever. As many as seven passenger cars carried a maximum 250 people a day the 21 miles from Mount Mitchell Station, located near what is now the town of Black Mountain, to the upper terminus at Camp Alice. The trip up took three hours and the return trip three and a half. In 1916, some 10,000 visitors disembarked at Camp Alice between mid-May and mid-October. In one week alone, almost 1,600 tourists made the trip.

Camp Alice consisted of a large, rustic dining hall and several platform tents for those who desired to spend the night. The dining hall served family-style meals to overnight visitors and prepared lunches for those who ascended the mountain. A moderately difficult 1-mile hike led from Camp Alice to Mount Mitchell's summit.

In 1919, the Perley and Crockett Logging Company, the owner of the logging railroad whose tracks were used for the excursion train, halted passenger service. When logging operations were completed, the tracks were removed and the grade was realigned for the Mount Mitchell Motor Road, which opened in 1922. The following year, nearly 13,000 people drove the 19-mile toll road to Camp Alice. Because the road was not wide enough for two-way traffic, an interesting set of rules developed. Automobiles were required to start their ascent between the hours of 8:00 A.M. and 1:00 P.M. They had to head down the mountain between 3:30 P.M. and 5:30 P.M. Visitors who stayed overnight were required to arrive at the lower terminus before 7:30 A.M. or wait for the 3:30 P.M. departure.

When the section of the Blue Ridge Parkway from N.C. 80 to Black Mountain Gap was completed in 1939, the state of North Carolina took over the Mount Mitchell Motor Road and removed the toll. When the present N.C. 128 was completed after World War II, it bypassed Camp Alice. The stone foundations are all that remain today. If you hike the trail to Mount Mitchell from Black Mountain Campground, you will pass the Camp Alice Trail Shelter near the foundations.

Return to N.C. 80 and continue in your original direction. On the left is the Mount Mitchell Golf Course, open to the public. It is 3 miles from the turnoff to Black Mountain Campground to Carolina Hemlock Recreation Area. Trailheads at the recreation area hook into Mount Mitchell State Park's trail system. But the real attraction at the recreation area is tubing on the South Toe River. During the summer months, tourists rent inner tubes from local grocery, gas, and convenience stores. The pastime is highly recommended; once you have your tube in hand, just follow the squeals of laughter. The United States Forest Service has constructed an easily accessible submerged-rock stairway leading into the pool formed by the South Toe near the campground, but most people take the well-worn path several hundred yards upriver and then sit atop their tubes and ride the rapids down to the pool. Docking areas are located farther downstream for those who want to continue past the campground, but most people prefer to simply hike back up the hill from the pool and come down again.

As you continue on N.C. 80, you will be following the South Toe River. Zeigler and Grosscup described their journey over the same route in 1883: "There are many spots of rare, sylvan beauty in the region of the upper Toe; many spots of wild and melancholy magnificence,—dells that seem the natural haunts for satyrs and fawns, and where a modern Walter Scott might weave and locate some most fascinating fictions."

Perhaps they were a bit carried away, but the valley is definitely picturesque—especially the section lying about 4.4 miles from Carolina Hemlock Recreation Area near the community of Celo. Located on the left at an elevation of 5,946 feet, Celo Knob (or Celo Peak) is awe inspiring. It was the first peak Dr. Elisha Mitchell climbed in his exploration of the Black Mountains. See "The Mars Hill to Burns-

Micaville Country Store

ville Tour" for more information about Dr. Mitchell and Mount Mitchell.

From Celo, it is 4.2 miles to Micaville. In the center of the community is an interesting structure known as the Micaville Country Store. Turn right at the store onto N.C. 80 North and drive a short distance to the intersection with U.S. 19E. Turn right.

Beginning in Micaville—as the name might suggest—and continuing through the remainder of the tour, you will witness constant evidence of the mining industry. This area can claim much of the mica and feldspar found in the United States. Some of the most productive mines even bear evidence of work done in ancient times. From an examination of the tunnels, the shafts, and the dump piles left behind, it appears that ancient miners sought mica that was in large, clear sheets. Zeigler and Grosscup recorded a theory about its use: "Many of the mounds in the North contain large sheets, over skeletons, from which it is inferred that it was used to cover the bodies of illustrious personages after interment, and that use may account for the zeal with which it was sought."

Among the famous local mines were the Ray Mine near Burnsville and the Clarissa Buchanan Mine in Mitchell County. Both show evidence of prehistoric digging. The Ray Mine was considered the best in the area. Samples gathered there won a prize at an international fair in Vienna, Austria. (For information about visiting the Ray Mine, see "The Mars Hill to Burnsville Tour.") The "Clarissey" was 300 feet deep; the mica at that depth was said to be of as fine a grade as that from the top. The Fannie Gouge Mine near Spruce Pine was also a heavy producer. A single block of mica taken there in 1926 weighed nearly 4,400 pounds.

Feldspar, a by-product of the mica mines, was discarded as waste and dumped in huge piles nearby for years. It eventually became more valuable than mica and is still important today. Although the mining sites do not lend much aesthetic appeal to this portion of the tour, their importance as local employers cannot be denied.

Continue on U.S. 19E into Mitchell County. Approximately 5.4 miles from Micaville, you will reach the community of Estatoe, named for an Indian princess whose story is detailed in "The Roan Mountain Tour." In abbreviated form, her name also survives in the Toe River.

About 0.2 mile past the Estatoe sign, turn left at the sign for the Penland School. It is 2.3 miles on Penland Road to the small community of Penland, situated between the Toe River and the railroad tracks. Drive 0.7 mile to Conley Ridge Road, turn left, and continue 0.8 mile to the school's visitors' center. You can drive through part of the 470-acre campus before reaching the end of the pavement. Though the studios are not open to the public, the visitors' center welcomes guests from early March to mid-December. If you wish to visit, call ahead or check out www.penland.org.

The Penland School of Crafts has been described as one of the leading shapers of the American crafts movement and a producer of some of the best artisans in the country. In 1914, a man named Rufus Morgan founded the Appalachian School. Morgan wanted to include handicrafts in his program of instruction. In visiting area homes, he discovered high-quality woven articles that had been discarded when store-bought cloth became available. He convinced his sister, Miss Lucy Morgan, to come to Penland from Chicago and learn weaving from a local woman, Aunt Susan Phillips, so she could teach the skill at his school.

Miss Lucy subsequently began instructing girls at the school and women in the community. She went on to found the Penland School with the goal of perpetuating the art of weaving and providing a source of income for local people. Miss Lucy also collected her students' wares and sold them to the outside world. In 1928, the school added a pottery department. By 1929, the sale of student-made goods totaled $18,000.

Today, the Penland School campus has over 40 buildings. It is open to stu-

Penland School of Crafts

dents during the spring, summer, and fall. Terms last from one to eight weeks, and the courses vary from year to year. The curriculum usually includes work in wood, glass, fiber, clay, metal, photography, and weaving. All are taught in rustic, yet professionally equipped, studios. At peak times, the Penland School has 160 instructors and students on campus.

If you browse the visitors' center, you will no doubt be impressed with the Morgans' vision in preserving traditional mountain crafts.

Return to U.S. 19E and turn left. It is 2.6 miles from the turnoff to the Penland School to the outskirts of Spruce Pine, a town that owes much of its prosperity to its role as the center of the mining industry. The town was founded in 1908 when the Carolina, Clinchfield, and Ohio Railway built a station on the Toe River, making Spruce Pine a shipping center for the region's extensive logging industry.

Two of the earliest settlers in the area were Isaac and Alice English, who established the Old English Inn, a landmark for travelers. The Englishes' daughter is credited with suggesting the name Spruce Pine because of the beautiful evergreens growing along the Toe River. The only problem was one of mistaken identity—the evergreens proved to be hemlocks.

The English family supposedly aided Union soldiers in escaping past Confederate lines during the Civil War. One of the escapees, Colonel J. M. Gere, returned after the war and joined Isaac English in opening up the area's mining industry. English and Gere were two of the first to mine mica and find markets for its use. Spruce Pine soon became known as the mineral capital of western North Carolina.

You can view the historic downtown area by turning left onto N.C. 226, which becomes Highland Avenue. After crossing the river, you will see the interesting configuration of Spruce Pine's commercial district. Turn right; the street splits into two different levels. The lower level, which runs parallel to the railroad tracks next to the river, is Locust Street. The upper level is called Oak Avenue.

One interesting shop is the Home of the Perfect Christmas Tree store, located at 262 Oak Avenue. In 2003, author Gloria Houston gave a foundation in Spruce Pine the rights to her award-winning children's book, *The Year of the Perfect Christmas Tree*. The foundation used the funds to create small businesses that produce handmade products. This store serves as a retail facility for the products.

Follow either Locust or Oak until the two merge and continue to Ward Street. Turn right onto Ward and drive one block back to U.S. 19E.

For a recommended side trip, turn right onto U.S. 19E and return to the intersection with N.C. 226. This time, turn south onto N.C. 226 and proceed approximately 5 miles to the Museum of North Carolina Minerals, located at Milepost 331 of the Blue Ridge Parkway. There, you can see some 700 of the state's finest mineral samples. New exhibits installed in 2003 focus on regional geology and spotlight early mining endeavors.

You can then hop on the Blue Ridge Parkway and head north to Milepost 328.2 to the Orchard at Altapass. This working orchard produces heritage apples. The best time to visit is early fall, when the apples are ripe. The orchard offers hayrides, storytelling, handmade crafts, jam, apple butter, cider, mountain honey, and

*Museum of
North Carolina
Minerals*

live music on weekends. Open from May through October, it has become a major tourist attraction in the area.

Continue north on U.S. 19E whether or not you chose to take the side trip. Just past the stoplight is a marker that indicates you are traveling on the Overmountain Victory National Historic Trail. For the rest of the tour, you will follow a route similar to the one taken by John Sevier's men.

It is 7.5 miles from Spruce Pine to a sign for the community of Ingalls in Avery County. In Ingalls, U.S. 19E intersects N.C. 194, or Three Mile Road.

An interesting character named Jacob Carpenter was born on nearby Three Mile Creek in 1833. From 1845 to 1919, "Uncle Jake" kept a record of local deaths, accompanied by brief annotations. People took to calling his notebooks "the Anthology of Death." The notebooks provide fascinating and often amusing glimpses into the lives of local inhabitants, as seen through the eyes of Jacob Carpenter. Here are some excerpts with a few adjustments to Uncle Jake's spelling and punctuation, as transcribed in the Federal Writers' Project's *North Carolina: A Guide to the Old North State*:

> Davis Frank ag 72 dide july 29 1842 ware fin man but mad sum brandy that warnt no good

> Abern Johnson ag 100.7 dide july 2 he war farmer and run forg to mak iron and drunk likker all his days

> Boon Pratt ag 28 dide sep 7 1906 work hard all life got rattel snak bite brandy cured it

> Frise Stamey ag 63 jan 9 1914 dide. Ware good Christen woman, She had 12 children

> Charles McKinney ag 79 dide may 1852 ware a farmer live in blew ridge had 4

womin married 1 live in McKinney gap all went to fields to mak grane all went to crib for corn all went to smok house for meat he cild 75 to 80 hoges a year and womin never had no words bout his havin so many womin if it war thes times thar would be har pulled thare ware 42 children belongin to him they all went to prechin together nothin said he mad brandy all his lif never had no foes got along fin with everibody nod him

Franky Davis his wife age 87 dide Sep 10 1842 she had fite wolves all nite at shogar camp to save her caff throde fire chunks to save caff the camp war haf mile from home now she mus have nerve to fite wolf all nite

Joe Sing age 70 dide nove 15 1890. He robed by nite made rales by day

Homer Hines age 28 dide july shot hisself cos of womin and whusky. Dogs run after him

The last entry read, "Jacob Carpenter took down sick April 1 1919."

Continue 4.4 miles on U.S. 19E to the community of Plum Tree, where the road takes a sharp right turn in front of the Vance Toe River Lodge, built in 1919 to house the Vance General Merchandise store. The current owners moved here in 1996 and transformed the historic building and its surroundings into a lodge, restaurant, and campground.

In 1989, this area provided most of the sites for the film adaptation of John Ehle's novel *The Winter People*. The movie, which starred Kelly McGillis and Kurt Russell, used the log cabin and the storefronts just around the curve from the lodge.

Beyond Plum Tree, the landscape opens into an expansive valley. An old Indian trail connecting the lands west of the mountains with the Yadkin and Catawba river valleys once passed through the valley.

One of the earliest settlers in the area was Samuel Bright, a rather rough and

Vance Toe
River Lodge

Church in the Plum Tree community

View of the Plum Tree community

lawless man but also one with a reputation for kindness toward strangers. Another early settler was William Wiseman, who served as the local justice of the peace. The story is told that Samuel Bright's wife was brought before Wiseman. She was charged with stealing a bolt of cloth from a traveling peddler. After the lady was convicted, Wiseman passed a sentence of "thirty-nine lashes, well laid on." The only problem was that Bright was so thoroughly feared that no one could be found to carry out the sentence.

Demanding justice, the peddler threatened to report the state of affairs to Judge Samuel Spencer in Salisbury. The peddler's threat apparently promised more trouble than did any scenario with Bright, so Wiseman resolved to carry out the sentence himself. Before he could do so, Bright and his family escaped over the mountains by way of the old Indian trail, which subsequently became known as Bright's Trace. The spring near the bald atop Yellow Mountain was called Bright Spring. Ironically, Wiseman eventually came to own part of Samuel Bright's original farm. The Overmountain Men traveled past Yellow Mountain over the same Bright's Trace.

View from Yellow Mountain

In 1785, Waightstill Avery of neighboring Burke County took out hundreds of grants covering the entire valley. Today, parts of the valley are still owned by the Avery family, who were early leaders in the region's venture into the Christmas-tree industry. The vigor with which local residents pursued that industry is evidenced by the considerable acreage currently in various stages of cultivation.

In 1784, Scottish botanist John Fraser came to the area in search of rare and exotic plant life. For a short time, he joined forces with French botanist André Michaux, but there seems to have been some competition or jealousy between the two. Michaux parted company with Fraser, using the excuse that his horses had strayed and that he needed to search for them. Though it is hard to envision now, the race among nations to find unusual plant species greatly resembled the space race of the 1950s and 1960s.

Fraser discovered the sturdy evergreen that now bears the name Fraser fir, a tree that has changed the economy of the mountain counties in northwestern North Carolina. The Fraser fir has become the Christmas tree of choice among consumers for several reasons—its sturdy branches can support heavy ornaments; it retains its needles long after it is cut; and it bounces back to its original shape after being wrapped for shipping. The Fraser fir grows only in areas of high rainfall (70 to 90 inches annually) at elevations above 3,500 feet. Given such a limited growing area, the trees bring a hefty price. Because much of northwestern North Carolina meets the criteria for growing the Fraser fir, local farmers quickly learned to plant every spare inch of their property with this lucrative crop.

It is approximately 3.4 miles from Plum Tree to a historical marker describing Yellow Mountain Road. Roaring Creek Road turns to the left and follows Roaring Creek to the base of Yellow Mountain; it also follows Bright's Trace and the course of the Overmountain Men, though the marker would have you believe that the historic route continues on U.S. 19E. The reason for the discrepancy is that the Overmountain Victory National Historic Trail was designed as a route that could be driven, and U.S. 19E was the local road that replaced Bright's Trace in transporting people from North Carolina into Tennessee.

If you are looking for a good day hike or a short route to the Appalachian Trail, drive up Roaring Creek Road for 3.6 miles to where the pavement ends. Continue on the gravel for 1.2 miles to the end of the road. On the right is the trailhead for the actual Overmountain Trail. The hike up to Yellow Mountain Gap takes only 30

to 45 minutes, but it is straight up the mountain, so be prepared for a gain of 800 feet in elevation in less than a mile. The trail follows a creek for the first part of the hike, then turns left at the bottom of an open field that goes to the top of the ridge. At the corner of that field is the road grade that will take you to the gap at the intersection with the Appalachian Trail. If you turn right at the gap and hike about 1.6 fairly level miles, you will find yourself at Little Hump Mountain, one of the most scenic balds in the whole mountain chain.

Once you either return to or continue on U.S. 19E, it is 4.2 miles from the historical marker to Minneapolis. In the 1930s, this community was noted for having the largest deposits of amphibole asbestos in North Carolina. The material was once used in fireproofing but has since gained a notorious reputation as a health hazard, so the industry has died out.

Continue 0.7 mile to the community of Cranberry. In 1826, Joshua, Ben, and Jake Perkins fled to North Carolina to escape arrest in Tennessee. In *A History of Watauga County*, John Preston Arthur wrote that the three brothers had been involved "in a rough play at a night feast and frolic. . . . After a log-rolling, [they] had attempted to remove the new flax shirt and trousers from Wright Moreland, and had injured him sufficiently to arouse his anger and cause him to take out a warrant for them."

That was probably the luckiest thing that ever happened to the Perkins brothers. They decided to support themselves while in North Carolina by digging for ginseng. Joshua Perkins set to work along the banks of Cranberry Creek, named for the abundance of berries in the vicinity. The Cherokees had come to the creek for centuries to collect cranberries for dye and war paint but had never eaten the fruit because the area was sacred to them. After the arrival of white men, the Cherokees changed their practice and began to use cranberries in their cooking.

It was iron ore—not ginseng or cranberries—that Joshua Perkins discovered. He and his brothers learned of a North Carolina statute that allowed any person who found ore on vacant land to build a tilt-hammer forge. When the person could prove that 5,000 pounds of iron had been produced at his forge, the state would grant a bounty of 3,000 acres covering the site. The statute was designed to encourage new mines, and it worked well.

Cranberry Forge was built in 1828. Zeigler and Grosscup quoted a state geological report describing the mine: " 'The steep slope of the mountain and ridges, which the bed occupies are covered with blocks of ore, some weighing hundreds of pounds, and at places bare, vertical walls of massive ore, 10 to 15 feet thick, are exposed. . . . The length of the outcrop is 1500 feet, and the width, 200 to 800 feet.' "

The mine was eventually sold to the Dugger family. The Harden family managed it during the Civil War, when iron bars used in the manufacture of axes were hauled to Camp Vance, below Morganton. Peter Harden was said to be the son of a Creek Indian brought to the Harden family after the Battle of Horseshoe Bend in 1814, though others believed him to be John Harden's illegitimate Negro son. Most months during the war, Peter Harden drove a four-horse load of iron bars to Morganton. When the mine was sold after the Civil War, he remained as caretaker. He was also the keeper of the local hotel—located near the old Cranberry High School—as well as postmaster, though he could neither read nor write. His wife did all the clerical work.

It is 0.7 mile to a junction with N.C. 194. This marks the end of the tour. The old Cranberry High School is on the right. You can turn right and follow N.C. 194 South into Newland, the county seat of Avery County, or you can turn left and follow U.S. 19E/N.C. 194 North. N.C. 194 North splits off from U.S. 19E after less than 1 mile and goes to Banner Elk. U.S. 19E continues to Roan Mountain, Tennessee.

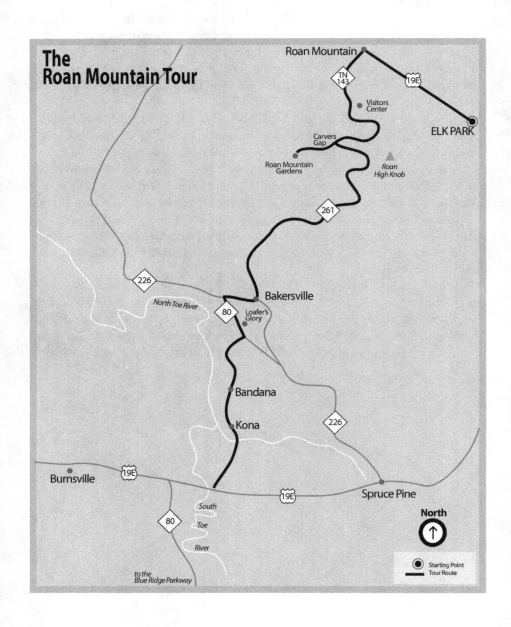

TOUR **15**

The Roan Mountain Tour

This tour begins in Elk Park near the North Carolina–Tennessee border and proceeds to the top of Roan Mountain. From the Roan, it travels to Bakersville, Loafer's Glory, Bandana, the Sink Hole Mine, and Kona, home of the legendary Frankie Silver. It leads ultimately to either Burnsville or Spruce Pine.

Total mileage: approximately 49 miles

To begin the tour, travel U.S. 19E heading north from Elk Park for 1.5 miles to the Tennessee line. Continue 4.3 miles to the community of Roan Mountain, then turn left onto Tenn. 143, heading south. Just after crossing the bridge, turn left onto Stratton Street and go two blocks.

The two-story white house on the corner of Stratton and Main streets was built in 1883 by General John Thomas Wilder for his family. Wilder was an industrialist, an inventor, a Civil War hero, and an influential figure in the development of East Tennessee. At age 19, he left his New York home to seek his fortune in the West. Eight years later, in 1857, he owned his own foundry and millwright establishment in Greensburg, Indiana. He also married the daughter of one of the town's founders.

When the Civil War began, Wilder closed his foundry and organized a company of local militia. Within a month, he was promoted to lieutenant colonel. His cavalry troops established such a reputation for speed and toughness that they came to be known as Wilder's Lightning Brigade. The brigade helped hold off victorious Confederate troops at the Battle of Chickamauga until the Union army retreated to Chattanooga. By the end of the war, Wilder was a brigadier general.

After the conflict, Wilder moved to Chattanooga. But he was not a carpetbagger. In 1867, he erected the first blast furnace in the South to use coke. He also started several successful manufacturing companies in the Chattanooga area.

General John Wilder's home in Roan Mountain

Sometime around 1870, Wilder purchased 7,000 acres along the top and sides of Roan Mountain at a cost of $25.15 per acre. He also acquired the Cranberry mine in nearby North Carolina (see "The Overmountain Victory Trail Tour" for information about the mine).

When Wilder's company began construction of the East Tennessee and Western North Carolina Railroad from Johnson City to his mine in Cranberry, Roan Mountain Station became a thriving community. He built the Roan Mountain Inn and a home for his family in the town. He also constructed the Cloudland Hotel atop Roan Mountain in 1885. For the same rate, guests could divide their time between the Roan Mountain Inn and the Cloudland Hotel, with horses and hacks providing transportation from the train station to the mountaintop. More information about the Cloudland Hotel is presented later in this tour.

The financial losses Wilder suffered in the panic of 1893 were so severe that his daughter was forced to drop out of college. Nonetheless, she went on to marry Arthur Hoyt Scott, who played a part in the development of the paper towels and tissues that made the Scott Paper Company known world-wide.

Despite Wilder's financial difficulties, his popularity remained high. He was chairman of the Chickamauga National Park Commission. He also intervened to prevent the arrest of former Confederate general Nathan Bedford Forrest on charges of parole violation. For this act, he was later rewarded honorary membership in the Nathan Bedford Forrest Post of the United Confederate Veterans. As one post member phrased it, "No man has done more than General Wilder in bringing order out of chaos."

Return to Tenn. 143 and drive 2 miles to an open field on the left. This is Shelving Rock Encampment National Historic Site. The property includes "the

shelving rock," an overhang where goods were stored to keep them dry. Approximately 1,000 volunteer Patriots known as "the Overmountain Men" camped here on September 26 and 27, 1780, while en route to the Battle of Kings Mountain. More information about the Overmountain Men is in "The Overmountain Victory Trail Tour."

Continue less than 0.1 mile on Tenn. 143 to Roan Mountain State Park's visitors' center, on the left. The excellent facilities at the park include a swimming pool, tennis courts, and cabins with rocking chairs on their porches.

For centuries, the 6,285-foot Roan Mountain has been an area landmark not only because of its height but also because of the distinctive appearance of its treeless summit. Generations of scientists have tried to explain why certain mountaintops in the 2,000- to 6,000-foot range in this part of the Appalachians will not support trees. Altitude and timberline are obviously not the answers, since nearby Mount Mitchell, at almost 7,000 feet, supports tree growth all the way to the top.

In 1938, a professor from Louisiana State University advanced the theory that wasp eggs laid in the trees were responsible for killing them off. Unfortunately, his theory failed to explain why the infestation did not spread and why eradication of the wasps did not result in reforestation. A botanist from North Carolina State University suggested that Indians had created the "balds" by continually burning off the mountaintop foliage for their settlements. But evidence from archaeologists and anthropologists showed that Indians preferred valleys near streams and never chose the tops of ridges for their villages.

As usual, where science failed, legend entered. In 1898, James Mooney recorded in his report to the Bureau of American Ethnology that the Cherokees had a mythological explanation for the origin of the balds. A Cherokee village was terrorized by a giant yellow jacket called Ulagu that swooped down, snatched up children, and quickly flew off into the distance. The ever-resourceful Cherokees posted sentinels on the tops of the mountains in order to track Ulagu to its lair, located in an inaccessible cavern. In this alternate version of the tale that appears in "The Nantahala Tour," the Indians prayed to the Great Spirit for aid. Suddenly, a bolt of lightning split off the side of the mountain where Ulagu hid. The Indians then quickly fell on the monstrous insect and destroyed it.

According to Mooney, the Great Spirit was so pleased with the Cherokees' "initiative in uncovering [Ulagu's] hiding place, their piety in appealing for Divine aid in their extremity, and their bravery in the final combat, that it was His decree that in the future the tops of the highest mountains be bare of timber, to better serve as stations for sentries should another such visitation occur."

The Catawba Indians, who also frequented the area, had a different explanation. In 1849, Charles Lanman recorded the following in *Letters from the Alleghany Mountains*:

> There once was a time when all the nations of the earth were at war with the Catawbas, and had proclaimed their determination to conquer and possess their country. On hearing this intelligence the Catawbas became greatly enraged, and sent a challenge to all their enemies, and dared them to a fight on the summit of the Roan. The challenge was accepted, and three famous battles were fought. The streams of the entire land were red with blood, a number of tribes became extinct, and the Catawbas carried the day. Whereupon it was that the Great Spirit caused the forests to wither from the three peaks of the Roan Mountain where the battles were fought; and wherefore it is that the flowers which grow upon this mountain are chiefly of a crimson hue, for they are nourished by the blood of the slain.

The Catawba legend is particularly accommodating because it accounts for another characteristic that helps draw thousands of visitors to Roan Mountain each year. On the top of the Roan are 600 acres of natural rhododendron gardens that put on a brilliant display of color each June.

In 1799, Scotsman John Fraser, under the patronage of the Russian government, made his third trip to the North Carolina mountains. During his journey up the Roan, he discovered a new plant, which he designated *Rhododendron catawbiense*. It is this plant with its crimson-colored blooms that attracts so many sightseers. Roan Mountain also boasts an 850-acre forest of Fraser fir and spruce. The Fraser fir, named after the same John Fraser who christened the Catawba rhododendron, has become the rage in the domestic Christmas-tree industry, spawning a whole new source of income for local landowners.

Fraser was one of many scientists who traveled to the area. The location offers an unusual assortment of plant life, as a number of species at Roan Mountain are rarely found outside the mountains of eastern Canada. Another famous botanist who visited the Roan was André Michaux, sent by the French government in 1785 to explore the United States and gather the seeds of trees, shrubs, and other vegetation for planting in the Park of Rambouillet. In 1786, Michaux established his central nursery in Charleston, South Carolina, then set about covering the entire country. He explored the area around the Roan in 1794. Some sources say it was Michaux who named the peak, after the Rhone River of his native France. Though this is doubtful, he did leave his mark on the area, teaching local settlers the value of the ginseng plant and showing them how to prepare it for the Chinese market. Still valued in Asia for its medicinal and aphrodisiac qualities, ginseng has provided supplemental income for the people of the mountains ever since Michaux's visit. A third well-known botanist who traveled to the Roan was Dr. Asa Gray, who visited twice in the 1840s. When Gray returned from one expedition, he called the Roan "without doubt, the most beautiful mountain east of the Rockies." While exploring the area, he discovered the unique species of lily that is still known as Gray's lily in his honor.

Just past the visitors' center, the road begins its steep ascent to the summit. The route hasn't changed much since Charles Dudley Warner described it in his 1889 book, *On Horseback*: "For six miles the road runs by Doe River, here a pretty brook shaded with laurel and rhododendron, and a few cultivated patches of ground and infrequent houses. . . . We mounted slowly through splendid forests. . . . This big timber continues till within a mile and a half of the summit by the winding road. . . . Then there is a narrow belt of scrubby hardwood, moss-grown, and then large balsams, which crown the mountain."

When Charles Lanman reached the summit, he offered an observation that still rings true: "It commands an uninterrupted view of what appears to be the entire world. When I was there I observed no less than three thunderstorms performing their uproarious feats in three separate valleys, while the remaining portions of the lower world were enjoying a deep blue atmosphere."

It is almost 11 miles from the visitors' center to Carver's Gap, where the crest of the ridge marks the Tennessee–North Carolina line. A parking area is on the right. Most visitors make the climb along the section of the Appalachian Trail that leads to the top of the Roan's bald, to the left.

If you turn right at the gap onto the forest-service access road, you can drive to the former site of the Cloudland Hotel and the rhododendron gardens. A small access fee is charged.

Traces remain of the foundation of General Wilder's Cloudland Hotel. Although accounts vary, the hotel had somewhere between 166 and 266 rooms. Guests could sleep in Tennessee and eat their meals in North Carolina without ever leaving the premises. The hotel was famous all over the East Coast, though guests had to endure a difficult journey to the summit by stagecoach or carriage. The Cloudland even ran a hack three times a week to the railroad in Johnson City, Tennessee. In 1885–86, the hotel sent out advertisements reading, "Come up out

Appalachian Trail seen from Carver's Gap on Roan Mountain

of the sultry plains to the 'land of the sky,' magnificent views above the clouds where the rivers are born, a most extended prospect of 50,000 square miles in six different states, one hundred mountain tops, over 4,000 feet high in sight."

Many visitors at the Cloudland Hotel witnessed strange happenings atop the mountain. Stories abounded of ghostly music and circular rainbows. The reports grew so widespread that Henry Colton, a scientist from Knoxville, Tennessee, came to investigate. Upon his return home, he reported his observations and conclusions to a Knoxville newspaper. "The sound was very plain to the ear . . . like the incessant, continuous and combined snap of two jars," he claimed. Colton offered the explanation that "two currents coming together in the open high plateau on the high elevation, by their friction and being on different temperatures, generated electricity. . . . The music was simply the snapping caused by this friction. . . . The heated air of the valley rises from eight in the morning until three or four in the afternoon. . . . As night comes on the current turns back into the valley, almost invariably producing a very brisk gale by three or four o'clock in the morning, which in turn dies down to a calm by seven o'clock and commences to reverse itself by nine o'clock."

Despite Colton's argument, the hotel's mountain neighbors continued to insist that the sounds came from angels, and that the circular rainbows that frequently appeared atop the Roan after thunderstorms could only be God's halo.

If you are in the area when the blooms are at their height in June, be sure to visit the natural rhododendron gardens. After viewing the gardens, return to Carver's Gap and turn right to continue down the North Carolina side of the mountain. Tenn. 143 becomes N.C. 261.

The route travels through a scenic farming valley for 23 miles to Bakersville, the county seat of Mitchell County. This entire area was late in opening to white settlement. Content to leave the land for the Cherokees and the Catawbas, the North Carolina legislature did not officially open the territory until 1793. Mitchell County was not created until 1861. The county seat was originally a community called Calhoun—later Childsville—but the people never liked that arrangement, so the location was switched to what is now Bakersville. Early court sessions met in a grove of trees that stood at the site of the present courthouse. A log courthouse was constructed in 1867.

Turn onto N.C. 226 North at the courthouse, heading toward Red Hill. After 2.6 miles, turn left onto N.C. 226A South/N.C. 80 South, heading toward Micaville. It is 1.9 miles to an area labeled Loafer's Glory on old maps. When researchers were sent into the area by the Work Projects Administration in the 1930s, they were impressed by the small community store owned by Nathan Deyton and Joe Wilson, located near the bridge over Cane Creek. Local men could be found at Deyton and Wilson's place on Saturdays, in the evenings, and on rainy days, as they played checkers, threw horseshoes, whittled, or just spun yarns. For that reason, the store and the area came to be known as Loafer's Glory. Though the original structure is gone, a small white storefront still stands at the intersection where N.C. 80 takes a sharp right turn toward Burnsville.

Follow N.C. 80 to the right. A drive of 2.4 miles on a winding road leads to the remains of the Sink Hole Mine, on the left. If you reach Silver Chapel Baptist Church, on the right, you have gone 0.2 mile too far.

Some historians have theorized that this mine was first worked by the Spaniards sometime between 1540 and 1690, during their search for silver in the area. A tradition among the Indians supported this theory; they told of white men coming on mules from the south during the summer and carrying off a white metal with them.

In *Western North Carolina*, John Preston Arthur described the mines as being "from sixty to eighty feet in diameter at the top. They extend along a ridge for one-third of a mile. They seem to have been a series of concentric holes. . . . Standing with their roots on some of [the] waste originally taken from these holes are several large trees nearly three feet in diameter."

In 1867, Thomas L. Clingman—United States senator, brigadier general in the Confederate army, and early explorer of area mountain peaks—started mining operations in the tunnels below the old excavations. In his *Speeches and Writings*, published in 1878, he gave testimony to the great age of the previous excavations and, by implication, to the possibility that Spaniards had mined the site: "Timber which I examined, that had grown on the earth thrown out, had been growing as long as three hundred years."

Though Clingman did not find silver at the Sink Hole Mine, a tinner named Heap took away a block of mica thinking it to be worthless, only to find a receptive market in Knoxville. Heap and a partner worked the site profitably for several years. The Sink Hole Mine was one of the first mica mines in the area, which soon prospered thanks to the new industry. Large pieces of the shiny, reflective metal can still be found on the Sink Hole Mine property. A dirt road leads all the way to the top of the abandoned shafts.

Across the road from Silver Baptist Church is a sign for Bandana. The story goes that this community received its name when a railroad worker tied a bandana

*Remains of the
Sink Hole Mine*

to a bush to mark the spot for a depot.

It is approximately 3 miles from the mine and Bandana to Kona. A small white church sits on a hillside to the left after a curve. Next to this church is the Silver Cemetery, where members of the Silver family are buried. Kona Road (S.R. 1176) is to the right. Kona Missionary Baptist Church is visible in the distance.

Located on Deyton's Bend, where the North and South forks of the Toe River meet, Kona was once a railroad stop. It was also noted for an infamous murder committed in 1831. Frankie Silver lived near here in a log cabin with her husband, Charlie, and their infant daughter. Though most early versions of the tale say she killed her husband with an ax in a jealous rage, recent research has proposed that Frankie may have acted in self-defense, since Charlie frequently beat her. Because women were not allowed to testify in court at that time, Frankie never got the chance to tell her side of the story on the witness stand.

Frankie supposedly chopped the body into small pieces and burned most of them in the cabin's fireplace. Charlie's family members suspected foul play and even consulted a Tennessee conjurer, who led them to the portion of the remains Frankie had been unable to destroy. Found guilty of murder, Frankie was hanged on July 12, 1833. She remains the only woman ever legally hanged in North Carolina. A printed ballad was handed out to the crowd of witnesses at the event. Its authorship was attributed to Frankie, though there is no evidence that such was actually the case. The ballad has been preserved in its entirety in North Carolina folklore collections, ensuring that the story of Frankie Silver will remain a part of the area's lore.

Continue 3.3 miles on N.C. 80 to the bridge that crosses from Mitchell County into Yancey County and spans both the railroad and the Toe River. The legend that surrounds the naming of the Toe relates that Estatoe, the daughter of an Indian chief, fell in love with the son of a rival chief. When her father refused to allow her to wed, Estatoe supposedly threw herself into the waters of what is now the Toe and drowned—which seems to be a common legend in the hills. The Indians then

Church in Kona

began calling it the Estatoe River, shortened to the Toe River by the white man. It is more probable that the name came from a well-traveled trading path that led from the South Carolina Indian village of Estatoe to the river. The Indians used the trail to reach mica deposits in the area. Archaeologists have discovered Indian ornaments with mica beadwork, as well as several Indian mounds containing sprinklings of mica.

It is another 2.2 miles to an intersection with U.S. 19E. This ends the tour. You have three choices. You can turn right onto U.S. 19E and drive 6 miles to Burnsville, or you can turn left and drive 8 miles to Spruce Pine. You might also continue on N.C. 80 until it intersects the Blue Ridge Parkway.

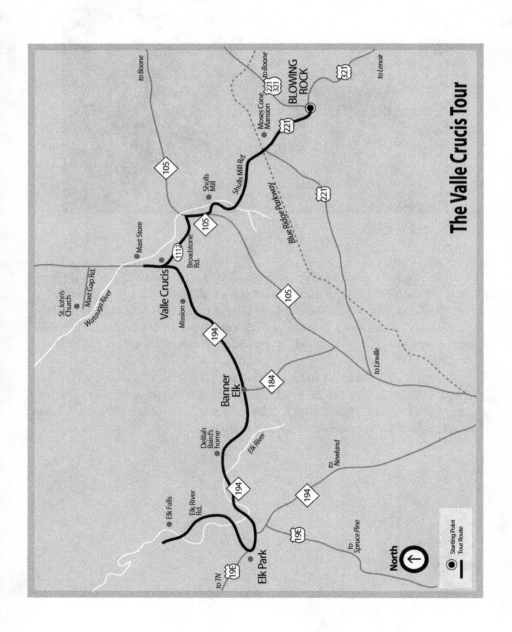

The Valle Crucis Tour

TOUR 16
The Valle Crucis Tour

This tour begins in Blowing Rock and travels along Shulls Mill Road to the area known as Valle Crucis. It continues to Banner Elk, follows the Elk River to the town of Elk Park, and ends at scenic Elk Falls.

Total mileage: approximately 35 miles

The tour begins in the town of Blowing Rock where U.S. 221, or the Yonahlossee Trail, heads toward Linville. Approximately 0.6 mile from Main Street on U.S. 221, a road on the right leads to the Bass Lake parking area, which gives access to many of the 25 miles of carriage trails on the Moses S. Cone Estate. A walking trail encircles what was formerly one of Cone's well-stocked trout ponds. The trail is especially popular in the summer and fall.

The trout ponds are just a small part of the 3,516-acre estate once owned by Moses and Bertha Cone. The eldest of 13 children born to a Bavarian immigrant who achieved success as a dry-goods merchant, Moses Cone started out as a drummer, or traveling salesman, who solicited orders for the family business. He discovered Blowing Rock on one of his sales trips.

He and his brother Caesar began to amass a sizable fortune when they switched their focus to the growing textile industry. Moses started buying land in Blowing Rock when he was 36 and continued to add to his estate for 35 years. He purchased most of his acreage between 1893 and 1899.

In 1899, the Cones began construction on their Victorian Neocolonial manor house atop nearby Flat Top Mountain. An impressive gabled home with Tiffany windows, it now houses the Blue Ridge Parkway Craft Center. The Cones built a self-sufficient estate on which they raised sheep, hogs, chickens, and milk cows. Their dairy was the first classified as Grade A in Watauga County. The estate was so

Trout Lake on the Moses S. Cone Estate

Bass Lake on the Moses S. Cone Estate

large that it supported 30 families. In an effort to introduce an alternate economy for local farmers, the Cones even experimented with apple orchards. At its height, the Cone estate had 10,000 apple trees of approximately 20 varieties.

When Moses Cone died, he left the estate to the hospital in Greensboro that now bears his name. His will specified that Mrs. Cone would have use of the estate until her death. The hospital later discovered that the money set aside for upkeep was insufficient, so it arranged to donate the house and surrounding land to the federal government. In 1949, the National Park Service took over the development and maintenance of the estate as a recreation area and public park.

To tour the Cone manor house on Flat Top Mountain, continue on U.S. 221 for 1 mile, then turn right, following the signs to the Blue Ridge Parkway. At the

Manor house on Moses S. Cone Estate

Grave site of Moses and Bertha Cone

View of Grandfather Mountain from the Moses S. Cone Estate

parkway, turn right and go approximately 1 mile to the entrance to the manor house parking lot. A popular and easy 2-mile round-trip hike leads from the parking area under the parkway to the Cones' grave site. If you wish to add another 4 miles to the hike, you can continue to the fire tower on top of Flat Top Mountain.

After visiting the manor house, head back toward U.S. 221. Just before the junction, turn right onto Shulls Mill Road, which travels under the Blue Ridge Parkway. Just beyond the overpass, follow Shulls Mill Road as it forks left. It is less than 0.1 mile to an unmarked road on the right. This is a one-way route to the parking area for Trout Lake—another lake in the estate's system.

From Trout Lake, return to Shulls Mill Road and turn right. The road winds its way through the woods and offers occasional vistas of Grandfather Mountain to the left. About 2.3 miles past the trout pond, it runs through the center of a resort development built on the former site of Camp Yonahlossee, one of the area's first summer camps for girls. Camp Yonahlossee began in 1922 under the direction of Dr. and Mrs. A. P. Kephart. The developers of the new resort have preserved much of the camp's original rockwork and many of its rustic buildings, including the barn, on the left, and the dam with its waterfall, around the curve on the right.

After another 1.5 miles, you will see the first signs of the Hound Ears Club. The fairways and greens of the club's golf course are visible through the trees on the left. Shulls Mill Road leads through the center of the property. The clubhouse and hundreds of expensive summer homes cover the surrounding hills. Atop one of the hills is the rock formation local residents were fond of comparing to a hound's ears before the deciduous forest grew up to cover it from view.

Just beyond the entrance to the Hound Ears Club and past Old Turnpike Road is a building across the road from Shulls Mill Baptist Church. This structure housed the community's general store. The former store and the church, both of which were built around 1850, are all that remain of a once-prosperous community that claimed a population of more than 1,000 at its peak.

Hound Ears Club

Shulls Mill began around 1835 when Phillip Shull, the grandson of a German immigrant who had moved to Valle Crucis in the 1770s, built a gristmill near his farm. It was during those days that some of the community's most colorful residents began to leave their mark on local folklore.

Around 1820, a man named James Aldridge arrived in the area and persuaded Betsy Calloway to marry him. They had seven children. All apparently went well until 1836, when another Mrs. James Aldridge appeared on the scene. It seems that Aldridge had deserted a wife and five children when he left the Big Sandy area in what is now West Virginia. A fur peddler traveling through Watauga County had recognized him and passed along his where-

View of Grandfather Mountain from Shulls Mill

abouts. As to Betsy's reaction when her husband's first wife showed up, John Preston Arthur recorded that "she was sulky, but that [Aldridge] himself was treating both women exactly alike, and had no doubt but that Betsy would soon get over it."

Sources disagree on whether or not she really did "get over it." The first Mrs. Aldridge returned to the Big Sandy. Shortly thereafter, three sons and a daughter from Aldridge's first family came to live in Watauga County. Aldridge spent the next few years bouncing back and forth between Shulls Mill and the Big Sandy until both wives grew unreceptive, at which time he started living with a third woman. Betsy struggled but managed to raise her children, and occasionally the children from her husband's previous marriage as well. She died in 1900 a well-respected woman. No one remembered much about James Aldridge by that time.

In 1859, another citizen of Shulls Mill entered the history books. John Preston Arthur described David Colvert "Cobb" McCanless as "a strikingly handsome man and a well-behaved, useful citizen till he became involved with a woman not his wife, after which he fell into evil courses." Arthur didn't supply the woman's name, but other sources identified her as Sarah Shull. Those sources also suggested it may not have been wholly Sarah Shull's fault that McCanless turned out the way he did.

In 1856, Cobb McCanless was elected sheriff. One of his duties was tax collection. In January 1859, he and Sarah Shull absconded with the funds he had gathered. Several months later, McCanless's brother took Cobb's wife—Mary—her children, her father, her mother, and his and Cobb's sisters west to join the fugitives. How Cobb managed to balance life with Sarah Shull and Mary is not clear, but he apparently achieved some measure of success until the Civil War, when word arrived that he had been killed in Kansas.

It wasn't until 1883 that locals learned Cobb had actually been killed in a shoot-out with Wild Bill Hickok. The McCanless gang had allegedly been impressing horses for the Confederate cause. Hickok, known to side with the Union, disagreed with those actions. In an interview in *Harper's New Monthly Magazine,* Hickok offered a description of Cobb McCanless: "You see this M'Kandlas was the captain of a gang of desperadoes, horse-thieves, murderers, regular cut-throats, who were the terror of every body on the border. . . . I knew them all in the mountains, where they pretended to be trapping, but they were there hiding from the hangman. M'Kandlas was the biggest scoundrel and bully of them all, and was allers a-braggin of what he could do." In December 1861, a shootout occurred between 10 of Cobb's boys and Wild Bill and his men. All but two of the McCanless gang were killed. Sarah Shull returned to Watauga County.

Shulls Mill was a regular stop on the toll road that ran from Lincolnton, North Carolina, to Abingdon, Virginia. Between 1855 and 1861, a nine-passenger stagecoach named Old Albany made daily stops at Joseph Shull's place. But by 1893, traffic was bypassing town, and the section of the turnpike from Blowing Rock to Shulls Mill was turned over to Watauga County to be maintained as a public road. In 1914, some local citizens, dissatisfied with what they considered county neglect, established the Valle Crucis and Blowing Rock Turnpike Company. This tour follows the route of the original toll road.

Shulls Mill began its finest hour in 1915, when William Scott Whiting, the owner of the Whiting Lumber Company, selected it as the site for a band mill. The same community that had listed a population of 25 in 1910 claimed 1,000 residents by August 1917. Though the town had previously boasted only a few stores (including the building on the left), a hotel, and a post office, the Whiting Lumber Company helped bring a train depot for the new railroad spur, a barbershop, a movie theater, a hospital, and housing for hundreds of workers.

By 1918, the lumber company had sawed over 1.6 million feet of lumber from 1,436 acres in the area. By 1925, timber close enough to the mill to allow the company to make a profit was growing scarce, and William Scott Whiting began moving his operation to alternate sites. He invited his workers to relocate at one of his other mills. Most accepted the offer. The flood of 1940 destroyed the majority of the buildings that remained.

Former store at Shulls Mill

Continue on Shulls Mill Road. At the stop sign just past the bridge, turn right onto Old Shulls Mill Road, which parallels the Watauga River, on the right. In the summer months, this part of the river is a popular swimming hole and fishing spot for local residents. It is 0.8 mile to an intersection with N.C. 105. Turn right and go 0.8 mile. At the traffic light just before the bridge, turn left onto Broadstone Road, heading toward Valle Crucis.

In 1883, Wilbur Zeigler and Ben Grosscup wrote in *The Heart of the Alleghanies* that "one valley in particular, by the Watauga, is of captivating loveliness. The mountains rise around it, as though placed there with no other purpose than to protect its jewel-like expanse from rough incursions of storm." Those who travel this part of the tour through the valley they described are likely to agree with that assessment.

It is 1.1 miles to where a green walkway goes over the highway. The walkway leads to part of Camp Broadstone. Bob Breitenstein, former assistant football coach at the University of Miami and future head coach at Appalachian State University, started an athletic camp here in 1956. In 1961, Appalachian State purchased the 55 acres for use in programs outside the traditional classroom. In 1975, ASU turned the property into an outdoor adventure and retreat center offering summer camp for the academically gifted.

The main entrance to the camp is 0.3 mile around the curve. Across the road is the original farm of the Shull family—the homestead established by Frederick Shull in the 1770s. The Shull home was a stagecoach stop on the route to Abingdon, Virginia. The recently renovated house on the right was built in 1888.

Continue 0.6 mile to the Mast Farm Inn.

In *Sketches of Early Watauga*, Betty MacFarland described how this farm complex grew from its humble beginnings as a simple log cabin built by David Mast in 1812: "With this building as a nucleus, the farm illustrates the progression of an enterprising pioneer family from this rude early house on a small homestead to

Frederick Shull Farm

Barn at Mast Farm

a larger more comfortable house, the seat of much larger landholdings. The complex includes one of the most complete and best-preserved groups of nineteenth century farm buildings in western North Carolina." The log house on the left in front of the large frame house is that original cabin. When the frame house was built in 1885, the log cabin was converted to a weaving house. A bedspread fashioned there was used in the White House during Woodrow Wilson's administration. Along with the barn across the road from the house, the farm consisted of a wash house, a springhouse, a meat house, a woodhouse, an apple house, and a blacksmith's shop—everything necessary for a self-sustaining farm complex.

Before long, the Mast Farm became recognized for the good food and hospitable lodgings it offered tourists seeking to escape the lowland heat. The tradition continues today. The Mast Farm Inn operates as a bed-and-breakfast inn featuring a restaurant noted for its excellent food.

It is 0.1 mile to the beginning of what might be called the commercial district of Valle Crucis. On the right is the old Valle Crucis Company store, erected in 1909. It now serves as an annex for the famous Mast Store. Across the street is Valle

Mast Farm Inn

Crucis Methodist Church, built in 1894 on the same site as its predecessor, an 1870 log church. In the 1940 flood, the church was washed off its foundation, but it was prevented from going downstream by the large sugar maples in the churchyard. These buildings and the school across the road are located on a tract settled in 1779 by Samuel Hix and his son-in-law, James Holtsclaw. The two men built a palisade of split logs to protect themselves from Indians and wild animals. Hix came to the wilderness to escape military service during the Revolutionary War; it is said he sided with the British. He eventually moved on to Banner Elk, where he became a well-known character who earned a living by hunting and making maple sugar. It is said he sold his landholdings for a rifle, a dog, and a sheepskin.

Continue 0.2 mile to the well-preserved Mast Store, built in the 1880s. The store is a popular tourist attraction that has spawned several imitators in the area. Goods touted in a 1940 advertisement for the store included "everything from toothpicks to caskets." Today's merchandise is equally eclectic. Many of the items mentioned in *Sketches of Early Watauga* can still be purchased here. "Even though it is now a general mercantile business, the store is a vivid commentary on early America in both goods and in atmosphere," Betty MacFarland wrote.

Mast Store

"Commodities typifying by-gone days include the following items: famed penny candy, cheese and crackers, fatback; Chesterfield hats in yellowed boxes, bolts of cloth, leather goods, washboards, washtubs, cast iron pots, kerosene lamps, cherry seeders, apple peelers, sausage grinders, saddles, horseshoes, sets of harness, turning plows and cultivators." Current owner John Cooper also carries skiing and outdoor clothing and equipment reminiscent of the popular L. L. Bean store in Maine.

On a hill diagonally across the road from the Mast Store is the Hard Taylor House. The original structure was built by Henry Taylor before the Civil War. The existing house was constructed in two stages by Henry's son, Thomas Hardester "Hard" Taylor, whose plan was to incorporate his father's two-room brick house as a nucleus. It was the first home in the valley to have closets in every room, indoor plumbing, and central heat.

On the left just past the Mast Store is the W. W. Mast home, built in 1903. Another 0.5 mile down the road is the Baird House, on the right. The original log cabin at the site was incorporated into this four-room, two-story house constructed sometime before 1873, when David and Elizabeth Baird moved in. Tradition says that this was the first home painted white in the area. The house and its barn serve as evidence of the prosperity of this farming valley.

Continue on Broadstone Road as it passes over the Watauga River. It is 0.8 mile from the Baird House to Mast Gap Road. Turn left, following the signs to St. John's Church. In 0.5 mile, Herb Thomas Road goes off to the left. Follow this gravel road that parallels the river for 0.6 mile to the church. Information about the history of the Episcopal Church in this area is presented later in the tour. This historic church was built in the mid-19th century by William West Skiles, who is also discussed later. The church is now operated as a summer chapel. Worship services are held each Sunday from Memorial Day to Labor Day. The church is also frequently booked for weddings.

Retrace your route for 2.6 miles past the Mast Store to Valle Crucis Elementary School. Turn right onto N.C. 194 South and head into the most scenic part of the valley. In *A History of Watauga County*, published in 1915, John Preston Arthur wrote, "There is, perhaps, more interest in this place and its romantic history than in any other in Watauga County. It is called the Valley of the Cross because

of the fancied resemblance to that symbol of our faith caused by two creeks, each flowing from an opposite direction into Dutch Creek. . . . There is a dreamy spell which hangs over this little valley." Arthur accurately captured the area's romantic overtones.

After 0.8 mile on N.C. 194, you will see the Squire Taylor House on the right. Taylor's first home, built in 1890, was located where Dutch and Clark's creeks flow together on the left side of the road. The 1940 flood destroyed the original structure, as well as Taylor's gristmill. The second house, built in 1911–12, survives as a bed-and-breakfast inn.

It is 0.1 mile to a restored barn that is part of the Valle Crucis Conference Center complex. Much of the history of Valle Crucis revolves around the work of the Episcopal Church. In the 1840s, L. Silliman Ives, the bishop of North Carolina, grew interested in this area. One of the best-known men Bishop Ives brought here was William West Skiles, a layman who later became a deacon. In 1842, Skiles wrote,

> The highland valley was magnificent in natural beauty. It lay in the elevated
> country between the Blue Ridge and the Alleghanies, nearly three thousand feet

St. John's Church

Squire Taylor House

above the sea, while grand old mountains of successive ranges, broken into a hundred peaks, rose to nearly double the height on either hand, many so near that their distinctive features could be clearly seen, while others were only dimly outlined in the distance. These mountain ranges were peculiarly interesting, differing in some particulars from those of any other parts of the country. The vegetation was singularly rich and varied. The valley, entirely shut in by forest-clad mountains, was watered by three small, limpid streams, two of them leaping down the hillsides in foaming cascades.

By 1844, Bishop Ives had used his own money to buy 2,000 acres of land and a sawmill in the area. He began building structures of adobe brick. As the buildings were completed, young men were brought in to study for the ministry and to serve as teachers in the boarding and day school. Ives also shipped in a herd of dairy cattle and hired Skiles, an experienced farmer, to supervise the operation.

About that same time, Ives established the Society of the Holy Cross, the first monastic order for men in the Anglican communion since the English Reformation in the mid-1500s. By 1849, authorities in the Episcopal Church were growing concerned that "the Mission at Valle Crucis had begun to drift away from the teachings of the Church, and was fast becoming a feeble and undignified imitation of the monastic institutions of the Church of Rome," as the bishops of North Caro-

Bishop Ives's cabin

lina stated in a report. Bishop Ives resigned in 1852, and the monastic order and divinity school were disbanded. But William Skiles, so impressed by Ives's mission that he had joined the monastic order and been ordained a deacon in 1847, elected to stay in Valle Crucis, where he ran a store, practiced medicine, and taught school until his death in 1862.

In 1895, Joseph Blount Cheshire, then the bishop of North Carolina, came to the area to revive the church's work. He built a dormitory and chapel with classrooms attached. A few years later, Junius Horner, bishop of the newly created Asheville district, encouraged the school even further. In 1903, the Episcopal Church bought 435 acres of the land previously owned by Bishop Ives. It began apple orchards and a dairy, built a sawmill and a wagon factory, and installed a hydroelectric power plant. The new school conducted classes from first grade through high school for both boarding and day students. A stone church, the Church of the Holy Cross, was built in 1926. Area public schools expanded by 1936, so the mission school dropped classes for the first six grades and became a boarding school for girls only. It closed in 1943, thanks in large part to World War II. The surviving facilities, many of which have been renovated and modernized, are now used as an Episcopal Church conference center.

Atop the hillside on the right are the mission-school buildings. Rounding the curve, you will come upon the Church of the Holy Cross on the right. Next to the

Apple barn at Valle Crucis

church is Bishop Ives's log cabin, the only structure surviving from his era.

Follow N.C. 194 as it climbs out of the valley. The steep, winding route makes for slow going, but the views to the left are beautiful. At the top of the ridge, N.C. 194 straightens out through a scenic valley dominated by a white farmhouse. It is 6.6 miles from the mission school to the town of Banner Elk. Continue through the traffic light. Lees-McRae College is on the left. Just past the campus is an intersection with N.C. 184; a right turn and a brief side trip will take you to the top of Beech Mountain, a popular resort and ski area. If you stay on N.C. 194, it is another 0.4 mile to the Elk River development, on the left. Beyond the entrance is a private airport runway. This valley, once known as the Big Bottoms of Elk, has a colorful history.

Though separating fact from legend is hard, the tale of Delilah Baird still makes a good story. In 1825, Delilah, the 18-year-old daughter of Colonel Bedent Baird of Valle Crucis, ran off with John Holtsclaw, the husband of the former Fanny Calloway and the father of their seven children. The story goes that Holtsclaw promised to take Delilah to Kentucky, and that, following their winding journey out of her home valley, she believed they had actually arrived there. After traveling from Valle Crucis to Banner Elk, you may appreciate how she was duped. Holtsclaw supposedly circled through Tennessee and returned to the valley of the Elk River, where he owned a 480-acre tract. You are now driving through that same valley.

One day, Delilah was out "sangin"—digging for ginseng—when she heard a cowbell that sounded remarkably like the one worn by her father's lead cow. Upon following the cow, she discovered how close she really was to Valle Crucis. She renewed her ties with her family but continued to live with Holtsclaw.

Soon afterward, Fanny Holtsclaw showed up asking her husband for work. She was willing to wash, weave, or do anything else to raise money to provide for her children. Holtsclaw's answer was to deed all his Elk River land to Delilah Baird. Ironically, one of Fanny's daughters, Raney, married the man who eventually came to own all of Delilah's land.

In 1881, at the age of 74, Delilah learned that her eccentric ways were leading her relatives to request hearings to determine whether or not she was capable of handling her own affairs. She wrote to Ben Dyer, the son of a neighbor, and offered

Delilah Baird's house

him a home and support for the rest of his life if he would come from Texas to defend her rights. "My folks are lawing me to death," Delilah put it. Ben Dyer, in his 70s himself, traveled to North Carolina the following year, only to return to Texas "loveless and forlorn" shortly thereafter. This last part is a known fact, since Dyer sued Delilah for his expenses in May 1882. A jury awarded him exactly $47.50, the price of railroad fare to and from Texas. Delilah lived until 1890 in a small log cabin that stood in front of the white house on the right that overlooks the airstrip today.

Continue 5.9 miles on N.C. 194 to an intersection with U.S. 19E. The Elk River flows beside this leg of the route much as it did in 1883, when Zeigler and Grosscup wrote,

> The scenery along the Elk has something decidedly romantic in its features. On one hand would be perched a moss-grown cottage on the mountain slope, with a few giant hemlocks, allowed to stand at the time of the general clearing, overshadowing it. Below, on the other hand, would lie fertile fields, watered by the noisy Elk, and enclosed on three sides by the dark and sober forests of the hemlock. The serenity of the evening was not disturbed by the farewell whistling of the quails; the rattling of the bells from the cows coming homeward across the pastures; the barking of a dog behind the barnyard fence, and the opening cry of the whip-poor-will.

Turn right on U.S. 19E and drive 1.2 miles to Elk Park. Approximately 0.2 mile past the center of Elk Park, a faded sign at the junction with Old Mill Road points to Elk Falls. Turn right, go 0.3 mile, and turn left onto Elk River Road. For 0.9 mile, the route follows what looks more like a creek than a river; when the road crosses a bridge, the rest of the route parallels the Elk River. It is 3.1 miles from the bridge to the end of the pavement at the parking area for Elk Falls. Park and make the 100-yard walk to the scenic falls.

Retrace your route to the stop sign at the end of Elk River Road. Turn left and wind your way for 0.5 mile to the business district of Elk Park and the intersection with U.S. 19E, where you will have three choices. A right turn will take you into Tennessee, heading toward Elizabethton and Johnson City. A left turn will take you to the junction with N.C. 194 South. There, you can follow U.S. 19E as it turns right toward Spruce Pine, or you can stay straight on N.C. 194 into Newland.

Elk Falls

The Globe Tour

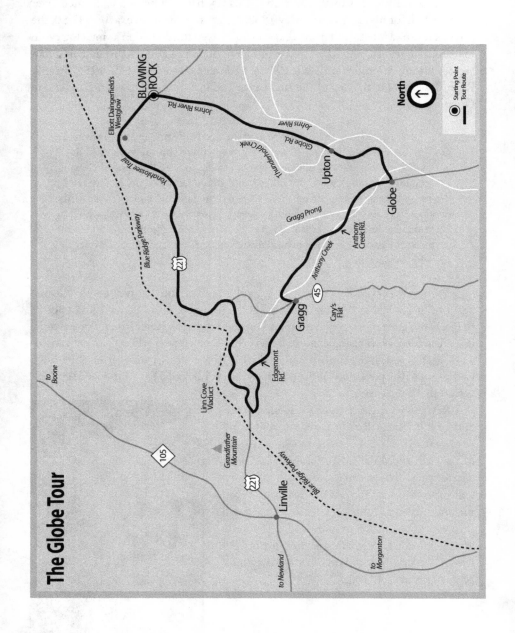

TOUR **17**

The Globe Tour

> This tour begins in the town of Blowing Rock and travels almost straight downhill into a valley known locally as "the Globe." It then proceeds back uphill to the foot of Grandfather Mountain and the crown jewel of the Blue Ridge Parkway, the Linn Cove Viaduct. From there, travelers can continue to Linville or return to Blowing Rock.
>
> Total mileage: approximately 32 miles

Although this tour stops at only one of Blowing Rock's many places of interest, the town is highly recommended as a place to spend days or even weeks. Developed in the 1880s, Blowing Rock is one of the oldest resorts in the southern Appalachians. A stop at the visitors' center on Valley Boulevard (U.S. 321) will provide you with information on several highly visible attractions.

This little-explored route begins at St. Mary's of the Hills Episcopal Church, located on the corner of Chestnut and Main streets two blocks from the town park. Inside St. Mary's is an interesting painting by Elliott Daingerfield, an artist who made Blowing Rock his home for several years. Daingerfield was one of North Carolina's best-known artists. His ecclesiastical and landscape paintings hang in many of the nation's best galleries, including the Metropolitan Museum in New York City and the National Gallery in Washington. He came to Blowing Rock in 1885 to recuperate from an illness and fell in love with the area. During his lifetime, he built three homes in the vicinity.

In 1918, William Stringfellow, a wealthy Alabaman who owned the Chetola Estate in Blowing Rock, made a donation for the construction of a new Episcopal church. He asked Daingerfield to contribute a painting. Daingerfield, long fascinated with a local legend about the Madonna of the Hills, began work at once. Using one of his homes as a backdrop and his wife as a model, he brought the legend to canvas. Blue Ridge natives say that on the summer solstice, the Madonna walks across the hills at dawn. If her coming is attended by blue skies, a rich harvest will

St. Mary's of the Hills Episcopal Church

follow. If clouds mask the peaks and mists cling to her feet, the year will be full of sadness and want. A miracle of beauty follows in her footsteps, for wherever her feet touch the earth, there grows a carpet of daisies, lilies, and rhododendron.

When Daingerfield donated his creation to the church, it was decided to name the new building St. Mary's of the Hills. The painting still hangs in this picturesque mountain church for all to see.

Across from St. Mary's is the equally picturesque Rumple Memorial Presbyterian Church. A few doors down, just before Blowing Rock Methodist Church, is a stop sign where Johns River Road leads downhill to the right and into the Globe. Turn right onto this road. The pavement ends a short distance into the descent. You will be on gravel roads for much of the rest of the route.

The first man to write a description of this area was Bishop August Gottlieb Spangenberg. Much of what he described in 1752 has remained the same. Bishop Spangenberg was sent by the Moravian Church to search for desirable land for a settlement. After reading what he had to say about his ascent out of the Globe, you will probably be thankful that the tour is heading downhill over the same terrain. "Here we have at length arrived after a very toilsome journey over fearful mountains and dangerous cliffs," Spangenberg wrote. "We came into a region from which there was no outlet, except by climbing up an indescribably steep mountain. Part of the way we had to crawl on hands and feet; sometimes we had to take the baggage and saddles and the horses and drag them up the mountains (for the horses were in danger of falling down backward—as we had once had an experience), and sometimes we had to pull the horses up while they trembled and quivered like leaves."

The unpaved road you are traveling has a washboard effect in places, but at

Rumple Memorial Presbyterian Church

least you are in no danger of falling backward. The reward comes during breaks in the foliage, when you will see a scene whose beauty has not diminished in the more than 200 years since Spangenberg's odyssey. "Arrived at the top at last," he wrote. "We saw hundreds of mountain peaks all around us, presenting a spectacle like ocean waves in a storm."

After 5 miles, you will reach the foot of the mountain, where Thunderhold Creek meets the Johns River. This is also the location of Upton. Johns River Missionary Baptist Church, built in 1892, is to the right. The church and some scattered homes are about all that remain of the once-busy community. Several gristmills were once along the route; the cleared areas where they stood are still visible. The last mill was destroyed by the flood of 1940 and was never rebuilt. The thriving enterprise in the area today is obvious from the landscape of the valley—tree and shrub nurseries have sprung up all along the river and creeks.

At the Upton fork, the road becomes Globe Road. "We are now in a locality that has probably been seldom trodden by the foot of man since the creation of the world," wrote Spangenberg, an observation still readily appreciated. "For 70 to 80 miles we have been traveling over terrible mountains, and along very dangerous places where there was no way at all. With respect to this place where we are encamped—one might call it a basin or kettle. It is a cove in the mountains and is very rich soil. Two creeks—one larger than the other—flow through it. Various springs of very sweet water form lovely meadow lands. . . . Our horses find abundant pasture among the buffalo haunts and grass among the springs, which they eat greedily."

It is 2.7 miles from Johns River Missionary Baptist Church to the intersection with Anthony Creek Road at Globe Baptist Church, organized in 1797. Like Upton, this area was a thriving community at one time. It even supported an outstanding preparatory school, the Globe Academy. The school opened to the public in 1882, but the 1916 flood washed it away.

The region had its most exciting history during the Civil War, thanks to the exploits of L. McKesson Blalock, better known by his adopted first name, Keith. When the war broke out, Keith Blalock joined the Confederate army to avoid conscription, but he harbored the idea of deserting and joining the Union forces. His wife, Malinda, didn't want to be left behind, so she, too, joined the 26th Regiment under Colonel Zebulon Vance—only she enlisted as Sam Blalock, Keith's brother. Her disguise worked.

Unfortunately, Keith and Sam did not get an opportunity to join Union forces as the days rolled by. Keith finally took matters into his own hands, sneaking into some bushes and rubbing himself with poison oak. He developed such a severe rash that the doctor took it to be a more serious condition and discharged him in 1862, only one month after his enlistment.

Brother Sam soon followed. Her discharge remains in the official records. She is listed as "Mrs. L. Blaylock [sic]," and beside her name is the notation, "Discharged for being a woman. This lady had done a soldier's duty without a suspicion of her sex among her comrades, until her husband, L. M. Blaylock, was discharged, when she claimed the same privilege and was sent home rejoicing."

But the war was just beginning for Keith. To prevent Confederate forces from finding him when his rash was cured, he and Malinda lived beneath Grandfather Mountain—"under the Grandfather," as the locals say—in a hut. The two fugitives were joined by several others trying to avoid conscription. Keith began recruiting for Unionist forces working out of Tennessee.

Whenever neighbors engage in guerrilla warfare, the affiliation of the observer seems to determine whether a fighter is a scoundrel or a savior. The mountain

*Cascade along
Edgemont Road*

Information sign in Gragg

people were fiercely divided in their loyalties. There were probably few areas in the country where the phrase "brother against brother" was more true than the southern Appalachians. Most of the blood feuds that have survived the generations had their origins during the Civil War.

Blalock and his band began raiding the Globe area. He was frequently seen wearing a Union uniform. Southern sympathizers felt he was a traitor and a deserter and made their feelings known. Many of Keith's enemies lived in the Globe and found themselves the victims of constant raiding by his forces. Malinda was wounded in one raid, and Keith lost an eye in another. Nonetheless, they managed to inflict more than their share of injury, to be sure.

The Southern forces retaliated by killing Keith's stepfather, which only inspired Blalock to increase his raids on the people of the Globe. After the war, he ambushed and killed the man he felt was responsible for his stepfather's murder. He was subsequently pardoned by the governor, a Union sympathizer. Keith Blalock's name is still remembered around these parts. How it is remembered often depends on which side people's ancestors took in the war. Blalock's grave is in Montezuma Cemetery, a few miles from Linville. Ironically, it is marked by a tombstone erected to honor him as a Confederate veteran.

Turn right at Globe Baptist Church and follow Anthony Creek Road. For the next 4.5 miles, the route climbs steadily back up the mountain and travels alongside Gragg Prong and, later, Anthony Creek. Beautiful cascades and small waterfalls are all along the route. Visitors have fashioned a number of turnouts along the road at scenic spots.

Just before the top of the mountain, you will drive a mile-long stretch of road where the trees on the adjoining hillside have been clear-cut. After enjoying the beautiful forest, this will prove a rude awakening. One benefit of the clear-cut area is that you can clearly see a waterfall that drops several hundred feet. When the water level is high, the waterfall is visible by looking back over your shoulder as you make the final climb to the ridge top.

At the top of the mountain, turn right onto Edgemont Road (S.R. 1514). You are now in the community of Gragg. You may not see any road signs here; on the other hand, a helpful hand-drawn road map may still be displayed on the information board at the time of your visit. This level area is also known locally as Cary's Flat. From here, you can look straight up into the face of Grandfather Mountain.

Stay on Edgemont Road as it runs past a former general store and New Hopewell Baptist Church. You are heading straight toward the Grandfather. Said to be over 140 million years old, Grandfather Mountain dominates the landscape of the entire area. In 1794, it affected French botanist André Michaux so profoundly that he wrote, "Climbed to the summit of the highest mountain of all North America with my guide, and sang the Marseillaise Hymn, and cried, 'Long live America and the French Republic! Long live liberty!'" Many people who hike to the top of the Grandfather today feel the same exhilaration, though they no doubt express it in humbler terms.

Pilot Ridge Road (S.R. 115) goes off to the right a little over 1 mile past New Hopewell Baptist Church. Stay on Edgemont Road (S.R. 1514), which continues straight. In another 0.2 mile, F.R. 192 goes left. Stay straight on Edgemont Road.

Driving this route, you will see both Grandfather Mountain and the Linn Cove Viaduct on the Blue Ridge Parkway straight ahead. The mammoth S-shaped

Linn Cove Viaduct

View of the Linn Cove Viaduct from former rock quarry

viaduct is one of the most complicated structures of its kind in the world. Its opening in 1987 completed the 470-mile parkway. For years, motorists had been forced to leave the parkway when they approached Grandfather Mountain and take a 14-mile detour. The delay in construction was caused by battles over rights of way and funding, as well as environmental concerns. After long years of hammering out a compromise, it took another four years and $10 million to complete the viaduct. But the wait was well worth it, as this section of the Blue Ridge Parkway is now proving one of the most popular.

Almost 5 miles past Gragg, you will see what remains of a rock quarry just below the viaduct. About 0.5 mile later, you will reach U.S. 221. You have three options in completing the tour.

You can turn left onto U.S. 221, go 0.4 mile to an intersection with the Blue Ridge Parkway, and head north on the parkway. A short drive will bring you to the viaduct and its incredible view. This route also leads past Price Lake and the Moses Cone Estate en route to Blowing Rock. For more information on these attractions, contact the Blue Ridge Parkway office (see the appendix).

Or you can turn left and stay straight on U.S. 221, which leads past the entrance to Grandfather Mountain. An admission fee is charged. The town of Linville is 2 miles beyond Grandfather's entrance on U.S. 221.

Your third option is to turn right onto U.S. 221 and follow it back to Blowing Rock.

U.S. 221 has an interesting history of its own. The road serves as testimony to how far techniques in building mountain roads have progressed. Also known as the Yonahlossee Trail—which translates from the Cherokee as "trail of the black

bear"—U.S. 221 looks like surveyors must have been tracking a bear when they laid out its course. Built by Hugh MacRae in 1889, it was originally a toll road designed to open MacRae's isolated resort of Linville to visitors in the Blowing Rock area.

MacRae ordered one of the last coaches ever made by the Wells Fargo Company and used it to transport tourists from Blowing Rock to Linville. The coach was to be called Awahili, meaning "eagle" in Cherokee, but the imprinter misread the instructions and the coach came back with "Awahili Cherokee" printed on its door. The stage held up to 18 people and made one trip a day, charging two dollars a head. MacRae also charged 25 cents for a two-horse wagon traveling his road and 10 cents for a rider on horseback. The toll road operated until 1920, when it became a public road.

Whereas a total of $24 million was spent on the final 8 miles of the Blue Ridge Parkway, MacRae's road cost only $18,000 to build. Ironically, his route served as the detour while all the controversy surrounding the construction of the last stretch of the parkway was being resolved. The Yonahlossee Trail took two years to build, and more than 300 men worked on it. The task was accomplished by bush crews, log crews, and shovel and mattock crews, in contrast to the heavy machinery that built the parkway now running above the old road. Although driving it takes a lot longer than the parkway, U.S. 221 may be your choice if you have already traveled the parkway and are looking for a change of scenery. If you choose a right turn off Edgemont Road, it is approximately 12 miles back to Blowing Rock along this route.

Near Blowing Rock on U.S. 221 is Westglow, one of the homes built by Elliott Daingerfield. This white Colonial mansion sits on the land that provided the back-

Westglow, the former home of Elliott Daingerfield

ground for his *Madonna of the Hills.* The two-story Grecian columns at the front of the house were imported from Italy. They were floated by river barge and hauled up the mountain by oxen. The stairwell and banister inside the house were designed by a French architect. The home was filled with antiques and Oriental rugs. It was completed in 1917 for a reputed cost of $20,000. Westglow now houses a top-rated luxury spa and a first-rate restaurant open to the public.

After glimpsing Daingerfield's summer home in Blowing Rock, you will have come full circle.

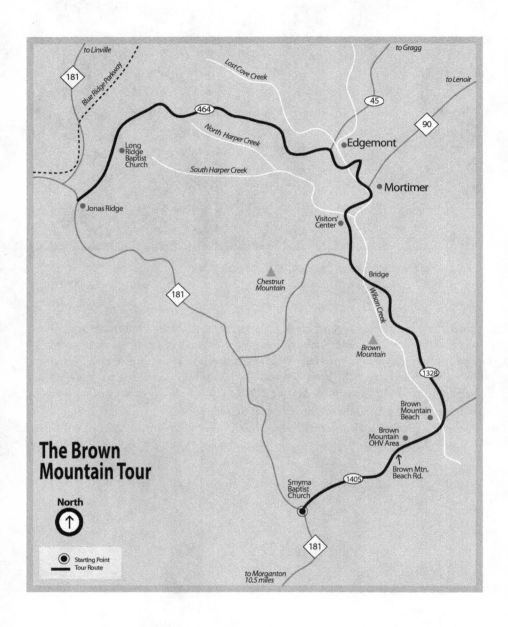

The Brown Mountain Tour

North

⊙ Starting Point
▬ Tour Route

TOUR 18
The Brown Mountain Tour

This tour travels along the foot of Brown Mountain, a ridge famous for the mysterious lights that have been spotted for generations. It also parallels scenic Wilson Creek, passes the virtual ghost town of Mortimer and the community of Edgemont, and climbs through the Harper Creek and Lost Cove wilderness study areas before ending at the community of Jonas Ridge.

Total mileage: approximately 42 miles

The tour begins on the outskirts of Morganton as N.C. 181 heads north toward the mountains. Drive 10 miles on N.C. 181 past the Kmart shopping center. You will see Smyrna Baptist Church as N.C. 181 makes a sharp curve to the left. Turn right onto Brown Mountain Beach Road (S.R. 1405) in front of the church.

After 3.5 miles, you will see signs for the entrance to Brown Mountain Off-Highway Vehicle Area, on the left. The area has 34 miles of trails and is the only place in Pisgah National Forest where ATVs and unlicensed trail bikes can be ridden. Some primitive campsites with tables and grills are available. Visitors must carry a dated fee stub or a season pass while on the trails. Passes are available for purchase at the self-service fee station at the entrance to the trail system. The area is open from mid-March through November and is crowded on weekends.

In 1.5 miles, turn left onto Brown Mountain Road (S.R. 1328) just after crossing a bridge. The road parallels Wilson Creek for the next 9 miles. In 2000, Wilson Creek was declared part of the National Wild and Scenic Rivers System. The river's 2.3-mile gorge is well known for its outstanding scenery, fishing, hunting, and challenging whitewater. The section that parallels the tour includes a difficult run of Class II–IV rapids suitable only for skilled paddlers.

All along the route are numerous trailheads, many for paths leading to scenic waterfalls.

View of Wilson Creek

Almost all the rest of the area covered in the tour is part of the Grandfather Ranger District of Pisgah National Forest. An excellent trail guide is available through the national forest district office (see the appendix). The guide can also be purchased at the visitors' center mentioned later in the tour.

Prior to 1750, this entire area was primarily an Indian summer hunting ground. Today, it is stocked with bears and wild turkeys and is once again a noted hunting area. The region has a large deer herd, as well as plentiful squirrels and grouse. Several miles of streams have been designated trophy, native, or general trout waters.

Approximately 0.8 mile from the turn, you will see Brown Mountain Beach Resort on the left. The "resort" is actually pretty rustic. The unusual rock buildings visible from the road serve as clues that this campground was in operation long before modern, full-hookup facilities came into being.

In 1916, the area was devastated by a major flood. That July, torrential rains fell for 36 hours. The Catawba River, fed by Wilson Creek, was said to have risen 45 feet. Because one of the main industries of the region was the clearing of timber, the heavy rain on the recently deforested hills caused landslides along Wilson Creek. The natural dams created by the landslides didn't last long, and their demise sent a violent rush of water deeper into the valley. Along with the water went buildings, bridges, railroad trestles, lumber, and boulders. A great deal of the debris landed at the present site of Brown Mountain Beach.

The summer resort was constructed on land scooped out by the disastrous flood. This has been a camping and recreation spot since the 1920s. As you travel past, you may be able to see the boulders that line the campground's drives. They are remnants of the 1916 flood.

Past the campground on S.R. 1328, you will enter Pisgah National Forest, where the paved part of the tour ends. For the next 4.5 miles, you will travel a gravel road with occasional cliffs on one side and Wilson Creek's gorge on the other. Designated parking areas are located all along the route. This area is a popular summer hangout for people from the surrounding counties because of its numerous natural swimming holes. It is advisable to drive this part of the tour early in the morning, before the crowds arrive. Most of the designated parking areas have trails that lead down to the rocky creek. Some have steps or railings, but most are still treacherous. You will

Paddlers shooting the rapids on Wilson Creek

probably notice a great many fishermen, swimmers, and sunbathers. If the water level is high, especially after heavy rains, you will see lots of paddlers.

As you pass through the gorge, you are traveling parallel to the ridge known as Brown Mountain, the supposed location of the renowned Brown Mountain Lights. Ask anyone who lives in the area about the lights and they will probably have a story to tell. Most will probably claim to have seen the lights. The only problem is that no two people seem to describe the same thing. Some say the lights

Brown Mountain Beach after the 1940 flood

are red at first, then change colors before they fade to pale blue. Some say they are white, while others say they are like big, shining stars. Some say they appear in groups of three, each light ascending, hovering for a brief period, and then vanishing. Despite the variations in description, there is little doubt about the lights on or near the mountain, the cause of which has yet to be explained.

In 1771, Gerard de Brahm, a German engineer and the first white man to explore the region, recorded his account of the lights. He wrote that "the mountain emits nitrous vapors, which are borne by the wind, and when the laden winds meet each other the nitre inflames, sulphurates, and deteriorates. This causes the lights to inflame." If Gerard de Brahm's version sounds a bit far-fetched, rest assured that it is no worse than some of the later theories.

The Reverend C. E. Gregory of New York is credited in some sources as being the first to bring the lights to the world's attention. In 1910, he built a cottage south of the mountain and soon told all his friends about the mysterious lights he saw from his home. By October 1913, popular interest had grown so strong that the United States Geological Survey sent D. B. Sarrette to make a study of the lights. Sarrette quickly concluded that they were simply the headlights of locomotives on the railway in the Catawba Valley below. Although many old-timers claimed the lights had been seen since Civil War times—before the railroad was built—Sarrette's theory was accepted by most of the educated public. Then the flood of 1916 wiped out all railroad transportation that summer. No one could explain why the lights continued to make their appearance in the absence of railroad activity.

During the next few years, numerous individuals conducted independent studies, each emerging with a different conclusion. The theories attributed the lights to will-o'-the-wisp, foxfire, St. Elmo's fire, Andes lights, and even radium emanations.

In 1922, the United States Geological Survey tried again. The new investigator, George Rogers Mansfield, took his assignment seriously. The first thing he did was set about refuting the theories advanced by independent investigators. Then, armed with a battery of surveying instruments, cameras, and topographical maps, he spent two weeks observing the lights and mapping their approximate origin. He reported that of the 23 lights he saw, seven were caused by locomotive headlights, since their times and location coincided with those of passing trains; 10 were caused by automobile headlights; two or three were caused by stationary lights in towns; and the remainder were caused by brush fires.

The 1916 flood may have washed out the railroad and temporarily eliminated it as a possible cause of the lights, but Mansfield dismissed that as an irrelevant point, since the lights witnessed during the period following the flood were probably caused by automobiles. The fact that there was little automobile travel in the area before the flood didn't seem to sway him. Though his findings may have accounted for some of the sightings, a great many remained unexplained. And Mansfield still hadn't answered the question of why the lights appeared only in one particular location. He did concede that although the lights originated from artificial sources, "they were given a supernatural aspect by reason of the particular and unique atmospheric conditions in the area."

Legendary explanations for the lights are plentiful, too.

According to Cherokee lore, the lights existed as far back as the year 1200, when the Cherokee and Catawba Indians fought atop Brown Mountain. The Cherokee version attributes the lights to the fallen braves' widows, who are still searching for their lost husbands today.

Lafayette Wiseman, a Civil War veteran who served under Robert E. Lee, is credited with transmitting the tale that the lights were the ghost of an old slave searching for his Low Country master, who had disappeared in the mountains while on a hunting expedition. Wiseman's great-nephew Scotty grew up to become a popular star at the Grand Ole Opry. He used the story to write "The Legend of the Brown Mountain Lights." Recorded by country-music star Tommy Faile, the song became a popular ballad in the early 1960s.

One favorite is the story of Belinda, as recorded by famous folklore collector Frank C. Brown. According to the legend, a man named Jim was the husband of Belinda and the father of her child. He had, however, been seeing another woman, Susie. When Belinda and her child mysteriously disappeared one day, many locals suspected foul play but couldn't refute Jim's claim that Belinda had just "put on her old bonnet and left the other day and she hasn't come back yet."

Soon after Belinda's disappearance, the mysterious lights began. Some residents finally decided to follow them to their source. They were led to a cliff, where they discovered what appeared to be the bodies of Belinda and her child. One witness to the discovery was the narrator of the version recorded by Frank C. Brown. That narrator remarked, "You know folks say the skulls of murdered people never decay, and I have heard all my life that if you ever took the skull of a murdered person and got it over the head of the person who murdered the one who was murdered, and asked them about it they couldn't tell a lie; they would have to tell the truth."

Jim was put to the test. He supposedly turned white as a sheet and began to tremble, but he wouldn't admit to murdering his wife and child. From then on, things went downhill for Jim. He began to lose his mind, constantly beating at the air and screaming for Belinda to "get away." He died a short time later. It is said that Belinda's soul still roams the ridge in the form of the mysterious Brown Mountain Lights.

Perhaps the moral to be gleaned from all these versions—whether grounded in science or folklore—is that the cause of the lights doesn't really matter. Most people like to conjure up visions of spirits and ghosts when they are sitting alone on a darkened mountain. Perhaps the more versions, the deeper and better the legend.

Approximately 3.5 miles from where the pavement ended, the route crosses the Wilson Creek bridge and reaches a fork in the road. Proceed to the right on Wilson Creek Road (S.R. 1328), following the signs for the town of Mortimer and Walker's Country Store. In 0.9 mile, you come to Walker's, on the left. The valley where the store is located was once the community of Hut Burrow, but the flood ended that town's existence, as it did so many others. The Wilson Creek Visitors' Center, open from April through November, is next to Walker's. It has an exhibit of historical photographs that show life in the area.

Continue 1.7 miles to a small parking area on the left. This is the trailhead for the Harper Creek trail system. Two of the most popular treks in the area lead to Harper Creek Falls and on to South Harper Creek Falls, for those who want a longer loop hike.

About 0.6 mile past the trailhead, you will begin to see the remains of the once-bustling community of Mortimer.

"Mortimer sprung up almost in a night and has flourished like the green bay tree. There are more than 100 houses in the place and some of them are as pretty as a fellow would find in a day's journey. I cannot imagine a better location for a little town than the one on which Mortimer is built." So wrote an admirer in 1905.

In 1904, the Ritter Lumber Company bought area land for its timber and developed the town of Mortimer to process lumber. In addition to buildings for its lumber operation, Ritter constructed a company store, a blacksmith's shop, a church, a school, a hotel, and numerous houses. Upon the arrival of the Carolina and Northwestern Railroad in September 1905, it even built a depot.

Some reports suggest that as many as 800 people were employed by Ritter and that the company had five engines bringing logs from the mountainside to the mill in the village. Things became so civilized that by 1906 Mortimer had two churches, a motion-picture facility, and the Laurel Inn, which attracted visitors for weekend stays. Teddy Roosevelt reportedly visited Mortimer and danced with Mrs. Bill Mortimer in the inn's ballroom. The Carolina and Northwestern added passenger

Wilson Creek Visitors' Center

service by 1910, bringing as many as 30 riders a day.

But disaster struck with the flood of July 1916. Much of the lumber company's operation was destroyed, along with many homes. Though more than 10 million board feet of lumber remained, most of it was badly damaged. The Ritter Lumber Company supplied the manpower that restored the rail service so vital to its operation, and the trains were running again as soon as August 29. Unfortunately, most of the virgin timber had already been cut, so Ritter began to slow its operation, staying only long enough to process the lumber on hand.

It appeared Mortimer was doomed, but the erection of a cotton mill about a mile below the village in 1922 made it a thriving community once again. The revitalization was short-lived. A fall in demand for the coarse yarn produced by the mill led its owners to close up shop in 1928.

Another burst of activity came in 1933, when the Civilian Conservation Corps (CCC) built a camp for 300 men engaged in constructing trails and roads and repairing many of the buildings in the village. In 1934, the old mill was reopened for the production of hosiery. The owner, O. P. Lutz, imported German-made machinery and even hired German technicians to run some of it, but his enterprise never really got off the ground. By 1938, the railroad closed.

The final blow came in 1940 with a second devastating flood caused by a hurricane that poured three days of rain on the area on August 12–14. Highway officials estimated that 90 percent of the bridges in Caldwell County were washed away. Wilson Creek reportedly reached a record flood stage of 94 feet. Few buildings in Mortimer survived, though the CCC camp somehow managed to escape destruction. The men of the camp stayed on through the early 1940s. One of their tasks was to take up the railroad tracks, which they reportedly shipped off for use in making war materials. The old railroad bed is now the road on which you are traveling.

Approaching Mortimer on S.R. 1328, you will see the remains of the hosiery mill stretching for about 0.1 mile on the right. Before crossing a small bridge, you can view the former site of the Laurel Inn on a hill on the left overlooking the creek. Though the inn collapsed from neglect, evidence of where it stood remains.

The village of Mortimer has been replaced by small cabins and trailers leased by fishermen and campers from the heirs of hosier O. P. Lutz. On the left just past the congested area of cabins and trailers is what remains of a bridge abutment. Mortimer's old school used to stand near this location. It was burned as a precaution after it was used to house patients during a smallpox epidemic. The old depot was located in the field near the present general store before it was moved to greener pastures as an exhibit at Frontier Village in Kentucky. The only two buildings that survived the 1940 flood are, on the right, the general store, and across the road, the white ranger station built by the United States Forest Service. The latter structure seems to be guarding the entrance to the campground area.

At the store, turn left onto N.C. 90, following the sign for Edgemont Baptist Church. The route passes Mortimer Recreation Area and its camping facilities and heads up the mountain to Edgemont. Because Edgemont escaped the brunt of the floods that hit Mortimer, greater evidence of past prosperity remains here.

On the left 2 miles past Mortimer is a white building with green shutters. Closer to the roadside is a small white building. The larger of the two is the old Edgemont railroad depot. It has been restored and now serves as a private residence. The smaller building, once the baggage house, is now a guesthouse. Since Edgemont was the end of the railway line coming up from Chester, South Carolina, it also became the rendezvous point for the hired carriages and wagons sent down to transport tourists to resorts in Linville and Blowing Rock. During the week of the Fourth of July, special excursion trains ran from South Carolina.

Continuing on N.C. 90, you will cross a creek just past the old depot. Turn right at another sign for Edgemont Baptist Church. You will soon see the picturesque white church built in 1916 sitting atop a small hill. Turn right again just before the church to see where the Edgemont Hotel once stood. Edgemont turned into something of a resort area upon the opening of the hotel, also known as the Rainbow Lodge. The hotel stood on this spot until a fire caused by vandals de-

Edgemont Baptist Church

stroyed it in the 1990s. In its glory days, it even offered cabins for Camp Rainbow, a summer camp for girls run by the Order of the Eastern Star. The camp was located in the large field in front of the hotel.

Return to N.C. 90 and turn right. You will soon approach Coffey's General Store, the focal point of what remains of the village of Edgemont.

The store is well worth a stop. It seems to have changed little since it was built in the early 1900s. Unlike many of the "restored" general stores cropping up for tourists in the mountains, Coffey's is the real McCoy. The store was originally located on the other side of the creek, but when the flood of 1916 changed the creek's course and necessitated the relocation of the road, the store's owner decided to move it to where it now stands. The store was actually placed up the road several hundred yards from its present location, but the floodwaters of 1940 moved it a second time. As Archie Coffey, who ran the store and the Edgemont post office for over 40 years, put it in a 1977 newspaper interview, the flood "picked up this store building and washed it up against a big tree. I didn't lose but about five or six cans

Edgemont Hotel before it burned in the 1990s

Coffey's General Store in Edgemont

off the shelves, but I never did get it level again. That's why the floor is buckled."

Buckled floor or not, the store still stands. Coffey's, like Walker's Country Store earlier in the tour, is a working store that serves its community. Both are recommended stops for travelers to sit a spell and ask questions about the history of the area. Coffey's has old photographs showing the effects of the two major floods.

When you have seen Edgemont, turn around and drive 0.6 mile back past the old depot. Just beyond the depot is Pineola Road (F.R. 464). Turn right onto this "narrow winding road with turnouts," as the sign correctly describes it. The steeply graded road travels through the wilderness study areas of Lost Cove and Harper Creek.

Thanks to the area's dramatic drops in altitude, many of the 25 trails around Wilson Creek offer hikers access to stunning waterfalls. Some of the most impressive are the 200-foot falls and cascades known as South Harper Creek Falls (whose trailhead was noted earlier), the exceptionally beautiful North Harper Creek Falls, the three-tiered Hunt Fish Falls, and the several sets of scenic falls along Gragg Prong. As you proceed up F.R. 464, you will see signs for the trailheads all along the road.

It is 3 miles to the parking area at the trailhead for Hunt Fish Falls, accessible via a hike of 0.8 mile. A drive of another 1.9 miles leads to the trailhead for North Harper Creek Falls, reached by an easy 1.1-mile hike. The waterfall drops 40 feet into a 50-foot-wide pool.

It is about here that the profile of Grandfather Mountain begins to break through the gaps in the forest on the right. If you look above the road to the left, you will also notice the sheer rock wall known as Little Lost Cove Cliffs. Continue 1.3 miles from the North Harper Creek Falls trailhead to a trailhead on the left. A difficult 1.3-mile hike leads straight up the hill to the cliffs. The elevation at the top of Little Lost Cove Cliffs is 3,400 feet. Hikers who make the climb have an excellent view of the mountain range dominated by the Grandfather.

It is 0.6 mile farther down F.R. 464 to a primitive campsite on the right. In another 0.9 mile is a trailhead on the right for a hike leading to Big Lost Cove Cliffs. Lost Cove Cliffs Overlook is a prime vantage point on the Blue Ridge Parkway for viewing the Brown Mountain Lights. An easy 1.7-mile hike leads to the cliffs, which have been designated a peregrine falcon nesting site and have well-marked areas where hikers and climbers should not go. Peregrine falcons were removed from the endangered species list in 1999. In 2009, some 12 pairs nested in the area, seven of them on forest-service lands. Only three of the 12 pairs produced fledglings, indicating that reproductive success continues to be a concern. Young chicks startled prior to acquiring full flight capability will run off the edge of the cliff attempting to escape the threat. Entering a closed site after the chicks have hatched but before they can fly will almost certainly cause this response. Entry into the areas defined by orange-painted boundaries is prohibited between January 15 and August 15. Be sure to heed the designated off-limits areas.

Continue 1.6 miles on F.R. 464 past the trailhead for Big Lost Cove Cliffs to Long Ridge Baptist Church, on the right. Turn left onto the paved road directly across from the church. About 0.6 mile up that road is Pittman Gap Community Church. Turn left and go 2.1 miles on Mortimer Road to the Jonas Ridge post office, on the left.

The naming of the community of Jonas Ridge is an interesting bit of trivia. The man for whom it was named, Jonas Braswell, did not own land, reside, or farm here. He did not even discover the place. His name has been stamped on the ridge because it was here that Jonas Braswell froze to death. Caught in a snowstorm on a camping trip in the 1800s, Jonas became ill and was forced to spend the night under a rock on a high ridge. The next day, he was carried to a nearby house, but he was too far gone to save. The evolution of the name from Jonas's Ridge to Jonas Ridge was a slow but logical one.

The tour concludes at "Jonas's Ridge." You are at the intersection with N.C. 181. An intersection with the Blue Ridge Parkway is 2.3 miles to the right. A left turn will take you down N.C. 181 to Morganton.

Waterfall on Gragg Prong in Lost Cove Wilderness Study Area

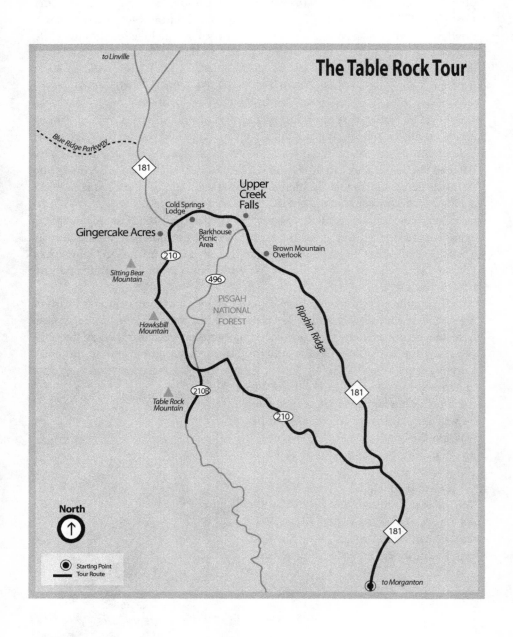

TOUR 19
The Table Rock Tour

This tour travels into the heart of Linville Gorge Wilderness Area. At points, it parallels the ridge that features Table Rock and Hawksbill mountains, both prominent peaks. It then turns onto a United States Forest Service road that travels past Hawksbill and to the top of Table Rock. The tour includes several recommended short hikes on trails with moderate grades but also allows drivers to enjoy an abundance of remarkable scenery without ever leaving their cars.

Total mileage: approximately 50 miles

The tour begins by heading northwest out of Morganton on N.C. 181 North. On the right at the corner of N.C. 181 and Bost Road just past the Kmart shopping center, you will see a stone monument in front of a restaurant parking lot. The monument memorializes Quaker Meadows.

Although it is hard to envision, this largely commercialized strip of road runs through what Bishop August Spangenberg described as some of the richest country he had seen in his search for land for a Moravian settlement in 1752.

According to tradition, the Indians cleared part of this broad and fertile bottom land and then allowed the wild grasses to grow, thus forming a large meadow, near which a Quaker camped before the French and Indian War. Spangenberg passed on purchasing this land because the war began the next year, making it unsafe to venture west of the Catawba River until after 1763.

In 1780, the fighters soon to be known as the Overmountain Men came from different locations to meet at Quaker Meadows. Isaac Shelby and John Sevier gathered at Sycamore Shoals, Tennessee, with over 400 men before marching here. William and Arthur Campbell of Virginia arrived here with another 400 to join the 160 men camped with their leader, Charles McDowell Jr. On September 30, those forces were joined by another 350 troops led by Benjamin Cleveland from

Wilkes County and Joseph Winston from Surry County. That night, the leaders met under a large oak tree to plan for their march to the Battle of Kings Mountain, where they were victorious against the British. The old tree, known as "the Council Oak," stood into the 20th century at the intersection where the stone marker now sits. For more about the march across the mountains from Tennessee, see "The Overmountain Victory Trail Tour."

Continue on N.C. 181. The highway roughly parallels a toll road built by Anderson Loven in 1889. Called "the Turnpike Road" by locals, it ran from Joy, a small community outside Morganton, to Pineola at the top of the ridge. Building the road through native rock was no small feat. Loven soon learned to pour boiling water over the rocks to crack them and make them easier to move. He did such a good job that his toll road existed until 1927.

Traveling N.C. 181, you will be aware of two uniquely shaped peaks dominating the landscape. The ascent begins to level off on Ripshin Ridge. You will see Table Rock and Hawksbill mountains so close on the left that it seems you could reach out and touch them. The areas on both sides of N.C. 181 and Ripshin Ridge are part of Pisgah National Forest. The forest is divided into various ranger districts; this tour travels through the Grandfather District. Between Ripshin Ridge and the ridge that includes Table Rock and Hawksbill is the deep river valley called Linville Gorge. The Linville River and the 10,975 acres that make up the gorge have been declared a wilderness area. Wilderness status carries with it regulations concerning road building and tree cutting, among other things, and it should ensure that this tour remains a backroad for some time to come.

The Linville River descends 2,000 feet in a 14-mile stretch. The whole gorge abounds in plant and animal life, including five species of rare plants, four species of rhododendron, and even virgin forests tucked in the rugged coves. Deer, bears, squirrels, raccoons, hawks, owls, copperheads, and timber rattlers can all be found in the forest.

Travelers in the area have long recorded their impressions, most of them focusing on the magnificence of Table Rock and Hawksbill. One such visitor was Charles Lanman, who toured the area on horseback in 1849. He was more impressed with Hawksbill than Table Rock. In his *Letters from the Alleghany Mountains*, Lanman wrote, "The prominent pictorial feature of the North Cove is of a mountain called the Hawk's Bill, on account of its resemblance to the beak of a mammoth bird, the length of the bill being about fifteen hundred feet. It is visible from nearly every part of the valley, and to my fancy is a more picturesque object than the Table Mountain, which is too regular at the sides and top to satisfy the eye. The table part of this mountain, however, is twenty-five hundred feet high, and therefore worthy of its fame." Actually, Table Rock measures 3,909 feet and Hawksbill 4,020 feet.

Another visitor, French novelist Jules Verne, found Table Rock especially memorable. In fact, he made it the setting for mysterious happenings in his novel *The Master of the World*. Published in 1904, one year before Verne's death, the novel opens with a description of a place called Great Eyrie. There is little doubt

View of Table Rock and Hawksbill from N.C. 181

that Verne was actually writing of Table Rock: "There, deep amid the Blueridge [*sic*] Mountains rises the crest called the Great Eyrie. Its huge rounded form is distinctly seen from the little town of Morganton on the Catawba River. . . . It rises rocky and grim and inaccessible, and under certain atmospheric conditions has a peculiarly blue and distant effect." Though no dastardly deeds take place inside Table Rock like in Verne's Great Eyrie, traveling alongside the mountain certainly suggests why he found it the perfect vehicle for his plot.

After the tour, you can decide for yourself whether you prefer Hawksbill or Table Rock.

Approximately 18.5 miles from Morganton, you will see an overlook on the right that is one of the recommended vantage points for the Brown Mountain Lights. As you look into the valley, Brown Mountain is the ridge to the right. A detailed discussion of the mysterious lights is in "The Brown Mountain Tour."

It is 0.4 mile past the overlook to a sign on the right for the popular Upper Creek and Greentown trails. Cars are often parked along the road. The trails are now part of the Mountains-to-Sea Trail, which when completed will stretch from the Great Smoky Mountains to the Outer Banks. The Grandfather District has 200 miles of trails, some of them with very little marking. The trails are usually obvious, but a forest-service topographical map is recommended to help solve dilemmas when they arise.

Continue about 0.4 mile on N.C. 181 to Barkhouse Picnic Area, on the left. Sheltered by trees and rhododendron, the picnic area has an interesting history. The name Barkhouse lingers from a home that stood for many years on the opposite side of what is now N.C. 181. The house was built by the same Anderson Loven of toll-road fame for a rich New Yorker named Kirkby. Legend has it that

Kirkby decked his place out with the best of furniture, silver, linens, and crystal, all for the benefit of his English bride. Upon being brought to the "bark house"— so named because it was weatherboarded with bark—Mrs. Kirkby was not duly impressed with either the scenery or the isolation. The house was deeded to her mother in New York but was inhabited solely by caretakers until it and 100 surrounding acres were sold to the forest service. The house was torn down, but the name somehow found its way to this picnic ground.

As you drive N.C. 181 near Barkhouse Picnic Area, you must negotiate a series of steeply banked curves. The mountain you are circling is Winding Stair Knob. Believe it or not, N.C. 181 was completely closed for several years while the road was "straightened" to its present form. Travelers will have little doubt about how the mountain received its name.

The land around Winding Stair Knob and Barkhouse Picnic Area was the scene of a Civil War skirmish that left local people calling the area "Kirk's Battle Ground." Both Union and Confederate supporters inhabited the mountains of North Carolina, a state of affairs that led to frequent dissension. In 1864, East Tennessee was captured by Union forces under Colonel George Kirk, who proceeded to conduct raids throughout Tennessee and western North Carolina. On June 29, Kirk made one of his most daring moves with a raid on Camp Vance, located near Morganton. Approximately 130 of his men marched into the camp under a flag of truce and tricked the lieutenant in charge into surrendering. Kirk's men immediately violated the terms of the agreement by burning every building except the hospital, whose kinder fate was attributed to the "blarney and ingenious persuasion" of the camp's surgeons. Some 279 prisoners were supposedly taken, including 240 unarmed and unorganized junior reserves.

After stripping the camp, Kirk and his men retreated up the mountain. The Burke County Home Guard, in hot pursuit, caught them at Winding Stair Knob. According to one source, Kirk left only 25 men—among them 12 Cherokee Indians—to engage the Confederates, since the Union position was so strong. The Burke County Home Guard had to march straight up the narrow road into a dense fog. They were strung out for a mile or more down the mountain, with no space to form except in the road. Kirk's men fired on the advance guard, killing William Waightstill Avery, one of Burke County's leading citizens. When the home guard retired, Kirk retreated into East Tennessee. Some local people say that for many years bullets from the skirmish could be found lodged in trees. Whether or not the action at Camp Vance constituted a strategic Union victory depends entirely on which side you believe.

Continue 0.8 mile up N.C. 181, where you will see a sign on the right for Upper Creek Parking Area, from which a moderately difficult trail leads to Upper Creek Falls. The round-trip distance is 1.6 miles and the estimated hiking time one hour. You can actually make a loop by starting at the trailhead on the left side of the parking area, which will take you to the upper part of the falls. From there, you can hike down alongside the creek until you come to the lower set of falls, then cross the creek and come back up the trail to the other end of the parking area. This nice side trip might prove a welcome respite from traveling in the car.

Lower level of Upper Creek Falls

Higher level of Upper Creek Falls

Follow N.C. 181 for 0.7 mile past Upper Creek Parking Area to the crest of a ridge, where you will notice a white building on the left. It stands where Anderson Loven built his lodge at the height of his toll-road business. Even after the days of the toll road, the Loven Hotel remained a successful summer resort and a bear hunters' paradise. It passed through several owners and a name change—to Cold Springs Lodge—before fire destroyed it in 1950. A new building was erected to be run as a lodge, but that structure was eventually turned into the private residence visible today.

Site of former Cold Springs Lodge

On the left 0.4 mile past the site of the former lodge is the entrance to Ginger-cake Acres via Old Gingercake Road (S.R. 1264). A sign directs travelers to Table Rock Picnic Area. Turn left onto this road, which leads through a residential area. At 0.3 mile, turn left at the first fork onto Gingercake Acres Road (S.R. 1265), which becomes F.R. 210 when the pavement ends 0.9 mile later. The rest of the tour is on gravel roads.

It is 1.3 miles from the end of the paved portion of road to the trailhead for the Sitting Bear Trail, which takes hikers to Sitting Bear Rock. This strange formation consists of a huge boulder 32 feet long and about eight feet thick balanced precariously on a pyramid-shaped stone 30 feet high. It is called Sitting Bear Rock because of its resemblance to a bear on its haunches. Though the resemblance isn't perfect, you will at least concede that it looks more like a bear than it does a slice of ginger cake. Early settlers in the area apparently thought differently, calling it Gingercake Rock. Gingercake Mountain was thus named for the singular pile of rock perched on its extreme summit. Charles Lanman wrote in 1849 that the "appearance of this rocky wonder is exceedingly tottleish, and though we may be assured that it has stood upon that eminence perhaps for a thousand years, yet it is impossible to tarry within its shadow without a feeling of insecurity." Lanman's observation still rings true.

Maybe the original name seems out of place because the perceptions of the character credited with christening the rock were a bit distorted. That character was a hermit known as Culgee Watson who lived in the gap between Gingercake and Hawksbill mountains. Watson died in 1816 and is supposedly buried somewhere in the area. It is said that he moved to this isolated spot because of a disappointment in love. That would go a long way toward explaining his aversion to the female sex, which was so extreme that he burned the rail of any fence a female touched and covered with dirt any place one sat. Watson was also well known in

Sitting Bear Rock

the area because he raised peacocks and used their feathers to trim his clothing. For some unknown reason, he called his suit covered with peacock feathers his "culgee"—hence the name by which he is popularly known. You probably won't see any peacocks, but a hike to Sitting Bear Rock is definitely worth the time nonetheless.

It is an additional 1 mile on F.R. 210 to the trailhead for the Hawksbill Mountain Trail. If you are in the mood for another hike, park your car, cross the road, and tackle the steep ascent of Lettered Rock Ridge. At 0.5 mile (after about 15 minutes of hiking), you will come to a junction marked only by a post in the middle of the trail. The marker may be misleading, but if you look back over your left shoulder, you will see the side trail you want ascending straight up the mountain. After 0.7

View from the top of Hawksbill

mile and another 15 minutes or so, the side trail reaches the summit of Hawksbill. It is worth every step, because you will find yourself on top of the world, with a 360-degree view of the area featuring Table Rock, Linville Gorge, Lake James at the end of the gorge, and Grandfather Mountain on the opposite side. The round-trip hike takes around an hour, depending on how you take to climbing steep trails. It is highly recommended.

About 2 miles past the parking area for the Hawksbill Mountain Trail, turn right off F.R. 210 onto F.R. 210B to access Table Rock Picnic Area. Before reaching the picnic area, you will pass a mildly confusing turn at 0.6 mile at the sign describing the North Carolina Outward Bound School, which is 0.5 mile to the right; you should follow the sign to the Table Rock summit and parking lot, which are 2.5 miles ahead. The last mile climbs a steep paved road, but the view from Table Rock is well worth the effort.

The parking area offers limited space. From it, you can see the beginning of a 1-mile route described on a sign as "hazardous cliff, rocky trail." The route leads to the top of Table Rock. Hiking time to the summit is approximately 30 minutes. Be forewarned that this is a popular area. Sometimes, cars are forced to park on the almost nonexistent shoulders as far as a mile from the trailhead. The fact that the parking area is frequently filled on weekends also means that the number of people who can make the trek to the summit is limited. Hikers are often rewarded with rappelling demonstrations. The United States Army brings some of its soldiers to Linville Gorge for wilderness-training exercises. They and students from the North Carolina Outward Bound School often rappel down the sheer face of Table Rock. But even if you find no action on the rocks, the view is the perfect culmination of this tour.

View of Linville Gorge

You have a few options in returning to civilization.

One course is to backtrack to the intersection of Old Gingercake Road (S.R. 1264) and N.C. 181; the Blue Ridge Parkway and the town of Linville are only a few miles to the left.

Or you may choose to retrace the tour all the way to Morganton, where you can pick up I-40.

If you want to continue exploring new territory, you can make a circle back to Morganton by turning right at the intersection of F.R. 210B and F.R. 210. This route leads 9 miles downhill over a winding gravel road; because of the road, the drive takes approximately 45 minutes. When you reach pavement, turn left off Table Rock Road onto Simpson Creek Road. It is 0.3 mile to an intersection with N.C. 181. If you turn right, it is 10.4 miles west to the monument for the Council Oak in Morganton.

The Old Buffalo Trail Tour

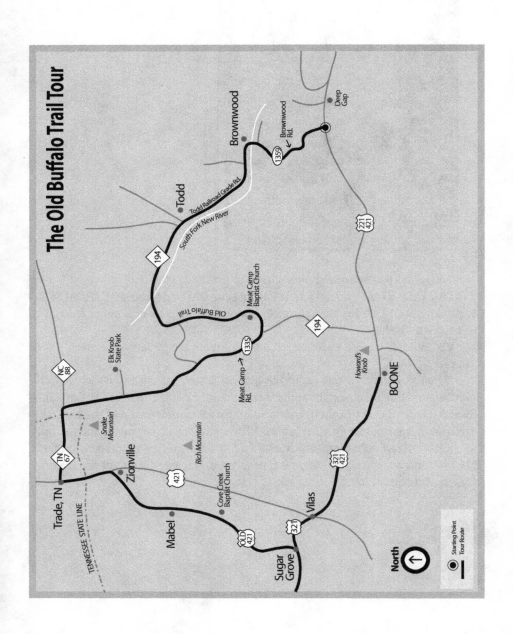

TOUR **20**
The Old Buffalo Trail Tour

This tour follows the South Fork of the New River to the community of Todd. From there, it weaves along the ridges, journeying on a trail originally cut by herds of buffalo. It passes an old hunters' camp called Meat Camp and goes to Elk Knob State Park and into Trade, Tennessee, before returning to North Carolina at Zionville. It continues to Cove Creek and ends at Boone.

Total mileage: approximately 126 miles

The tour starts on U.S. 421 near Deep Gap at Brownwood Road, which is 2 miles from the stoplight at the intersection of U.S. 421 and U.S. 321, 2.6 miles from the Blue Ridge Parkway at U.S. 421, and 7.3 miles from the U.S. 421 and N.C. 194 intersection on the outskirts of Boone.

Turn onto Brownwood Road and follow the creek through scenic farmland and rolling hills cleared for pasture. After 2 miles on Brownwood Road, you will reach a sign marking the boundary between Watauga and Ashe counties. The actual border is the South Fork of the New River, on the left. Follow the river through the scenic valley for a mile to Cranberry Springs Road, on the right. On the left is the A. S. Cooper Farm, listed on the National Register of Historic Places. At the stop sign after passing the farm, turn left onto Todd Railroad Grade Road. The building on the corner is the former R. T. Greer and Company Root Warehouse, also on the National Register.

The route travels 3.8 miles along the New River to the community of Todd. In 1914, the Norfolk and Western Railroad decided to lay tracks from Abingdon, Virginia, to Todd. The arrival of passenger, mail, and express trains made Todd a center of activity. All the interest centered around the timber business; the railroad was built to enable timber companies to export the area's lumber. At one point in

Barn on A. S. Cooper Farm

its history, Todd boasted two hotels, nine stores, a bank, four doctors, a dentist, a druggist, a Masonic lodge, an Odd Fellows hall, a post office, a mill, and even a rent-a-buggy service for hotel guests who wanted to venture into the community.

Entering present-day Todd, the first building you will see is a stately white house on the left as Big Hill Road enters on the same side. Over 100 years old, the building was once an elegant hotel. It is said that a huge turntable was built into the kitchen wall to allow the cooks to rotate food into the dining room. That feature and a private power generator ensured that guests were treated in fine style.

Across the road from the old hotel is Todd's General Store, established in 1914. Although the store now caters mainly to the tourist trade, it still manages to suggest the community's former prosperity.

Former hotel in Todd

Todd's General Store

Straight ahead as the road curves to the right is Todd Mercantile, built as a cooperative store by a group of area businessmen around 1910. Both this store and the general store are sheathed in pressed tin.

On the left farther down the road is the old railroad depot, next to the post office. Until the railroad was built, the town was known as Elkland or Elks Crossroads. The railroad company changed the name to Todd in honor of Captain J. W. Todd, an eminent lawyer and leading citizen of Ashe County.

In 1933, the timber ran out, and the railroad pulled up its tracks and left, taking most of the area's businesses with it. Besides the depot, some old rail cars are the only evidence left of the railroad. The area in front of the depot is supposedly the place where three strong men using a turntable rotated the train each day for its 5 A.M. departure to Virginia.

John Preston Arthur's *History of Watauga County*, written in 1915, preserves some interesting tales about Peggy Clawson, one of Todd's most colorful characters. No record of her husband's name survives. "Her evident inclination was to have him simply the 'husband' of Peggy Clawson," Arthur wrote. Domestic tranquility was apparently unknown in the Clawson household. As Arthur delicately put it, "Tradition says, in a most friendly spirit, that they occasionally 'fell out and

Todd Mercantile

Former depot at Todd

kissed again with tears.' " Arthur also related that Peggy was excommunicated from Three Forks Baptist Church in July 1832 for "beating her son." But the following October, she "made open acknowledgment for her transgression and was restored to full membership."

Personal life aside, Peggy left her mark on regional folklore for an incident that occurred while she was in the woods making maple sugar (some sources say she was gathering ginseng) on a cliff overlooking the New. Arthur wrote that "a dog chased a bear into the river, and [Peggy] got into the canoe tied near by, poled out to the bear swimming in a deep hole at the base of the cliff, and drowned it by holding its head under the water with the canoe pole. After this exploit, it being Saturday, she walked down to the Old Fields Baptist Church in time for morning service." This was definitely a woman who could take care of herself. She left such an impression that the story is still told in the vicinity.

Beyond Todd, the road ends at the stop sign at N.C. 194. Turn left, heading south. Approximately 5.2 miles down the road, you will crest a hill in the area near Hopewell Church Road. Nearby is a rock cave known as Wolf's Den. Though it is overgrown by forest today, people who grew up in the area can still remember playing inside the large cave.

During the late 1700s, members of the Lewis family were well-known local wolf hunters. At that time, the county paid $2.50 for each wolf scalp brought in by bounty hunters. Since a scalp from a cub brought the same bounty as that from a mature wolf, the Lewises followed the same female to her lair each year, took her six to 10 cubs, and allowed her to escape. When asked why he never killed the mother wolf, Gideon Lewis answered, "Would you expect a man to kill his milch-cow?" Because the cave inhabited by the female wolf proved so lucrative for the Lewis family, it became known as Wolf's Den.

It was also the site of the only Revolutionary War military engagement in what is now Watauga County. The Patriots, or Whigs, were the revolutionaries of their time, of course, while the Loyalists, or Tories, were the conservatives or tradition-alists. The Patriots around Wolf's Den had already organized their own militia to fight the British by the time actual conflict broke out. Between 1770 and 1780, a number of British sympathizers living in the mountains secretly organized their own Tory militia. Small-scale skirmishes between mountain people who were longtime neighbors were the result.

One of the earliest Patriot militia groups was led by Colonel Benjamin Cleve-land, a man preceded by his reputation. Before the Revolutionary War, the local militia spent most of its time defending frontier settlements against Indian attacks. On one foray into Indian country, Cleveland and his men had been attacked and robbed of their horses and most of their belongings. Unlike most men in such situations, Cleveland possessed the fortitude to return to the scene of the attack, where he regained his possessions and even managed to wangle an apology from one of the Cherokee chiefs.

A strong performance at the Battle of Kings Mountain followed. Cleveland then turned his attention to Tory activity in the mountains. Historian Lyman Draper wrote that "Colonel Cleveland was active at this period in sending out strong scouting parties to scour the mountain regions, and, if possible, utterly break up the Tory bands still infesting the frontiers."

Cleveland also had a reputation for being inhumanly cruel. One legendary punishment came after he captured two men described as "Tory horse-thieves." He hanged the first man without any semblance of a trial. He then turned to the second and offered him the kinder fate of cutting off his own ears. The second man chose self-mutilation over hanging, and the legend of Cleveland's cruelty grew.

In April 1781, when local Tory leaders learned that the infamous Cleveland was in Ashe County visiting his New River farmlands, they could not resist the temptation to capture him and take him to South Carolina, where they knew the British would pay a handsome reward.

Led by Captain William Riddle, the Tory group caught up with Cleveland at the Perkins farm. They stole his horses and set up an ambush, knowing he would follow. Draper described the scene: "Cleveland from his great weight—fully three hundred pounds—knew he could not run any great distance, and only be too prominent a mark for Tory bullets, dodged into the house with several Tories at his heels." When one of the attackers seemed to find the thought of killing Cleveland on the spot more enticing than the promise of a future reward, Cleveland "instantly seized Abigail Walters, who was present, and by dint of his great strength, and under a high state of excitement, dextrously [sic] handled her as a puppet, keeping her between him and his would be assassin." At that point, Captain Riddle intervened and assured Cleveland that he would not be harmed if he surrendered peacefully.

After traveling up the New River with their captive, Riddle and his men decided to camp for the night at Wolf's Den. According to Draper, the next morning found Cleveland "sitting on a large fallen tree, engaged, under compulsion, in writing passes for the several members of Captain Riddle's party, certifying that each was a good Whig to be used, when in a tight place." Cleveland harbored a strong suspicion that his usefulness would run out as soon as all the passes were written, so "naturally but a poor penman, he purposely retarded his task as much as possible, hoping to gain time for the expected relief, apologizing for his blunders." His stall tactics worked, as his rescue party was soon at hand. When "the Whigs rushed up, yelling their loudest yells, Colonel Cleveland, comprehending the situation, tumbled off the prostrate tree, on the side opposite to his friends, lest their balls might accidentally hit him." Riddle and his men fled, and Cleveland was saved.

Some sources say Cleveland eventually caught up with Riddle and strung him up on the famous "hanging oak" in Wilkes County. The mountain where Wolf's Den is located is called Riddle's Knob to this day, while the creek flowing past it is known as Riddle's Fork.

Cleveland went on to lose his North Carolina lands and move to South Carolina. He apparently ballooned to 450 pounds and died at age 69 while sitting at his breakfast table.

Leaving Wolf's Den, travel downhill for 2 miles on N.C. 194. On the left just before Hubert Norris Road is an old, nearly illegible marker stating that this is the location of the Old Buffalo Trail of Watauga County. There is evidence that large herds of buffalo roamed east of the Mississippi hundreds of years before the arrival of Columbus. The herds supposedly wintered on the Atlantic coast and migrated westward across the Appalachians for the summer. Some of the buffalo passed through Watauga County and left distinctive trails that can still be seen today.

Relics found along the Old Buffalo Trail attest that Indian hunters also used the well-defined trail. As white settlers moved closer to the area, groups of men known as long hunters came into the mountains to hunt for extended periods. Records of a camp—Meat Camp—erected before the Revolutionary War serve as evidence that they used the Old Buffalo Trail. Meat Camp supposedly derived its name from its status as a primitive packing house. Hunters stored their dressed animal carcasses there until they were ready to return to their homes in the lowlands. The location became so well known that the community is still known as Meat Camp.

Between 1790 and 1800, the main road from the Yadkin River Valley near Wilkesboro to Trade, Tennessee, followed the Old Buffalo Trail. Buffalo traveled the mountain ridges and tended to avoid the swamps and laurel thickets along the creeks. They often laid out steep grades on dry land. When the road to Tennessee was plotted, it avoided such grades. Where the buffalo had established a good trail along the crests and sides of mountains, the road followed exactly the same course.

It is 1.1 miles from the old trail marker on N.C. 194 to Meat Camp Baptist Church, located on a hill on the right. The church was organized in 1851. It and the store and volunteer fire department 0.4 mile farther down the road serve as the center of the Meat Camp community today.

At the intersection where the store is located, turn right onto Meat Camp Road, which follows Meat Camp Creek for 1.8 miles. At the intersection with Hopewell Church Road, you will see what appears to be a group of abandoned buildings in such bad disrepair that they may be piles of old lumber soon. The first building is an old gristmill built by Jacob Winebarger in 1873. At one time, similar mills were all over the mountain region.

Continue the climb up the mountain on Meat Camp Road for 1.7 miles to a sign on the left for Rich Mountain Road, a gravel road that climbs up and over Rich

*Meat Camp
Baptist Church*

Winebarger Mill in earlier days   *View of Tennessee from Rich Mountain*

Mountain Gap between Snake Mountain (elevation 5,574 feet) and Rich Mountain (5,372 feet). Both are void of large trees, due largely to the fact that they have been used as pasture for cattle for decades. The ridges now resemble natural balds and boast beautiful stands of rhododendron and laurel in late June. The gravel road was used as a turnpike for travelers crossing the mountains into Tennessee as late as 1902. However, it is a much easier and equally scenic drive to continue on Meat Camp Road.

Drive 1.8 miles to the entrance to Elk Knob State Park. Beginning in the late 1990s, this 1,800-acre tract was targeted for development until concerned citizens and The Nature Conservancy worked to purchase it. In 2003, it was donated to the state of North Carolina. Because it is one of the state's newest parks, development is still in its early stages. However, travelers can enjoy a 4-mile round-trip hike to the summit that offers stunning views. On clear days, the view extends up to 60

View from Elk Knob

miles. Plans call for some back-country camping in the near future.

Continue on Meat Camp Road as it goes over and down the mountain. Meat Camp Road eventually merges into Sutherland Road as it passes through a long, scenic valley. The Sutherland family arrived in the area in 1807 and became prosperous raising cattle, sheep, and horses in the fertile valley.

It is 6.2 miles from Elk Knob State Park to the intersection with N.C. 88 at the end of the valley. As you approach the intersection, you will see the picturesque Sutherland Methodist Church sitting atop a small knoll. Built in 1854, it is said to have been one of the first churches in Ashe County to promote camp meetings, the forerunners of what are now called revival meetings. The movement became popular in the aftermath of the Civil War. Because people traveled to

Sutherland Methodist Church

the meetings from good distances, they camped near the gathering places. The nonstop services resulted in high emotions, which in turn led to new converts.

Turn left on N.C. 88, heading west. It is 4.2 miles to the North Carolina–Tennessee state line, at which point the road becomes Tenn. 67. Continue 1.6 miles to the intersection with U.S. 421 in the town of Trade. Turn left on U.S. 421 and drive 0.7 mile to the North Carolina line. Just past the "Welcome to North Carolina" sign, turn right onto Old 421 Road.

This section of U.S. 421 running from Boone to Trade is basically the same route taken in 1673 by the first English-speaking white men in Tennessee. James Needham, an indentured servant named Gabriel Arthur, and eight Indians set out on an exploration sponsored by Abraham Wood, who maintained Fort Henry at what is now Petersburg, Virginia. Their mission was to explore the mysterious western frontier and to establish a post for trading with the Cherokees.

The Needham party traveled along what historian John Preston Arthur described as "a well-worn Indian trail which was almost level." The group passed through a gap in the mountains between Zionville and Trade described by Arthur as being "so low that one is not conscious of passing over the top of a high mountain."

The route through Trade proved so practical that Daniel Boone followed it on his famous trailblazing expedition to Kentucky in 1769. Because of its location on one of the most traveled routes into the wilderness, Trade flourished as a resting place. It is the oldest community in Tennessee.

One other flirtation with notoriety came in July 1866, when a man traveling from North Carolina stopped at the home of Colonel James Grayson near Trade. The man's shoes were almost completely worn out, so Grayson hired him to work on his farm for a few days until he could pay for new ones. After the man left, authorities from Wilkes County, North Carolina, came to Grayson's farm looking for Tom Dula, who was wanted for the murder of Laura Foster. Grayson agreed to help them look for Dula. They caught up with the fugitive about 9 miles west of Mountain City, Tennessee. He was sitting on a rock in a creek, soaking his feet. His new shoes were undoubtedly not made for a long hike. Grayson took Dula back to his farm and the next day returned him to Wilkes County for trial. Dula was convicted and hanged for murder on May 1, 1868. As the lyrics of the famous ballad report, if it hadn't been for Grayson, Dula might have been in Tennessee.

Immediately after turning right onto Old 421 Road, you will see Zionville Baptist Church on the left. You are now entering Zionville, where the Daughters of the American Revolution (DAR) erected one of a series of monuments marking the trail Daniel Boone followed in the 1700s as he cut across the mountains on his way to the fabled land of Kentucky. It is 0.2 mile from the church to Emory Greer Road. The marker is beside Emory Greer Road in the front yard of a brick house on the left.

Continue on Old 421 Road through Mabel and Mast. As you drive through Mabel, you will see the community's old school on the left.

Former schoolhouse in Mabel

Henson's Chapel
Methodist Church

It is 5.6 miles from Zionville to Amantha. The road curves around Henson's Chapel Methodist Church, organized in 1858. The present building was erected in 1926.

It is 0.8 mile farther to Cove Creek Baptist Church, formed in 1799, then 0.6 mile to the Western Watauga Community Center, on the right. Next to the community center is another of the DAR stone monuments set out to designate Daniel Boone's trail, which you have been following since Zionville. The Cove Creek marker, however, is different from the other DAR markers. It shows Daniel sitting with his gun. His dog is nearby. Below Daniel's plaque is a plaque of a buffalo. The DAR apparently realized that the Old Buffalo Trail and Boone's trail intersected. Unfortunately, whoever installed the markers in 1913 put the one that should be in Zionville at the Cove Creek location. All things considered, it doesn't really matter, since you can still have your photograph made in front of the monument no matter where it is.

DAR marker in Cove Creek for
Daniel Boone's trail

Ahead is the stone Cove Creek School, built by Work Projects Administration laborers in 1937. When the school was threatened, a nonprofit group formed to preserve it. Since 1998, the group has held an annual music festival honoring musician Doc Watson to raise money for the school.

It is 0.7 mile past the school to the center of Cove Creek. The names on the buildings may cause some confusion. The Cove Creek Volunteer Fire Department is near the Sugar Grove post office. The explanation is that the first post office for Cove Creek was located in an area known locally as Sugar Grove because of its sugar maples. The Sugar Grove post office thus became a permanent part of the Cove Creek community.

Turn left onto U.S. 321, drive 1.2 miles to the intersection with U.S. 421, and turn right. As you travel the 6-mile stretch into Boone, you will begin to see Howard's Knob on the left. At 4,451 feet, the mountain towers above the town. Its name comes from Benjamin Howard, who fled to a cave at the base of a low cliff a quarter-mile north of the knob when American Patriots pressed too hotly for his assistance during the Revolutionary War. Accounts say he sheltered himself in his cave rather than join the fighting. It is also said that his daughter, Sallie, was the real heroine because she was willing to endure a severe switching rather than reveal her father's hiding place. Howard finally took the oath of allegiance in 1778. His hideout retained his name.

In addition to serving as an area landmark, Howard's Knob has been the site of energy experiments designed to assess the potential of giant wind-powered generators. In 1978, an experimental wind turbine was built by General Electric and managed by NASA. The turbine was 131 feet tall and had 97-foot-long steel blades that rotated at 35 miles per hour. It was designed to power 300 to 500 average-sized homes. Local people complained about the whooshing noise made by the blades, which caused windows to vibrate audibly. There was also evidence that the windmill disrupted television reception. In 1983, the experiment was abandoned, the turbine dismantled, and the site turned over to the county for use as a park.

Upon reaching Boone, the home of Appalachian State University and the commercial mecca of the region that bills itself as "the High Country," you should be able to find the modern conveniences you may have missed while traveling the Old Buffalo Trail.

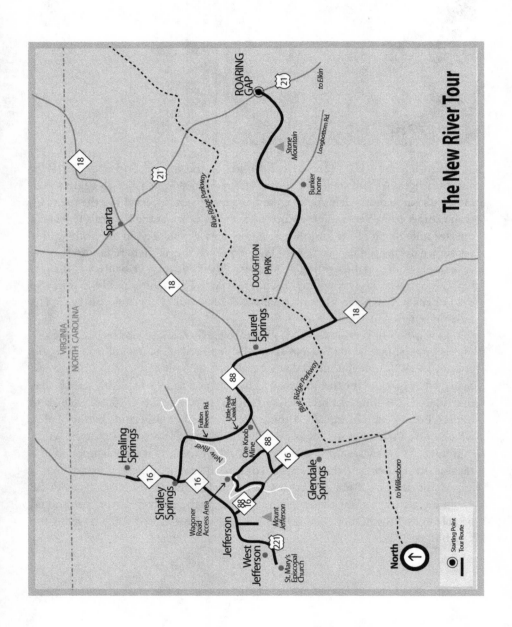

The New River Tour

TOUR 21

The New River Tour

This tour begins near Sparta and goes to Roaring Gap, Stone Mountain State Park, the Ore Knob Mine, Shatley Springs, Healing Springs, Mount Jefferson State Natural Area, and West Jefferson. It then visits the frescoes at Beaver Creek, travels to New River State Park, and ends at the frescoes in Glendale Springs.

Total mileage: approximately 125 miles

The tour begins where the Blue Ridge Parkway intersects U.S. 21 about 7 miles south of Sparta, the county seat of Alleghany County. Head south on U.S. 21. You can also begin the tour by taking the U.S. 21 exit from I-77 at Elkin and driving north to Roaring Gap.

The area encompassed by this tour has been known historically as "the Lost Provinces." When the earliest settlers in Ashe, Alleghany, and Watauga counties were building roads and railroads, the most practical routes took them into southwestern Virginia. While Ashe and Alleghany were officially part of North Carolina, many of the counties' trade and business connections were with Virginia and Tennessee.

The unusual features of the New River also contributed to the area's unique development. The New is the only river in the eastern United States that flows northward to the Midwest. Development proceeded in the same direction. The fact that the path of commerce was westward instead of eastward created a growth pattern different from that of the rest of the North Carolina mountains.

The New is the oldest river in America. At one time, it held the headwaters of the mighty Teays River; hard to believe as it is, scientists say that the Ohio and Mississippi rivers were once tributaries of the prehistoric Teays. Scientists also say that the New has changed little since it was first seen by settlers, a claim that seems to be supported by the writings of Bishop August Spangenberg, an early traveler sent by the Moravian Church to find land for a settlement. In his account of his journey, Spangenberg recorded his impression of a river that was undoubtedly the New. His December 14, 1752, entry stated,

> We virtually lost ourselves in the mountains, & whichever way we turned— we were literally walled in on all sides. . . . We had nothing but bleak mountains, & dry valleys to traverse, & because we followed the river several days in hopes of escaping from the mountains, we were only getting down deeper all the time, for the river flowed N. & S. & E. & W., in short all points of the compass. At last we determined to keep a course between E & S., to scramble across the mountains as well as we could. One mt. rose up beyond the others, & thus we pursued our way, between fear on one side—& hope on the other.

Spangenberg's remarks ring true to anyone who has ever traveled the back-roads along the New.

Many of the original settlers along the river were Revolutionary War soldiers who were given grants. Much of the land in the area still remains in the hands of the descendants of those early grantees. As a result, the region has had one of the most stable populations in North Carolina for 200 years. Only recently have real-estate developers and land speculators invaded this section of the mountains as they have the rest of western North Carolina. The relative isolation that existed until recent decades enabled the land to retain its charm.

After 4 miles on U.S. 21, you will reach the community of Roaring Gap. On the right is the post office. On the left is the entrance to the Roaring Gap Club, one of the oldest summer resort communities in the mountains. Because of the town's proximity to the Piedmont cities of Winston-Salem and Greensboro, many wealthy industrialists and businessmen chose to build summer homes in Roaring Gap. Since the late 1890s, the cool summer days have attracted the Reynolds and Hanes families, among others.

Oral tradition tells that the first settlers in Roaring Gap came for a different reason. A man named Absalom Smith left England for America in 1775. Because he could not afford his passage, he labored as an indentured servant for a rich planter near Norfolk, Virginia. While working off his seven-year obligation, Absalom fell in love with the planter's daughter, Agnes. Knowing that her father would never ap-prove of the relationship, Agnes eloped with Absalom to the mountains. It is said they were accompanied by a horse and an old Negro servant who had been with Agnes for many years. Along their journey, they escaped an Indian attack, perhaps only because the Indians were too thoroughly amazed at the sight to pursue them in earnest—Absalom was swimming the Yadkin River leading Agnes on the horse, while the Negro servant, who could not swim, clung desperately to the horse's tail. The Smiths built a home and lived out their lives in Roaring Gap. Their graves are nearby in the cemetery at Antioch United Methodist Church. It seems fitting that Roaring Gap, born of such romantic beginnings, should have proven a prosperous community.

Stone Mountain State Park

If you are driving south from Sparta on U.S. 21, you will see signs for Liberty Knob Baptist Church and the John P. Frank Parkway about 0.2 mile from the entrance to the Roaring Gap Club. Turn right onto Old Gap Road (S.R. 1100) just past the sign marking the Eastern Continental Divide (elevation 2,972 feet); the turn comes up quickly, so be alert. The road becomes Oklahoma Road in about 1 mile. On the right is Liberty Knob Baptist Church, formed in 1884. After approximately 2.3 miles, you will reach a church and the intersection with the John P. Frank Parkway. Turn right into the entrance to Stone Mountain State Park.

If you are starting the tour from Elkin at I-77, you may want to skip the uphill drive to Roaring Gap and go straight to Stone Mountain State Park. It is 10 miles from the U.S. 21 exit off I-77 to Traphill Road, on the left, where you will see a sign for the state park. Travel 4 miles on Traphill Road to the right turn onto the John P. Frank Parkway. It is 3 miles on the parkway to the park entrance.

You can pick up a park map at the visitors' center, located 0.7 mile from the entrance. It is then 2.3 miles from the visitors' center to the parking lot for the actual mountain. Visitors who arrive early in the day can park closer to the base of Stone Mountain than those who arrive later. But even those who have to use the lower lot and walk up find it worth the hike.

Stone Mountain, elevation 2,305 feet, is a dome-shaped granite mass that rises 600 feet from base to summit. Since most of the surrounding valleys have elevations of 1,400 to 1,600 feet, the huge, sheer wall seems even more impressive. The circumference of the base of Stone Mountain is nearly 4 miles. Permanent maps directing visitors to a series of first-rate hiking trails are located at the base of the mountain. The valley at the base is an excellent vantage point from which to watch rock climbers negotiating such colorfully named routes up the rock as Electric Boobs, Grand Funk Railroad, and Purple Daze. It seems the routes must have been

Farmhouse built by Eng and Chang Bunker

named during the late 1960s or early 1970s.

After viewing Stone Mountain, take a left out of the bottom parking lot and continue on Stone Mountain Road. It is 0.9 mile to a marker for the Widows Creek Trail, on the right. The hike to a small, sheltered waterfall is a relatively short one, but be forewarned if you decide to cross the stream—the slippery rocks may be the reason for the name Widows Creek.

The pavement ends 1 mile past the Widows Creek trailhead. Continue 1.1 miles to an intersection with S.R. 1737 (Longbottom Road). Turn left and drive 2 miles to Roaring River Baptist Church. You can park in the lot to view the white two-story farmhouse next door. This was the house built by Eng and Chang Bunker, the original Siamese twins.

Born in Siam, now Thailand, in 1811, the twins began touring the world at age 16. In 1829, they came to America. When they decided to retire after 10 years of touring, they chose to settle near Wilkesboro, one of the towns where they had been exhibited. They arrived with $10,000 and purchased a retail store. They subsequently gave up the store and began farming on land near where the farmhouse stands. In 1839, they became American citizens and adopted the last name of Bunker. About the same time, they met Sallie and Adelaide Yates. The couples courted for several years before marrying and moving into the farmhouse. Nine months later, Eng and Sallie had their first daughter. Six days after that, Chang and Adelaide had their first daughter. Eng and Sallie eventually had 11 children; Chang and Adelaide had 10.

Eventually, things fell apart. Eng and Chang built two separate houses in Surry County. The wives lived apart; the twins would spend three days with Sallie and three with Adelaide. In 1874, Eng woke to find his brother dead; he passed away a short time later. They are buried in Surry County.

Farm on Longbottom Road

Return to the back entrance of Stone Mountain and continue straight on Longbottom Road. It is 2.6 miles to Double Creek Baptist Church, on the left. You will enter a scenic, pastoral valley dotted with fairly new homes. The road makes a 90-degree turn in front of a beautiful, well-maintained, late-19th-century white farmhouse with two-tiered porches and decorative woodwork.

One mile from the farmhouse, you will see a trail entrance for Doughton Park on the right and a parking area on the left. Doughton Park is one of the most popular attractions on the Blue Ridge Parkway, though most visitors see only the upper part of its 6,000 acres. The trail entrance provides access to the lower half by way of several of Doughton Park's hiking trails. Visitors can enjoy short hikes up some relatively deserted routes or plan a longer trek that takes advantage of the loops throughout the park. The park offers primitive back-country camping areas. Interested visitors should check with park officials to reserve one of the popular campsites.

Doughton Park was named for Robert L. Doughton, who served in the United States House of Representatives from 1911 to 1953, during which time he was the powerful head of the House Ways and Means Committee. Doughton is credited with being the power behind the passage of the Social Security Act, which he considered the hallmark of his career. In 1953, Doughton Park was dedicated to the man who was largely responsible for bringing the parkway through this part of North Carolina.

From the parking area for the hiking trails, continue 6.5 miles to an intersection with N.C. 18. Turn right, heading north. It is 2 miles to an "N.C. Gamelands" sign, which directs travelers to Thurmond Chatham Wildlife Management Area. The 6,403-acre game refuge is well known by deer hunters.

Continue 4.4 miles to an intersection with the Blue Ridge Parkway. Just past

Wild Woody's

the parkway are Station's Inn on the right and Freeborne Inn on the left. Both establishments cater to motorcyclists in the summer and fall. Next to Freeborne Inn is Wild Woody's, which has been owned and operated by Linda Woody since 1971. Her family has lived in this area for seven generations. Among other eclectic items for sale, the store has a collection of vintage record albums from the 1960s and 1970s.

Continue north on N.C. 18 for 1.7 miles to Doughton-Hall Bed and Breakfast, on the left. The Queen Anne–style house was the home of Congressman Robert L. Doughton. It was built in 1898 and became a national historic landmark in 1972.

It is 0.1 mile to the Laurel Springs post office, on the right. Turn left onto N.C. 88. You will pass the Upper Mountain Research Station, established in 1944. The station has 454 acres of land at an elevation higher than 3,200 feet. The research focuses on Christmas trees, burley tobacco, small fruits, small grains, organic vegetable production, mushrooms, and a vineyard.

Doughton-Hall Bed and Breakfast, the former home of Congressman Robert L. Doughton

After 4.3 miles on N.C. 88, you will see a historical marker on the right for the Ore Knob Mine. Just past the marker, turn right onto Little Peak Creek Road (S.R. 1595). You may be able to see the remains of the famous Ore Knob Mine on the left after a little less than 1 mile. The area is overgrown, and the shafts have been closed down and fenced off, but the mound of earth is still there.

The Ore Knob Mine had a rather inauspicious beginning. In 1800, a French mining engineer came to Ashe County in search of iron. Though his undertaking was quite successful, his judgment failed him where the 300 acres at Ore Knob were concerned. He bought the tract thinking it showed promise of bearing iron, only to abandon it after determining that whatever iron was there was so badly adulterated by copper as to be virtually worthless. The property was therefore sold. After he paid his taxes, the Frenchman was left with a balance of $11, which was split equally among his 11 children. In 1870, two capitalists from Baltimore purchased the tract and began to make a huge profit once copper started bringing a high price.

In January 1982, news of a sensational murder involving the notorious Outlaws motorcycle gang hit the media. An undercover informant told police that in December 1981, he had unwillingly participated in the murder of a man whose body was thrown into a deserted 200-foot shaft at the Ore Knob Mine. A second body was also believed to be in the shaft. Investigators examined the vicinity but were unable to corroborate the informant's story. It was proposed that someone be lowered into the hole for a closer look, but mining officials judged the shaft to be too unstable.

In one of those cases where fact is stranger than fiction, it just so happened that a man who called himself "the Nashville Flame" learned of the dilemma while watching television in a motel. The Flame was performing as a stunt man on a local thrill-show circuit. Finding himself in the right place at the right time, he offered his climbing talents to the authorities, who eventually accepted his offer. One of his quirks was that he allowed the media to photograph him only when his face was covered by a helmet or a ski mask.

When the Flame really did find two bodies at the bottom of the shaft, one of the most sensational series of murder trials in the history of western North Carolina was launched. It ended with the murder conviction of four men, including the original informant. The Flame continued to insist that more bodies were in the mine, but the attorney general of North Carolina made the wise decision to permanently seal the dangerous shaft, and the final chapter in the saga of the Ore Knob Mine was officially closed.

In recent years, the Environmental Protection Agency has been active in determining the extent of contamination from the mine and in preventing its expansion.

Continue on Little Peak Creek Road for 2.8 miles, then turn left onto South J. E. Gentry Road for a quick 0.3 mile. Just before the bridge, turn right onto Fulton Reeves Road, a gravel road that parallels the South Fork of the New River. On this scenic route, the New River is frequently only a few feet from the road. This part of the tour allows you to see the beauty of the New up close—so close that you'll almost

New River seen from Fulton Reeves Road

feel you're canoeing the river. Since the second edition of this book was published, more development has moved into this area. Numerous new homes overlook the river. As a result, the drive is not as bucolic as it was in past years.

The route passes the Yellowknife Ranch, on the right. After 2 miles, you will come upon a dead-end sign, but don't panic. Follow the main road as it makes a 90-degree turn and crosses what resembles a pontoon bridge. The bridge is safe. For the next 1.5 miles, you will drive on a paved road directly beside the New.

At the intersection, turn left onto U.S. 221, heading south. Just past a small bridge 1.5 miles down U.S. 221, turn right onto East Shatley Springs Road (S.R. 1571). When the road forks 1 mile later, bear left onto Tom Fowler Road (S.R. 1572). After less than 0.5 mile, turn right onto N.C. 16, heading north. It is 0.5 mile to a sign on the left announcing the entrance to Shatley Springs Inn.

Though the family-style country cooking served at the inn is the primary attraction at Shatley Springs today, the healing waters that once drew people from near and far still bubble. In the 1880s, a chronic sufferer named Martin Shatley wheezed into the area dragging his considerable ailments like a ton of bricks. Shatley was long-winded and graphic in describing his condition, but a brief sampling should suffice to establish that he was not a well man. "I first broke out with pimples," he wrote. "Soon my skin got scaly, when I rubbed my hand briefly over my skin I could see hundreds of scales fly off my skin. . . . My eyes were most of the time red and swollen. Sometimes I had to hold my eyelids up with my hands to see my way to walk."

Shatley's long search for a cure ended when he bought a farm in Ashe County. One day, he was out walking and stopped to bathe his irritated face in a cool spring. Within an hour, his condition was so markedly improved that he returned and im-

Shatley Springs Inn

mersed his whole body. Within three days, the man the doctors had given up on was completely healed. Needless to say, word of Shatley's miraculous cure swept the countryside, and a resort was established at the site. Countless gallons of spring water have since been carried away by people who believe in its curative powers. Whether or not the water has healing power, it certainly does taste good.

Refreshed by the miracle water, return to N.C. 16 and turn left, heading north. It is 2.1 miles to Healing Springs Road, on the right. Turn onto Healing Springs Road and drive 1.3 miles to the former resort of Healing Springs. You will see some of the cottages and the old springhouse, but everything is in a state of disrepair from abandonment. The property is for sale.

Old springhouse at Healing Springs

In 1884, Eli Barker and his son discovered the springs here. Thompson's Bromine-Arsenic Springs Company out of Saltville, Virginia, began to sell the water in cases of 12 half-gallon bottles that went for six dollars. According to a company brochure that sounded strangely similar to the one about Shatley Springs, the water could cure "inflammation in the Neck of Bladder, Brick Dust Deposits in Urine, Pain in Loins and Kidneys," among many other ailments.

By 1888, a 75-room hotel served visitors who wanted to stay and "take the waters." They could ride a train to Seven Mile Ford, Virginia, 35 miles east of Bristol, then take a hack to the hotel. The hacks left the station for the springs on Mondays and Thursdays. The price of boarding at the hotel was $2 a day and $12 a week; for four weeks or more, the cost was $10 a week.

After viewing Healing Springs, return to N.C. 16 and drive south. It is 6.6 miles to the intersection where U.S. 221 South joins N.C. 16. The two highways run conjunctively for 1.3 miles before U.S. 221 splits off to join N.C. 88. Turn right and follow U.S. 221/N.C. 88 heading west. The huge mountain on the left is Mount Jefferson. Stay on U.S. 221 South as it bears left, bypassing Jefferson's business district. After 3 miles, you will see a sign on the left for Mount Jefferson State Natural Area. Follow Mount Jefferson State Park Road (S.R. 1152) for 2.1 miles to the summit.

In 1827, Dr. Elisha Mitchell climbed Mount Jefferson and recorded in his diary that he had never seen anything more beautiful than the view from the big rock near the summit. For more than 100 years after Mitchell's visit, the summit remained inaccessible except by difficult trails. Then the Work Projects Administration came to Ashe County in the 1930s. Local citizens hoping to attract tourists proposed that a road be built. When supporters of the project learned that federal funds could not be used to construct a road to private property, they set out to

View from Mount Jefferson State Natural Area

acquire the 26 acres at the top for use as a public park. The land was donated and the road built. Due to a lack of maintenance funds, it soon fell into disrepair. In 1941, local citizens petitioned the North Carolina government to accept the acreage as a state park. The effort was unsuccessful at first, but the group finally convinced the government to designate the Mount Jefferson land as a state recreation area. When North Carolina later passed a law requiring a minimum 400 acres for state-supported parks, local citizens once again set out to meet the challenge. They secured financial contributions and land donations of the necessary acreage, and Mount Jefferson State Park was born. It has since been changed to a state natural area. In recent years, budget woes have threatened the continued existence of the park. It would be a true loss, as the views from the summit on clear days are magnificent. Displays at the various overlooks help visitors identify the mountains in the distance. If visibility is good, guests can see far into Virginia and Tennessee and view much of the Blue Ridge range.

Even the naming of the mountain was the subject of controversy. For a long time, Mount Jefferson was known locally as Nigger Mountain or Negro Mountain. In his book *Ashe County: A History*, Arthur Fletcher credited tourism, not racial enlightenment, for the change. He stated that the members of various committees were afraid that potential visitors would get the idea that the new park was for blacks only and stay away. It was finally suggested that the mountain be named for the two towns at its base, which were themselves named for a great president. The issue was thus resolved.

The reason for the original name is also a subject of debate. Most sources say the mountain served as a station on the Underground Railroad during the Civil War and that it was named for the runaway slaves who hid there. Historians have discredited that view, since land grants predating the Civil War carried references to Negro Mountain. The most likely explanation for the name comes from the fact that the mountain is a solid black color during winter. Because of the high elevation, most of its trees are stunted. When their foliage is off, the bare black rocks are all that can be seen.

Return to U.S. 221 and turn left, heading toward West Jefferson. It is 1.3 miles

Downtown West Jefferson

to an intersection with N.C. 163/194 at a stoplight; remember this intersection, as you will return to it later in the tour. Turn right onto U.S. 221/N.C. 194 and head into West Jefferson. It is 1.5 miles to the third stoplight, located at the corner of Main and Jefferson streets in the center of town; the Ashe County Visitors' Center is on the corner. Turn right on East Main Street. The Ashe County Cheese Company's factory and outlet store are half a block down East Main. A tour of the factory reveals how cheese is made. Freshly made samples are available at the outlet store.

In the early 1900s, Ashe County farmers learned that raising dairy herds could be a profitable industry. Upon the increase of milk-producing herds in the area, the North Carolina Department of Agriculture promoted the establishment of cheese factories. Cheesemaking demonstrations were met with enthusiasm. The first factory opened in 1915. Soon, small operations began throughout the county. Unfortunately, the widely scattered locations of the factories and the poor mountain roads prevented cheesemakers from reaping much of a profit. All but one of the plants is now closed. The Ashe County Cheese Company carries on the longstanding tradition alone.

Retrace your route to N.C. 163. Just before the intersection, you will see a McDonald's on the right and a sign indicating the route to the "Church of the Frescoes." Turn right onto Beaver Creek School Road just before the intersection, following the signs for the frescoes.

It is 0.8 mile to St. Mary's Episcopal Church. Though this small, picturesque mountain church houses one of the area's main tourist attractions, it was not always the focus of community pride. Milnor Jones was an Episcopal minister and active missionary who organized the first Episcopal church in Ashe County, the Church of St. Simon the Zealot. On June 21, 1896, Bishop Joseph Blount Cheshire came from Raleigh to conduct services. He was met at the church by an unexpected

Ashe County Cheese Company

St. Mary's Episcopal Church in Beaver Creek

greeting committee. He wrote, "I was assaulted and forcibly prevented from entering this building by a mob of between fifty and one hundred men which had been gotten together for the express purpose of preventing our service that day. And the reason they gave for this action was that they 'did not like Mr. Jones' doctrine' and they understood that I taught the same doctrine." Cheshire further noted that he "met with the most violent opposition, accompanied with bitter abuse from Methodists and Baptists, especially the latter." Milnor Jones went on to organize a school at Beaver Creek. His quaint Church of St. Simon the Zealot, later renamed St. Mary's, was eventually abandoned for lack of funds until a different sort of notoriety came its way.

In the summer of 1980, artist Ben Long returned to the United States to train others in a dying art form. For seven years, he had studied fresco painting in Italy with a master of Renaissance technique. Long relocated to Ashe County, where he took on as many as 20 apprentices at one time and used two Episcopal churches in the area as his studios.

Fresco painting is a tedious and complicated process, which explains its rarity in today's world. Natural ground pigment is mixed with distilled water, thinned with lime, and painted onto damp plaster. As the plaster dries, the lime and pigment bind chemically, so that the wall literally becomes the painting. This unusual technique produces an interesting effect; many say that fresco walls seem to glow. The drawback is that the pigment is absorbed the moment brush touches plaster, so a mistake can necessitate the removal of an entire section of wall.

Long imported lime from the same site in Florence, Italy, that Michelangelo used for the Sistine Chapel. He mixed the lime with North Carolina sand to make his plaster. Local people served as models for the characters in his frescoes; Long himself took the role of Doubting Thomas. The results are so impressive that over 200,000 people a year visit the out-of-the-way chapels to view Long's frescoes. *Mary, Great with Child*; *John the Baptist*; and *The Mystery of Faith* are featured at St. Mary's. Despite the possibility of encountering a busload of tourists, St. Mary's is a worthwhile stop. Since gaining prominence with his Ashe County work, Long has

Frescoes in St. Mary's: The Mystery of Faith *(center) and* St. John the Baptist *(right)*

created frescoes throughout the state. There is even an official Ben F. Long Fresco Trail, which includes frescoes in seven counties in western North Carolina.

Retrace your route past Mount Jefferson State Natural Area but continue straight when the road becomes N.C. 16 South/88 East. In 2.9 miles, you will cross the North Fork of the New River. Turn right onto N.C. 16 South. You will see a dirt parking area beside the road, next to a general store. Turn immediately right onto Bill Bledsoe Road (S.R. 1588), a gravel road that passes under the bridge you just crossed. The road travels beside the New River for 2.1 miles. Fifteen years ago, no development existed along this route. Now, the hillside across the river is dotted with large resort homes. At the intersection where the road ends, turn left onto Wagoner Access Road to reach Wagoner Road Access Area and the New River State Park office. The access area is the best place to reach the state park by automobile. If you feel adventurous, renting a canoe will provide you an opportunity to see the river from an entirely different perspective.

In 1965, the Appalachian Power Company applied for a license to dam the New and build reservoirs in Virginia and North Carolina. What followed was a case study in grass-roots opposition. Citizens' groups, environmentalists, federal agencies, and the states of North Carolina and West Virginia joined forces to lobby against the proposed damming. In 1975, North Carolina declared the 26.5-mile stretch of the New from its confluence with Dog Creek (near Wagoner Road Access Area) to the Virginia line a state scenic river. In 1976, that section became part of the National Wild and Scenic River System. The New remains free-flowing today.

From the park office, retrace Wagoner Access Road past Bill Bledsoe Road and continue straight for 0.6 mile to the junction with N.C. 88. Turn right. The road

Development along the New River

splits after 1.6 miles; follow N.C. 16 to the left. You may encounter construction while this road is widened, so be prepared for a possible detour. About 3.6 miles after the turn onto N.C. 16, you will start to see a new set of "Church of the Frescoes" signs. Turn right onto J. W. Luke Road (S.R. 1162).

On the left is the Church of the Holy Trinity, the second Episcopal church housing Ben Long frescoes. Long's interpretation of the Last Supper occupies the entire front wall.

Around the side of the church is the entrance to a new facility in the basement. It is called the Chapel of Christ the King. The name comes from a large mosaic created by architectural sculptor John Early in 1920. The mosaic was given to the church by a visitor. The chapel also features *The Departure of Christ*, a fresco created by Ben Long student Jeffrey Mims in 1984.

Church of the Holy Trinity in Glendale Springs

Ben Long's fresco of the Last Supper

The Departure of Christ *in the Chapel of Christ the King at the Church of the Holy Trinity*

Another interesting, if unrelated, portion of the basement is the columbarium. If you've ever contemplated having your remains cremated but can't decide what should be done with your ashes, the columbarium at the Church of the Holy Trinity provides one unusual alternative.

Continue on J. W. Luke Road for 0.1 mile to N.C. 16. At the intersection is the historic Glendale Springs Inn, built in 1895 by Daniel W. Adams. On July 30, 1998, President Bill Clinton and Vice President Al Gore showed up with a group of dignitaries to proclaim the New River an American Heritage River. While they were in the area, they chose this inn for their weekly, private "Thursday lunch." The inn has been closed and for sale since late 2008.

Cross the intersection onto Trading Post Road. It is 0.3 mile to an intersection with the Blue Ridge Parkway at the Northwest Trading Post. The trading post is sponsored by the Northwest Development Association. Its mission is to keep alive the old mountain crafts. The shop sells over 250 types of handmade crafts by more than 500 craftsmen from 11 northwestern North Carolina counties.

The tour ends here. If you return to the intersection with N.C. 16 and turn left, it is approximately 24 miles to U.S. 421 just outside North Wilkesboro.

Glendale Springs Inn

Appendix

Federal Agencies

Andrew Pickens Ranger District, Sumter National Forest
USFS
1112 Andrew Pickens Circle
Mountain Rest, S.C. 29664
864-638-9568
http://www.fs.usda.gov/scnfs

Blue Ridge Parkway Headquarters
199 Hemphill Knob Road
Asheville, N.C. 28803-8686
828-271-4779 or 828-298-0398 (information line)
http://www.nps.gov/blri/contacts.htm

Cradle of Forestry Interpretive Association
66 South Broad Street
Brevard, N.C. 28712
828-877-3130
http://www.cradleofforestry.com

Great Smoky Mountains National Park
107 Park Headquarters Road
Gatlinburg, Tenn. 37738
865-436-1200
http://www.nps.gov/grsm

Nantahala National Forest
www.fs.usda.gov/nfsnc

> Cheoah Ranger District
> 1070 Massey Branch Road
> Robbinsville, N.C. 28771
> 828-479-6431

> Nantahala Ranger District
> 90 Sloan Road
> Franklin, N.C. 28734
> 828-524-6441

Tusquitee Ranger District
123 Woodland Drive
Murphy, N.C. 28906
828-837-5152

Pisgah National Forest
www.fs.usda.gov/nfsnc

Appalachian Ranger District
P.O. Box 128
Burnsville, N.C. 28714
828-682-6146

Grandfather Ranger District
109 Lawing Drive
Nebo, N.C. 28761
828-652-2144

Pisgah Ranger District
1001 Pisgah Highway
Pisgah Forest, N.C. 28768
828-877-3265

Tennessee Valley Authority
400 West Summit Hill Drive
Knoxville, Tenn. 37902
865-632-2101 or 828-498-2234 (Fontana Dam Visitors' Center)
http://www.tva.com

North Carolina Agencies

Chimney Rock State Park
P.O. Box 220
Chimney Rock, N.C. 28720
GPS coordinates: 35.432799, -82.250260
828-625-1823 or 828-625-9945
http://www.chimneyrockpark.com
Email: chimney.rock@ncdenr.gov

Division of Parks and Recreation
Physical address: 512 North Salisbury Street, Archdale Building, Seventh Floor, Room 742, Raleigh, N.C.
Mailing address: 1615 Mail Service Center, Raleigh, N.C. 27699
919-733-4181
http://www.ncparks.gov
Email: parkinfo@ncmail.net

Division of Tourism, Film and Sports Development
North Carolina Department of Commerce
Physical address: 301 North Wilmington Street, Raleigh, N.C. 27601-1058
Mailing address: 4301 Mail Service Center, Raleigh, N.C. 27699-4301
800-visitnc (800-847-4862)
http://www.visitnc.com

Elk Knob State Park
5564 Meat Camp Road
Todd, N.C. 28684
GPS coordinates: 36.332586, -81.69064
828-297-7261
Email: elk.knob@ncdenr.gov

Gorges State Park
N.C. 281 South
P.O. Box 100
Sapphire, N.C. 28774-0100
GPS coordinates: 35.1133, -82.9563
828-966-9099
Email: gorges@ncdenr.gov

Grandfather Mountain State Park
2050 Blowing Rock Highway
P.O. Box 9
Linville, N.C. 28646
GPS coordinates: 36.11139, -81.81250
828-737-9522
http://www.grandfather.com
Email: grandfather.mountain@ncdenr.gov

Mount Jefferson State Natural Area
1481 Mount Jefferson State Park Road
West Jefferson, N.C. 28694
GPS coordinates: 36.397660, -81.473466
336-246-9653
Email: mount.jefferson@ncdenr.gov

Mount Mitchell State Park
2388 State Highway 128
Burnsville, N.C. 28714
GPS coordinates: 35.7528, -82.2737
828-675-4611
Email: mount.mitchell@ncdenr.gov

New River State Park
358 New River State Park Road
Laurel Springs, N.C. 28644
GPS coordinates: 36.467680, -81.340350
336-982-2587
Email: new.river@ncdenr.gov

Stone Mountain State Park
3042 Frank Parkway
Roaring Gap, N.C. 28668
GPS coordinates: 36.3873, -81.0273
336-957-8185
Email: stone.mountain@ncdenr.gov

Chambers of Commerce and Visitors' Centers

Alleghany County Chamber of Commerce
58 South Main Street
P.O. Box 1237
Sparta, N.C. 28675
800-372-5473 or 336-372-5473
http://www.sparta-nc.com
Email: info@sparta-nc.com

Ashe County Chamber of Commerce
1 North Jefferson Avenue, Suite C
P.O. Box 31
West Jefferson, N.C. 28694
888-343-2743 or 336-846-9550
http://www.ashechamber.com
Email: ashechamber@skybest.com

Avery County Chamber of Commerce
4501 Tynecastle Highway, Unit #2
Intersection of N.C. 105 and N.C. 184
Banner Elk, N.C. 28604
800-972-2183 or 828-898-5605
http://www.averycounty.com

Beech Mountain Chamber of Commerce
403A Beech Mountain Parkway
Beech Mountain, N.C. 28604
828-387-9283
http://www.beechmtn.com

Blowing Rock Chamber of Commerce
7738 Valley Boulevard
P.O. Box 2445
Blowing Rock, N.C. 28605
877-750-4636 or 828-295-4636
http://www.blowingrock.com
Email: Marcia@visitblowingrock.com

Boone Chamber of Commerce
208 Howard Street
Boone, N.C. 28607
828-264-2225
http://www.boonechamber.com
Email: info@boonechamber.com

Brevard/Transylvania Chamber of Commerce
175 East Main Street
Brevard, N.C. 28712
828-883-3700
http://www.brevardncchamber.org
Email: Prentiss@brevardncchamber.org

Bryson City/Swain County Chamber of Commerce and Visitors' Center
210 Main Street
P.O. Box 509
Bryson City, N.C. 28713
800-867-9246 or 828-488-3681
http://www.greatsmokies.com

Carolina Foothills Chamber of Commerce
2753 Lynn Road, Suite A
Tryon, N.C. 28782
828-859-6236
http://www.polkchamber.org
Email: info@polkchamber.org

Cherokee County Chamber of Commerce
805 West U.S. 64 Highway
Murphy, N.C. 28906
828-837-2242
http://www.cherokeecountychamber.com
Email: info@cherokeecountychamber.com

Clay County Chamber of Commerce
388 Business Highway 64
Hayesville, N.C. 28904
828-398-3704
http://www.ncmtnchamber.com
Email: info@ncmtnchamber.com

Franklin Chamber of Commerce
425 Porter Street
Franklin, N.C. 28734
866-372-5546 or 828-524-3161
http://franklin-chamber.com
Email: facc@franklin-chamber.com

Graham County Travel and Tourism
12 North Main Street
Robbinsville, N.C. 28771
800-470-3790 or 828-479-3790
Email: info.GrahamCounty@frontier.com

Haywood County Chamber of Commerce
28 Walnut Street
P.O. Box 600
Waynesville, N.C. 28786
828-456-3021
http://www.haywood-nc.com/chamber.asp
Email: info@haywood-nc.com

Henderson County Chamber of Commerce
204 Kanuga Road
Hendersonville, N.C. 28739
828-692-1413
http://www.hendersoncountychamber.org/contact-us.html

Henderson County Travel and Tourism Visitors' Information Center
800-828-4244 or 828-693-9708
http://www.historichendersonville.org/index.htm

High Country Host Visitors' Center
1700 Blowing Rock Road
Boone, N.C. 28607
800-438-7500
http://www.highcountryhost.com
Email: info@highcountryhost.com

Highlands Visitors' Center
269 Oak Street
Highlands, N.C. 28741
866-526-5841
http://www.highlandschamber.org

Jackson County Chamber of Commerce
773 West Main Street
Sylva, N.C. 28779
800-962-1911 or 828-586-2155
http://www.mountainlovers.com

Mitchell County Chamber of Commerce
79 Parkway Maintenance Road
P.O. Box 858
Spruce Pine, N.C. 28777
800-227-3912 or 828-765-9483
http://www.mitchell-com

Polk County Travel and Tourism
20 East Mills Street
P.O. Box 308
Columbus, N.C. 28722
800-440-7848 or 828-894-2324
http://www.nc-mountains.org

Yancey County/Burnsville Chamber of Commerce
106 West Main Street
Burnsville, N.C. 28714
828-682-7413
http://www.YanceyChamber.com

Others

Appalachian Trail Conservancy Headquarters
799 Washington Street
P.O. Box 807
Harpers Ferry, W.Va. 25425-0807
304-535-6331
http://www.appalachiantrail.org

Ben Long Fresco Trail
www.benlongfrescotrail.org

Benton MacKaye Trail Association
P.O. Box 53271
Atlanta, Ga. 30355-1271
http://www.bmta.org

Cherohala Skyway
105 College Street, Suite 6
Madisonville, Tenn. 37354
800-245-5428 or 423-442-9147
http://www.cherohala.org

Cherokee County Historical Museum
87 Peachtree Street
Murphy, N.C. 28906
828-837-6792
cchm@webworkz.com

Fontana Village Resort
300 Woods Road
P.O. Box 68
Fontana Dam, N.C. 28733
GPS coordinates: 35.432264, -83.821199 or 35° 25' 56.1504", -83° 49' 16.3158"
828-498-2211
http://www.fontanavillage.com
Email: info@fontanavillage.com

John C. Campbell Folk School
One Folk School Road
Brasstown, N.C. 28902
800-365-5724 or 828-837-2775
https://www.folkschool.org

Junaluska Memorial and Museum
1 Junaluska Drive
Robbinsville, N.C. 28771
828-479-4727

Mast General Store Home Office
Highway 194
Valle Crucis, N.C. 28691
828-963-6511
http://www.mastgeneralstore.com

Nantahala Outdoor Center
13077 Highway 19W
Bryson City, N.C. 28713
888-905-7238
http://www.noc.com

North Carolina Bartram Trail Society
P.O. Box 968
Highlands, N.C. 28741
http://ncbartramtrail.org

Oconee State Park
624 State Park Road
Mountain Rest, S.C. 29664
864-638-5353
http://www.southcarolinaparks.com

Orchard at Altapass
P.O. Box 245
Little Switzerland, N.C. 28749
888-765-9531 or 828-765-9531
http://www.altapassorchard.com
Email: billcarson@altapassorchard.com

Penland School of Crafts
P.O. Box 37
Penland, N.C. 28765-0037
828-765-2359
http://www.penland.org
Email: info@penland.org

Roan Mountain State Park
1015 Highway 143
Roan Mountain, Tenn. 37687
800-250-8620 or 423-772-0190
http://www.tn.gov/environment/parks/RoanMtn

Alderman, Pat. *In the Shadow of Big Bald*. Mars Hill, N.C.: Bald Mountain Development Corp., 1972.

Alexander, Nancy. *Here Will I Dwell: The Story of Caldwell County*. By the author, 1956.

Allen, Martha Norburn. *Asheville and Land of the Sky*. Charlotte, N.C.: Heritage House, 1960.

Alley, Judge Felix E. *Random Thoughts and Musings of a Mountaineer*. Salisbury, N.C.: Rowan Printing Company, 1941.

Appalachian State University. *Forever Alive: Mountain People, Mountain Land*. 1978.

Arthur, John Preston. *A History of Watauga County, North Carolina*. Richmond, Va.: Everett Waddy Company, 1915.

———. *Western North Carolina: A History from 1730 to 1913*. Raleigh, N.C.: Edwards and Broughton Printing Company, 1914.

Ashe County Heritage Book Committee. *The Heritage of Ashe County, North Carolina*. Vol. 1. Winston-Salem, N.C.: Hunter Publishing Company, 1984.

Blackmun, Ora. *Western North Carolina: Its Mountains and Its People to 1880*. Boone, N.C.: Appalachian Consortium Press, 1977.

Bradley, Jeff. *A Traveler's Guide to the Smoky Mountains Region*. Boston: Harvard Common Press, 1985.

Burke County Historical Society. *The Heritage of Burke County, 1981*. Winston-Salem, N.C.: Hunter Publishing Company, 1981.

Buxton, Barry M. *A Village Tapestry: The History of Blowing Rock*. Boone, N.C.: Appalachian Consortium Press, 1989.

Caldwell County Heritage Book Committee. *The Heritage of Caldwell County, North Carolina*. Vol. 1. Edited by E. Carl Anderson Jr. Winston-Salem, N.C.: Hunter Publishing Company, 1983.

Carpenter, Cal. *The Walton War and Tales of the Great Smoky Mountains*. Lakemont, Ga.: Copple House Books, 1979.

Cherokee County Historical Museum. *The Heritage of Cherokee County, North Carolina*. Vol. 1. Edited by Alice D. White. Winston-Salem, N.C.: Hunter Publishing Company, 1987.

———. *Marble and Log: The History and Architecture of Cherokee County, North Carolina*. Edited by Dr. Carl Dockery. Murphy, N.C.: Cherokee County Historical Museum, 1984.

Colton, Henry E. *Mountain Scenery: The Scenery of the Mountains of Western North Carolina and Northwestern South Carolina*. Raleigh, N.C.: W. L. Pomeroy, 1859.

Cooper, Horton. *History of Avery County, North Carolina*. Asheville, N.C.: Biltmore Press, 1964.

———. *North Carolina Mountain Folklore and Miscellany*. Murfreesboro, N.C.: Johnson Publishing Company, 1972.

de Hart, Allen. *North Carolina Hiking Trails*. 2d ed. Boston: Appalachian Mountain Club Books, 1982, 1988.

Dykeman, Wilma. *The French Broad*. Knoxville: University of Tennessee Press, 1955.

Federal Writers' Project of the Federal Works Agency Work Projects Administration. *North Carolina: A Guide to the Old North State.* Chapel Hill: University of North Carolina Press, 1939.

FitzSimons, Frank L. *From the Banks of the Oklawaha.* 3 vols. Hendersonville, N.C.: Golden Glow Publishing Company, 1976–79.

Fossett, Mildred B. *History of McDowell County.* Marion, N.C.: McDowell County American Revolution Bicentennial Commission Heritage Committee, 1976.

Freel, Margaret Walker. *Our Heritage: The People of Cherokee County, North Carolina, 1540–1955.* Asheville, N.C.: Miller Printing Company, 1956.

Frome, Michael. *Strangers in High Places.* New York: Doubleday and Company, 1966.

Genealogical Society of Watauga County. *The Heritage of Watauga County, North Carolina.* Vol. 1. Winston-Salem, N.C.: Hunter Publishing Company, 1984.

Graham County Centennial 1972, Inc. *Graham County Centennial, 1872–1972.* 1972.

Griffin, Clarence W. *History of Old Tryon and Rutherford Counties: 1730–1936.* Spartanburg, S.C.: Reprint Company, Publishers, 1977.

———. *Western North Carolina Sketches.* Forest City, N.C.: *Forest City Courier,* 1941.

Hannum, Alberta Pierson. *Look Back with Love: A Recollection of the Blue Ridge.* New York: Vanguard Press, 1969.

Henderson County Genealogical and Historical Society. *The Heritage of Henderson County, North Carolina.* Vol. 1. Edited by George Alexander Jones. Winston-Salem, N.C.: Hunter Publishing Company, 1985.

Jackson County Historical Association. *The History of Jackson County.* Edited by Max R. Williams. Sylva, N.C.: Jackson County Historical Association, 1987.

Johnson, Earline. *Jonas Ridge History.* Banner Elk, N.C.: Pudding Stone Press, 1974.

Journal of Cherokee Studies 4 (Fall 1979).

Kephart, Horace. *Our Southern Highlanders.* 1913. Reprint, New York: Macmillan Company, 1957.

Lanman, Charles. *Letters from the Alleghany Mountains.* New York: G. P. Putnam's Sons, 1849.

Macon County Historical Society, Inc. *The Heritage of Macon County, North Carolina, 1987.* Edited by Jessie Sutton. Winston-Salem, N.C.: Hunter Publishing Company, 1987.

Marsh, Blanche. *Historic Flat Rock: Where the Old South Lingers.* Asheville, N.C.: Biltmore Press, 1961.

McIntosh, Gert. *Highlands, North Carolina . . . Walk into the Past.* Highlands: By the author, 1983.

Medford, W. Clark. *The Early History of Haywood County.* Asheville, N.C.: Miller Printing Company, 1961.

———. *Haywood's Heritage and Finest Hour.* Asheville, N.C.: Daniels Graphics, 1971.

———. *Land o' the Sky: History, Stories, Sketches.* Waynesville, N.C.: By the author, 1965.

———. *The Middle History of Haywood County.* Asheville, N.C.: Miller Printing Company, 1968.

Miller, Clyde C. *The Old Buffalo Trail of Watauga County, North Carolina, Bicentennial, 1976.*

Mooney, James. *Myths of the Cherokee.* One of several papers accompanying the Nineteenth Annual Report of the United States Bureau of American Ethnology to the Secretary of the Smithsonian Institution in 1897–98. Washington: Government Printing Office, 1900. Reprint, New York: Johnson Reprint Corp., 1970.

Morgan, Lucy, with LeGette Blythe. *Gift from the Hills.* New York: Bobbs-Merrill, 1958.

Morgan, Robert Lindsay. *The Lure of the Great Smokies.* Boston and New York: Houghton, Mifflin and Company, 1927.

Morley, Margaret W. *The Carolina Mountains.* Boston and New York: Houghton, Mifflin and Company, 1913.

Mull, J. Alex. *Mountain Yarns.* Banner Elk, N.C.: Pudding Stone Press.

Padgett, Guy. *A History of Clay County, North Carolina.*

Parris, John. *Mountain Bred.* Asheville, N.C.: *Citizen-Times* Publishing, 1967.

———. *My Mountains, My People.* Asheville, N.C.: *Citizen-Times* Publishing, 1955.

———. *Roaming the Mountains.* Asheville, N.C.: *Citizen-Times* Publishing, 1955.

———. *These Storied Mountains.* Asheville, N.C.: *Citizen-Times* Publishing, 1972.

Patton, Sadie Smathers. *A Condensed History of Flat Rock.* Asheville, N.C.: Church Printing Company, 1961.

———. *Sketches of Polk County History.* Spartanburg, S.C.: Reprint Company, Publishers, 1976.

———. *The Story of Henderson County.* Asheville, N.C.: Miller Printing Company, 1947.

Peattie, Donald Culross. *Pearson's Falls Glen: Its Story, Its Flora, Its Birds.* Tryon, N.C.: Tryon Garden Club, 1962.

Peattie, Roderick, ed. *The Great Smokies and the Blue Ridge: The Story of the Southern Appalachians.* New York: Vanguard Press, 1943.

Phifer, Edward W., Jr. *Burke: The History of a North Carolina County, 1777–1920.* Morganton, N.C.: By the author, 1977.

Polk County Historical Association, Inc. *Polk County History.* Edited by D. William Bennett. Dallas, Tex.: Taylor Publishing Company, 1983.

Reeves, Eleanor Baker. *A Factual History of Early Ashe County, North Carolina: Its People, Places and Events.* West Jefferson, N.C.: By the author, 1986.

Reid, Christian [Frances Christine Fisher Tiernan]. *"The Land of Sky"; Or, Adventures in Mountain Byways.* New York: D. Appleton and Company, 1876.

Reynolds, T. W. *Born of the Mountains.* 1913.

———. *Highlands.* 1964.

Rights, Douglas L. *The American Indian in North Carolina.* 1947. Reprint, Winston-Salem, N.C.: John F. Blair, Publisher, 1957.

Schenck, Carl Alwin. *The Birth of Forestry in America, Biltmore Forest School, 1898–1913.* Santa Cruz, Calif.: Forest History Society and the Appalachian Consortium, 1974.

Schwarzkopf, S. Kent. *A History of Mt. Mitchell and the Black Mountains: Exploration, Development, and Preservation.* Raleigh: North Carolina Department of Cultural Resources, Division of Archives and History, 1985.

Southern Appalachian Historical Association. *The Heritage of Watauga County, North Carolina.* Vol. 1. Edited by Curtis Smalling. Boone, N.C.: Hunter Publishing Company, 1987.

Street, Julia Montgomery. *Judaculla's Handprint and Other Mysterious Tales from North Carolina*. Chapel Hill, N.C.: Briar Patch Press, 1975.

Swain County Genealogical and Historical Society. *The Heritage of Swain County, North Carolina, 1988*. Winston-Salem, N.C.: Hunter Publishing Company, 1988.

Teacher Training Class of Burnsville, 1930. *History and Geography of Yancey County*. 1930.

Thomasson, Lillian Franklin. *Swain County: Early History and Educational Development*. Bryson City, N.C.: 1965.

Tinsley, Jim Bob. *The Land of Waterfalls: Transylvania County, North Carolina*. Brevard, N.C.: J. B. and Dottie Tinsley, 1988.

Van Noppen, Ina W., and John J. Van Noppen. *Western North Carolina Since the Civil War*. Boone, N.C.: Appalachian Consortium Press, 1973.

Walser, Richard. *North Carolina Legends*. Raleigh: North Carolina Department of Cultural Resources, Division of Archives and History, 1980.

Warner, Charles Dudley. *On Horseback: A Tour in Virginia, North Carolina, and Tennessee*. Boston and New York: Houghton, Mifflin and Company, 1889.

Wellman, Manly Wade. *The Kingdom of Madison: A Southern Mountain Fastness and Its People*. Chapel Hill: University of North Carolina Press, 1973.

Wheeler, John H. *Reminiscences and Memoirs of North Carolina and Eminent North Carolinians*. Columbus Printing Works, 1884. Reprint, Baltimore, Md.: Genealogical Publishing Company, 1966.

White, Newman Ivey, ed. *The Frank C. Brown Collection of North Carolina Folklore*. 5 vols. Durham, N.C.: Duke University Press, 1952.

Zeigler, Wilbur G., and Ben S. Grosscup. *The Heart of the Alleghanies or Western North Carolina*. Raleigh, N.C.: Alfred Williams and Company, 1883.

Index

1916 flood, 242, 244, 245-46, 247
1940 flood, 247

A.S. Cooper farm, 263, 264
Adam Shoals, 93
ALCOA, 12, 98
Alderman, Pat, 178-79
Aldridge, James, 219
Allanstand, 169
Allanstand Industries, 169
Alligator Rock, 118
Aluminum Company of America. *See* ALCOA
Amantha community, 272
American Heritage River, 291
American Prospecting and Mining Company,
    64
Ammons Branch Campground, 88
Anderson, J.W., 175
Andrews, N.C., 24, 35
"Anthology of Death," 198-99
Antioch United Methodist Church, 276
Apalachia Dam, 43-44
Apalachia Lake, 43-44
Appalachian Power Company, 288
Appalachian Trail, 28, 56, 57, 161, 165, 167,
    176-77, 180, 201-2, 209
Appletree Group Campground, 22
Argyle, 130
Armstrong, Lucy Camp, 119
Armstrong, Robert, 20
Arrowhead Glade Picnic Area, 72
Art Loeb Trail System, 113, 114
Arthur, Gabriel, 270
Arthur, John Preston, 202, 211, 219, 224-25,
    265-66, 270
Asbury, Francis, 159, 162
Ashe County Cheese Company, 286
Asheville Farm School, 166
Atahita. *See* "Shouting Place"
Atakullakulla, 31, 63, 69-70
Avery, Waightstill, 201
Avery, William Waightstill, 256
Awahili Cherokee, 238

Babcock Land and Timber Company, 28
Baird House, 224, 225
Baird, Bedent, 228
Baird, David, 224
Baird, Delilah, 228-29
Baird, Elizabeth, 224
Bald River Falls, 28-29
Balds, 207-8
Balsam Grove community, 117
Bandana community, 211-12
Banner Elk, N.C., 228
Baring, Charles, 122, 127-29
Baring, Susan Heyward, 122, 123, 127-29
Barker, Eli, 284
Barkhouse Picnic Area, 255, 256
Barnard, Hezekiah, 173
Barnett, William, 71, 72

Bartram Trail, 21, 70, 71
Bartram, William, 66, 69-70
Bartram's Travels, 70
Bass Lake, 215, 216
Bat Cave community, 146
Battle of Chickamauga, 205
Battle of Cowpens, 189
Battle of Horseshoe Bend, 19, 20
Battle of Kings Mountain, 189, 190, 206, 254,
    266-67
Battle of Round Mountain, 139, 155
Bear's Town, 3
Bearwallow Overlook, 92
Beaumont Estates, 127
Bechtler, August, 147
Bechtler, Christopher, 147
Beech Gap, 116
Beech Mountain, N.C., 228
Beechertown, 69
Belinda (Brown Mountain Lights), 245
Bell Institute, 166
Bellew, Pitt, 135
Ben F. Long Fresco Trail, 288
Ben Hur, 148
Bennett, Thomas, 124
Benton MacKaye Trail, 28
Betsey's Gap, 161
Big Bald Mountain, 177-78
Big Bear Farm. *See* Bear's Town
Big Bear, Chief, 3
Big Lost Cove Cliffs, 251
Big Tom Mountain, 185
Big Tom Wilson Motor Road, 184, 186
"Big View," 97, 98
Billingsley brothers, 80
Biltmore Estate, 108
Biltmore Forest Fair, 112, 113
Biltmore Forest School, 112, 113
Biltmore Industries, 140
Birth of Forestry, The, 113
Black Balsam Knob, 114
Black Mountain Crest Trail, 193
Black Mountains, 183-86
Black Rock Mountain, 89
Blalock, L. McKesson "Keith," 234-35
Blalock, Malinda "Sam," 234
Blannahassett Island, 172
Block House Steeplechase, 141
Block House, 138, 139, 141, 142
"Bloody Madison," 169-70
Blowing Rock, N.C., 215, 231-32
Blue Boar Lodge, 14-15, 16
Blue Ridge Escarpment, 94
Blue Ridge Heritage Area, 183
Blue Ridge Parkway, 186, 193, 194, 197
Blue Ridge Parkway Craft Center, 215
"Blue Wall," 94
Bluff community, 161
Bobby N. Setzer State Fish Hatchery, 109
Bonnefoy, Antoine, 31-32
Boone, Daniel, 270, 271, 272
Bottomless Pools, 154
Boudinot Boundary, 161
Boudinot, Elias, 161
Brant Island Shoal Light, 182

Brasstown Carvers, 52
Brasstown community, 50-52
Braswell, Jonas, 251
Breitenstein, Bob, 221
Bridal Veil Falls, 77-78
Bright Spring, 201
Bright, Samuel, 200-201
Bright's Trace, 201
Brinkley, John, 100-102
Brinkley, Sally, 100-101
Brittain, William, 57
Brittain's Cove, 169
Broad River. *See* Rocky Broad River
Brotherhood of Railway Clerks, 136
Brown Brothers Lumber Company. *See* Murchison Lumber Company
Brown Mountain, 243-45
Brown Mountain Beach, 242, 243
Brown Mountain Lights, 243-45, 251, 255
Brown Mountain Off-Highway Vehicle Area, 241
Brown, Carter P., 140, 141
Brown, Frank C., 245
Brown, James, 128-29
Bruckmann, Fred, 14-15
Bryson City, N.C., 3, 4-5
Bryson City Cemetery, 8
Buck Creek Gap, 192
Buncombe Turnpike, 122, 129, 162, 167
Bunker, Adelaide Yates, 278
Bunker, Chang, 278
Bunker, Eng, 278
Bunker, Sallie Yates, 278
Burnett, Frances Hodgson, 147-48
Burns, Otway, 182
Burnsville, N.C., 181-83
Burnt Rock Mine, 92
Burrells Ford, 85
Butler, Marguerite, 51
Byrne, John B., 72

Cable Cove Recreation Area, 10
Calderwood Dam, 12
Calderwood Lake, 12
Caldwell, David T., 171
Calhoun, John C., 95
California Creek church, 176
California Creek, 176
Calloway, Betsy, 219
Camp Alice, 193-94
Camp Alice Trail Shelter, 194
Camp Broadstone, 221
Camp Daniel Boone, 114
Camp Rainbow, 249
Camp Santeetlah, 16
Camp Vance, 256
Camp Wilson, 186
Camp Yonahlossee, 218
Campbell Boyd home, 125-26
Campbell, Arthur, 253
Campbell, John C., 51
Campbell, Olive Dame, 51-52
Campbell, William, 190, 253
Camping and Woodcraft, 7-8
Cane River, 180, 184, 186

Canton, N.C., 114, 115
Carl Sandburg National Historic Site, 123-25
Carolina and Northwestern Railroad, 246, 247
Carolina Hemlock Recreation Area, 194
Carolina Mountain Club, 114
Carolina Special, 135, 138
Carolina Spruce Company, 186
Carolina, Clinchfield, and Ohio Railway, 197
Carpenter, Jacob, 198
Carr, Louis, 108
Carson House, 190-92
Carson, John, 190-91
Carson, Mary Moffitt McDowell, 190
Carson, Rachel, 191
Carson, Samuel Price, 191
Carter, Edward, 175
Cartoogechaye Creek, 57, 58
Carver's Gap, 209
Cary's Flat, 236
Cashiers, N.C., 94-95
Cataloochee Trail, 159
Catawba Indians, 208
CCC, 16-17, 64, 72, 86, 109-10, 247
Celo community, 194
Celo Knob, 184, 194
Central House. See Old Edwards Inn and Spa
Champion Coated Paper Company, 113, 114-15
Champion Fibre Company. *See* Champion Coated Paper Company
Chapel of Christ the King, 289
Charles Hall Museum, 29
Chattahoochee National Forest, 82
Chattanooga, Tenn., 205
Chattooga River, 81, 82, 85, 88
Chattooga Town, 81
Chatuge Dam, 55
Chatuge Lake, 54, 55
Cheoah Dam, 11, 12
Cheoah Mountain, 10
Cheoah Ranger Station, 16
Cheoah River, 13
Cherohala Skyway, 26-29
Cherohala Skyway Visitors' Center, 29
Cherokee County Courthouse, 42, 47, 48
Cherokee County Historical Museum, 48-49
Cherokee National Forest, 168
Cherokee Removal, 4, 20, 26, 40-41, 52
Cheshire, Joseph Blount, 227, 286, 287
Chestnut Bald, 111
Chickamauga National Park Commission, 206
Chimney Rock, 150-51
Chimneytop Mountain, 94
Chota, 32
Chunky Gal Mountain, 56
Chunn, Sam, 71, 72
Church of God of Prophecy, 44
Church of St. John in the Wilderness, 127-29
Church of the Holy Cross, 227
Church of the Holy Trinity (Glendale Springs), 289
Church of the Messiah, 49-50
Citico Creek Wilderness Area, 28
Civil War, 23, 42, 48, 59, 124, 125, 126, 127,

308   129, 145-46, 155, 163, 169-70, 190, 205, 233-36, 256

Index

Civilian Conservation Corps. *See* CCC
Clarissa Buchanan Mine, 195
Clawson, Peggy, 265-66
Clay County, 53-54
Clay County Historical and Arts Center. *See* Old Jail
Clay County Recreation Park, 55
Clemson University, 84
Cleveland, Benjamin, 190, 253-54, 266-67
Cliffside Lake Recreation Area, 77
Clingman, Thomas L., 184, 211
Clinton, Bill, 291
Cloudland Hotel, 206, 209-10
Coffey, Archie, 249-50
Coffey's General Store, 249-50
Coker Creek, 32-33
Cold Mountain, 113, 114
Cold Springs Lodge, 257, 258
Cole, Matthew, 69
Colton, Henry E., 149, 173, 210
Columbia Marble Company, 36-47
Columbus, N.C., 154-57
Commissioner Rock, 88
Cone, Bertha, 215, 216, 217
Cone, Caesar, 215
Cone, Moses S., 215, 216, 217
Connemara. *See* Carl Sandburg National Historic Site
Coolidge, Calvin, 152
Cooper House, 7
Cornwell Hall, 175
Cottage Industries Guild, 169
Council Oak, 254, 261
Courthouse Creek, 116
Courthouse Falls, 116
Cove Creek Baptist Church, 271
Cove Creek community (Haywood County), 159
Cove Creek community (Watauga County), 272
Cove Creek School, 272, 273
Cover, Franklin Pierce, 35
Cowee (Cherokee town), 65-67
Cowee Mound. *See* Ralph Preston Historic Cowee Mound
Cowee Valley, 64-65
Cowee/West's Mill Historic District, 63-64
Crabtree community, 160
Cradle of Forestry in America, 112
Cranberry community, 202
Cranberry Forge, 203
Cranberry mine, 205
Crescent Lane and Timber Corporation, 91
Crockett, Davy, 191
Cullasaja community, 75
Cullasaja Gorge, 76
Cullasaja River, 75
Cullowhee, N.C., 102-3
Cuming, Alexander, 30-31, 61-62

Dahlonega, Ga., 33
Daingerfield, Elliott, 231-32, 238-39

DAR, 21, 271, 272
Daughters of the American Revolution. *See* DAR
Davidson River, 108-9
Davidson River Campground, 108
Davidson, Alan, 23
Davidson, Benjamin, 108
Davis, Jefferson, 124, 125
de Brahm, Gerard, 244
de Choiseul, Charles, 125-26
de Choiseul, Joseph Marie Gabriel St. Xavier, 125, 127
de Schweinitz, Frederick, 29-30
De Soto, Hernando, 38, 76, 97
Deal's Gap, 11-12
Deep Gap (Clay County), 56
Deer Killer, 42
Demeré, Paul, 63
Departure of Christ, The, 289, 290
Devil's Courthouse, 86, 96, 116
Devil's Old Fields, 116
Deyton, Nathan, 210
Deyton's Bend, 212
Dills, William Allen, 104
Dillsboro, N.C., 103, 104
Dirty Dancing, 152
Dixie Highway, 165
Dodgen, Adam, 92-93
Dodgen, Eliza, 92-93
Dorland Institute, 166
Dorland Memorial Presbyterian Church, 166
Dorland, Luke, 166
Dorland-Bell Institute, 166
Doubleday vineyard, 138
Doughton Park, 279
Doughton, Robert L., 279, 280
Doughton-Hall Bed and Breakfast, 280
Draper, Lyman, 266-67
Drayton, John Grimké, 128
Drift Falls, 92
Drowning Bear. *See* Yonaguska
Dry Falls, 77
Duché, Andrew, 65
Dugger family, 203
Duke Energy Access Trail, 21
Duke Energy, 91, 92, 94
Duke Power. *See* Duke Energy
Dula, Tom, 271
Dyer, Ben, 228-29
Dykeman, Wilma, 165-66

Earle's Fort, 138, 139
Earls Ford, 82
East Flat Rock, N.C., 121
East Fork of Pigeon River, 113-14
East Tennessee and Western North Carolina Railroad, 205
East Tennessee Railroad, 164
Eastern Band of the Cherokee Indians, 3, 6, 67
Edgemont Baptist Church, 248
Edgemont community, 248-50
Edgemont Hotel, 248, 249
Edgemont railroad depot, 248, 249
Edison, Thomas, 119

Edmonds, R.H., 137
Ehle, John, 199
Elizabeth II, 176
Elk Falls, 229
Elk Knob State Park, 269-70
Elk Park, N.C., 229
Elk River, 229
Elkland. *See* Todd community
Elks Crossroads. *See* Todd community
Ellicott Rock Trail, 88
Ellicott Rock Wilderness Area, 88
English Chapel, 108
English, A.F., 108
English, Alice, 197
English, Isaac, 197
Ernestville, Tenn., 178
Eskota community, 186
Esmeralda Inn, 147-48
Estatoe (Indian), 212-13
Estatoe community, 196
Estatoe Trail, 118
Euchella, 5, 6, 20, 67-68
Euchella v. Welch, 67

F.P. Cover & Sons Tannery, 24, 35
Faile, Tommy, 245
Fairbanks, Douglas, 148
Fairy crosses, 50-51
Fannie Gouge Mine, 195
Farmer, Henry T., 129
Featherstonhaugh, George, 36
Feldspar, 195-96
Ferebee Memorial Recreation Area, 69
Ferguson Supply Store, 160
Ferguson, Patrick, 190
Ferguson's Field, 4
Fields of the Wood, 33, 44-45
Fillmore, Millard, 146
Fine, Peter, 160, 161
Fines Creek community, 160, 161
Fitzgerald, F. Scott, 152
FitzSimons, Frank, 146
Flag Pond community, 178
Flat Rock, N.C., 121-31
Flat Rock Hotel. *See* Woodfield Inn
Flat Rock Playhouse, 123-24
Flat Rock Rockers, 129
Flat Top Mountain, 215, 216, 217
Fletcher, Arthur, 284
Flinsch, Margaret, 146-47
Flint Ridge, 178
Flying Squirrel, Chief, 149
Fontana Dam, 10, 11
Fontana Village, 10, 11
Foothills Equestrian Nature Center (FENCE), 141
Foothills Trail, 93-94
Ford, Harrison, 12
Ford, Henry, 119
Ford, Tom, 80
Forest Heritage National Scenic Byway, 105-18
Fort Butler, 25, 41, 47
Fort Frederica, 32
Fort Hembree, 54-55
Fort Lindsay, 5

Fort Loudoun, 63
Fort Montgomery, 25
Fort Prince George, 62-63
Foster, Kennedy "Kan," 179-80
Foster, Mary, 179
Foster, William S., 6
Foster's Racepath, 154
Fothergill, John, 66
Founders Hall, 175
Francis Asbury Trail, 160
Francis, Allan, 84-85
Francis, Henry, 84
Francis, James, 84
Franklin Gem and Mineral Museum, 72-73
Franklin, N.C., 58-59, 72-73
Fraser fir, 201
Fraser, John, 201, 208
Freeborne Inn, 280
Freeman, Gertrude, 146
Freeman, Jerome B. "Rome," 150
Freeman, Thomas, 100
French Broad Baptist Institute. *See* Mars Hill College
French Broad River, 118, 162, 165, 166-67, 168, 173
French, Aaron, 142, 155
Frontier Village, 248
FROTH (Friends of the Horsepasture), 92
Frozen Creek Access, 92
Fugitive, The, 12

Gable, Clark, 148
Garber, Jan, 192
General Electric, 273
Gentry, Jane, 164, 165
George VI, 176
Gere, J.M., 197
German prisoners-of-war, 164
Gerton community, 146
Gingercake Mountain, 258
Ginseng, 208
Glade Gap, 56
Glassy Mountain, 125, 126, 127
Glen, James, 32
Glendale Springs Inn, 291
Globe, The, 233-36
Globe Academy, 233
Globe Baptist Church, 233, 235
Gneiss community, 76
Goodrich, Frances, 168-69
Gore, Al, 291
Gorges State Park, 92
Government Services, Inc., 11
Gragg community, 235, 236
Gragg Prong, 250, 251
Graham County, 10
Grandfather Mountain, 236, 237, 250, 251
Granny Lewis Creek, 178-79
Grant, James, 63
Grant, Ludovick, 31, 32
Grassy Ridge Access, 92
Gray, Asa, 93, 208-9
Gray's lily, 209
Grayson, James, 271
Great Eyrie, 254-55

Great Smoky Mountains National Park, 10, 11, 159, 160
"Great Yellow Jacket," 71
Green River, 133, 154
Greentown Trail, 255
Greer, David, 177-78
Greer's Bald. *See* Big Bald Mountain
"Greer's Potato Hills," 178
Gregg, Norman, 150-51
Gregory Bald, 12
Gregory Bald Trail, 12
Gregory, C.E., 244
Grey, Jennifer, 152
Greystone Inn, 119
Griffiths, Thomas, 65
Grimshawes post office, 87, 88
Grosscup, Ben, 76, 87, 88-89, 95, 172, 192, 195, 203, 221
Guasili, 38
Guice, Peter, 133

Hadley, J.V., 126
Hall, James, 113
Hampton Legion, 95
Hampton Place, 95
Hampton, Wade II, 85, 95
Hampton, Wade III, 95
Handmade in America, 183
Hanging Dog community, 41-42, 48
Hard Taylor House, 224
Harden, John, 203
Harden, Peter, 203
Harmon Den Wildlife Mangement Area, 161
Harper Creek Falls, 246
Harper Creek Wilderness study area, 250
Harper's New Monthly Magazine, 179-80
Hart, William S., 148
Hawksbill, 254, 259-60
Hawksbill Mountain Trail, 259-60
Hayes, George, 53
Hayesville, N.C., 53-54
Healing Springs, 283-84
Heap, Mr., 211
"Helper, the," 135, 136
Hemlock woolly adelgid, 13-14
Henderson County, 145
Henderson, Bayles, 69
Henderson-Brevard Railroad, 118
Henry, Robert, 167-68
Henson's Chapel Methodist Church, 272
Hickok, Wild Bill, 219-20
Hickory Nut Falls, 151
Hickory Nut Gap, 145
Hickory Nut Gap Farm, 145
Hickory Nut Gorge, 148-51
Hidden, W.E., 64
Higgins community, 181
Higgins, Holland, 177
Higgins Ridge, 178, 179
"High Bridge," 133
High Hampton Inn, 94
Highlands, N.C., 78-81
Highlands Inn, 79, 80
Highlands Nature Center, 89
Hikers' Hostel, 165

Hiwassee Dam, 42, 43
Hiwassee Lake, 42-43, 44
Hiwassee River, 33, 37, 38, 39, 40
Hix, Samuuel, 223
"Hog Greer." *See* Greer, David
Hogarth, William, 31
Holtsclaw, Fanny, 228
Holtsclaw, James, 223
Holtsclaw, John, 228
Holtsclaw, Raney, 228
Home of the Perfect Christmas Tree store, 197
"honey locust place," 75
Hooper Bald, 15, 27
Hooper House, 103-4
Hooper, Delos Dexter, 103-4
Horner, Junius, 227
Horse Cove, 88, 89
Horse Cove Campground, 13
Horsepasture River, 92, 93
Horsepasture River Gorge, 92
Hot Springs, N.C., 162-67
Hot Springs Resort and Spa, 166-67
Hound Ears Club, 218
Houston, Gloria, 197
Howard Gap Road, 134, 139
Howard, Benjamin, 273
Howard, Sallie, 272-73
Howard, Thomas, 139
Howard's Knob, 273
Huger, Daniel, 161
Hunt Fish Falls, 240
Hunter, A.R.S., 40
Huntington. *See* Murphy, N.C.
Hut Burrow, 245
Hutchinson, C.C., 78-79

"Immortals." *See* Nunnehi
Indian Boundary Recreation Area, 28
Indian Grave Gap, 67
Indian Removal Act, 24-25
Ingalls community, 198
Ingersoll, Bob, 148
Iron bridge (Chattooga River), 88, 89
Iron Duff community, 160
Issaqueena, 84-85
Issaqueena Falls, 83-84, 85
Ives, L. Silliman, 225, 226-27

Jackrabbit Mountain Recreation Area, 55
Jackson County Courthouse, 103
Jackson, Andrew, 19, 24, 182
Jarrett House, 104-5
Jarrett Springs Hotel. *See* Jarrett House
Jarrett, Nimrod S., 69
Jarrett's Station, 69
Jeffrey's Hell, 28
Jennings, E.H., 118
Jeptha. *See* Toxaway, N.C.
Jesuit House of Prayer, 165, 166
Jewel Hill, 166, 171
Joanna Bald, 26
Jocassee (person), 94
Jocassee Gorges, 91
Jocassee village, 94
John C. Campbell Folk School, 51-52

John Rock Scenic Area, 109, 110
John the Baptist, 287, 288
Johns River Missionary Baptist Church, 233
Johnson, Andrew, 146
Johnson, Andrew Jr., 163
Johnstone, Andrew, 127
Johnstone, Elliott, 127
Jonas Ridge community, 251
Jones, Evan, 52
Jones, Milnor, 286, 287
Jones, Tommy Lee, 12
Joyce Kilmer Memorial Forest, 13-14
Judaculla, 102, 116
Judaculla Rock, 102, 116
Junaluska, Chief, 19-21, 22, 26
Junaluska Creek, 20, 22
Junaluska Memorial Museum, 19, 21

Kalakaleskies, 78
Kanawha Hardwood Company, 24
Karuga, 84
Keith House, 51, 52
Keith, James, 170
Kelsey, Samuel T., 78-79
Kemp, Hal, 192
Kenmure, 130-31
Keowee River, 94
Kephart, A.P., 218
Kephart, Horace, 6-7
Kephart, Mrs. A.P., 218
Kilmer, Joyce, 14
King Creek Falls, 85
King, Margaret, 122
King, Mitchell Campbell, 129-30
King, Mitchell, 122
King, Susan, 122
Kirk, George, 256
Kirk's Battle Ground, 256
Kirkby, 255-56
Kituwah Indian Mound, 3
Kona community, 212
Kudzu, 136-37
Kulsetsiyi. *See* "honey locust place"
Kunz, George Frederick, 64
Kuykendall, Abraham, 126, 127
Kyser, Kay, 192

La Morte, Alexis, 128
Lake Adger, 154
Lake Cheoah, 11
Lake Glenville, 98, 99
Lake Jocassee, 92, 94
Lake Keowee, 92
Lake Logan, 114, 115
Lake Lure, 152
Lake Lure Inn and Spa, 152, 153
Lake Santeetlah, 16
Lake Tahoma, 192
Lake Toxaway, 91
Lake Toxaway Company, 118-19
Lake Toxaway Country Club, 119
Land Trust for the Little Tennessee, 67
Lanier, Sidney, 143
Lanier Club, 140
Lanier Library, 140

Lanman, Charles, 149, 150, 163, 208, 209, 254, 258
Lapland. *See* Marshall
Last of the Mohicans, 151
Last Supper, The, 289, 290
Laurel Inn, 246, 247
LBJ Civilian Conservation Center, 72
Ledges Whitewater River Park, 173
Lee, Robert E., 165
"Leech Place," 39, 40
"Legend of the Brown Mountain Lights," 245
Lettered Rock Ridge, 259
Lewis family (Ernestville), 178-79
Lewis family (Watauga County), 266-67
Lewis, Gideon, 266
Lewis, Joseph V., 64
Lewis, William, 178-79
Lindsey, W.T., 138
Linn Cove Viaduct, 236, 237
Linville, N.C., 238
Linville Gorge, 254, 260
Linville River, 254
Little Hump Mountain, 202
Little Lost Cove Cliffs, 250, 251
"Little People," 50-51, 149
Little River Road, 124-26
Little Tennessee River, 67, 68
"Lizard Place." *See* Joanna Bald
Loafer's Glory, 210
Loeb, Art, 114
Log Cabin Inn, 155
Long, Ben, 287-88, 289, 290
Look Homeward, Angel, 8-9
Looking Glass Falls, 110-11
Looking Glass Rock, 109-10
Lookout Loop, 165
Lord Ashburton, 122
Lost Cove Wilderness study area, 250
Lost Provinces, The, 275
Loven, Anderson, 254, 255, 257
Loven Hotel. *See* Cold Springs Lodge
Lover's Leap, 167
Lovin, Joel, 80
Lower Cullasaja Falls, 76
Lower Satulah Falls, 81, 82
Lower Towns, 81
Lowndes family, 124
Lunsford, Bascom Lamar, 175-76
Lutz, O.P., 247, 248
Lynn community, 142
Lyttleton, William Henry, 63

Mabel community, 271
MacFarland, Betty, 221, 223
MacKaye, Benton, 28
MacRae, Hugh, 238
Madison County Courthouse, 173
Madonna of the Hills, 231-32, 238-40
Mansfield, George Rogers, 244
Maple Springs Observation Point, 13
Marble community, 36-37
Markle Handicraft School, 180, 181
Markle, John, 181
Mars Hill, N.C., 175
Mars Hill College, 175

312   Marshall, N.C., 172-73

Mary, Great with Child, 287, 288

Mast community, 271

Mast, David, 221

Mast Farm, 221-22

Mast Farm Inn, 221-22

Mast Store, 222, 223-24

Mast Store Annex, 222, 223

Master of the World, The, 254-55

Max Patch Mountain, 161

McAboy, Leland, 142, 143

McAboy House, 142, 143

McCabe family, 130

McCanless, David Colvert "Cobb," 219-20

McDowell County, 186-92

McDowell House, 189-90

McDowell, Charles Jr., 253

McDowell, Hunting John, 189, 191

McDowell, Joseph, 167-68, 189, 190, 191

McDowell, Silas, 151-52

McDuff, Aaron, 160

McGillis, Kelly, 199

McGuire, Cotton, 16

Meat Camp Baptist Church, 268

Meat Camp community, 268

Meigs, Return J., 100

Mellon, Andrew, 13

Melrose Junction, 135, 136

Memminger, Christopher Gustavus, 124, 125, 128

Memminger, Edward, 126

Merrimon, Augustus, 170, 171

Micaville Country Store, 195

Micaville community, 195

Michaux, André, 93, 184, 201, 208, 236

Middle Prong Wilderness Area, 115, 116

Middle Towns, 40, 63, 67, 99-100

Mill Farm Inn, 142

Mill Spring community, 154

Mills, Ambrose, 154

Mills, Columbus, 142, 154-55

Mills, John, 142

Mimosa Inn, 142, 143, 155

Mims, Jeffrey, 298

Minneapolis community, 202

Mission Farms, 52

Mitchell County, 210-12

Mitchell, Elisha, 184-85, 284

Moccasin community, 80

Moccasin War, 80-81

Montezuma Cemetery, 235

Montgomery, Archibald, 63

Montvale Lumber Company, 10

Moodys Spring, 85, 86

Mooney, James, 4, 5, 6, 25, 39-40, 41, 55, 58-59, 63, 69, 75, 96-97, 100, 159, 207

Moore Cove Trail 111

Moore Creek Falls, 111

Moore, George Gordon, 15

Moore, William, 100

Moreland, Wright, 202

Morgan, Lucy, 49-50, 196

Morgan, Rufus, 196

Morgan, Thomas, 162

Morley, Margaret, 180

Morristown (Asheville), 109

Morse, Lucius, 150, 151

Mortimer community, 245-47

Mortimer Recreation Area, 248

Mortimer, Mrs. Bill, 247

Morton, George Edward, 137-38

Moses S. Cone Estate, 215-18

Moss, Henry, 36

Mount Beulah Hotel. *See* Jarrett House

Mount Jefferson, 284-85

Mount Jefferson State Natural Area, 284-85

Mount Mitchell, 182, 184, 185-86, 193

Mount Mitchell Motor Road, 104, 185, 186

Mount Mitchell Railroad, 193

Mount Mitchell State Park, 186, 193-94

Mount Mitchell Station, 193

Mount Pisgah, 113

Mountain Dance and Folk Festival, 176

Mountain House, 193

Mountain Lodge, 122, 127

Mountain Magnolia Inn, 166

Mountain Park Hotel, 164

Mountain Rest, S.C., 83

Mountain Waters Scenic Byway, 76-77

Mountains-to-Sea Trail, 255

Moytoy, 30-31

Mud Creek Baptist Church, 127

Murchison Boundary, 185

Murchison Lumber Company, 186

Murchison, David, 185

Murchison, K.M., 185

Murphey, Archibald D., 47

Murphy, N.C., 39-40, 47-50

Murray Branch Recreation Area, 167

Museum of North Carolina Minerals, 197

Mussendine Matthews, 167-68

Mystery of Faith, The, 287, 288

Nantahala Gorge, 21, 68-69

Nantahala Lake, 22, 70

Nantahala Outdoor Center, 69, 167

Nantahala Power and Light Company, 98

Nantahala River Launch Site, 21, 69

Nantahala River, 22, 70

NASA, 273

Nashville Flame, 281

Nathan Bedford Forrest, 206

National Register of Historic Places, 23, 47, 53, 82, 136, 142, 175, 176, 263

National Speleological Society, 153

National Wild and Scenic Rivers System, 92, 241, 288

National Wilderness Preservation System, 113

Nature Conservancy, 147, 269

Needham, James, 270

New Echota, Ga., 41

New River, 263, 264, 275-76

New River State Park, 288

Nicie, 20, 21

Nikwasi Indian Mound, 58-59, 61-62, 67

Ninety-Six, S.C., 85

Nolichucky Jack. *See* Sevier, John

Norfolk and Western Railroad, 263-64

Norman Wilder Forest, 138

North Carolina Outward Bound School, 260

North Fork of the New River, 288
North Harper Creek Falls, 250, 251
Northwest Development Association, 291
Northwest Trading Post, 291
Norton, Barak, 86-87
Nunnehi, 55, 58-59
Nu-Wray Inn, 181-82

O'Connell, Jeremiah Joseph, 83
Oconee State Park, 85, 94
Oconee, Chief, 94
Oconostota, 63
Old Albany, 220
Old Buffalo Trail, 267-68
Old Edwards Inn and Spa, 80
Old English Inn, 197
Old Hunting Country, 140-41
Old Jail (Hayesville), 53, 54
Old Joe, 175
Olmsted, Frederick Law, 23, 107
Oochella. *See* Euchella
Orchard at Altapass, 197-98
Orchard Inn, 136
Ore Knob Mine, 281
Our Southern Highlanders, 8
Outlaws motorcycle gang, 281
Overhill Towns, 29, 30, 69
Overmountain Men, 190, 201, 206, 253-54
Overmountain Victory National Historic Trail,
  190, 198, 201

Pace family, 134
Pace's Gap, 134, 135
Pacolet Area Conservancy, 138
Pacolet River, 134, 136
Pacolet River Valley, 137
Paint Creek Corridor, 168, 169
Paint Mountain Turnpike, 168
Paint Rock, 167-68
Palmer, Arthur, 49
Palmetto Trail, 136
Pardo, Juan, 39
Parris Gap, 147
Parris, John, 172
Patterson Lumber Company, 168
Patton, James, 162
Patton, John, 162
Patton, William, 193
Paulownia, 137
Peachtree community, 37
Peachtree Creek, 38
Peachtree Mound and Village Site, 38, 39, 50
Pearson, Charles William, 134, 136
Pearson's Falls, 136
Peattie, Donald C., 136
Penland community, 196
Penland School of Crafts, 196-97
Pensacola community, 184, 186
Peregrine falcons, 95, 251
Perkins, Ben, 202-3
Perkins, Jake 202-3
Perkins, Joshua, 202-3
Perley and Crockett Logging Company, 185,
  194
Pheasant Branch, 126

Phillips, Susan, 196
Pickens, Andrew, 88
Pickford, Mary, 148
Pigeon River, 160
Pinchot, Gifford, 107-8
Pine Crest Inn, 140
Pink Beds, 108
Pink Beds Picnic Area, 113
Pisgah Astronomical Research Institute, 117
Pisgah Center for Wildlife Education, 109
Pisgah Forest, N.C., 107
Pisgah National Forest, 107, 108, 113, 118,
  168, 241, 242, 243, 254
Plamondon family, 141
Pleasant Gardens, 189, 190
Plum Tree community, 199-200
Polk County, 138, 154
Polk County Courthouse, 155
Poplar Cove, 14
Pratt, Joseph H., 64
Priber, Christian Gottlieb, 31-32
Pump. *See* Gerton community

Quaker Meadows, 253
Qualla Cherokees, 68
Quilt squares, 183

R.T. Greer and Company Root Warehouse,
  263
"Rabbit Place," 12
Rabbit Skin community, 160
Rainbow Falls, 93
Rainbow Lodge. *See* Edgemont Hotel
Rainbow Springs, 57
Ralph Preston Historic Cowee Mound, 67-68
Rattler Ford Campground, 14
Ray Mine, 183, 195
Red Marble Gap. *See* Topton
Red Stick Creeks, 19
Removal of 1838. *See* Cherokee Removal
"reservees," 20
Reynolds, Henry, 162
Rhododendron catawbiense, 208
Rich Mountain, 268-69
Riddle, William, 267
Riddle's Knob, 267
Ripshin Ridge, 254
Ritter Lumber Company, 57, 246, 247
Riverwood Shops, 104
Roan Mountain, 205-10
Roan Mountain community, 205
Roan Mountain State Park, 206-10
Roan Mountain Station, 206
Roaring Gap community, 276
Robbinsville, N.C., 19-21
Robertson, Reuben, 113, 114-15
Rocky Bluff Recreation Area, 161-62
Rocky Broad River, 146, 148
Roosevelt, Franklin D., 152, 176
Roosevelt, Theodore "Teddy," 108, 246
Rosman community, 118
Rosman Research Center, 117
Ross, John, 40-41
Round Top, 152
Rudolph, Eric, 10

Rumbling Bald Mountain, 152-54
Rumbough, Bessie, 163
Rumbough, Carrie, 163, 166
Rumbough, James, 163, 164, 166
Rumple Memorial Presbyterian Church, 233
Russell Farmstead, 81-82
Russell, Jane Nicholson, 82
Russell, Kurt, 199
Russell, William Ganaway, 82
Russian wild boars, 16
Rutherford Trace, 100
Rutherford, Griffith, 67, 99-100, 113
Rutland, 166
Ruxton, Frederick, 156

Saluda Cottages. *See* Campbell Boyd home
Saluda Gap, 191
Saluda grade, 134-36
Saluda River, 138
Saluda, N.C., 133-36
Sam's Gap, 176
San Souci. *See* Campbell Boyd home
Sand Town Cherokees, 58
Sandburg, Carl, 123, 124, 125
Sandburg, Paula Steichen, 125
Santeetlah Dam, 16
Santeetlah Gap, 14
Santeetlah Overlook, 27
Santeetlah, Chief, 57-58
Sapphire Inn, 91
Sapphire Valley Mining Company, 91
Sapphire, N.C., 91-92
Sargeant, C.S., 93
Sarrette, D.B., 244
Satulah Mountain, 81, 82
Schenck, Carl A., 108, 111-13
Schoolbred, J.G., 126
Scott, Arthur Hoyt, 206
Scott, Winfield, 5, 25, 41
Sears, Roebuck and Co., 103-4
Seigling, Rudolph, 126
Sequoyah Dam, 78
Seven Months a Prisoner, 126
Sevier, John, 100, 178, 190, 253
Sharp, Cecil, 164
Shatley Springs Inn, 282-83
Shatley, Martin, 282-83
Shelby, Isaac, 190, 253
Shelton Laurel Massacre, 169-70, 176
Shelving Rock Encampment National Historic
    Site, 206, 207
Sherman, William T., 88
Sherrill, Bedford, 145
Sherrill's Inn, 145-46
Shining Rock Wilderness Area, 113, 114, 115
Shook's Campground, 160
Shooting Creek, 55
Shortia, 93
"Shouting Place," 71
Shull, Frederick, 221
Shull, Joseph, 220
Shull, Phillip, 219
Shull, Sarah, 219-20
Shulls Mill community, 219, 220
Shulls Mill community store, 218, 220

Shunkawauken Falls, 157
Siler John, 58
Siler, Jacob, 57-58
Siler, Jesse, 58
Siler, William, 58
"Sitting Down Place," 96-97
Silver family cemetery, 212
Silver Run Falls Access, 94
Silver, Charlie, 212
Silver, Frankie, 212
Silvermine Trail, 167
Silversteen, Joseph, 118
Simms, William Gilmore, 93, 94
Singer Sewing Machine Company, 91
Sink Hole Mine, 211, 212
Sitting Bear Rock, 258, 259
Sitting Bear Trail, 258
Skiles, William West, 224, 226, 227
Skyuka, 139, 155
Skyuka Hotel, 155
Slaughterhouse Curve, 135
Slick Rock Falls, 110
Slick Rock Trail, 88
Slickrock Wilderness Area, 14
Sliding Rock Recreation Area, 111-12
Smith Hotel. *See* Highlands Inn
Smith, Absalom, 276
Smith, Agnes, 276
Smith, Richard Sharp, 173
Smithsonian Institution, 38, 75-76
Snake Mountain, 269
Snap Dragon, 182
Snowbird community, 16, 26
Snowbird Mountain Lodge, 14
Snowbird Mountains, 10, 14-15, 26, 36
Snowbird Valley Railway Company, 24
South Fork of New River, 263, 281-82
South Harper Creek Falls, 246, 250
Southern Highland Craft Guild, 105, 169, 181
Southern Mountain Handicraft Guild, 169
Southern Railroad Company, 135-36
Spangenberg, August Gottlieb, 232, 233, 253
Spearfinger, 97
Spencer, Samuel, 200
Spivey Creek, 179-80
Spivey Gap, 180
Spivey Gap Recreation Area, 180
Spoonauger Falls, 85
Spring Creek community, 161
Spring Mountain Park, 155, 157
Spruce Pine, N.C., 197
Squire Taylor House, 225, 226
St. John's Church, 224, 225
St. Mary's Episcopal Church (Beaver Creek),
    286, 287
St. Mary's of the Hills Episcopal Church,
    231-32
Stairway Falls, 92
Standing Indian Campground, 57
Standing Indian Mountain, 56
State of Franklin, 178
Station's Inn, 280
Stearns Park, 155
Stearns, David, 142, 155
Stearns, Frank, 155

Stecoah, 10
Steichen, Edward, 125
Steiner, Abraham, 29-30
Stone Mountain State Park, 277-78
Stone Store House, 80
Stoneman, George, 190
Stratton Bald, 27
Stratton Ridge Overlook, 27
Stratton, John, 27
Stringfellow, William, 231
Strother, David, 179-80
Strother, James, 167-68
Stuart, John, 138
Stumphouse Tunnel Park, 83-85
Sumter National Forest, 82
Sunburst Campground, 115
Sunburst, 114, 115
Sunset Rock (Columbus), 157
Sunset Rock (Highlands), 89
Sutherland family, 270
Sutherland Methodist Church, 270
Swain County Courthouse, 4
Swanson, Gloria, 148
Swayze, Patrick, 152
Sycamore Shoals, Tenn., 190, 253
Sylva, N.C., 103-4

T.M. Rickman General Store, 64
Table Rock, 254, 255, 260-61
Table Rock Picnic Area, 260
Tahlequah, Okla., 32
"tail of the dragon," 11-12
Tallassee Power Company, 12
Tanasee Bald, 102, 116, 117
Tapoco community, 12, 13
Tapoco Lodge, 13
Tatham Gap Road, 24-25, 26
Tatham, James, 25
Tau Rock Vineyard, 138
Taylor, Thomas Hardester "Hard," 224
Tecumseh, 19
Tellico Plains, Tenn., 27-29, 30
Tellico (Cherokee village), 32
Teneriffe, 126
Tennessee Valley Authority, 11
Thomas Legion, 6
Thomas, Will, 4, 5, 6, 16
Thompson's Bromine-Arsenic Springs Company, 284
Thomson, Peter G., 114
Thorpe Lake. See Lake Glenville
Thorpe, J.E.S., 98
Thurmond Chatham Wildlife Management Area, 279
Tiernan, Frances Christine Fisher, 163
Tiffany's, 64
Tlanusiyi. See "Leech Place"
Todd community, 263-65
Todd Mercantile, 265
Todd, J.W., 265
Todd's General Store, 264
Toe River, 196, 197, 212, 213
Toe River Arts Council, 183
Tompkins, George, 177
Topton community, 21

Toxaway (person), 94
Toxaway Falls, 118-19
Toxaway River, 111, 119
Toxaway, N.C., 118-19
Trade, Tenn., 270
Traditional Medicine Trail, 19, 21
Trail of Tears, 20, 24, 43, 49
Tranquility, 126
Transylvania County, 111
Treaty of New Echota, 25, 52
Troast, Girard, 33
Trout Lake, 216, 218
Trust community, 161
Tryon Garden Club, 136
Tryon Hounds, 141
Tryon Peak, 138
Tryon Riding and Hunt Club, 140, 141
Tryon Toymakers and Woodcarvers Shop, 140
Tryon wooden horse, 140
Tryon, N.C., 138-42
Tryon, William, 138, 139
Tsali, 4-5, 6, 68
Tsali Campground, 9
Tsali Recreation Area, 9-10
Tsistuyi. See "Rabbit Place"
Tuckasegee community, 99
Tuckasegee River, 4, 98, 99
Tunnel Hill, 83
Turner, Tom, 147, 148
Turnpike Road—Joy to Pineola, 254
Turtleback Falls, 93
Tusquitee Bald, 55
Tusquitee community, 55

Uktena, 68-69
Ulagu, 207
Ulagu. See "Great Yellow Jacket"
Ulunsuti, 69
Uncle Jake. See Carpenter, Jacob
Underground Railroad, 284
Unicoi Crest Overlook, 27
Unicoi Mountains, 10, 27-28
Unicoi Turnpike National Millennium Flagship Trail. See Unicoi Turnpike
Unicoi Turnpike, 40, 42, 43, 49
United Daughters of the Confederacy, 165
United States Forest Service, 108, 112, 194
United States Geological Survey, 244
Unto These Hills, 6
Upper Bearwallow Falls, 92
Upper Creek Falls, 256, 257
Upper Creek Trail, 255
Upper Mountain Research Station, 280
Ustenaka, 138
Utlunta. See Spearfinger
Utsala. See Euchella

Vadderland, 164
Valentine Museum, 38, 102-3
Valhalla community, 137
Valhalla Fruit Farm, 138
Valle Crucis and Blowing Rock Turnpike Company, 220
Valle Crucis community, 221-27

Valle Crucis Conference Center Complex, 225-27
Valle Crucis Methodist Church, 223
"Valley of Rubies." *See* Cowee Valley
Valley River, 36, 39
Valley River Mountains, 36
Valley Towns, 40, 41
Valley Towns Baptist Mission, 52
Valleytown, 24
Van Buren, Martin, 41
Van Hook Glade Campground, 77
Vance Toe River Lodge, 199-200
Vance, David, 167-68, 173, 177
Vance, Eleanor, 140
Vance, Robert B., 191
Vance, Zebulon, 170, 234
Vanderbilt, George, 107, 108, 113, 118, 137
Verne, Jules, 254-55
Vineyard Mountain, 55
von Bismarck, Otto, 129

W.W. Mast home, 224
Wagoner Road Access Area, 288
Walcott, Russell, 142
Walhalla, S.C., 80
Walhalla Road, 81
Walhalla State Fish Hatchery, 86
Walker Inn, 22, 23
Walker, Margaret Scott, 22-23
Walker, William, 22-23
Walker, William Pitt, 24
Walker's Country Store, 245
Wallace Gap, 67
Wallace, Lew, 148
Walnut community, 171
Walters, Abigail, 267
Warner, Charles Dudley, 181, 185, 209
Warren Wilson College, 166
Warrior Monument, 155, 156
Warrior Mountain, 139
Wasituna, 5
Watauga (Cherokee town), 67
Watauga River, 221
Watson, Culgee, 258-59
Watson, Doc, 272
Waugh, John, 22
Wayah Bald, 70-71
Wayah Bald fire tower, 72
Wayah Gap, 70, 72
Webster, N.C., 103
Wedgwood, Josiah, 65
Welch, Joseph, 67
Wellman, Manly Wade, 163
West Fork of Pigeon River, 115
West Jefferson, N.C., 285-86
West, Herman, 49
West, William, 63-64
West's Mill, 63-64
Western Carolina University, 102
Western North Carolina Railroad, 164
Westglow, 238-39
Wetmore, George Peabody, 28
Wheeler, John H., 189
White Oak Mountain, 155

Whiteside Cove, 88, 89
Whiteside Mountain, 86, 87, 95-96
Whitewater Falls Scenic Area, 93
Whiting Lumber Company, 220
Whiting Manufacturing Company, 15, 16
Whiting, William Scott, 220
Widows Creek Trail, 278
Wilcox, Lemuel, 143
Wild Woody's, 280
Wilder, John Thomas, 205-6
Wilder's Lightning Brigade, 205
Williams, Frances Nevins, 142
Williams, Joe, 147
Williams, Old Bill. *See* Williams, William
     Sherley
Williams, William Sherley, 156
Williamson, Andrew, 67
Wilson Creek, 241-47
Wilson Creek Visitors' Center, 246
Wilson Lick Ranger Station, 71
Wilson, Big Tom, 185
Wilson, Ewart, 185-86
Wilson, Joe, 210
Wilson, Woodrow 82, 89, 222
Winding Stair Gap, 57
Winding Stair Knob, 256
Winding Stair Road, 134
Wind-powered generators, 273
Wine Spring Bald, 71
Winebarger, Jacob, 268
Winston, Joseph, 254
Winter People, The, 199
Wiseman, Lafayette, 245
Wiseman, William, 200-201
Wolf Clan, 68
Wolf's Den, 266-67
Wolfe, Thomas, 8-9
Wood, Abraham, 270
Wood, Mrs. George Leidy, 10
Woodfield Inn, 129
Woodfin, N.C., 173
Woody, Linda, 280
Work Projects Administration, 172, 182, 210,
     272, 284

Yale, Charlotte, 140
Yancey County, 179-86, 192-95
Yancey County Chamber of Commerce,
     182-83
Yancey County Courthouse, 181
Yellow Creek Mountains, 10
Yellow Mountain, 201, 202
Yellow Mountain Gap, 202
Yonaguska, 3-4
Yonahlossee Trail, 237-38
Young's Fort, 138, 139, 154
Yunwi Tsunsdi. *See* "Little People"

Zachary, Mordecai, 86
Zachary-Tolbert House, 86
Zeigler, Wilbur, 87, 88-89, 95, 172, 192, 194,
     195, 203, 221
Zionville Baptist Church, 271
Zionville community, 271

CPSIA information can be obtained
at www.ICGtesting.com
Printed in the USA
JSHW040828210321
12725JS00001B/1